Starting an iPhone® Application Business

FOR DUMMIES®

Starting an iPhone® Application Business

FOR DUMMIES®

by Aaron Nicholson, Joel Elad, and Damien Stolarz

WILEY

Wiley Publishing, Inc.

Starting an iPhone® Application Business For Dummies®

Published by
Wiley Publishing, Inc.
111 River Street
Hoboken, NJ 07030-5774

www.wiley.com

Copyright © 2010 by Wiley Publishing, Inc., Indianapolis, Indiana

Published by Wiley Publishing, Inc., Indianapolis, Indiana

Published simultaneously in Canada

For general information on our other products and services, please contact our Customer Care Department within the U.S. at 877-762-2974, outside the U.S. at 317-572-3993, or fax 317-572-4002.

For technical support, please visit www.wiley.com/techsupport.

Wiley also publishes its books in a variety of electronic formats. Some content that appears in print may not be available in electronic books.

Library of Congress Control Number: 2009936809

ISBN: 978-0-470-52452-7

Manufactured in the United States of America

10 9 8 7 6 5 4 3 2 1

WILEY

FEB 0 2 2011

About the Authors

Aaron Nicholson is the Creative Director at Perceptive Development (www.perceptdev.com), a Los Angeles-based consultancy that develops iPhone software and accessories. He is an interactive media designer/developer, a musician, and a theater geek who lives at the intersection of culture and technology. His interactive media boutique, Open Secret Communications, has developed online properties for top entertainment companies, Fortune 500 firms, and many small- and medium-size businesses. He holds a BA from the University of Southern California's Annenberg School for Communication.

Joel Elad has written five books about various online topics, including *LinkedIn For Dummies*, *Starting an Online Business All-in-One Desk Reference For Dummies*, and *Web Stores Do-It-Yourself For Dummies* (all from Wiley). He is the head of Real Method Consulting, a company dedicated to educating people through training seminars, DVDs, books, and other media. He holds a master's degree in business from UC Irvine and a bachelor's degree in computer science and engineering from UCLA. He has contributed to *Entrepreneur* magazine and Smartbiz.com, and has taught at institutions such as the University of California, Irvine.

Damien Stolarz is an inventor with a decade of experience in making different kinds of computers talk to each other. After studying computer science and electrical engineering at UCLA, Damien co-founded Blue Falcon Networks (formerly Static Online, Inc.), where he supervised, architected, and developed networking software for seven years. He has written and spoken at conferences about Internet video, content delivery, and peer-to-peer networking, and he created Robotarmy in 2002 to provide high-technology consulting in these areas.

Dedication

Aaron dedicates this book to his father, whose steadfast love and support have helped him more than words can say.

Joel dedicates this book to one of his best friends, Michael Bellomo. Not only did you get me started in this crazy world of being an author, but you always support me, make me laugh (with the big joke — you know the one) and believe in me. Thank you for the e-mails, the two-hour conversations on the phone, all the laughter, and (sniff sniff) the inspiration that tells me I can climb any mountain!

Publisher's Acknowledgments

We're proud of this book; please send us your comments through our online registration form located at www.dummies.com/register/.

Some of the people who helped bring this book to market include the following:

Acquisitions, Editorial, and Media Development

Project Editor: Pat O'Brien

Acquisitions Editor: Kyle Looper

Copy Editors: Teresa Artman, Barry Childs-Helton, Jen Riggs, Virginia Sanders, Beth Staton, Brian Walls, Rebecca Whitney

Technical Reviewer: Kira Hamilton

Editorial Manager: Kevin Kirschner

Editorial Assistant: Amanda Graham

Sr. Editorial Assistant: Cherie Case

Cartoons: Rich Tennant (www.the5thwave.com)

Composition Services

Project Coordinator: Katherine Crocker

Layout and Graphics: Timothy Detrick, Joyce Haughey, Melissa K. Jester

Proofreaders: Caitie Copple, Sherry Massey

Indexer: ConText Editorial Services, Inc.

Publishing and Editorial for Technology Dummies

Richard Swadley, Vice President and Executive Group Publisher

Andy Cummings, Vice President and Publisher

Mary Bednarek, Executive Acquisitions Director

Mary C. Corder, Editorial Director

Publishing for Consumer Dummies

Diane Graves Steele, Vice President and Publisher

Composition Services

Debbie Stailey, Director of Composition Services

Contents at a Glance

Table of Contents

Introduction

· ·

*W*hen Apple opened its App Store along with the iPhone 3G in the summer of 2008, it took a mere three days for iPhone users to generate 10 million downloads from the 800 apps that were available, averaging 12,500 purchases per application. Barely a year later, the App Store has swelled to 65,000 applications and boasts over 1.5 billion app downloads. In short, the App Store is its own economy. Perhaps you've heard of the iPhone or you own one, or even several, applications and you want to see how you can take advantage of this 21st century gold rush. Perhaps you're a software developer looking to create something for this booming economy. Perhaps your company is looking to reach out to new and existing customers. To all of you, welcome to *Starting an iPhone Application Business For Dummies*.

When the iPhone launched in June of 2007, it was a smash success. The ability to use a handheld device that was a real Apple computer enthralled Apple enthusiasts. The device's sleek, leading-edge design and innovative features elevated it to a status symbol quickly in the eyes of the general public. But there was only one problem. What about all that space for more apps? Apple hadn't made it possible to install additional apps and was mum about the subject.

By the time the iPhone SDK (Software Development Kit) was announced in March 2008, the thirst for apps on the iPhone was palpable from both consumers and developers. As soon as the SDK was released to developers, the mad dash to develop apps for the upcoming unveiling of the App Store resenbled the land grabs of the homestead days out West.

The success of the App Store is not the only source of excitement about iPhone apps. iPhone apps are fun to develop and use! A robust mobile platform that rivals the power of a laptop computer with an innovative easy-to-use interface is a real game changer in both technology and lifestyle. The fact that you or anyone else can sign up cheaply, learn what you need to know for free, put your ideas into action, and sell mobile computing software supported by a world class leader like Apple is an opportunity unlike any other in the world.

We've written this book to help you with the aspects of iPhone development you can't find on Apple's Developer Connection Web site: How to start and operate an iPhone app business.

You do not need to be a programmer to read this book!

Like anything else, this is a business and many of the modern business rules apply, with some Apple twists. We hope you enjoy the process of creating your very own iPhone software business. It's fun, challenging, and rewarding.

About This Book

This book covers all aspects of creating, launching, and marketing an iPhone application. There's a lot of advice and many concepts, but also some step-by-step instructions to get things done, and it's all right here in this book.

This book is organized as a guide. You can read each chapter in order or read only specific chapters. Throughout the process of building an iPhone application, you can think of this book as a reference, where you can find the chapter you need that applies to your situation and the knowledge nugget you need to know, and then be on your merry way. We do a fair amount of cross-referencing too, so if you need to look elsewhere in the book for more information, you can easily find it.

In writing this book, we assume that you know a bit about computers, as most folks do today. But you may be utterly fresh to the concepts of programming an iPhone application and submitting it to the App Store. Despite what you may think, you do not need to be a programmer to create an iPhone application. (Naturally, though, it can make the process simpler if you are a programmer.) This book is designed to help everyone, from the aspiring entrepreneur who wants to enter this exciting world to the programmer who knows how to write XCode but needs help with the business and marketing aspects of the iPhone application to the company that wants to reach out to the iPhone user community and extend its brand with its own application.

We divide this book into six handy parts:

- Part I starts with the basics, as we talk about the world of the iPhone, the App Store, mobile computing in general, and a crucial step in the process: how to price your iPhone application.

- Part II goes into the idea generation process, helping you come up with your winning idea, figuring out what you can bring to the table, and identifying which market forces may affect your development. We describe how to craft the core of your iPhone application and make a competitive analysis of the idea and then show you resources where you can learn more.

- Part III is designed to get the necessary stuff done up-front so you don't have to worry about it later. We talk about how to register with Apple, gather all the development tools, and think about all the different team members you may need to help create your iPhone app.

✔ Part IV takes everything we've covered and gets you into the nuts and bolts of turning your idea into a functioning iPhone application. We'll talk about how to flesh out a concrete app specification, hire developers to write the code, put together a budget and figure out how to fund this project, and keep everything running as the developers are writing code and the designers are creating graphics.

✔ Part V talks about everything you need to focus on after your iPhone app launches in the App Store. We talk about different ways to get publicity for your app and have it reviewed by different sites, and we help you build buzz by using the latest in social networking, blogging, and talking to the user community. We'll show you some effective paid marketing options and describe how to build your business for the future.

✔ Part VI is the traditional *For Dummies* Part of Tens — our lists detail a number of iPhone application review sites to consider and traits we found in highly successful applications.

And Just Who Are You?

We assume that you know how to use your computer for the basic operations, like checking e-mail, typing up a document, or surfing the great big World Wide Web. If you are worried that you will need a Ph.D. in Computer Operations to write an iPhone app, relax. If you can look at a Web site, you can use LinkedIn.

We use the words *app* and *application* interchangeably, to refer to the same thing.

This book assumes that you have a computer that can access the Internet; any PC or Macintosh computer will be fine, as well as Linux or any other operating system with a Web browser.

Programming for the iPhone requires a Mac. This book doesn't.

We do not get into the core specifics of the programming necessary to build an iPhone application. In some parts of the book, we talk about specific applications, like Microsoft Excel, so we assume that if you have Microsoft Excel, you know how to use it for the purposes of building a spreadsheet and entering data, for example.

This book doesn't describe the basic operations of a computer, accessing the Internet, or using an Internet Web browser like Safari, Internet Explorer or Firefox. We've tried to keep the information here specific to Apple, the iTunes store, and the App Store. Beyond that, if you need more information about connecting to the Internet or using a Web browser, check out *The Internet For Dummies*, by John R. Levine and Margaret Levine Young (published by Wiley).

Icons Used in This Book

The Tip icon notifies you about something cool, handy, or nifty or something that I highly recommend. For example,

A dancing clown out front doesn't mean that it's the best restaurant on the block.

Don't forget! When you see this icon, you can be sure that it points out something you should remember. For example,

Always check your fly before you walk out on stage.

Danger! Ah-oogah! Ah-oogah! When you see the Warning icon, pay careful attention to the text. This icon flags something that's bad or that could cause trouble. For example,

No matter how pressing the urge, no matter how well you know these things, do not ask that rather large woman next to you when she is due.

This icon alerts you to something technical, an aside or some trivial tidbit that we just cannot suppress the urge to share. Feel free to skip this incredibly unimportant technical information. For example,

It would be as ludicrous for us to recommend the 802.11q standard as it would be for me to insist that 1 is a prime number.

Where to Go from Here

You can start reading this book anywhere. Open the table of contents and pick a spot that amuses you or concerns you or has piqued your curiosity. Everything is explained in the text, and information is carefully cross-referenced so that you don't waste your time reading repeated information.

Part I
Surveying the Marketplace

The 5th Wave

By Rich Tennant

"You ever notice how much more streaming media there is than there used to be?"

In this part . . .

Hey, if you're wondering, "What does surveying have to do with creating an iPhone app?" then let us explain. The best analogy we can give is the saying, "To know where you are going, you first have to know where you are." Reviewing the current state of this market will only help you build a better iPhone application.

In this part, we cover the exciting world that Apple has created for iPhone applications by looking at the App Store and the accompanying world of the iPhone app developers. We even take a look at the big picture of mobile application development to see how the iPhone has created some unique offerings that can change the market. We then describe one of the most challenging aspects current developers have had to face — how to price an iPhone application in the market. Trust us, this part lays a solid foundation for you to build your great idea on.

Let's dig in!

Chapter 1

The Wide, Wide World of iPhone App Development

*I*n July 2008, Apple Computer launched two momentous events. The first was an updated version of its hit iPhone product, the iPhone 3G. That same day, Apple launched something far more important to the success of its product: a central repository where iPhone users could purchase or download applications that could run on their iPhone. In simpler terms, Apple opened the App Store, where third-party developers from around the world could now have access to this new and growing market of iPhone owners who were eager to spend cash and get more capabilities from their gee-whiz phone.

In less than a year, Apple's U.S. App Store alone has seen more than 40,000 applications approved and available on the store, and Apple celebrated its billionth application download in less than a year.

In this chapter, we present the App Store to you and talk about the different ways you can see or categorize the applications already present. We'll talk about the link between the iPhone's hardware and the applications that use it, and show how the development of the iPhone itself has affected the application development world. Sit back and enjoy!

Touring the Apple App Store

Let's dive into the selling environment that makes the world of iPhone applications go 'round. (If you're already familiar with the App Store, you can skip ahead to Chapter 2.)

If you don't already have it, download iTunes here: www.apple.com/itunes/download/.

You can uncheck the check boxes on the left that will put you on Apple's mailing lists and skip entering your e-mail address if you like, or keep them and fill in your address if you'd like to get news from Apple. Then just click the large Download Now button. The application will download to your Desktop or Downloads folder. Then you can double-click to install it.

Go ahead and open up iTunes. To get to the App Store, you'll first need to enter the iTunes Store by clicking the first link under the store heading on the left menu pane. Then click App Store in the menu pane that appears to the right of where you just clicked, and you should see something like Figure 1-1.

Figure 1-1: The general layout of the App Store.

Perusing the storefront

Just below the App Store menu item you've just clicked, you'll see the Categories menu. The center of the screen is dominated by featured applications grouped into sets. And the right column of the screen shows Quick Links, Top Paid Apps, and Top Free Apps.

Two other powerful ways to explore the App Store are Searching and Browsing, which are available in the Search pane at the top right of the interface, and in the Quick Links Section.

Each of these forms of navigating the iTunes store is useful as we plan our application, surveying the marketplace, sizing up the competition, and seeking to promote our finished app.

Categories

The Categories menu on the left gives us a quick way to browse the store by subject matter. If you know, for example, that you will create a news gathering application, hanging out in the News category will immerse you in the existing ecosystem of apps in your category. If you have an app that doesn't fit in one category in mind, you might need to refine how your idea relates to the given categories or explore multiple categories.

The digital end cap

The large center area of the App Store can be described as a digital end cap, similar to the areas in a traditional music store at the ends of each aisle and surrounding the cash registers that feature products the retailer is trying to promote.

Each grouping of apps in this section has a See All button at the top right. Use it to see a grid layout of all featured apps in that category.

The Quick Links section contains the Browse and Power Search options, in addition to links to manage your iTunes account.

Browse

Clicking Browse takes you to a plain-looking interface that is not unlike the Finder interface on an Apple Computer. Browse functionality allows you to

- Further divide your category exploration into subcategories
- Sort applications by Name, Release Date, Artist (Creator), Category, and Price

This can be powerful if you want to look at all apps in your category that are in the same target price range as your app, for example, or if you want to see all apps from a given development company.

To sort by the various headings, such as Price, simply click that heading. You should see something like Figure 1-2. You can click again to reverse the sort order.

Search and power search

The quickest and simplest way to search the store is by clicking in the search text field at the top right of the application, entering your search term, and hitting the Return key. This will yield a search of the entire iTunes Store for your term. The search is visually broken into sections, so it is fairly easy to see the result. If you are looking for an app with the word *hello* in the title, for example, you can easily get to the app simply by following this method, as seen in Figure 1-3.

For a more advanced, targeted search, click Power Search in the Quick Links menu. Then you'll be presented with a strip of search options. Because we're starting in Applications, the search starts out confined to that area. You can fill in the remaining text fields and drop-downs to get a more specific search.

This gives you a much more useful display of your search results, and allows you to easily filter by developer once the results are in.

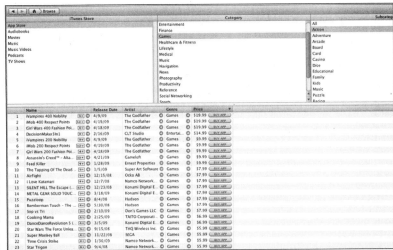

Figure 1-2: Sort the list of apps by different criteria.

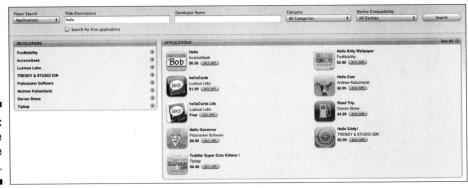

Figure 1-3: Search the App Store by keyword.

This advanced search method is handy for Competitive Analysis. We show you the details in Chapter 6.

Top applications

The final stops on our tour of the App Store storefront are the two Top Apps categories. These two panes on the bottom right give you a quick way to see what's hot at any given time in the paid and free genres.

Checking back often and downloading/purchasing as many apps as you can afford is a great way to stay on top of winning design and development ideas and keep your finger on the pulse.

The App Store on the iPhone

Each iPhone and iPod Touch has a mobile version of the App Store on the device, which works over Wi-Fi and cellular connections. Your app can be an impulse buy anytime, anywhere.

Browsing the App Store on the phone is slightly different from browsing on iTunes:

✔ Featured Apps are grouped into the What's New and What's Hot sections.

✔ Search is limited to a simple search within the App Store.

✔ There is no special Browse functionality to drill down into subcategories and list sorting.

If you have a device, playing with the App Store for a few minutes will have you navigating like a pro once you've learned your way around the App Store in iTunes on your computer. You can see different versions of the iPhone screen when browsing in Figure 1-4.

Figure 1-4:
Search the
App Store
from your
iPhone.

A word about updates

Most application developers release free updates to their app which contain bug fixes, extended functionality, or new design elements.

You *can* update your apps directly on your phone with the Updates tab in the App Store. We do not recommend this. Depending on your connection to the internet, it can take a long time and tie up your bandwidth in an annoying way.

For your enjoyment and sanity, particularly if you have a lot of apps, we recommend updating in iTunes. Click the Applications link in the Library category in the leftmost menu in iTunes. At the bottom right you'll see a link that says Updates Available. Click that link; then click Download All Free Updates in the upper right of the screen. You'll be asked to enter your password; then the updates will begin to download. The Downloads menu item in the Store category to the left will have a circled number, like the number 10 in Figure 1-5. Clicking Downloads will allow you to see the progress of the downloads. Once all of the downloads have completed, sync your device. You're set!

Figure 1-5: See what downloads are ready for you!

Apple's Free Marketing

The ad buy that will get you the most bang for your buck for promoting your iPhone app is *nothing!* The commercial culture that Apple has ingeniously built around iPhone applications is one in which potential buyers primarily look directly to the App Store to browse, search for, and make their minds up about what apps to buy. As the store gets more crowded with the rising popularity and mainstream appeal of the iPhone, iPhone entrepreneurs are increasingly looking to traditional forms of advertising to get their app seen. So far, however, it is placement in the store itself that has fueled the boom many have experienced since the release of the App Store.

That most certainly doesn't mean, "Don't worry about promoting your app." What it does mean is that you should focus primarily on your application's quality over your marketing plan. The quality will get your app noticed initially, get people recommending it to friends, generate buzz, and put it on Apple's radar for one of its coveted "Featured App" slots on the App Store storefront, like the ones featured in Figure 1-6.

Figure 1-6: Apple features several iPhone Apps in its store.

Like most of Apple's business practices, how apps get picked for the featured slots is largely a mystery that is not disclosed to the public. Even top iPhone entrepreneurs who have been featured multiple times claim that their selection was the luck of the draw. However, there's a pattern: the best and most interesting apps end up on the Featured App lists. Some of the biggest selling points of the iPhone are third-party apps like the one you are about to create. It is in Apple's interest to put the best of those apps forward, so prospective buyers and existing users continue to get the best experience of the iPhone.

Who do you call to get your app featured in the App Store? The best planners, designers, and developers you can get your hands on!

If you watch Apple's online and TV ads and commercials associated with the iPhone, you'll notice a lot of those little application icons flying around. This is also a tremendous source of publicity for those apps fortunate enough to get put in the ad. Again, there is no trick but being one of the best to make this happen.

Another promotional caper you can shoot for is winning the Apple Design Award at Apple's annual (World Wide Developers Conference) WWDC convention. Winning the competition will put you at the top of Apple's mind for its marketing campaigns and score you tons of free press. You'll have a runaway hit on your hands at that point!

Check out the requirements, evaluation standards, and application details at `http://developer.apple.com/wwdc/ada/index.html`, as seen in Figure 1-7. Good luck!

Figure 1-7:
Apple's
Conference
offers
Design
Awards.

The Frictionless Selling Experience

A primary driver of virtually every new selling innovation has been an increase in the ease of bringing a product to market. Henry Ford profited from the assembly line. The music industry started becoming wealthy with the advent of audio recording and distribution, and until recently, profited immensely with every advance in the medium from vinyl, to tape, to CD. Lately, we have experienced the dawn of the digital age. For many, including the music, film, and news industries, this has been a major bummer. Sales have plummeted as consumers increasingly look to the Internet to meet their media needs. Because these industries profit on the relative *scarcity* of what they produce, the more easily available it is, the more they have to lose.

As an iPhone entrepreneur, you stand to profit from this same phenomenon. The more *abundantly* your software is available, the more you will make. This is true, within the context of the App Store, because Apple has handled the scarcity side of the profit equation for you by making a relatively tamper-proof commerce environment. It is not for someone to steal, lend, or find a cheap alternative to an iPhone app. That being the case, the easier it is for people to get your app, the more you make. Also, the easier the process of buying and installing your app, the fewer buyers will drop off before completing the sale.

Apple had exactly these principles in mind when it created the App Store and its commerce model. Apple has made buying your app easy for consumers the same way it has made its operating systems and software products the most seamless to use in the industry. Once users set up their billing information with the App Store initially, buying an app is as simple as clicking and confirming, like in Figure 1-8.

Figure 1-8: Find your app; then click and buy!

Global Distribution

At the time of this writing, the iPhone is available in 88 countries worldwide. That's great for people in those countries, but it's also great for you! You can sell to them all without changing a thing!

Most of the apps in the App Store today are only in English. There is a tremendous opportunity for you, however, if you internationalize your app. You could allow the users to specify their language, or release multiple versions in different languages. How could that be better than having all the languages in one app? People speaking a given language are naturally drawn to apps presented in their own language. If you release the app in their language and write the app description text in their language so they can see that in the App Store, then if they have a need for an app of your app's kind, your app is much more likely to be the one they will choose.

You can check out the exact countries where the iPhone is available here: www.apple.com/iphone/countries/.

How iPhone App Developers Positioned Themselves

When we look across the spectrum of iPhone applications on the market, there are a number of ways to slice the market up in order to get a handle on it. We call these *market differentiators*. We'll take a look at price points, market purpose, quality level, mass vs. niche market, and whether the app is a port of existing functionality to iPhone vs. novel functionality.

Price points

One way to segment the market is by price point. We'll look deeper at this in Chapter 3 from the perspective of how to price your app. For now, we'll take a look at how some existing apps are priced, and how that distinguishes them in the market.

Free apps

There are a number of reasons an app might be priced free. The developer may have just been cutting their teeth on the app. They may be using a free app as a trial version of a paid app they hope to hook customers on before requiring a purchase. The app may exist only to support some other product such as a medical device, social network, publication, or banking product. The app might be trying to generate a large user base for later conversion to paid subscriptions or the like. The app might be functioning as an advertisement for a specific brand. The app might be free to customers, but companies might pay to be featured in the app. Or the app may be a platform for rotating advertisements.

Let's take a look at some popular apps in each of these categories.

✔ **Developer cutting teeth:** Though they aren't making any money from their apps, certain app developers now have one major advantage over many other developers: they have launched an app in the App Store. Now when these developers seek to be hired to develop applications for another company or raise money for new apps, they have a foot in the door, can point to their reviews, and easily direct prospects to their work. These applications become important to the developer's portfolio and future, and consumers get the benefits of their work for free. Two examples of apps in this category include:

- **Space Deadbeef:** *Space Deadbeef* is a graphically rich fly and shoot game by a group called I.D.P. It's evident from the application description that the designers and developers only created the app for credit. The game has terrific graphics and satisfying game play, but only has a few levels and no companion paid app. It appears to be a portfolio piece for some game developers to get into working with the iPhone.

- **FastShop:** Emmanual Berthier's FastShop occupies the crowded space of list management for the iPhone. A simple and direct implementation of a shopping list application, FastShop is free and frill-less (see Figure 1-9). But if you need a shopping list, it might be just what the doctor ordered.

✔ **Trial Version:** One of the most popular ways that iPhone app developers have promoted their paid applications is to create a trial, or "Lite," version of the same application for free, so consumers can download and try out the application. If they find the app useful, then they can pay and download the full version. So is releasing a free trial app worth it? That's going to depend on your marketing strategy, target audience, niche, and more, all of which we'll be discussing further on in this book. Two great examples of trial apps include:

- **Balloonimals Lite:** One of our favorite games for the iPhone. It was made for 5-year-olds, but watch what happens when you pass it around at a party! The premise of the game is creating balloon animals that you can blow up, play with, and then pop. The Lite version comes with only one animal; then presents a link to the paid version in the App Store.

- **MLB.com at Bat Lite:** MLB.com at Bat is a popular baseball fans' resource for looking up team standings, player stats, and videos of top plays. The Lite version lacks game day pitch-by-pitch, box scores, and live game day audio that are present in the paid version.

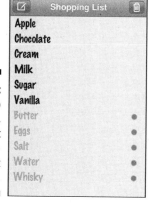

Figure 1-9:
FastShop
is a simple,
free list
manage-
ment
iPhone app.

✔ **Supporting another product:** With the advent of iPhone 3.0 and hardware support, this category will be exploding. If you have a desktop application or hardware device that could be integrated with the iPhone, it may be in your interest to develop an app for it and give it away for free or cheaply. iPhone compatibility and market presence has *cache* (coolness) value, and gives you a great new marketing platform and something to toot your horn about. The iPhone is about lifestyle integration, which is something every consumer brand should strive for. A free app to support existing products can be a great way to do that. Two examples of iPhone applications in this category include:

- **Daylite Touch:** Market Circle's Daylite Productivity Suite for Mac is a full-featured time and team management application which sells for around $200 per user. Daylite Touch is its free companion application for the iPhone that allows one to tie into the desktop data of the full application over the Internet (see Figure 1-10). This is a common example of a company with a retail product extending the product's value with a free iPhone app, and simultaneously generating interest in its desktop products via the App Store.

- **Remote:** Apple's Remote app has a simple but powerful premise: allow you full control over iTunes from your phone. It has a slightly different market purpose than Daylite Touch. It simply bridges the gap between iTunes and the iPhone, offering an obvious and useful value proposition that probably would have been filled by a third-party developer had Apple not beat them to it. What's this doing for Apple? It simply enhances its already abundant cool factor and over-delivery on lifestyle functionality to support its iPhone platform.

Figure 1-10:
Daylite
Touch
provides
desktop
calendar
data on your
iPhone.

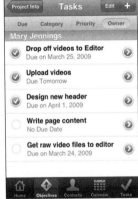

✔ **Generating a user base for later conversion:** Think "free" can't make money? Just ask Facebook, which had been valued as high as $15 billion, or YouTube, which was purchased by Google for $1.65 billion. The reason why companies pay all these dollars for a free service can be summed up in one word: Eyeballs. Once you have the attention of a large audience, the advertising and marketing possibilities for your company skyrocket. Another popular model in this space is similar to the Trial Version model, but involves giving early users a service for free with the hope of later converting some of them to pay for the same service after some initial period expires or get them to buy upgrades to the free base service. Two specific apps that fit this category include:

- **Soonr:** Soonr is a "cloud sharing" application that polls user-defined folders on your computer for new or modified files and posts them to a secure account on a Soonr server on the Internet, or "cloud." You can then access them on a Web browser or your iPhone for review, sharing, and printing. Initially it was totally free. Now the original version is free, but you can pay a monthly fee for more storage.

- **Loopt:** Another vowel-deficient app title, Loopt is a social networking application that overlays your location and that of your friends over a Google-style map (see Figure 1-11). You and your friends can send updates with photos and text tags up for others to see. If you allow your location to be seen, friends can see your GPS position and track your activity. Of course, it has the proper privacy controls. Loopt has been free since its inception, leading us to believe that its real product is Loopt's base, which it'll use for marketing.

✔ **Promoting a Specific Brand:** This medium of app is part of the arsenal of a brand immersion campaign It's a form of marketing that seeks to involve consumers in a brand in passive forms, such as games, gimmicks, and productivity applications that have value on their own, but also create a positive association or strong recognition with a certain brand in the mind of the consumer. The idea is that if you play with it, you'll remember it. Two specific applications that fit this category include

- **Rhinoball:** Rhinoball is a game based on the Disney film *Bolt*. In the game, you play one of the supporting characters who has to roll toward the goal while sticking as close to possible to a given path.

- **Magic Coke Bottle**: This is The Coca-Cola Company's take on the old magic 8-ball. Its hope is that users will play with the app in groups, promoting the Coke brand. The user experience is fun and smooth, making good use of the iPhone's unique interface shake and slide functions.

Figure 1-11:
See where
your friends
are with
Loopt!

✔ **Paid Feature:** Let's say you want to serve information to consumers who aren't necessarily willing to pay for it — but the providers of the information stand to benefit from being seen. This is the revenue model of the Yellow Pages and classified newspapers of the world. If you can provide an information base that entices consumers while essentially serving as advertisement for your data providers, think about reversing the equation and serve the customers television has always served, the advertisers and product placers.

One example of an application in this category is YPmobile, a Yellow Pages mobile application. Perhaps the longest-standing form of provider-paid information, the Yellow Pages make its money by charging companies to be listed. This app takes it a few steps farther by featuring live events in your area, offering a planning notebook, displaying ratings and reviews, and more.

✔ **Advertising Platform:** Embedding ads in iPhone apps is a popular combination with free applications. You can find your own advertisers and program their ads into your app, or use a service such as AdMob (www. admob.com), which handles this for you. AdMob claims to have served over 76 billion impressions. Two applications that fit in this category include:

- **Bloomberg:** Bloomberg is a popular market tracking application by the New York financial news organization of the same name. Its classy interface and no-nonsense information delivery have made it a favorite of investors. It features non-invasive placement of rotating advertisements on the lower right of the screen.

- **Where:** Where is like a Swiss Army knife for geolocation applications. Using the familiar map interface, Where allows you to toggle between several geolocation services, such as Yelp, a Starbucks finder, Zipcar, and Yellow Pages, and other points of interest on the map around you. It features ads superimposed over the top of the map interface, which move to the bottom of the screen in certain views.

Cheap apps

On the iPhone, cheap means $.99. It's that simple. There are not nearly as many reasons for creating a paid app as there are for a free app, but the one main reason makes up in importance for them all: make some money. $.99 is the ultimate impulse buy price on the iPhone. I recently had a teenage theater clerk try to educate me on how to jailbreak the iPhone and steal applications. When I said I wouldn't be doing that because I am a developer and encouraged him not to do so as well, he chimed, "I'll buy *your* app — if it's $.99!" That pretty much says it all.

Here are two examples of popular cheap iPhone applications:

✔ **Koi Pond:** Koi Pond by Blimp Pilots is a beautiful time-killing lifestyle game that allows you to observe and play with a koi pond. Wiping your finger across the screen gently disturbs the water and scatters the fish. A properties screen allows you to customize your pond. As one of Apple's top paid iPhone apps, $.99 has added up pretty quickly for these developers.

✔ **Ocarina:** The iPhone startup Smule has captured hearts and pocket-books with its gorgeous Ocarina. A digital representation of the simple indigenous wind instrument, Ocarina lets you use the microphone like a wind hole and place your fingers on the screen to finger various note patterns (see Figure 1-12). As you play, others around the globe can tune in to hear you in real time. If you are tired of playing, you can switch modes and just listen to others play. It's a "small world" experience.

Figure 1-12: Play your iPhone like an Ocarina!

Midline

Any app priced from $1.99–$9.99 has an average price point. Often companies choose to price apps higher in this range if they gain strong popularity or are more involved. This is also the price range in which you will see companies offering apps at reduced prices for a period of time to boost interest and sales. Two examples apps include:

- ✓ **Hero of Sparta for $5.99:** Gameloft's 3D third-person action adventure game pits you against hordes of monsters.

- ✓ **Weightbot for $1.99:** One of the best-designed iPhone apps, Weightbot allows you to simply enter your weight for the day and track it over time with a line graph. Setting a goal weight gives you a second line on the graph as a target. The beauty of this app is in the beauty and amusement of its design qualities.

Premium

Premium apps range from $10.99 up to hundreds of dollars, but most fall in the $10 to $50 range. Certain full-featured specialty apps go up into the hundreds. Apps in this range are counting on being valuable enough to the consumer that they are no longer an impulse buy, but more of an investment. Two examples of premium apps include:

- ✓ **Omnifocus for $19.99:** Omnifocus for the Mac is a full-featured, innovative task management app that can be networked between machines across the Internet. Omnifocus for iPhone is the full-featured cousin that synchronizes with the desktop application, allowing on-the-go networked time management. Its four star rating indicates that its higher price isn't a deterrent for many.

- ✓ **Netter's Anatomy Flash Cards, for $39.99:** A beautifully drawn application for learning anatomy, this application will appeal to med students, doctors, and biology enthusiasts. Its higher price reflects the depth of specialized data it presents so thoroughly and beautifully.

Excessive

While there are a lot of applications that offer a reasonable price point, there are a few apps that are just plain expensive in price.

At one time this category was typified by the infamous "I am Rich" application, which sold for $999 and simply displayed a glowing red gem. While a select few saw this as a useful tool, Apple has taken it down due to customer disputes.

Now, this category is mostly dominated by industry-specific specialty apps, such as:

- ✓ **MyAccountsToGo for $499.99:** This is a tool for Microsoft Great Plains or SAP client relations management software. We sure hope those sales reps close some big contracts to afford this on their phone! But then again, it is probably the only app of its kind for these systems.

✔ **iRa Pro for $899.99:** This mobile video surveillance app turns your phone into one of those video walls that security guards fall asleep in front of in movies. If you have a complex surveillance situation going on, we're sure this would be pretty handy. Take a walk while you monitor that parking garage for intruders!

Market purpose

Another way to slice the marketplace is by the purpose the app was created for. Here, we mean whether the app fills an existing need, attempts to improve on an existing application, creates a new demand for something, supports other elements of a business, or simply was created for one's own enjoyment or particular use and to share with the world. Some of these categories intersect with the previous sections in the Free Apps category.

Here are some of the different areas that define market purpose:

✔ **Filling an existing but unfulfilled need:** This is gold in any market, and that's particularly true for software, because once a piece of software is available it is available to everyone all at the same time. It's not like neighborhood restaurants that don't have to compete with the same type of restaurant in another city. Once a need is met well in the software world, it's hard to compete against it. If you can get in to fill a need before anyone else, and do it well, you can really dominate that area.

One example of filling an existing need is shown with the Instapaper application (see Figure 1-13). Ever come across an article online you want to read, but not right now? It's just an article and might not be worth bookmarking. Besides, are you really going to go back to that bookmark? That's what Instapaper is for. This simple app is combined with a bookmark that you put on your bookmark bar in your browser. When you come across such an article, hit the bookmark once; it is saved. Then the article pops up in a list in your free or pro version of the iPhone app.

Figure 1-13: Keep track of news articles with the Instapaper app!

✔ **Making an existing app better:** If there is an app, how does it do it well? Does it neglect functionality? Is it high quality or kind of junky? Perhaps there is a niche market that can be served by a more specialized version. All of these questions, and more, are valid when looking at getting into a field already occupied by one or more apps. The App Store is a meritocracy, so coming in with a better app can be rewarding.

✔ **Creating a new demand:** Great ideas have to start somewhere. Some of them might as well start with you. If you strike a chord with your idea, you might start a demand that people didn't even know they had. For example, there's an iPhone app called Eternity that helps you with time tracking. A lot of freelancers track how much time they spend on projects. But who tracks how much time they spend at *everything*? That's the purpose of Eternity: helping you see how you are spending your days. You can track anything from work time to playtime, family time, whatever. Then run reports and look at logs of how you whiled away the hours. While some people may see this as unnecessary, others who are addicted to time management become hooked.

✔ **Supporting other elements of a business:** The iPhone can act as a mobile extension of an existing business operation. Many companies are getting into iPhone development simply to have a presence in that space. Or they see the iPhone as a new tool with which they can extend their offerings. For example, SalesForce, a leading online client relations management platform, created an iPhone app that simply brings the functionality of the online version to the iPhone as a convenient application with which to access the same features.

✔ **Doing it for their own enjoyment/reasons:** If you've invested in this book, you are probably not releasing an app just for the heck of it, but many developers do. The open source software movement has led to many programmers getting used to creating things for their own use and then releasing them to the rest of us essentially just to contribute to society. They get the fun/usage of their app, and then they get the recognition and gratitude when others use it, too. For example, encryption is a coder's tool for turning readable text into unreadable forms (such as a hash) for secure transmission. Armin Teoper's HashToHash does just this on the iPhone simply and elegantly, but he seemed to write this application simply because he determined he could, and not for financial or advertising gain.

Quality level

Another way to parse the market in the App Store is by quality. There are a lot of quality apps out there, but also a surprising number that leave something to be desired. To a certain extent, quality is a matter of taste, so don't be offended if yours differs from ours.

✓ **Amateur Design:** Take a look around the App Store and take an assessment of relative graphics quality, thoughtfulness of approach to the app's subject matter, attention to detail, and so on. A close read will reveal a lot of amateur design efforts out there. Be aware, though, that an amateur design can be one of the best-selling applications out there.

For example, Ethan Nicholas created an iPhone game called iShoot. Ethan did not invest in developing the best graphics. Yet his app struck a chord with gamers, and he made almost a million dollars in its first year on the App Store. While the app is not as graphically compelling as many others, iShoot's game play has excited and addicted fans, proving that your app doesn't have to be perfect to be a hit. (It can help, though, if you focus on design.)

✓ **Professional Design:** A vast majority of apps on the App Store look good with a professional design, but are not terrifically well executed. Even apps by major companies such as Facebook find themselves panned by reviewers. The line between professional and premium may be in the eye of the beholder, but it's still a worthy distinction to make as you survey the market.

For example, let's look at 24 — Special Ops. This iPhonification of the popular television series has fun, retro style, and game play, but doesn't shine in terms of attention to detail. The text dialogue is often fragmented and grammatically incorrect. The posterized-looking graphics, though interesting, don't fit the style of the show. Overall, however, it is a fun game that makes decent use of the *24* characters and plot style.

Another example is iFitness. This popular fitness app shines in that it features a pretty comprehensive list of exercises with photos of each, some stock exercise routines, a logbook, and the ability to put together your own routines. It's a good app, but its interface lacks character, there are few written instructions, and it doesn't have any particular branding or point of view to distinguish it in the marketplace. These missing attributes leave the door wide open to competition in this market space.

✓ **Premium/Exceptional Design:** We all know a great thing when we see it. It seems to transcend the competition, go further than it needed to in terms of quality and thoughtfulness, and it is presented in a near-flawless fashion. The best example of this is the iPhone itself. Premium applications live up to this standard and perhaps even push it a little further.

One example of a premium design is the Touchgrind application. An innovative skateboarding game from Illusion Labs, Touchgrind makes terrific use of the iPhone's form-factor and multitouch interface. In the game you get a top-down view of your board as if you were riding it looking down. Finger movements move the board and trigger different jumps and tricks. The graphics are stellar, game play is fun and challenging, and the concept is innovative and novel.

Another example is the FourTrack application (see Figure 1-14). Remember those old four-track tape recorders from back in the day? Even the Beatles recorded their first records with just four tracks. FourTrack from Sonoma Wireworks brings four-track action to the iPhone in a beautiful interface perfect for the songwriter, band, or doodler to get more than just one track down on new songs, song sketches, etc. Then you can easily transfer your masterpiece via Wi-Fi to your computer for use in Sonoma's companion application. The app makes elegant use of the touch interface, the iPhone's audio capabilities, and desktop interoperability to help you create a masterpiece.

Figure 1-14: Make beautiful music with the FourTrack app.

Market size

Certain apps are made for the masses; and some are made for specific interest groups, professions, and other niche markets. Just because an app targets a niche market doesn't mean it has limited potential. In today's specialty-oriented culture, targeting a niche is one of the best ways to be noticed and perceived as relevant.

One example of an iPhone App for the masses is the WebMD application. The popular Web reference for everything medical is cleverly ported to the iPhone. Use the 3D symptom checker, or just do a good old search to find out just what ailment you *might* have. Then go to your doctor before you get too scared about that red bump.

One example of an iPhone App for a niche market is the Normal Lab Values application. At the time of this writing, Normal Lab Values (the fourth most popular paid medical app) has a simple interface that displays normal lab values for medical tests that doctors can use to interpret test results, like in Figure 1-15.

Figure 1-15: See Normal Lab Values on your iPhone.

Emulating existing products

Many apps on the iPhone were great products or apps elsewhere first. As more and more consumers pick up an iPhone, moving an existing application to the iPhone platform is a great way to keep and/or extend your application's user base, plus it becomes a great marketing and branding tool to say that you also "exist" on the iPhone, as you may simply keep your existing customers from trying a competitor's program.

For example, Pandora Radio is an application that allows you to pick a favorite band or musical preferences and then hear a custom radio station composed of music that has similar characteristics to the music you chose. If you like something, you can click to buy it on iTunes, or rate the song to affect future music selections on your custom channel. This program has been popular on the Internet for years. Pandora decided to create an iPhone application of its service that works seamlessly with its Internet Web version. If you created an account on Pandora Radio and then download its iPhone app to your iPhone, you can log on with the same account and enjoy the same stations on your iPhone as well as your computer. You can also create new stations from your iPhone just as easily as using their Web application. Now Pandora can turn your iPhone into a radio.

Extending your product or brand to the iPhone is not just for entrepreneurs and up-and-coming products. The iPhone version of Google offers voice-powered search and one-touch access to Google's Web apps. Other big companies such as eBay are joining the iPhone application mix, too, to offer their products and services to the iPhone user community.

Entering the Marketplace with a New Application

The first thing to consider when looking at creating a new app is whether you can add new functionality or content into the marketplace or improve upon existing functionality/content out there. The last thing App Store consumers need is yet another tip calculator — unless you know you can create one that will blow the competition out of the water!

The only area of exception to this rule seems to be games. Games are the most popular category of iPhone apps by far. As of this writing, 16 of the top 20 paid apps of all time are games, and the others are entertainment apps. What's special about games? They are entertaining; they are an impulse buy; and, most importantly to you, they eventually lose their allure. Unlike a productivity app that a consumer will cling to increasingly as they integrate it into their lifestyle, a person can beat a game, become bored with it, or simply want something new. This leaves the door open to you to create new and interesting games.

Take a look around the App Store and spot apps that fall into the categories we've listed in the previous section, in addition to getting a deeper feel for the app categories that are built into the store. Getting an intuitive feel for the environment you will be entering into is invaluable as you move forward with your process. At a certain point, you will have a moment when you see an opening that you are the perfect person to fill. Stop and write that idea down!

You don't have to set out to beat the largest, well-funded companies creating apps. The App Store is still driven on ideas. To compete, your execution must be great, but, unless your app absolutely demands it, you're not going to need to invest in a team of 3D wizards to pull it off well. When you know you've hit on something that will work and people will love (or at least find useful), just jump in there and start the process we've outlined in the rest of this book.

You don't need to come up with an idea that will please everybody. In fact, the more targeted you can make the profile of the person you are seeking to serve with your app, the easier it will be to assess and hit that target's needs.

Finding your fit or unmet need

There are essentially three approaches for entering the idea phase of developing your app:

- Identifying needs in the marketplace
- Looking around your environment for needs that can be met by an app
- Taking an inventory of what you can offer

You can work exclusively with one approach, or you can work them all back and forth until you have a winner. We recommend working all three angles, because this will yield you the best combination between something that is needed in the marketplace, something that connects with the world around you, and something that connects with who you are, your background, and what you can offer.

We've started, somewhat counterintuitively, with assessing the market before we assess the environment and your own interests. Before you look around in your life for applicability of the iPhone, we want you to have a firm grasp of the context of the iPhone and its app universe. This will both limit and expand your ideas, as your understanding of the device will shape the lens through which you view your world. You don't want to waste your time getting hyped about coming up with something nobody has ever thought of only to find out that, oh yes, they have. Conversely, having developed a depth of knowledge of the iPhone, you might well see an angle on a real-life situation or problem you might otherwise overlook.

Alternately, on your first pass, we don't want you to just go in like a laser beam, only looking at apps you know are going to be in your related fields of knowledge. There are a few reasons for this. As we mentioned previously, you might discover interesting features or weaknesses in an app from a category you didn't expect. Additionally, you might find a market need that isn't already in your repertoire, but that makes perfect business sense for you to pursue. In the act of idea generation, we are starting with the general and moving toward the specific, like using a large fishing net to gather all the inspiration and knowledge we can, rather than going out there with a fishing pole hoping to snag a sturgeon.

Identifying needs in the marketplace

As you go through the App Store to identify needs, here are some points to consider:

✔ **Scour the App Store for opportunities.** We suggest taking a half an hour a day for a week to explore the App Store. Give yourself a system. The easiest place to start is by checking out the top apps (free and paid) in each category starting at the top of the list, like in Figure 1-16. Doing three categories a day will take exactly seven days. Some categories may be irrelevant to anything you might want to do. You can feel free to skip those, but taking the time to go through them might give you inspiration where you didn't expect to find it. You might see an interface style in the medical category that would be perfect for a coloring book application, for example. The more you know your environment, the more intuitive you will be in that space. (We discuss doing an extensive review of the App Store in Chapter 6.)

✔ **Learn through buying.** In addition to reading app descriptions and looking at screenshots, you'll need to buy and play with some apps. Give yourself a budget; something easy to bite off for you, but large enough to give you plenty of options. Make a list of apps you'd like to buy. Then at the end of your session, go back and buy as many of them as will fit into your budget. Obviously, grab as many free apps as you want. And don't hesitate to buy a few apps you think might be flops. You'll need to know some specifics about what you don't like as well as what you do.

Figure 1-16:
Review the
top paid
(and free)
apps for
ideas and
info.

✔ **Write down your impressions and comparisons.** You can take as many notes as you like, but mostly you're just trying to get a lay of the land at this point. As you hone in on an area you might want to enter into, you can do more specific assessments of existing apps in that space.

Keep in mind the market differentiators we covered in the last part of this chapter. How are apps priced relatively to each other? What purpose is an app filling in the marketplace (filling an existing need, improving on existing apps)? Is this a high-quality app, junky, or in between? Is this app for everybody, or just a specific group? And, as far as you can tell, is this an iPhonization of something already out there, or does this app represent totally new functionality?

✔ **Pretend you're the customer.** As you explore, try to put yourself in the shoes of someone who might use that application. This will be hard for areas that are totally foreign to you, but those are areas you are probably not going to want to develop for anyway, so don't sweat it. For areas you can identify with, role-play a bit and think about how you might use that application in your life. What would you be looking for in an application?

What problem would you want to solve by having such an application? Look at the apps in a given category in this context and holes will start to emerge:

- "There's no app that does X!"

- "This app doesn't do X very well."

- "This app could be presented way better."

- "I would want this app to also do Z."

- "The interface on this app is non-intuitive."

- "This app is going after the wrong demographic."

✔ **Keep exploring.** When you feel you've fully explored the top apps, dig a bit deeper and look at apps that didn't make that list. Why do you suppose they are not rising to the top? How many apps in a category are essentially filling the same purpose? No need to be exhaustive or scientific here. That would turn you into an academic instead of an entrepreneur. Just get a depth of experience in the market space so that you know what you are getting into. We'll get more specific and scientific when you identify your application idea.

Assessing the environment

As you move through your work and personal life, try as often as possible to look through iPhone-tinted glasses and see an opportunity. You can use the people and events in your daily life to help you start your path toward developing a killer iPhone app. Here are some specific things you can start to do right now:

✔ **Find the pain points.** Every time you think, "Dang that's annoying!" think about how you could alleviate that annoyance with a clever application. Every "I wish I could" thought is a seed of inspiration. Keep an *iPhone Inspiration* list in your notes application on your phone and add to it with impunity. Just note anything down that occurs to you as you move through life. Many people have found purpose (and profit) by solving other people's pain points.

✔ **Tap your personal network.** Ask the people around you what problems or wishes they'd like to solve in their life. However, don't ask them about it in the context of an iPhone application. Just ask them for the raw request they have to fix those problems, like "I wish I could organize my shoes" or "I want a way to keep track of my kid's friends." You can think about how that request could relate to an application later. Take notes. We're just gathering data from the world around us. Some of it will be thrown away or ignored later, but we don't know which parts yet. Keep it all for now.

✔ **Daydream.** We're not condoning job slacking, but if you're doing it anyway, you might as well make it work for you! This works equally well on the couch instead of watching TV. If you're into gaming, imagine yourself in an alternate universe in which you play the main character. What does it look like? What are your goals? What is your character like? Open your eyes and make notes; then close them again to further explore your imagination. Allow details to emerge in your mind. Repeat. If you are more of a productivity-oriented person, imagine an amazing tool for getting something done. Don't confine your imagination to the iPhone yet. When you've got it really rich in your head, write it down. Then, you can take it apart and see how you could do that with your iPhone. Don't just think of software; the iPhone can interact with external hardware as well. While you daydream, the sky is the limit! Put off worrying about how to do what you are think about for later in the process.

Taking an inventory of what you can offer

At this point, you might already have an idea for the type of app you'd like to pursue. But we also encourage you to do this part of the process anyway. You might discover things about yourself that you weren't thinking about. You might find a new angle to add to your concept. And, if this first venture works out well, you are probably going to want to create more apps. Having fully invested yourself in the process will give you a greater depth to draw from and give you more to work with.

Start by writing a brief life history. This doesn't have to be an autobiography. Bullet points are great. You can draw a timeline to help yourself remember sequentially, or just start writing a list of everything that comes to mind. You've had millions of life experiences. Even by just scratching the surface, you will unlock areas of interest, knowledge, and expertise that you might not be focusing on in your present-day life, particularly if you've had multiple careers, as many people have.

Now, like our fishing net analogy, we are dredging up past experience so we can have as much raw material on the table as possible to start from. Otherwise, you might focus just on your immediate interests and miss something that could be a gold mine. If you are reading this book, you are probably interested in making some sort of change in your life or career. A great place to start with this is by bringing back to life things you were interested in as a child, but have let go by the wayside. Dig out your old records. Go through your old stuff. Even reconnect with old friends. Make an initial list and keep it around to add to and play with.

Now let's hone in a little bit more. Take an area of interest from your past or present and drill down on it. This might be your present career or hobby. Or it might be something you used to do, but haven't done for a while. Just take something that sparks your interest and inventory everything you know about it. Even if you don't realize it, you probably have specialized knowledge in at least one area. This doesn't have to be something serious. It could be a mastery of miniature golf, card tricks, or a video game. But, of course, it can also be something related to your career or hobby.

You are also welcome to start with something you have an interest in but don't yet have a lot of experience with. This will make your process longer, because you'll have to become an expert or find experts in the area, but it might be worth it to you.

If you are working with a partner or team, it may be that only one or some of you are experts in the area you choose to pursue. That is okay. Knowledge in the subject matter of your app is only one job in the many that will need to be done. It can actually be helpful for one or more of your team not to start out as experts, so that they can catch things and pose questions that those who have worked with a subject for a long time are prone to make assumptions about or overlook.

Try to wrap up this part of the process with a set of multiple interest areas and angles on those interests. We want to have more than one, because now we will combine the three approaches we have taken and try to come up with the optimal fit between

✔ Your particular interests

✔ The needs and wants of the environment around you

✔ The existing marketplace in the App Store

Synthesizing the approaches to find your idea

Let's start with your interest list. Take each of the major areas you've come up with and condense them each into a short phrase, like these:

✔ Gold mining

✔ Dart throwing

✔ Action-adventure games

✔ Managing the combustion process for nuclear power plants

Now let's do the same for the discoveries you've made about your environment. Dig out that *iPhone Inspiration* note from your Notes application and compile them the same way:

✔ It's annoying to keep track of my notepad and my phone while I'm gold mining.

✔ Judy would like a way to know where to find the cheapest gas in her neighborhood.

✔ I wish I had a quick way to look up nuclear reactor core temperatures.

✔ I wish I had a way to learn music on my phone.

✔ I want to catalog my bug collection and compare it to an online database.

And the same for any realizations we had while checking out the App Store:

✔ I like apps that let me pinch and zoom the screen.

✔ I find shaking the iPhone annoying.

✔ There is no iPhone app for nuclear power plants.

✔ Science apps tend to look very basic and don't have great graphics.

✔ I love the way kids' app X looks and works.

✔ Task management apps have been really overdone.

Once you've thoroughly gone through and catalogued your discoveries from each of these processes, you can start to look for patterns and connections. In our preceding list, the most obvious pattern is that we have a level of expertise with nuclear power plants, we wish we had a tool to help us manage part of a nuclear power plant, and there is no software for nuclear power plants. Your lists may not yield as obvious a connection between each other, but they will help you to cross-reference. The thing we are looking for is something that connects with us personally, fills a real need in the real world (which includes the digital world as well), and has not been overdone in the App Store. Once you find ideas that meet all of these criteria, you are ready to move into more specifically assessing the market for your app by determining demand, getting specific about the competition, targeting your demographic, and envisioning your app in detail. This book guides you through the process.

Connecting with Apple's Strategy and Vision

Apple is notoriously close to the chest with even near-term announcements, let alone long-term strategy. But a look at the historical context out of which the iPhone was developed, combined with observation of how Apple has staged the release of functionality for the device so far, can paint a picture of Apple's strategy and vision.

Unlike Microsoft, which is a software company, Apple has created itself as a lifestyle company that specializes in hardware and software. The difference is important. Every move Apple makes is informed primarily by how its products will integrate into the lives of its customers. Whereas Microsoft puts a premium on its operating system being compatible with any number of hardware systems, Apple creates its own hardware that is engineered to be the optimal fit for its operating system. Where Microsoft emphasizes a diversity of products, Apple focuses on product lines it feels matter most to a broad range of consumers, and leaves specialty applications to third-party developers. Whereas Microsoft relies on a whole industry of third-party companies to service its products, Apple makes great service and repair a central theme of its business operation. The list goes on. Take a moment to make your own list of qualities that make Apple unique and express its approach to the market. You can compare it to many other companies besides Microsoft.

As an iPhone entrepreneur, it is important for you to *grok* (deeply understand) the ideology that informs the Apple brand so that your products can find synergy with Apple, and thus the expectations of your customers. That will help propel you to the forefront by making you a co-innovator with Apple, not just someone trying to do something with the iPhone.

Connecting between iPhone hardware and applications

We explore the various novel hardware and software features of the iPhone in Chapter 2. For now, we want to help you get onboard with Apple's vision for the iPhone and why it created it the way it did, so that you can participate with Apple in this exciting new medium, rather than simply going along for the ride.

The iPhone is a computer, nothing less. Indeed, the fact that it is called a *phone* is a bit of a misnomer. Apple engineered the iPhone to be the leading-edge mobile computing platform from the ground up, based on its venerated OS X operating system that runs its desktop and laptop computers. Because the iPhone is really essentially a miniaturization of a laptop computer, it has a rich subset of all of the capabilities of Apple's standard computers, including fast processing power, strong graphics rendering, and robust input/output capabilities.

 As you approach the platform from a development perspective, you should be looking at the iPhone as a tiny computer, not a phone that can run some software. This differentiates the iPhone strongly from Blackberry, Nokia, and other "smart phones." The iPhone is differentiated from Palm because of the robustness of its hardware and operating system and from Microsoft's Windows CE platform because of its usability, which we discuss next.

In order to create a device small enough to fit in your pocket and still give the level of user experience that is at the core of the Apple brand, Apple got creative with the iPhone's hardware design, particularly its input hardware. If you have an iPhone, you are familiar with its multitouch touch screen. You also know that that you can control certain things on the device by moving it in space. This is accomplished with the iPhone's accelerometer, a device that measures the phone's relative position over time and its position relevant to gravity.

Some iPhone applications even use sound as an input, such as Smule's *Ocarina*, which allows you to use the mic like a wind instrument, and *Google*, which uses voice recognition for searches, like in Figure 1-17.

Figure 1-17:
Do a Google
search on
your iPhone
with your
voice.

These novel input methods, combined with the size and shape of the iPhone's screen and its ergonomic characteristics (the way it fits into your life physically), demand certain behaviors and characteristics of the software that is developed for the iPhone. The iPhone also has methods to communicate to the world outside, including cellular, Wi-Fi, Bluetooth, and its dock connector. Some or all of these will need to be contemplated in your application development process.

The iPhone is the hub of Apple's contemporary realization of a concept called the Personal Area Network. Similar to Local Area Network (LAN), such as the network in a typical office, and Wide Area Network (WAN), one that connects multiple locations across a distance; the Internet itself; or a company's intranet), the concept of the Personal Area Network (PAN) is that, in a computer-enabled society, individuals can be the center of their own network of interoperating devices.

Until iPhone 3.0, the iPhone was simply a LAN and WAN device: It allowed one to connect with the world, but had no direct interoperability with hardware or devices in its local vicinity, except in the context of a LAN (connecting with your computer over Wi-Fi, for example). Once Apple opened up access to the iPhone's Bluetooth port, it became a PAN device (though Apple doesn't describe it in these terms).

Bluetooth is a network protocol (a way of sending and receiving information) for devices that are within about 60 feet apart. You are most certainly familiar with Bluetooth headsets for cellphones. But a phone headset is only one of dozens of possible Bluetooth profiles. There are profiles for all sorts of doodads, including headphones, microphones, keyboards, mice, game controllers, sensors, and printers. The fact that the iPhone supports Bluetooth means that you can walk into a room and control an iPhone-supported printer, stereo system, home appliance, or nearly any other type of device simply and seamlessly from your phone. You can also interoperate with devices you carry with you in a pocket or purse — even computerized clothing.

In addition to Bluetooth, iPhone 3.0 opened up the opportunity for developers to use the iPhone's dock connector to interoperate with various devices. The dock connector allows a more discreet, secure connection to the phone, and allows access to video and audio out. The dock connector interface also is cheaper to implement. because you don't need to embed Bluetooth hardware in the device you want to interoperate with.

As you move forward with your iPhone projects, keep in mind that you are helping to advance the evolution of an entirely new computing model. The iPhone exists in a space that is related to both cellphones and standard computers, but is really a transcendence of both: mobile computing. Imagine out three to five years. What kind of amazing ways could you, the people you know, and humanity at large, use a computer network that is composed of millions of tiny interoperating devices, all of which are connected, aware of each other, able to command and be commanded by other devices, and able to process huge amounts of information simultaneously? How does this shape what it is like to be a citizen, consumer, worker, entrepreneur, etc.? That's where we want you to put your head, because, as an iPhone entrepreneur, you are helping to create that future.

Following iPhone releases has affected the app world

In the beginning, there was a twinkle in the eye of Steve Jobs. Then there was an iPhone that looked like it should be able have apps installed on it, but couldn't. Then there was an iPhone that you could hack, or jailbreak, so you could put apps on it. Then there was iPhone 2.0, which legitimized putting apps on the iPhone and started an industry. Then there was iPhone 3.0, which allowed all sorts of new functionality, including the ability to connect to external devices.

A new version of iPhone hardware/software is released approximately each year, in the summer. Similarly, a new version of the iPod Touch is also released each year. The iPod Touch has most of the functionality of the iPhone, but lacks its cellular connectivity. Both run the same operating system, and the iPod Touch is compatible with most apps available for the iPhone. For simplicity's sake in this book, we will typically refer to applications running on the iPhone, but the iPod Touch is another market for your app.

Let's look at the progression of the iPhone:

- ✔ **Phase 1: The iPhone Is Born.** When the iPhone was first released, it was met with excitement and critical acclaim, but it featured only a few proprietary Apple applications: Calendar, Phone, Mail, Text, Clock, Camera, Pictures, Settings, Safari, iPod, Maps, Stocks, and iTunes.

  The remaining slots available on the home screen caught the imaginations of users and developers, but Apple offered no plans for opening up the device for third-party development. Instead, Apple touted the third-party creation of Web apps, which are Web sites optimized to fit the iPhone's screen and make use of some of its features. Many Web apps were created, and they are still relevant today, but people were underwhelmed. Many an ireful blog bemoaned such a capable device lacking such an obvious function as third-party apps.

- ✔ **Phase 2: The Users Strike Back.** To get around the frustration, some developers began *jailbreaking* iPhones, a process that removes Apple's roadblocks to installing third-party apps on the device, and reverse engineering the iPhone Software Development Kit (SDK), a set of applications that allow a developer to program an iPhone application. Before long, it became cool to jailbreak your phone and use third-party applications developed by programmers using the hacked SDK.

- ✔ **Phase 3: The iPhone 2.0 Cometh!** In March of 2008, lo and behold, Apple revealed that it had planned to support third-party developers all along, and unveiled

- iPhone OS 2.0, which allowed the installation of third-party apps

- Its iPhone Developer program, which supports and assists iPhone developers

- The App Store

It could almost be said that iPhone 1.0 was merely a prologue and that the release of iPhone 2.0 was the real beginning of the iPhone story, because iPhone apps have become such a central driver of the iPhone's sales, narrative, and appeal. Upon the release of iPhone 2.0, the App Store exploded with activity and has made several individual developers millionaires, spawned dozens of new companies specializing exclusively in iPhone development, and become a cultural phenomenon.

✔ **Phase 4: The Users are Still Restless.** After the App Store had been around for a while, consumers and developers began to wonder why it was so hard to interact with the iPhone on a hardware level. The iPhone wouldn't even support a stereo Bluetooth headset, let alone more interesting devices. In that spirit, companies such as Perceptive Development (where Damien and Aaron currently work), along with several others, set out to find a workaround for Apple's locked-down hardware. Perceptive came up with a way to communicate with the iPhone through its audio port using FSK, the same type of technology used in the now-antiquated serial modem. Remember *bee-do-beeeee-squaaaaash-bee-do-beeeeee?* That's code being sent as an audio signal, and it's how our software called Tin Can allowed devices to talk to the iPhone and for iPhones to communicate with each other.

✔ **Phase 5: The Dawn of iPhone 3.0.** Shortly after Perceptive worked out the kinks, however (what do you know?), Apple announced iPhone 3.0, which has support for hardware interaction. At the writing of this book, the release of iPhone 3.0 portends to unleash a similar if not so frenzied torrent of iPhone-related activity as developers plunge in to make hardware for the iPhone and take advantage of other features of the new OS, including in-app purchase.

If you think the iPhone would be better with a certain attribute, it's probably on the radar of the folks at Apple. Some of the earliest releases on the App Store were apps that had been developed with the hacked SDK for jailbroken iPhones. Once Apple opened up the phone to apps, those developers simply had to port their code to the legitimate SDK; they were instantly ahead of the pack. As for our hardware workaround, it has some uses, even in the context of 3.0, and it shows off our programming prowess, but the release of 3.0 makes it somewhat irrelevant on a commercial level. The moral of the story is that, to a certain extent, you can anticipate that Apple will eventually release the cool features that "everyone" thinks it should. Planning accordingly can really help your business.

Writing for current or future functionality

Given the development history of the iPhone, several people begin to wonder whether it's important to write for the current functions available to iPhone application developers, or to plan an application that would work with potential future functions of the iPhone. If you can prove the concept of an app like the Tin Can app, then you'd be a step ahead of everyone else when the new hardware function is announced.

When you are looking at whether to focus on current or future functionality, keep in mind that Apple announces new upgrades to the iPhone to everyone all at once. You can follow the speculation on blogs and other resources mentioned later in the book, but in order to get the real news that you should act on, you'll need to wait with everyone else for one of Apple's announcement events. It's a good idea to jump on new features early if you can, but don't gear your business toward new functionality that is only speculation.

Stay right on top of the wave, instead of ahead or behind it.

That said, many features that are desired by the development community, but not yet enacted by Apple, are still being utilized with jailbreaking. Keeping your eye on these developments can give you a good idea of what Apple has in store, so you can be anticipating that in your planning.

In other words, it's up to you, but your focus should be on what your app will provide, not necessarily what functions you can write code for on the iPhone. Your application should make sense to the user community and provide some sort of utility or entertainment. If you need a function that's not available, look for a workaround first. When and if Apple announces a new feature, you'll be better positioned to incorporate and use that new feature.

Chapter 2

Understanding the iPhone Platform

In This Chapter

▶ Accessing GPS location information

▶ Sensing user input

▶ Providing application navigation options

▶ Employing new iPhone 3.0 business strategies

*I*f you want to develop an iPhone application, it helps to have a big-picture idea of the platform for which you're developing an app. The iPhone is simply the newest entry into the field of mobile computing, so a look at the roots and capabilities of mobile computing may help stir up an idea or two, or at least help guide you to the elements of your application that you need to plan for in advance.

This chapter discusses the different capabilities and useful functions that mobile computing has brought to users. We go through different categories of functionality that include networking, hardware, gaming, and user-generated content. Then the focus shifts to the iPhone itself — and its exclusive functionality that you should keep in mind when you design your iPhone application; you may be tapping into one or more of those features yourself.

Apple's Entry into Mobile Computing

Waiting to enter the market allowed Apple to observe the successes and failures of other products:

✔ Observing the pitfalls of trying to fit pre-existing approaches to computing onto a tiny device, Apple went back to the drawing board on user-interface design, making the screen fill the entire face of the device and increasing the screen resolution to 160 pixels per inch, well beyond a standard monitor's 72 pixels per inch.

✔ To accommodate the screen, Apple engineered its own predictive text engine, which allowed even large fingers to manipulate a small onscreen keyboard, and the multitouch touch screen, which (in effect) increases usable screen size by allowing the user to zoom, pan, and rotate the onscreen image seamlessly.

✔ Apple created user-interface methods for use on a smartphone, which were foreign to the desktop experience — in particular:

- An accelerometer measures the effects of motion and gravity; to manipulate data on the phone, the user has a new range of input methods for the device: *shaking, rotating, moving,* and *orienting.*

- An embedded GPS receiver is integral to the phone's "location-aware" capabilities, which we discuss later in this chapter.

In short, the iPhone represents the first true mobile computing platform because of its combination of

✔ Computing power

✔ Robust operating system

✔ Uniquely handy interface features in a handheld device

High on the list of those handy features is the iPhone's location awareness. Read on.

iPhone Location-Aware Capabilities

Since the iPhone is a cellphone, a computer and a GPS device, it is a no-brainer that it should have functionality that is based on where the user is located geographically. To this effect, hundreds of apps that are already out there use this awareness to locate the nearest movie theater, tell your friends where you are, give you directions, and so on.

As you conceive of your application, consider whether location awareness is going to be a very important feature. (Is location *truly* irrelevant? Are you sure?) In fact, location awareness is one of the attributes that makes the current generation of mobile computing transcend previous computing standards. As a location-aware device, a mobile computer adds a dimension to the computing experience that didn't have much of a place (so to speak) on a stationary computer. By using your geography as a sorting mechanism for the vast array of data available on the Internet, the computer that is your iPhone acts as a mobile guide that knows more about your surroundings than you do. Just thinking of ways to utilize this capability can be a great springboard for app ideas.

Telepresence

Telepresence is the notion that a person can be virtually "present" in an environment that's geographically somewhere else. This is accomplished through projecting actions and senses (input and output) through the Internet in real time. A Webcam provides a form of telepresence by allowing the user to video-chat with another person over the Internet. But what about when you aren't just sitting around at your computer? That's where the iPhone and other mobile computers come into play:

- ✔ Twitter is a form of telepresence that uses the simple format of short text messaging to let you give interested people a small window into your world, and you can even Twitter from your iPhone nowadays (see Figure 2-1).

- ✔ Ever take a picture on your phone and send it via SMS to a friend right then? That, too, is a form of telepresence.

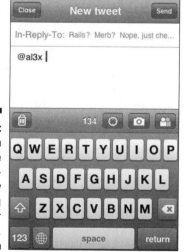

Figure 2-1:
You can achieve telepresence by Twittering on your iPhone.

The telepresence revolution has only just begun. As mobile computers such as the iPhone get more capable, and the types of data that are conveyed get more robust, telepresence will mushroom into a way of life for most people in developed nations. For a fascinating look at a potential future for telepresence, check out the movie *Sleep Dealer*, a dystopic fantasy set only a few years in the future. We believe the future of telepresence to be far less grim than depicted in the movie, but it still portrays an amazing vision for how a person's entire set of senses could be digitized and transmitted through the Internet to distant locations.

Even the senses of touch and smell may soon be showing up on your computer from a distant (or even synthetic) environment. Mobile computing already fits into this equation: Anyone with a mobile computer can grant telepresence to anyone else with a computer. This is applicable to both work and interpersonal situations. Using your cellphone to ask your spouse what to get while you're at the grocery store is already a rudimentary form of telepresence, but what if you could provide the full sensation of being right there with you? How would that change how you communicate with your friends, family, and society? As an iPhone entrepreneur, you have the opportunity — right now — to help to shape the leading edge of this exciting new phenomenon.

Telematics

Most prevalently used when referring to navigation systems in automobiles, the term *telematics* simply means the long-distance transmission of computer information. Anyone who has used a GPS system has used telematics, and since the 2.0 release, the iPhone has itself been a GPS device. But in the world of mobile computing — especially of the iPhone — telematics takes on a much deeper meaning. The fact that the iPhone can give you directions is itself revolutionary, but that's only the tip of the iceberg. In collaboration with location awareness and telepresence, telematics allows the user to step inside a meta-universe of data available to them about their environment at any given time. By meta-universe, or metaverse as it's sometimes called, we mean a universe of data that is superimposed on top of our everyday universe — literally it means a universe of universes. So what are we getting at here? Armed with your iPhone, you can drop into any location in the world and within a few minutes know more about that location than most of the locals:

- Your exact geographical location to within a few meters
- Routes from that location to anywhere
- The history of the area
- Translations for common phrases
- Current news and events
- The structure of the government
- The exact location of every public bathroom in town
- All the subway and bus stops
- Anyone's phone number
- Where to get the best food of any type

The list goes on and on — Figure 2-2 is just an example — and that's just information related to your physical location! You barely need to move a muscle to receive this information, or even to contribute your own information back to the public at large. You are literally an intelligent, mobile node in a vast super-computer called the Internet.

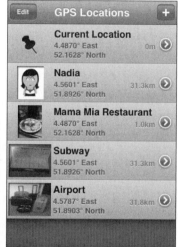

Figure 2-2:
Find out what's close by with telematics on your iPhone.

Business automation

Even before the advent of the iPhone, mobile computing has quietly revolutionized business as we know it. Any business activity that takes place across distances has been touched by mobile computing. Some of the most obvious examples are in the distribution and tracking of products and packages:

- ✔ **FedEx:** Ever used tracking for your FedEx packages and wondered how they knew exactly where your package was on its route? The answer lies in the handheld device the delivery guy had you digitally sign after he scanned your package with it. FedEx implements a massive mobile computing network composed of these devices, all of which are tied to their central computer network wirelessly over cellular. Each time a package changes hands or passes a checkpoint, it gets scanned again. Each package has a unique bar code that's correlated to your shipping data, so the system can track the movement of your package through space and time. This allows precise location of your package, but also a high degree of flexibility for rerouting around bad weather and other obstacles. In a pinch, your package can even be tracked down en route to your destination and sent to a different address if needed. Now FedEx allows consumers to use their smartphones to tie into the same data network, further spreading logistical awareness through the FedEx organization directly to the end-user. An example of FedEx Mobile for the iPhone can be seen in Figure 2-3. This same mobile computing methodology is used extensively throughout the commercial shipping industry.

✔ **RFID:** Short for *radio-frequency identification*, RFID is another manifestation of mobile computing in business automation. Rather that manually scanning a barcode to receive package information, RFID systems rely on tiny microchips embedded in products (or even under the skin — yikes!) to transmit data about an item to receivers that can be mobile or positioned at specific waypoints. In advanced RFID systems, the microchips themselves are unpowered, but receive power from energy waves emitted from the receiver. Once given power, the microchips transmit data that the receiver then sends into a database to be processed with all of the other data points coming into it. The result is pinpoint-accurate tracking, identification, and logistical information passively being computed at any given time.

If you've obtained a passport in the last few years, you take an RFID device with you every time you go on vacation.

Figure 2-3: Use FedEx Mobile for the iPhone to automate shipment tracking.

But business automation doesn't only have to do with tracking and logistics. It also has to do with communication and collaboration:

✔ **Project management:** Perceptive Development uses an online service called BaseCamp to help it manage and organize all of its software-development projects. Using an iPhone app called Encamp, employees (such as authors Damien and Aaron) can call up that same system on the device for management and assignment of tasks — from anywhere, as shown in Figure 2-4.

✔ **Managing client relationships:** Perceptive also uses a client-relations management package called SalesForce in the same way. Every time one of its employees takes a meeting with a client, he or she immediately uses an iPhone to enter notes from the meeting into a SalesForce account. That way the passing of time doesn't blur the details of the meeting for the attendees or let them forget to enter the data. In addition, since that company is spread across three states and two countries, its representatives can use audio conferences to conduct meetings between themselves or with their clients. A business meeting conducted in an elevator is an example of business automation facilitated by mobile computing — but sending the client the contract, getting a digital signature, and setting the first milestones for your development team *during that same call* — from the same device (in the same elevator) you're calling from is a whole new ball game.

Figure 2-4: Manage your task list from your iPhone remotely.

For many people, the business automation facilitated by mobile computing is already a part of everyday life. But taking a step back from to consider the broader implications can be truly staggering — and (more importantly) open your mind to new ways you can further and enhance this cultural shift with your own iPhone products.

iPhone Networking Capabilities

What we generally think of as the Internet today is only the tip of the iceberg. Today's Internet is based on the concept of *hyperlinking* — linking related documents dynamically, whether by clicking on those onscreen strings of blue text we are so familiar with, or with other forms of linking such as images and video. Hyperlinking is incredibly powerful, and has spawned a total revolution in communication. But Tim Berners-Lee, the man who invented the concept of hyperlinking — and literally evangelized the subject into mainstream use (and thus largely shaped the Internet we use today) — has a new frontier he would like us to tackle: the linking of *data*.

While millions of documents are linked together on the Internet now, Berners-Lee invites us to conceive of the vast oceans of existing data that are *not* interconnected. All that data is unavailable to anyone but its immediate owners, unable to be readily synthesized, practically invisible to the rest of us — and the pictures painted by that data could increase the intelligence level of humanity hundreds of times over. Berners-Lee is now on a quest to get companies, governments, and other institutions to participate in new systems that open their data to usage by the masses.

Mobile computing brings its capabilities of location awareness, telepresence, telematics, and business automation to the quest. The realization of Berners-Lee's latest vision for the Internet would increase the robustness of these capabilities dramatically, by tying the mobile computer user into the very heartbeat of humanity in a very accurate fashion that could be fine-tuned to specific needs.

But there's even more to this. Not only can mobile computing allow us to tie into the vast array of documents and data available on the Internet, it can allow us to do things with that data and to do things together. It can do this in several ways including communication between devices, crowdsourcing, cloud computing, and collaboration.

Communication between devices

Innovation in communication is especially exciting in the realm of mobile computing because it ties in so closely with — and expands on — the interpersonal communication we cherish but take for granted. How can you, the iPhone entrepreneur, improve people's lives by helping them communicate better with the iPhone?

Well, how about turning an iPhone into a virtual ocarina? Believe it or not, it's been done. It may sound goofy, but there's more to it than novelty: The most touching example of inter-device communication we've seen so far is the *explore* mode of Smule's Ocarina app: Tapping the globe icon brings you to a view of the earth from space, which features colored ribbons of light emanating from various geographic locations. The light is accompanied by a melody played by a person in that location using the program as a musical instrument. You can also see shimmering lights covering the globe where people are playing the instrument, but which are not being currently broadcast to you. There's no better way to get a feeling of "it's a small world" than watching and listening to this app for a while.

What's going on here? On a technical level, as an individual plays, the fingerings on the screen and the wind pressure exerted on the microphone are being sent to a server in real time. As the app scans the globe, it taps into one of these data streams and sends the data to your iPhone at the same time. Then the app interprets the data and converts it to sound for you to hear. Pretty simple technologically, but a major leap culturally. The ability to listen in passively — from anywhere in the world — on people's personal moments doodling with a virtual flute is rather revolutionary. On a technical level, it's simply a real-time communication between two computers, no less than text chatting or videoconferencing. On a cultural level, well . . . it's a small world!

As technologies such as the iPhone deepen the capabilities of such devices, the horizon for inter-device communication expands exponentially. Here are some examples:

- **Staying in virtual touch with your business:** These days a large company with employees in the field can now track those employees' physical locations down to the meter, and furthermore, anyone with a mobile device in that company can see the location of all the other employees. Many companies have employed this on a social level on the iPhone for the purposes of location-based social networking and location-based games. Of course, iPhone applications can be set to ask the user before their location is shared. But it is probably still possible for Apple and the phone carrier (and thus possibly the government) to see users' locations, inspiring interesting privacy debates.

- **Mobile videoconferencing:** One of the very much-anticipated potential features of the iPhone is mobile videoconferencing. Imagine being able to be anywhere and in direct video contact with friends, associates, and family. Videoconferencing hasn't taken off in the mainstream yet, but when it hits mobile devices, it surely will.

- **Mobile networking:** With the advent of iPhone 3.0, devices can now communicate directly to each other over the air between them rather than tunneling through the Internet. This opens the door to in-person multiplayer games, sending and receiving data such as contacts and other data directly between devices, and pairing devices together to create ad hoc (on the fly) networks. The possibilities are truly immense.

Imagine some interesting ways that iPhones could communicate with each other:

- What methods of communication would work best — voice, sound, video, images, data, text?
- How would these be useful/fun?
- Is there a business use?
- Is there a novelty factor?

The phenomenon of crowdsourcing uses inter-device communication — and the social dimension of the iPhone — in unique enough ways that it calls for a closer look.

Crowdsourcing

Crowdsourcing is using the communications and organizational power of the Internet to have people across various locations engage in synchronized or related activity with each other.

Perhaps the earliest great example of crowdsourcing is eBay. eBay took the rummage sale, combined it with auctioneering, and facilitated it with the Internet — to create perhaps the most powerful customer-driven commerce engine in the world. Every transaction that happens on eBay positions end users on both sides of the equation! The only job that the eBay company has (and don't get us wrong, it's still a big one) is to act as an intermediary between end users (in this case, between buyers and sellers). They simply provide the forum, payment methods and dispute resolution, and let the users do the rest.

eBay pioneered crowdsourcing on a grand commercial scale, but now that it's a large corporation, it's more focused on protecting and enhancing its current platform. Since then, crowdsourcing has expanded into niche markets such as photography (www.istockphoto.com), arts and crafts, and even furniture. Internet Web sites you are probably very familiar with, such as Flickr, FaceBook, and Wikipedia, are also crowdsourcing applications.

All this activity has happened on standard computers across the standard Internet. But the advent of mobile computing — Internet-connected telephony in particular — has dramatically changed crowdsourcing. Now crowdsourcing is not only a commercial and open-source activity, it's also a social tool and performance-art medium. The term *flash mob* has taken on a new meaning the last five years as cellphone text messaging has been used to gather huge crowds spontaneously in randomly specified urban locations.

Sometimes these crowds are composed of individuals who are pre-rehearsed to do a certain group dance routine or other behavior in a public place such as a train station. The participants have never met each other, but have simply learned the moves at home. When they are alerted (via their cellphones) where and when to show up — sometimes just moments before — they spontaneously unite to fill the area with coordinated dance. Or perhaps they all just spontaneously freeze or strike a certain pose. The effect of this kind of apparently spontaneous group activity is rather breathtaking, even when viewed through the distortion of a YouTube video. To see it, search YouTube for *flash mob* or check out www.improveverywhere.com.

Companies are even beginning to use the concept of flash mobs for advertising purposes. Mega–ad firm Saatchi and Saatchi recently featured the singer Pink in a mobile-phone ad campaign staged in London's Trafalgar Square, into which poured a thousand people who had received a mobile-phone alert, as seen in Figure 2-5.

Figure 2-5: Crowd-sourcing comes to Trafalgar Square as a marketing event.

Mobile computing takes all aspects of crowdsourcing to the next level by putting real computing power in the palm of the hand. Thousands of eBay entrepreneurs now use mobile computers to handle every aspect of the selling process — from locating products to taking photos, posting descriptions, running auctions, and making bank transfers. Many mobile computer users use their devices exclusively for managing blogs, maintaining and promoting a presence on social networks, and updating their Twitter status.

In the near future, entire cottage industries will revolve around people spread all over the globe using their pocket devices to create and sell products and services, generate social media, and create happenings. Perhaps they could be doing all or some of that with your upcoming mobile application!

Cloud computing

Cloud computing is a term that evolved out of the distribution of computing power and data storage away from the end-user's desktop and onto servers connected to the Internet. Because engineers often depict the Internet as a cloud when they diagram networks on paper, computing that took place "in the cloud" meant computing that took place *on the Internet* rather than on a user's local computer.

Just as a cloud is a vague subject, so is the term *cloud computing*. And it's used to mean different things in different contexts. To people concerned with mobile computing, however, it simply means the capability of a mobile device to make use of data and computing power not stored locally on the device.

The iPhone comes with a pretty large hard drive, but it's not large enough to store (for example) all the data you might store on a personal computer at home — some of which you might want to access from your phone. A company called Soonr, along with several others, has intermediated this difficulty by creating a service that replicates your desktop computer's files on an Internet server (see Figure 2-6). When you want to access a file on your iPhone, the software asks the server for the file and it's downloaded to the device. It's is an example of "the cloud" serving data to your computer.

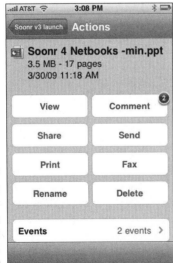

Figure 2-6: Using Soonr to store files away from your iPhone.

To find an example of computing power being administered via the cloud, we can look to Skype. If you download and install the iPhone version of Skype on your phone, you will find a somewhat familiar interface that combines the attributes of the iPhone's chat and phone applications. Dialing a phone number or Skype buddy on a Wi-Fi network will connect you to that person just as if you were talking to that person on your phone, except the connection is happening across the Internet.

Neither the desktop nor iPhone versions of Skype know anything about placing a call across the Internet, however. Both applications simply act as a conduit through which information that's generated and processed on Skype's *servers* is delivered to you. When you dial a number, that bit of information is sent up to the server, which in turn runs software that opens the phone or Internet connection to the person you're calling, and then opens a port from the audio channel it has created for you to the software you're running. It's kind of like sending a piece of mail: All you have to know is how to put on a stamp and drop it in the box. The Post Office has all the intelligence (no postal jokes, please) needed to route and track that piece of mail. That's how cloud computing pertains to computational power.

The model is similar to the mainframes (servers) and terminals (local computers) that typified early large-scale computing, except that

- ✔ The servers and computers can connect to each other from anywhere at anytime.
- ✔ Instead of the local computers being "dumb terminals" that only know how to request, send, and display data, modern cloud-computing scenarios generally involve fully capable computers *on both ends*. If you consider the Internet as one huge global computer (on the one end), then your iPhone (the computer on the other end) lets you tap into the power of the Internet — to varying degrees — at any time.

Mobile computers represent an ideal way to take advantage of cloud computing: The less power (and thus bulk) needed on the device itself, the smaller and more lightweight it can be. More importantly, all these devices running around drawing data from — and contributing data to — the cloud make for a dynamic and evolving data network on a global scale.

iPhone Hardware and Accessories

Mobile computers were born to be accessorized. However, before the iPhone 3.0, most accessories had nothing to do with computing power, but more to do with convenience: headphones, stereos, audio devices on armbands, and so on. With the advent of iPhone 3.0, the sky is the limit for truly useful devices that can be paired with the computing power and connectivity of the iPhone. Medical devices such as glucose and heart monitors; gaming devices such as joysticks and various novel controllers; specialized gear for photography, diving, flying — you name it — all can and will be developed for the iPhone. The hardware and accessory world is the "personal" side of the Personal Area Network.

As an iPhone entrepreneur, you don't have to start with software. You can start with an interesting hardware idea and then conceive of the iPhone software that will support your hardware.

After all, cellphones only gained a mass-cultural foothold in the late nineties; mobile game consoles have been around since the beginning of that decade. If you consider even more primitive gaming devices (such as the little rudimentary games that play from a built-in chip), mobile gaming has been around since the seventies. *Pong*, *Pac-Man*, *Space Invaders*, *Galaga*, and thousands of other arcade games have found new homes — or have been specifically developed for countless pocket video-game devices — in the last 40 years. You may have to look to an antique store or collector to find most examples of these types of devices, but they're still being sold as key fobs and other cheap novelty items in drug stores and toy stores.

A device lineage that's more apt as a precursor to the iPhone, however, really began with Nintendo's GameBoy. The GameBoy was the first high-quality game console that was adapted for mobile use. The original GameBoy even had the same form factor as many cellphones: a square screen on top and the control buttons on the bottom. The GameBoy had a card-slot on the back, into which the user could plug any number of video games (*Mario Bros.* and *Donkey Kong*, anyone?). To this day, you can find little kids running around with one hand practically glued to a GameBoy.

There have been many iterations of the mobile console game device: the most advanced one to date is Sony's PSP (PlayStation Portable), which offers a powerful processor, high-resolution graphics, and networking capabilities. Simple, cheap games on cellphones have been around for a number of years, but the iPhone is the first mobile computer to embrace mobile gaming in a way that offers serious competition to specialized gaming hardware devices from leaders such as Nintendo and Sony.

So the iPhone has fully entered the mainstream as a mobile gaming platform. It will be interesting to see what the video-game console manufacturers do next to outmaneuver Apple. Or will they face the same fate as music stores in the face of iTunes?

Games are by far the top-selling app category on the iPhone. So the most potentially lucrative question you have to ask yourself is this: Had any great game ideas lately?

Unique iPhone Capabilities

If you deconstruct the iPhone to its components, you won't find a lot of features that aren't found in other devices. The unique features it does have, however, are game-changers. The iPhone itself is an evolutionary step technologically — but culturally the iPhone is absolutely revolutionary. That's because the iPhone is more than the sum of its parts. Apple didn't just combine features found in pre-existing mobile computing platforms; it combined them elegantly and functionally. Result: a device that's truly useful as a mobile companion for business, social interaction, and play — just what the marketplace has yearned for.

We've already covered many of the unique capabilities of the iPhone — its functionality as a robust gaming platform on a PDA-style device, location awareness, robust connectivity to the Internet and other devices, and more. The hub of all of these capabilities, and the core of what truly makes the iPhone unique, is its operating system.

The operating system

The *operating system* is a layer of software that runs on a computer as (essentially) the host to all other software running on that computer. It manages resources between applications, the operations of the hardware, and offers various services to applications. The operating system is not only the bedrock upon which a programmer develops an application, but is also necessary for the application to run. The more capable the operating system, the more capable the programs that can be written for it.

iPhone OS, the operating system for the iPhone, is an only-slightly-limited version of OS X, the operating system that runs on all of Apple's standard computers. This is revolutionary because OS X is the most stable and high-performance operating system in existence. Years ago, Microsoft attempted to *port* (transfer to a different environment) its operating system to the mobile world with Windows CE, but missed the boat in terms of stability and usability. Rather than mimicking the surface mechanisms of OS X for the iPhone, such as the use of windows and menus, Apple utilized the underpinning of the operating system — and completely redeveloped the *user interface* (how a person interacts with the computer) that runs on top of it. This combination set the stage for a highly usable and enjoyable computing experience on a tiny mobile device — something that has been attempted many times before but never achieved with such aplomb.

iPhone OS thus affords developers an incredibly rich set of tools, including

- ✔ Hardware-rendered 3D graphics
- ✔ Powerful sound capabilities
- ✔ Networking capabilities
- ✔ Databasing
- ✔ Seamless integration with the hardware of the device, including its novel input/output capabilities.

What's more, Apple supports and trains developers. Result: It's as easy as possible to go from never having programmed an app before to creating a beautiful finished app ready for sale. This is still a complicated process, but Apple provides documentation, instructional videos, and support every step of the way. For developers already familiar with OS X, coding for the iPhone is simply an extension of abilities they already have. And because the iPhone is a bona fide computer, it can run other programming languages as well (Java, for example), making it a truly flexible environment for nearly any app you can dream up and develop.

The accelerometer

The *accelerometer* is a tiny component embedded in the iPhone that can tell various things about the device's position in space, including

- ✔ Its relative orientation over time
- ✔ Its orientation to the ground (gravity)
- ✔ Its speed as it travels through the air

But don't throw your iPhone unless you can afford a new one!

It works just like a set of tiny springs with an object mounted between them. Imagine taking two springs and connecting them to the upper and lower surfaces of a brick. If you moved the set up and down, you would see one spring stretch and the other contract, and then the other spring do the same as the brick traveled up and down between them. If you could measure the degree of stretch and contraction of each spring, you could then calculate how fast the brick was moving (speed) and how fast its speed was changing (acceleration). This is exactly how an accelerometer works, except it uses electromagnets instead of springs, a tiny speck instead of a brick, and it measures movement in three dimensions.

The iPhone is the first mobile computer to utilize an accelerometer — and in a fascinating way. Developers have created motion-sensitive apps (as shown in Figure 2-7) that can

- ✔ Calculate your compass direction
- ✔ Use the phone like a steering wheel
- ✔ Rotate the screen contents
- ✔ Sense when the phone is shaken or bumped

Figure 2-7: The accelerometer lets your apps do some amazing things.

Accelerometer

iPhone responds to motion using a built-in accelerometer. When you rotate iPhone from portrait to landscape, the accelerometer detects the movement and changes the display accordingly. The accelerometer also gives you amazing game control.

What uses can you think of for the types of measurements the accelerometer calculates for the iPhone?

Multitouch

Touch screens have been around for quite some time. But the ability for a touch screen to interpret more than one gesture at a time is relatively new. Apple capitalized on this innovation in its quest to overcome the limits of a small screen, by intimately embedding multitouch support into the iPhone's operating system. This handy feature puts zooming, panning, rotating, and stretching in your application easily within your grasp.

iTunes Store

iTunes makes the iPhone unique by extending the seamless selling experience directly to the iPhone in the form of the instantaneous purchase and downloads of music and applications over Wi-Fi and cellular phone networks. Some smartphones and PDAs through the years have had the technology to offer this type of service, but no other has rivaled the quality of downloads, nor the seamless experience of downloads, available on the iPhone.

iPhone 1.0, 2.0, 3.0, and Beyond

Camping out at the Apple store for the new iPhone became an instant tradition in the summer of '07 when the iPhone was first released. Now, with two more years of new iPhones — and new software releases to match — the tradition is firmly entrenched.

The first version of the iPhone was a closed device, and only people who engaged in iPhone "hacks" could add new programs to teach their phone new tricks. With the 2.0 firmware followed by the iPhone 3G, people could install third-party programs; before long, over a billion downloads solidified the success of Apple's new computing platform.

Recently with the advent of 3.0, Apple has added a number of fantastic new features — and methodically added some features that should have been there from the beginning, such as copy and paste, laptop tethering, video recording, and picture messaging. But gripe as people will about limitations, some of the new features *are* truly revolutionary, even if only from a market perspective.

The 3.0 firmware significantly enhanced the Bluetooth story for the iPhone. Originally, the iPhone would only communicate with in-vehicle Bluetooth, hands-free Bluetooth, and do a limited address sync with the car. It didn't even support A2DP, the stereo-Bluetooth standard, so everyone with fancy wireless Bluetooth headphones could only connect to calls, not to music. That's changed — now the iPhone supports stereo Bluetooth. And that's not half the story, as will be detailed in a minute.

The 3.0 firmware has come out almost simultaneously with the newest iPhone, the 3GS. Fortunately for case manufacturers, the iPhone 3GS has the same dimensions and case size as the 3G. And aside from internal enhancements to speed, battery life, and memory, the hardware is very similar, except for the notable addition of a compass and a video-capable camera.

The video camera is a significant addition. The new iPhone's video is smooth 30 frames per second, at 640 x 480 resolution — essentially VHS quality, which is pretty impressive for a phone. With up to 32 GB of storage, that's a significant amount of video. The application possibilities opened by adding a high-quality camera to the phone are significant.

To be fair, the first iPhone was technically capable of video, at low frame rates, but only hacked phones had that capability.

The compass has a lot of implications:

- ✔ The fast-moving Google Map Streetview features demonstrate just how amazing technology has become: Turning the phone instantly swivels the map to correspond to the phone's new position in space (see Figure 2-8); the compass opens amazing new opportunities for location awareness and fine-grained pedestrian guidance and interactive mobility.

- ✔ Some of the natural applications of a truly direction- and location-enabled phone are tele-guidance for pedestrians as well as *augmented reality*, where your phone adds additional layers of information, context, data, and media to where you are and provides details about what you're facing.

- ✔ With the combination of accelerometer, compass, GPS, and the possibility of some sort of wireless beacons, it won't be long before in-building personal navigation is enabled. Imagine going to a museum, downloading its free app, and your iPhone automatically downloads and narrates your journey through the museum — tuned to your interests, in your language, and down to the exact picture or sculpture you're looking at.

Figure 2-8:
The compass adds a new dimension to maps on the iPhone.

One of the most significant enhancements to 3.0 is that Apple launched a program to encourage hardware interactions with the iPhone, allowing hardware companies to develop devices that connect to the dock connector, or communicate over Bluetooth, to applications on the phone. Early on, all you could buy for your iPhone were basics like batteries, speakers, and video cables. These days, any device you could imagine wanting to connect to a touch-screen display — be it a pool-chemical tester, a turkey-temperature reader, or a remote control for your mini-helicopter — can be developed and sold along with an App Store application.

Bluetooth is the basis of the new peer-to-peer communication features of the iPhone. It used to be that to accomplish head-to-head gaming, or any other kind of peer-to-peer communication, both phones had to be on the same Wi-Fi network. Too bad if two kids in the back seat of the minivan wanted to play. No longer — Bluetooth allows the devices to find each other and play right away.

The major story for iPhone application development is that more of the features used by other applications can be integrated into your own apps now. Want to integrate Google maps? Go ahead. Want to use cut-and-paste in your app? Feel free.

For many application developers, the limitations they were experiencing weren't technical obstacles so much as business restrictions. They had the app, but in order to do a "trial" app they had to call it "lite" and then hope people could be convinced to upgrade to the new apps. Or they had a whole range — a lite, a medium, a premium, and a deluxe version — and this created a bit of end-user confusion — which one should I buy? And why can't I get a credit if I upgrade?

Apple has introduced a new business model as a possibility for app purchases: If you sell an app — even for 99 cents — you can offer in-application purchases of upgrades, data, enhancements, or features. This allows you to sell a single, paid version, offer all your upgrade paths, and give the user both the opportunity and rationale to upgrade — right within the app. Free apps are still free, to avoid "bait-and-switch" type confusion, but there's a lot that can be done with the new model.

For starters, here are six revenue models that can take advantage of the iPhone in-app purchase option:

- ✔ Sell a basic app for an initial price and then sell a full version for more money.
- ✔ Sell an online version of the app for an initial price and then allow the user to download the data for an additional fee.
- ✔ Sell an ad-subsidized "lite" version, and then offer an ad-free version for an additional fee.
- ✔ Create a content-sales space within your app, where you can sell extra (and specific) content for an additional fee.

✔ Sell additional "consumable" digital content for an additional fee, such as extra levels in a game, additional sound banks for a synthesizer application, or additional cards for an e-card application.

✔ Sell premium access to content, even on a monthly rental basis — for instance, a mapping application could give access to premium maps, or a newsmagazine could grant 30 days of access for $5.

These models have just come out and are being tested by Apple, consumers, and developers alike, but there are lots of creative ways to use them. The primary opportunity is the same: When you've got customers into your app's world, you have the opportunity to offer them more right there in your application. If you have something great to offer, the friction between asking for the sale and getting it is all but eliminated.

Chapter 3

Pricing and Revenue Models

*E*ver since the App Store was launched, developers kept asking the hot question "What should I charge for my application?" No single correct answer exists, but the question can affect your development, your future as an iPhone application developer, and your success with this application.

Tens of thousands of applications are in the App Store, so you can find all sorts of pricing levels. The key is to determine what makes sense for your situation and apply a price that can help you meet your goals.

Identifying Revenue Streams

Whatever skill and sweat you put into an iPhone app, you probably want a way to receive a tangible reward for it. You can cash in on an iPhone app in two ways:

✓ **Paid applications:** Generate income directly from the App Store when users download them.

✓ **Free applications:** Generate income only from other business activities, such as

- Increasing sales of related products

- Selling advertising

- Building your own reputation

The best revenue model for your app depends on your needs and how your application matches up to the current offerings in the App Store.

Paid apps

The obvious way to get a return from selling an iPhone app is a transaction in the App Store:

1. You set the price.
2. The user pays that price.
3. Apple keeps some of the money.
4. Apple deposits the rest in your bank account.

Evaluating how much to charge for your app involves balancing many variables against each other to determine the optimal fit. It involves both

- **Hard data:** Market research, for example
- **Intuition:** A "gut feeling" about the amount that people would be willing to pay

Consider how much time, money, and intellectual property you invested in the app. If those elements are a substantial barrier to possible competitors, you can charge more.

Even if you already know the amount you want to charge, completing this process helps you objectively evaluate your pricing:

- You might change your mind.
- If you don't change your mind, you can justify your decision to partners and investors.

The Apple design for the App Store and the way it has chosen to market the store essentially puts application development in the same business genre as music production.

The App Store is now a hit-driven market with Apple positioned as the primary tastemaker, just as the record industry of old had a few large record labels positioned as gateways and tastemakers. If you want to create an award-winning app, and thus draw the attention and energy of Apple, you can find a lot of information about how to do so in the Apple Human User Interface (HUI) Guidelines and other documentation provided to app developers. Apple essentially tells you exactly how you can impress them and how you might turn them off.

Implement the Apple guidelines, even if you aren't setting out to be featured in the next Apple commercial.

The problem is that Apple doesn't support every good application, which leads to the other side of the music business metaphor: the indie label or solo band. Just as indie labels and do-it-yourself musicianship has taken off dramatically alongside the iTunes store, in order to be successful you must also become, to a certain extent, your own marketing department. Find out as much about marketing your app as you do about creating it in the first place, and then apply that knowledge to your task. Get your team together and hit the street to ensure that your app is seen and used. Don't already target "the usual suspects" — look for ways for your app to interest people who aren't already looking for one. The iPhone is a pop culture phenomenon: If your app is "right up the alley" of someone who isn't using an iPhone, seeing or hearing your ad, promo, or product buzz could prompt that person to make the switch, just to be able to use your app.

✔ **Barriers to entry**

Development costs are barriers that can hinder you or help you:

- If your development costs are high, you must price your app high enough and sell enough copies to recoup your costs before you will make a profit.

- High development cost can prevent competitors from copying your idea.

The same concept holds true in software and hardware development: If you come up with an idea that requires a large investment and can fund the project, you cut out a large portion of your potential competition.

Exclusive content is a powerful defense against competition. If you can latch on to a niche that others can't easily get into (industry-specific data feeds, exclusive pricing data, or editorial content that you have exclusive rights to, for example), you can make hay on that data with little competition as long as a market for it exists.

✔ **Unique offerings**

Companies that offer higher-priced apps have information or services that cannot be easily replicated by another company. These kinds of assets are distinct from the design and development of the apps themselves, but are the bases for the apps. Discover your core competencies and identify unique offerings that only you can provide. This business of selling a unique offering is one in which you can truly profit because, absent those attributes, another company can't come along and compete with your app on price.

Becoming popular in the App Store is a bit of a self-fulfilling prophesy: A popular app might be featured in a digital endcap, become quite visible by earning a spot on the Top 100 list, or be featured in the first few pages in its category in the App Store.

Like Google searchers, most App Store browsers don't look past these displays and the first few pages of a category listing before making their purchasing decision. Therefore, if your app doesn't become popular right away and you're relying on browsing consumers to find it, it may never become popular. This situation is a key factor in the race-to-the-bottom phenomenon, because price has such an important role in determining how many people download an app. So, it *appears* that you should price your app as low as possible so that you can rack up a lot of purchases as soon as it comes out, and thus ride a wave of popularity in the App Store. Let's examine this theory further, though.

If you price your app at 99 cents and sell 10,000 copies, you make roughly $7,000 gross, after Apple takes its 30 percent cut off the top. If you sell the app for $9.99, you need to sell only 1,000 copies to reach the same revenue. But, at 1,000 copies, your app has a far lesser chance of being in the top of its category than if you price it lower and your competition can then copy it, sell it for a lower price, and potentially become more popular than you — further driving its sales and popularity against yours. These factors combine to make quite a good argument for pricing your app as low as possible.

But then ask yourself this question: How many people can you reasonably expect to buy your app? Because roughly 10 million iPhones are now in circulation, you're dealing with a large but limited market, and your app is most likely to appeal to only a small percentage of them. If you sell your app cheap and saturate your market, you have no way to go back and charge more for the copies people have already bought. You can raise your price for future copies, but you risk suffering a backlash as customers find out that they could have paid less, and you reduce the amount of potential customers who would buy your application because of the perception that your app is only worth the lower price, due to the copies you've already sold cheap.

You can choose one of two solutions:

- **Make sure that your app is marketable.** It should be interesting, well designed, and targeted at a market segment that's large enough to give you the number of sales you need.

- **Promote your app outside the App Store.** The App Store is a gift to you as a business owner because it offers free promotion. But engaging in some good old-fashioned (and newfangled) advertising and promotion gives you more control over the presentation and salability of your app. Highlighting its features and benefits to your particular target demographic helps you justify the price in their minds so that you can charge the appropriate amount for it.

Price ranges

Your pricing should reflect the impression a consumer is likely to have about your app. For example, if you're selling a simple game with fairly "flat" graphics and game play that hinges primarily on simple variables, such as the speed of play, your app probably will be regarded like a candy bar at a supermarket checkout: a fun way to kill a bit of time but not worth much of an investment. This "novelty" or "impulse" quality puts your app in the $.99-1.99 category.

Don't dismiss this category quickly. Candy bars are big business!

The same concept applies to relatively shallow-featured utility applications, books, and other apps that are equivalent to buying a small bauble or tool.

You can justify a higher price by increasing the quality of your design and the cleverness of your implementation, but this kind of app gravitates to the lower end of the $1–5 range if it doesn't provide some advanced or sophisticated game playing features, proprietary information, or advanced and useful functionality usually reserved for a full-fledged computer.

If you were to try to receive a higher price for the app in our simple game example, you would run the risk of defying the expectations of your audience and missing the mark. For example, an independent developer named Owen Goss revealed that a game in which he invested $32,000 (including the value of his time) grossed only $535 in its first month. His *Dapple* is a beautifully crafted matching game in which the user mixes colors to create matches. We believe that two factors were at work in this application's faltering:

- *Dapple* **is quite similar to the popular iPhone game** *Aurora Feint.* This type of puzzle game is a classic genre. *Aurora Feint* and others like it (*Bejeweled, Tetris Attack, Trism*) have somewhat saturated that market.

- **The price of** *Dapple* **was too high.** At $4.99, a puzzle game is too expensive for the average consumer to buy just to try it out. Because many other alternatives are priced lower in the puzzle game genre and no trial option is offered in order to hook shoppers before the purchase, the price may have proved to be too much of a barrier because it eliminated the app from the impulse-buy category.

A lifestyle app named *Shopper,* on the other hand, in a similar impulse-buy category, is priced at $1.99, an easily digestible amount for a shopping list application. Rather than serve as just a list app, however, Shopper also identifies which store you're in by geolocation and modifying your options accordingly, as shown in Figure 3-1.

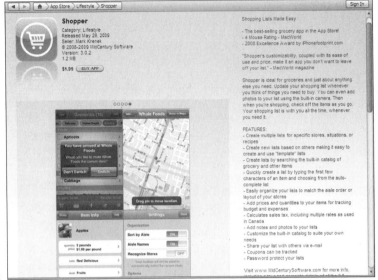

Figure 3-1:
An impulse
buy with
cool fea-
tures can
earn you
money.

✔ **$.99 to 1.99**

About half the apps in the Top 100 cost 99 cents. These applications are
"nice to have" in the sense that they're entertaining or solve a simple
need but don't necessarily excite consumers enough to want to put
down more than the price of a cup of coffee.

Even low-priced apps must be of high quality in order to be seriously
considered by customers for purchase.

✔ **$4.99 to $6.99**

Successful apps priced over $2 may seem similar to cheaper apps, but
they have a couple of key differences:

Games in this price category deliver an experience that isn't duplicated
for less money. The recent iPhone version of the incredibly popular
Cyan Worlds game *Myst* is an example in this price range (see Figure 3-2).
The game of *Myst* is simple by current standards. You're presented with
various choices and puzzles as you navigate through a world composed
of static images. Each navigation point loads a new image rather than
send you through a seamless 3D environment, like most modern adventure games offered by game publishers today.

The beauty of *Myst* lies in its narrative and graphics, however. It's an
absolutely beautiful and interesting game. For this reason, it also has a
huge, long-standing following that Cyan Worlds capitalized on for this
release. *Myst* is one of many examples in which a slightly higher-than-
average price is justified by stunning graphics, a factor that affects your

bottom line. In a way, the app industry resembles the fashion industry: People often pay top dollar for brilliant or crystal-clear intuitive design. Wouldn't you pay a bit more for an app that gives you something nice to look at rather than something plain or poorly designed?

Myst isn't just an example of great graphic design, however. There are currently many games that top its graphics, which were so leading-edge when it was first released. *Myst* is an example of great *overall* game design. The concept and execution behind *Myst* combine to create a game that engages users for hours and makes them feel like they are on an exotic quest that they want to keep diving deeper into. Thus it inspires word of mouth and great reviews, which fuel sales. This X factor is something that's hard to engineer. It requires artistry. And this is one of the things that are vital to making great apps great, and thus commanding and justifying a higher price point in their genre.

Nongame apps that succeed at a higher price level don't necessarily leverage proprietary or specialist-level data or provide absolutely unique functionality. They do their job better than most of the competing apps for a similar function, or provide a function or utility that most other apps don't.

Any app priced at $4.99 or more should have an accompanying free trial app, to allow users to get hooked on it before they invest in the full version. Otherwise, you could leave a lot of potential customers on the table. Even if some trial users don't buy your full app, the buzz that's generated by having more people trying your app and writing reviews is worth it, if your app is good. Trial apps are covered later in this chapter.

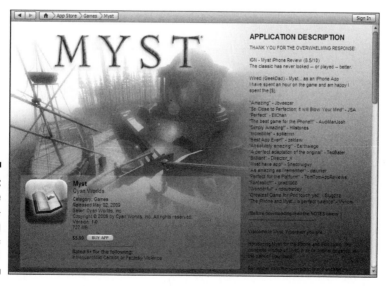

Figure 3-2: Simple game + stunning graphics = success!

As you edge up the price of your app, you aren't always eliminating potential buyers. A higher price isn't necessarily a bad thing. If your app helps divers evaluate water conditions, for example, you have a specialized target market. If you craft your app better than the competition does, your public will appreciate the extra care you put into your app to fit their precise needs in the most effective, fun-to-use way, and they may select your app over the competition's by virtue of your app's higher quality and commensurate price.

✔ **$7.99 to 9.99**

To do well in this price range, your app must be not only a leader in its field but also meet a strong demand from the public.

Every app in the Top 100 costs $9.99 or less, but few of them are priced at $8.99. A consumer who will pay $8.99 probably will pay $9.99, so cutting the price a dollar doesn't increase total income.

You encounter stiff competition from these two types of companies (known euphemistically as BigDevCo or BigCo):

- **Large software companies:** Electronic Arts and Apple, for example

- **Established iPhone companies:** Ngmoco, for example

These larger companies have established development teams, successful properties on other platforms that they can port to the iPhone, and deep pockets to take risks. They can turn out top-quality products for a fraction of the price that smaller companies and individuals can, and they have access to the related funding they need.

Don't be intimidated by big competitors. You have your own advantages:

- You can move rapidly to respond to market changes.

- You can try things they aren't willing to try.

- You don't have an existing product line to support that would distract you from building a new application.

- You can write software for niche markets where they won't invest.

✔ **More than $10**

If your app has required you to spend a lot of money in research and development (R&D), accesses and displays targeted "specialized" information or exclusive content, connects with a specialized or proprietary system such as a corporate software program, and has an audience that's small but willing to pay for that kind of functionality on their phones, you may need to (and be able to) charge tens or hundreds of dollars for your application.

Apps priced over $9.99 are for specialized markets, not for every type of iPhone user. Reduce your costs and widen your target demographic to bring your app to less than $9.99 if you want to sell it in large numbers.

If you're considering pricing your app over $10, you need two things:

- **A good idea of *exactly* who will buy your app and why**

  Buyers in this category usually need a product for work or a technically sophisticated recreation (such as digital music). There are only about five games in the App Store over $9.99.

- **A marketing strategy that gets your app in front of potential buyers and convinces them to buy**

  If your app is an extension to an existing product line, such as the OmniFocus task management software, you have a built-in customer base to promote to. If not, you need to identify how to reach the people you're targeting with your app.

The medical field probably has the highest concentration of apps in this category. Medical professionals need specialized tools, resources, and information, and are used to paying for them.

Many other demographics fit some or all of this description. Engineering, science, or professional areas like nursing, real estate, and law can benefit from a well-designed application. Recently, the ProRemote app, which provides an iPhone interface with the ProTools digital audio recording software, got quite a bit of attention — and rave reviews — for around $130. Beatmaker, a mobile rhythm machine for musicians and music enthusiasts (see Figure 3-3), has had similar success by charging $19.99.

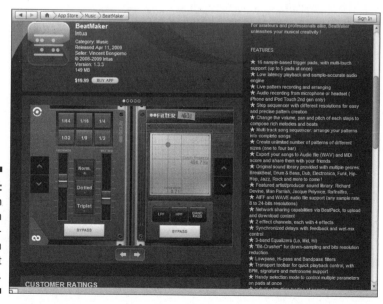

Figure 3-3: Premium apps with lots of features can succeed at high prices.

Free apps

You have many reasons, from a business perspective, to create a free application. A good free application provides a benefit, whether it's

- ✔ Monetary (from advertising support)
- ✔ Promotional (to support another product or iPhone application)
- ✔ Brand building (to increase mindshare without directly selling)

Free trial iPhone apps are a helpful tool for selling paid applications, so they're covered in this chapter with paid applications.

- ✔ **Choosing an advertising platform**

    Advertising is the most popular reason to give away an app.

    Dedicated companies such as AdMob have already sprung up to provide and support iPhone advertisements. Mobile advertising platforms, such as MillenialMedia that were serving mobile ads even before the iPhone came along, are also getting into the iPhone game. Enough of these providers now exist that AdWhirl, a company that helps you aggregate streams from numerous mobile ad providers, is providing a one-stop shop for mobile advertising. In the first part of 2009, AdWhirl claimed more than 8 million advertising impressions served.

    If you want to find and implement an ad network to manage the advertisements in your ad-supported iPhone application, check out these providers:

    - • **AdMob:** www.admob.com
    - • **AdWhirl:** www.adwhirl.com
    - • **MediaLets:** www.medialets.com
    - • **Millennial Media:** www.millennialmedia.com
    - • **PinchMedia:** www.pinchmedia.com

AdWhirl claims that the top 100 apps can average between $400 and $5,000 a day. Your income depends on the initial interest in and the average amount of time your customers spend using your app.

Mobile advertising is quantified by these measurements:

- • **Click-through rate, or CTR:** A click-through is generated only when a user clicks an ad to open the page where a product is advertised.

- • **Cost per thousand, or CPM:** This term refers to the number of passive impressions an ad receives, or the number of people who only see the ad regardless of whether they click it. (M is the Latin numeral for 1,000, by the way.)

Sometimes, advertising agencies refer to *eCPMs,* which refers to how much the app itself is generating in ad revenue per thousand ad views. CTR and CPM fees are included in one general calculation so that you can easily quantify total revenue.

AdWhirl says that the eCPM of iPhone applications ranges between $.50 and $4.00, depending on the app:

- Apps in which the user performs a complex, longer-lasting set of tasks or games tend to make between $1.00 and $4.00 eCPMs.

- Apps in which the user simply checks the status of something and then quits tend to make between $.50 to $1.00 eCPMs.

If your application generates 100,000 ad impressions over a given period with an eCPM of $1.00, your total revenue for that period is $100.

If your income comes from selling advertisements, you need to boost two numbers: impressions and click-throughs. Your ability to increase your impressions depends on how many people download and use your app. Increasing the number of click-throughs seems to depend on how engaging your app is, and the relevance of the ads to your target customer. Your advertising effectiveness depends on the quality of your app in terms of its filling a niche with consumers and delivering on the promises that prompted them to download it in the first place.

Just because your app is free doesn't mean that you can invest less energy and ingenuity if you want it to make money for you.

✔ Free trial versions

If you're releasing a completely new type of app into the market, we highly recommend creating a free trial version. There is no better way for users to find how your product operates and sell themselves than letting them play with it themselves:

- No description can give users the exact experience.

- Users are unlikely to pay more than 99 cents for an app to try it.

In the iPhone world, most try-before-you-buy apps utilize the limited functionality model and are distributed as two separate apps:

- A trial or "light" version

- A regular or Pro version

Some companies even release three or more apps with titles such as Free, Standard, and Pro all with different prices and sets of available functionality. For example, the Mitch Waite group has 9 different versions of its iBird Explorer app, with prices ranging from Free to $29.99, as shown in Figure 3-4.

The free, try-before-you-buy or Lite version should give users a useful experience but also compel them to buy the full version. Consider these options:

- **Limit the number of game levels.** A free game version can allow one or two levels of play and then remind users about the paid version of the app. If a user enjoys one or two levels, she might be motivated to buy the complete game.

- **Limit the number of uses.** You can limit actions, such as the number of times a user can repeat a certain action (opening a file in a given session, for example).

- **Limit functions.** You can limit the number of times a user can save or print information or limit the number of documents he can create. For a creative app, such as a drawing or writing program, you may want to allow potential buyers to use all the tools but prevent them from saving, printing, or sending their work without buying the paid application.

  If you have a gaming app, consider limiting its weapons.

- **See how other apps divide their features between their free and paid versions.** As you experiment with trial apps in the App Store, keep an eye out for the different ways that developers implement limits in their apps. You see a wide variety. Note which ones make you want to buy the paid version, which ones are so limiting that you don't want to bother, and which ones are so unrestricted that you don't feel you need to buy the paid versions.

In your app's trial version, you want to hit the "sweet spot," where its users feel that it's "theirs" but their options are limited enough that they pony up for the full version.

Apple doesn't allow time-limited trials (unlimited use for a week or a month, for example).

✔ **Supporting another product**

If you have an existing service or product line that you want to help you move into the iPhone market, use this category as your starting point, but don't necessarily limit yourself to making your app free. Ask yourself these questions:

- Will my customers feel justified in spending more money on my iPhone app on top of what they pay for my other offerings, or will they feel "nickel-and-dimed"?

- Does my app represent a new service, or is it really a value-add to an existing service?

- Will having an iPhone app push new business to my existing divisions and therefore justify the expense, or does it need to make money itself in order to be viable?

- Is the prestige of having an app in the App Store worth the expense to me?

- Does my iPhone app help me sell a non-iPhone product that recoups my iPhone expenses?

- Will my free iPhone app be used to upsell users to buy optional hardware or software or services from me?

Answering these questions can guide you to decide whether to price your app or make it free. You're deciding whether to use your app as either

- A product in its own right

- An extra platform to run other products and services

For example, paid software applications, such as Salesforce.com have a free iPhone app (see Figure 3-5) to make their software more valuable by enabling access through the sales team's iPhones.

Paid apps can promote for you. Electronic Arts created an iPhone version of its Trivial Pursuit game but didn't give it away. Its iPhone app (see Figure 3-6) is a full version of the game that reinforces the line of Trivial Pursuit board games.

Even if your app isn't free or a self-sustaining advertising vehicle, placing a free iPhone app in the App Store is a tremendous opportunity to generate PR and keep your company "fresh." Particularly if your company exists in an industry that isn't already prevalent in the mobile computing scene, promoting your new iPhone app can give you a good reason to hit the streets with ads and articles about your company, which can attract a lot of attention.

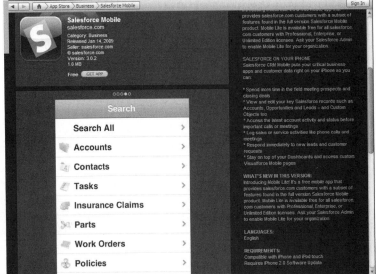

Figure 3-5: Support a paid product with an iPhone app, such as Salesforce.com.

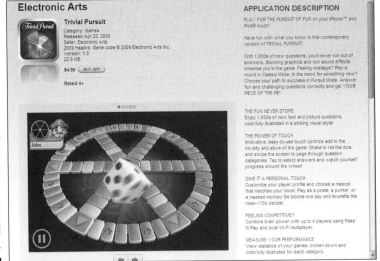

Figure 3-6: Your iPhone app can generate money and brand recognition.

Create an advertisement inviting people to download your free app. It's a helpful way to put your company in the forefront of people's minds. You can even use your app the way marketers have used refrigerator magnets and free pens, to put your app's name in front of people's faces. If you make a product that people use regularly and that is sponsored by your company, you ensure that they think of you every time they use it.

✔ **Generating a user base for later conversion**

An app can build a loyal user base of customers; then earn money from this customer base down the road. This category can be seen two ways:

- **The social networking model:** Users are viewed as a targeted demographic group that can receive other advertisements.

  This model sees users themselves as a commodity to be traded rather than as simply a captive audience for the app they purchased from you. You're building a customer base that you will later convert into paying customers for a related product or service, or just sell outright to another advertiser.

- **The trial model:** In this context, the trial model is a bit different from the trial or Lite version discussed earlier. You start with a standard version of your app and offer all its standard features for free to your customers. When you have a large user base, you can start upselling those users to more advanced features. For example, Soonr sells more disk space on its servers for user files.

  Which advanced features you offer depends on your specific application. With the release of iPhone 3.0, Apple has built this model directly into the operating system. Game designers, for example, can allow users to purchase (with real money) new clothing or weapons for characters, new abilities, and new levels for example. This *app purchase* relates directly to the model of converting free users to paying users by offering enhanced functionality or content.

If you want to implement the In App Purchase option in your application, you cannot offer your app for free. You must charge at least 99 cents so that you can offer something for sale as an add-on purchase while the user is "in-app", or using the application. So you'll need to give the app at least enough perceived value so that people will want to buy it, and then you can attempt to up-sell them.

✔ **Promoting a brand**

Free iPhone apps are increasingly being used as promotional tools. Web sites such as eBay, Facebook, and LinkedIn offer free iPhone apps to extend the power of their offerings to their users who have iPhones, so you can always check your auctions, update your profile, or write on your friend's wall — all from the comfort of your iPhone.

If you're wondering whether you (or your company) should spend this much expense and effort to create a promotional piece, the following sections present some "buzz-worthy" concepts that other companies have experienced by creating promotional iPhone applications.

- **Viral marketing**

  Viral marketing is the digital age equivalent of the word-of-mouth marketing method. Rather than just let it happen by itself, by virtue of the value of the product or service, however, these days marketers are taking matters into their own hands, by creating campaigns designed to stimulate the activity of people passing information about a product or service to each other. One way they do this is to create an ad campaign that's so shocking or different that people just start talking about it. If the campaign is interesting enough, it may even draw press coverage, particularly if it sparks controversy.

Flash games or "mini" applications that can be embedded in social networking sites such as Facebook and MySpace are the latest online marketing rage. The idea is that after people embed these widgets on their pages, their friends find them and embed them in their own pages.

Similarly, advertisers have been using the iPhone app as a micro site. A user can't easily spread an app to other users, the way she can spread a social networking widget, but in the busy App Store marketplace, a good free app can catch on and draw lots of attention to the app and its sponsor. When people use the Dance Mixer iPhone app from Psyclops, for example, to create and e-mail their own dance videos to their friends (see Figure 3-7), those friends learn about, and can buy, Dance mixer themselves.

- **Stickiness**

  For a promotional app to take root, it must be *sticky*. (Don't worry: Nothing oozes from the iPhone.) This term simply refers to apps that people find so useful or entertaining that they *stick* with them longer and return to them repeatedly. This concept is easier to achieve in the app world by understanding several key factors.

  Reviews: Reviews have a major effect on purchasing decisions at the App Store. Even someone who never uses an app after the first time will probably give it an unfavorable rating when prompted to rate the app before deleting it. Bad reviews can work against the viral popularity and success of your app.

  Effectiveness: If your iPhone app is sticky, you (or your company) see the benefit because your customers are exposed longer to your brand, your products, or whatever you're promoting by way of your app. If your app is barely used or holds a user's attention for only seconds rather than minutes (or hours), the app isn't promoting anything.

  Conversion: The point of a promotional tool is to eventually encourage another action, whether it's to buy a product, examine a brand further, or continue using a particular company's products or services. You enjoy a better conversion or success rate with sticky apps than with ones that are never launched again.

- **Soft promotion**

    When you target advertising to a consumer indirectly, you engage
    in *soft promotion*. Rather than hit consumers over the head with
    overt appeals, such as "Drink Coke," a soft promotion places the
    brand name in front of consumers by other means without making
    an appeal. "Brought to you by" and "Powered by" are soft promo-
    tion lead-ins that position one brand with another. Sponsoring a
    softball team is a form of soft promotion. So is buying the naming
    rights to a baseball field.

    The goal of soft promotion is to ingratiate a brand or product into
    the hearts and minds of consumers by way of non-invasive, non-
    confrontational interactions that simply put the brand or product
    in front of consumers without asking anything of them. The idea
    is that later on, a consumer who is asked to make the sale will
    already be familiar with the brand and will therefore be comfort-
    able making a purchase.

    Perhaps the most relevant form of soft promotion to the iPhone
    market is the concept of brand interaction. Anyone who has
    bought a Dodger Dog at Dodger stadium, for example, has engaged
    in brand interaction. You are, in a sense, "eating" the Dodger
    brand. On the Internet, brand interaction often comes in the form

of Flash games that let users investigate Web sites. The game is composed of colors, characters, and themes that are connected with the brand being advertised. Bono's Product (RED) campaign is an example of noncommercial brand interaction in the commercial space: Having convinced many top companies to sell Product (RED)– branded products and give some of the proceeds to charity, Bono has caused consumers to engage with (RED)-branded products and helped raise awareness of (RED) causes.

The idea is that a consumer who has a positive or fun experience that involves your brand will be more likely to remember and associate with it in the future. It's based on the same concepts that drive team-building exercises in the corporate culture, after which an employee might say, "I trust Bob because we worked together to scale that rock cliff together."

The iPhone is ripe territory for brand interaction because it's the most interactive computing device. You hold it. You move your fingers across it. You play with it. You work with it. It's integrated into your daily life. Putting your app in the same context can be a recipe for memorable familiarity with your brand. For example, rather than use the light from your iPhone screen as a flashlight, install and use the Coleman Lantern app (see Figure 3-8) and experience the light of a Coleman-brand lantern as you camp or look for your keys.

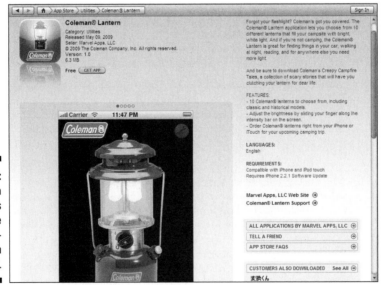

Figure 3-8: Coleman lanterns let iPhone users interact with their brand.

- **Paid feature**

  Rather than have users pay for content, content providers who use the paid feature concept pay you to get users to see their content. Yellow Pages and coupon books are good examples. Applications that aggregate commercial data, such as where to find the closest Starbucks or classified ads, have the opportunity to charge for promoting that data to consumers.

  You're essentially selling advertising in this approach, so the standard advertising models apply. You can charge a flat monthly rate, charge per user of your product (a few cents per user, for example), or charge per impression.

  If you charge per impression, you need to build into your software the ability to track particular clicks and views so that you have accurate metrics. Because this is one of the newest uses of a promotional iPhone application, we expect to see more examples after the features of the iPhone 3.0 OS are fully integrated into recent iPhone applications.

Estimating Income

The amount of money you will make directly from an iPhone app is hard to predict, for a couple of reasons:

- **Users must adjust to the newness of the App Store.** At the time his book was written, the App Store had been around for a little more than a year, so little historical data is available to show sales figures and trends. In that period, new versions of the iPhone have been released, and the 3.0 version alone comes with new revenue opportunities that haven't yet been truly quantified. Without much historical data because of the newness of the store, it's important to listen to other developers and companies to get some comparison numbers.

- **Apple is the "tastemaker."** Because only one avenue (the App Store) now exists for iPhone users to buy iPhone apps, Apple, the store's owner, has set itself up as the de facto consumer tastemaker. Apple inherently gives its favorite applications prime real estate, whether it's on the App Store home page under the Staff Picks label, in a full-page, full-color ad in *Time* or *USA Today,* or in an appearance in its catchy and effective TV spots. (Apple now gives dedicated App Store home page space to the apps featured in their ads, as shown in Figure 3-9.) That promotion from Apple can launch your app into the truly profitable category, but it's something you can't necessarily count on when you begin the development process. The key is to follow as many guidelines as Apple publishes in order to catch the eye of the tastemaker.

There's more than money

Your first iPhone app may be released for free, and for many good reasons. The benefits you receive from may be measured not in dollars and cents but, rather, by these other benefits:

✔ Leads that pan out in iPhone developer contract work

✔ The visibility to launch another business

✔ Increased ad revenue

Figure 3-9: Featured Apple ads get more visibility.

Determining your application's price point

Regardless of what you know about pricing in general, how do you know exactly how much to charge for *your* app? Surveying comes in handy for this task, and it boils down to these steps:

1. **Identify the type of person who is likely to buy your application.**

   Or, "Know your demographic." Does it consist of moms between the ages of 25 and 45? Is it high school boys who have a bent for gory games? Be as specific as possible without narrowing out people on the edge of your demographic who would still be strong potential customers.

   You can even create fictional personas to make these demographics more lifelike. For example, you might create for your lifestyle application a character named Cindy, who's a vegan and a yoga student. Then fill in as much fictional detail about the character as you can: age, background, or favorite musicians, for example. Then create a few more characters who would also be good prospects for your app. You can use these personas in role-playing scenarios to discover interesting additions to your app in addition to its survey and marketing uses.

2. **Find a group of likely buyers in the real world that match your targeted demographic.**

   The larger the set of people (or *sample size*), the more accurate your survey, but don't go overboard. A sample of 5 to 10 people works well. But even if you can find only a couple of representative customers, start there. Don't let the gathering of a group become a barrier to determining a price for your app.

   Don't just rely on your immediate friends and family.

   Don't let inhibition hold you back, either. Grab a clipboard and go to the local coffee shop or use a relevant e-mail list and poll them. Ask a qualifying question to make sure their opinion counts. For instance, if you're targeting general iPhone users, you could ask, "Do you own an iPhone?" If you're targeting business users of iPhone, you might ask, "Do you use your iPhone for business productivity?" The closer you can get to your target market, the smaller sample you can do, but if your app has broad appeal, then your survey can target anyone with an iPhone. Most people think to offer their opinions and provide this type of feedback. If possible, get the participants' contact info so that you can complete follow-up research for advertisements. You can even offer the app for free for responding to your surveys.

3. **Show your app to your potential customers and ask how much they would pay for it.**

   If you don't have your app ready yet, describe it in as much detail as possible and provide images, if you have them. Make sure you ask the same questions for every survey. If this method is too vague for your respondents, complete this step later, when you're closer to having a finished product. Gather the group's responses and find an average respond. If you feel that it's appropriate, you can weight some responses more heavily than others based on how likely respondents are to buy any application in the first place.

   Start with these four questions:

   - Would you pay $X.XX for this application?

   - What is the most you would pay for this application?

   - What is the least you would pay for this application?

   - On a scale from 1 to 5 (1 is 'Definitely No', 5 is 'Definitely Yes'), how likely are you to buy this application?

You can use this data to reconcile differing opinions among respondents and as a guide if you choose not to price your app at their average suggested price levels.

4. **If possible, price your app according to your survey results.**

   Sometimes, you may find that the cost of building the application exceeds what people will pay. You may need to factor other variables, such as development costs, into your final price, or the price of other competitive applications. The consumer isn't always the final decision maker on price. You also must feel that your price is correct, despite group members' input. You can rely on their too-high and too-low pricing numbers to help guide your decision. If you later have trouble selling, you can refer to your survey data and adjust accordingly.

   If no significant barrier exists to pricing your app according to your survey, however, do that. You already have objective proof that people who match the type you're looking for and who would buy your app would consider buying it at the specified price.

5. **Market to the people you surveyed.**

   After your app is for sale and you launch your marketing campaign, use your demographic descriptions and personas to market to those people. Make marketing pieces that would appeal to the people you surveyed.

Test your marketing pieces on the same people you surveyed. They give you valuable feedback about how your message lands and how they might be compelled to respond to it.

Different demographics may be willing to pay completely different prices for the same functionality. For instance, a clever note-taking application might be perceived as a 99 cent application by consumers, but business users might pay $4.99. Depending on your survey, you may benefit from making multiple versions of the application, with different graphics and marketing campaigns, so that you can target these different segments of your market.

Predicting an application's revenue

Each pricing method comes with its own revenue model or chart. Rather than try to condense all possible options into one neat chart, we discuss the issues you should keep in mind as you come up with your own revenue projections. (For the purposes of this discussion, we focus on paid applications in this section, where revenue equals sales from selling your app directly to users.)

When you're ready to start formulating revenue estimates, the following concepts can influence your numbers:

✔ **Sales can "pop" after an event.** Whenever your iPhone application receives a positive review on one of the major review sites or is featured in an iPhone ad, you could see a significant same-day increase in sales. Though it's impossible to know on exactly which day a single review will be posted and the effect it can have on sales, you can incorporate into your revenue projections a predicted set of events based on

 • Your marketing plan

 • The number of reviews that similar apps have gotten before yours.

✔ **Reaching the Top 100 Lists can help your application stay there.** Many application developers have noted that after their applications reached the Top 100 list, their presence on the list generated steady sales to keep them there. In other words, if you can crack the Top 100, you may see steady sales that are generated literally by your presence on the list. Again, you can't guarantee that kind of placement, but if you think your app can reach and stay in the Top 100, you should predict a period of constant, steady sales.

✔ **Plan to have a marketing budget.** We don't discuss in this chapter how to generate a budget for developing your iPhone app, but we can say that one way to help ensure steady revenue for your application is to create or allocate a portion of your budget for marketing expenses. Though some marketing efforts don't cost money, others, such as Google AdWords, can pay for themselves from increased revenue, especially because you can track certain marketing efforts against sales to calculate their effectiveness. Perhaps you can revisit your pricing model and allocate a portion of each sale toward marketing the app for future buyers.

✔ **Work backward from your costs or goals**. Many people come up with their revenue projections by first determining the size of the budget they need in order to develop their app and then estimating the number of sales they need in a given period to cover that budget. For example, you might determine that your app must generate $10,000 in one year. You determine that you will charge $9.99 per app, which generates about $7.00 ($9.99*70%) per sale for you. You therefore need about 1,429 unit sales, or 120 sales per month.

What might your revenue projection look like? The following examples use an application priced initially at $9.99, and you receive a 70 percent share for each sale.

Example A:	Build an Audience with Several Positive Events after 60 to 90 Days		
Month	Units Sold (per Day)	Revenue/Sale	Total Revenue
1	90 (3)	$7.00	$630
2	150 (5)	$7.00	$1050
3	300 (10)	$7.00	$2100
4	300 (10)	$7.00	$2100
5	150 (5)	$7.00	$1050
6	90 (3)	$7.00	$630
7	90 (3)	$7.00	$630
8	60 (2)	$7.00	$420
9	60 (2)	$7.00	$420
10	60 (2)	$7.00	$420
11	60 (2)	$7.00	$420
12	60 (2)	$7.00	$420
Year 1 Total	1470		$10,290

Example B:	Hit the Marketplace Fast and Strong and Discount Over Time		
Quarter	Units Sold	Revenue/Sale	Total Revenue
1	1800 (20)	$7.00 (9.99*.70)	$12,600
2	1350 (15)	$7.00 (9.99*.70)	$9450
3	450 (5)	$4.90 (6.99*.70)	$2205
4	450 (5)	$4.90 (6.99*.70)	$2205
Year 1 Total	4,005	$26,460	$26,460

You can make projections more accurate by adding revenue from

- People who convert from a trial version to the fully paid version
- Ads in your application
- In-purchase revenue — the sale of additional items inside your application

Testing estimates

The best prediction in the world can't replace the experience of having your app sell in the App Store, receiving favorable reviews that drive sales, or watching it hit number one on the Top 100 list with an accompanying big payday. As you put your plan into effect, and especially if you must justify your budget to your company or backers, you need to know whether your revenue projections are realistic and achievable.

After you come up with a projection, you need to ask yourself, "Can I realistically achieve these numbers?"

You have a couple of ways to validate your projections:

✔ **Pricing surveys**

Find a set of people who match your intended customer base, and ask these five important questions:

- Would you pay $X.XX for this application?

- What is a fair price for this application?

- What is the highest dollar amount you would pay for this application?

- What is the lowest dollar amount you would pay for this application?

- On a scale from 1 to 5 (1 is 'Definitely No,' and 5 is 'Definitely Yes'), how likely are you to buy this application?

If you already surveyed a group to determine your application's initial price, specify the price you're considering, to see whether their answers change. If the group members rate their likelihood of buying as 4 or 5, you could potentially consider it a sale. (If 50 percent of your test group says that they would buy your app and you then determine that you can reach a target market of Y people, can you achieve sales numbers of 0.5*Y based on your projections?)

After you launch your app into the App Store, you can change your app price and see how it affects your sales, if any, and update your projections accordingly.

✔ **Competing products**

By looking for free or paid reports over the Internet, you can find out the sales history of other iPhone applications from their developers who talk about their experiences. If they have apps that are similar to yours, you can compare your revenue projections to their sales to see whether your numbers are feasible or completely unrealistic.

If your applications are similar, you can achieve better results by creating a better marketing or launch plan.

Maximizing Sales

Once you have submitted your iPhone application to Apple for approval, and they get back to you (usually within four weeks) with notification that your application has been posted on the App Store, you can log onto the App Store and monitor daily download statistics for your app.

Once you get notification, your marketing campaign should kick into high gear and you should be promoting your app immediately. Because of the rapidly changing market, we recommend spending no more than one week studying the sales data before taking action to maximize sales. One or two days' data is too little, but studying the situation for two weeks could be too long. If sales are disappointing after one week (unless a lot of your marketing initiatives haven't really hit yet), look into ways to maximize your sales.

Though price may be the reason that your app isn't selling, you can give your sales a jolt by following other avenues instead of discounting. Read on.

Participating in a promotion

Simply being in the App Store isn't enough. Thousands of apps are available. Even being featured for a few days on the digital endcap usually isn't enough promotion. Even for a relatively inexpensive app, some targeted advertising can truly pay off.

Starting an iPhone Application Business For Dummies delivers many marketing and promotion tips specifically for iPhone applications.

Writing reviews

People tell you rather quickly what they like and don't like about your app. Identify holes quickly and patch them:

- ✔ **You may need to invest in a second round of development.** You have to bring your application up to the standards that your customers want.

- ✔ **You need to make continual incremental updates.** You have to do this even if you don't have problems with your app that are generating bad reviews.

As you plan your app, budget for this round of development.

Offering a trial version

If you don't already have a trial version, make one.

Then promote your new trial version. Getting people to use your app, and talk about it, can provide the bridge they need to make the purchase. This strategy can work even when a price reduction doesn't.

Repricing

If customers are complaining about the price of your app, listen to them.

Some consumers believe that all software should be free and that any price is too high. You're the judge: Decide whether their feedback is legitimate.

If your app is priced higher than your competition's, is your price justified? If so, make your case to compel customers to choose you. Outstanding design is an effective way to give customers the instant impression of quality.

If your higher price isn't justified or you think that you can still profit from a lower price, consider adjusting the price of your application.

Revising revenue projections

Part of the reason that you should enter all the initial revenue projection numbers into a spreadsheet is so that you can change one number, such as the unit price, and see the effect that a single change would have on your entire projection. By updating the price of your product, its estimated sales quantity, or your total budget or target revenue, for example, you can see in real time the other figures necessary to meet your goals.

This revenue revision process is particularly important after your application has launched, in case you want to use your revenue projections to help validate whether you set the right price point. Your customers need to feel that they're receiving an appropriate value for the paid application you plan to sell, and adjusting that price point can mean the difference between success and failure.

This concept is known as *price elasticity:* Changing the price of your application changes the actual buying demand of people wanting to purchase your app. If you lower the price and see a rise in the number of purchases or downloads, your app is price elastic.

Don't drop the price too low just to encourage a burst of buying activity. Use spreadsheets to test different prices to help determine the new price and to understand what the new price will mean to your revenue projections.

Suppose that you launch a paid app at $9.99 and see about 150 downloads in its first month of availability, or about 5 downloads per day. You then experiment with a sale in the second month, by lowering the app price to $7.99, and you then see 250 downloads the next month, or roughly 8 downloads per day. So far, your revenue looks like this:

Month	Price	Revenue per Sale	Quantity Sold	Revenue
1	$9.99	$6.99	150	$1,049
2	$7.99	$5.59	250	$1,398 ($349, or 33 percent, gain)

However, suppose that you lower the price of your app and people download it only 175 times during the second month. Now your revenue chart looks like this:

Month	Price	Revenue per Sale	Quantity Sold	Revenue
1	$9.99	$6.99	150	$1049
2	$7.99	$5.59	175	$978 (down $70+ from Month 1)

Even though the quantity of applications sold spiked slightly, the price reduction wiped out any benefit you received from those higher sales. In the previous example, you could have sold 140 applications at $9.99 apiece, or a 7 percent decline from Month 1, and still made the same amount of money as lowering the price to $7.99. For this price reduction to have been worthwhile, you would have needed 188 downloads at $7.99 apiece to earn the same revenue in Month 2 as you did in Month 1.

Here's a quick list of steps to follow in your quest for the perfect price point:

1. **Launch your app and measure initial sales by scrutinizing daily download statistics.**

2. **Calculate the initial results and compare them to your projections.**

3. **Conduct pricing tests and measure new download statistics and revenue.**

4. **Calculate new results and compare them to your initial results.**

Your application may experience sales ups and downs caused by external factors such as positive reviews, aggressive marketing practices, or the inclusion or exclusion of your app from the top lists. Because this market is relatively new, not much historical data is available to create fancy equations and perform statistical analyses. You can run pricing tests that last only one week or perform multiple tests in one month.

From here, you can explore several options:

- ✔ **Lower the price to reach a monthly sales goal.** If you see that lowering the price creates enough additional demand to cover the decreased amount of revenue per sale, you could lower the price until you reach your necessary goal of sales per month or quarter.

- ✔ **Keep the original price point and add more features.** If your calculations indicate that lowering the price isn't feasible based on your break-even point or sales figures, perhaps you need to update your application by trying to add features that could prove appealing enough to earn a higher number of sales at your app's original price point.

- ✔ **Combine price sales with marketing initiatives.** Depending on your marketing budget, you can employ a selective number of temporary price sales to coincide with your marketing initiatives so that you're lowering the price only when you're also generating a lot of attention toward your application. Then you can slowly raise or reset the price after the promotion period ends, to see whether you can sustain download numbers with your initial price point.

If you cruise the App Store, you encounter lots of apps advertising that they're on sale for a limited time. Putting something on sale can temporarily draw interest to it, overcome certain consumers' price objections, and fuel more sales. This can in turn drive up purchase numbers, increase the number of reviews, and generate a boost in sales revenue.

Putting your application on sale is a perfectly legitimate way to do all these things. But don't contribute to (or be victimized by) the race-to-the-bottom mentality. In the App Store, many "sale" prices become permanent prices because competitors follow suit. You're operating in a community of sellers who are trying to make a living by virtue of attracting consumers.

- ✔ If you collaborate with your fellow merchants and they do the same, the App Store can be a viable selling environment for many years.

- ✔ If price slashing wins out, the overall value of the store plummets.

Put your app on sale when you think it's appropriate, but don't undercut your price to make a fast buck in a way that erodes the marketplace for everyone.

Moving on

If you try boosting your promotional efforts and dropping your app's price and you *still* don't produce the results you were after, chalk it up to experience and move on to your next project.

To prepare for your next project, ask yourself if there was a possibility that you executed something wrong on this project. Look back over your development and marketing efforts:

- ✔ Did you provide an application that had better functionality, a unique offering, or a better price than the competition?

- ✔ Was the market overcrowded or not in demand by the time the application launched?

- ✔ Did lowering the price have a noticeable effect on sales? Could you have sustained profit for your application at the lower sales price?

- ✔ Did reviews point out shortcomings or flaws that you could have fixed?

Target your strengths and weaknesses, and how you took advantage of any opportunities and reacted to any opponents or competition. Sometimes, the issue will have nothing to do with the price of your application.

Once you have evaluated your efforts, you could reread our book *Starting an iPhone Application Business For Dummies*. Find out where you didn't fully apply something and apply it more fully. Do as much research as you can in addition to reading this book as well and apply it. Remember, being an iPhone entrepreneur isn't just about software development. It's as multifaceted as any business. Keep your chin up and keep growing as a business person. The 90% rule still applies! (10% inspiration, 90% perspiration). Just keep in mind that perspiration not only applies to physical labor, but really becoming informed about your field and delivering at the top level that you possibly can.

Part II
Pinpointing the Business Offering

"Okay, the view's just up ahead. Everyone switch to 'America the Beautiful' on your Media playlist."

In this part . . .

In this part, we help you narrow down all the possibilities out there into an iPhone application you plan on creating by using a three-step approach. First, we talk about coming up with the idea itself, using a variety of methods and research and some good ol' fashioned thinking. Once you've fleshed out your idea, you should look at what you can bring to the table. By *you*, we mean your company, your experience, and your connections. Finally, we look at how your application will compete in the existing market and what competitive advantages you can see (or create) in your idea.

Chapter 4

Coming Up with a Winning Idea

*A*fter you create an app idea, as described in Chapter 1, you have to describe it in detail so that you can evaluate whether it can be successful and decide how to go about creating the application.

In this chapter, we drill down into specific app categories, show you how to approach the process of creating an idea for an application, and start you thinking about which idea would make a great iPhone App. After you come up with an idea, you have to create some form of competitive advantage, of course, by thinking of ways to make it harder for the competition to battle you. Finally, you should know which legal safeguards can help you protect your idea as you move toward assembling your team of developers and artists to turn your idea into a working iPhone app.

Analyzing Your Competition

To start developing specific ideas about what features and capabilities to include in your application, simply get hold of every app in the category where your iPhone app idea would fall, and use it. As you do, keep notes about these items for each app:

- ✔ Features you wish it had
- ✔ Features that are superfluous or annoying
- ✔ Design elements that keep you engaged
- ✔ Design elements that turn you off

As you develop a list, you can make a spreadsheet to catalog your observations:

- ✔ Along the top row, list the names of the apps you review.
- ✔ Along the left side, list the attributes you're checking.

This spreadsheet creates a jumping-off point to develop the specific features of your app, as shown in Figure 4-1.

Use this spreadsheet in your business plan as a competitive analysis tool. We describe it in Chapter 7.

Don't get so bogged down in what everybody else is doing that you can't think of your own ideas. If this happens to you, review what you wrote about you're your ideas while reading Chapter 1 and just let yourself daydream about your app.

The purpose of this exercise is twofold:

- ✔ **Understand your app category** so that you don't just reinvent the wheel or repeat other people's mistakes.

- ✔ **Find inspiration in other developers' work** so that you can include elements of the better features of other apps in your app.

	A	B	C	D	E	F	
1	**OmniFocus**	*Concept*	*Purpose*	*User Interface*	*Design*	*Usability*	*Interop*
2	*Strengths*	Fills a need in the marketplace.	Ability to keep lots of tasks organized rather than in one huge list.	Simple and direct navigation of a large set of data.	Fancy transitions don't delay getting to your data.	Easy to get around even a complex set of tasks.	An effe tasks u one's c environ
3		Uses a proven task-management methodology rather than just a standard to-do list format.	Ability to sync with the desktop and other team members.	Relatively easy to add new tasks.	It is easy to see what buttons do and how to use them.	Fast to put in new tasks and assign attributes to them.	One-bu informa
4			Ability to sort on context.			Audio and photo options give nice depth to tasks.	You ca webser it suppo Dreamh
5						Ability to sort tasks by geolocation is cool.	It does users t tasks a from ea
6						Syncing with desktop data is very helpful.	If you h tasks, e can inc downlo; you syr
7							To sync desktop buy the OmniFo about $
	Weaknesses	It may be a bit too complicated.	Drilling through layers of projects and categories can be overwhelming on the	One has to click multiple times to get to tasks grouped into	The app is somewhat dry to use.	Syncing with the server can take a long time and blocks using the app while it	

Figure 4-1: Capturing competitive analysis with a spreadsheet.

After you complete your spreadsheet, don't try to look too deeply into it, as though you're reading tea leaves. Your new spreadsheet is an important guide, but it is only a reference tool — don't let the information on it trap you in old ideas.

To help you get started, we take apart a few apps in each of several popular categories, to see what makes them tick.

Studying an app's strengths and weaknesses

Because the iPhone is a terrific device for helping people organize and navigate their lives, many application developers have capitalized on its power, interface, and Internet connectivity.

We assume in our example that you want to create a task management application. We hope that you will, by studying the apparent strengths and weaknesses of an existing app, gain some ideas to be used in developing your own application. In the example, we study the OmniFocus task management application, shown in Figure 4-2. We show you how to study the strengths and weakness in various categories of application design, such as the application's concept, purpose, user interface, and graphic design.

It may be helpful for you to purchase an app you want to evaluate and follow along with our outline by discovering the interface yourself. In our example, if you don't want to buy the OmniFocus app, get a similar app such as Things and compare its features to what we outline here for Omnifocus.

Figure 4-2:
The powerful OmniFocus task management app.

Concept

The richly featured OmniFocus task management application was inspired by David Allen's book *Getting Things Done*. Users can use OmniFocus to look at tasks through the lens of project (doing the dishes, for example) or context (housework, for example).

OmniFocus is a useful example of a productivity application on the iPhone because it's a stand-alone application *and* a Web-driven app. You can use it only on the phone or connect it with your desktop version of the app by allowing it to communicate with a server on which both apps update the data. Each member of your team, if you have one, can connect to the same data, making it possible to share projects and to-do items.

Strengths

- ✔ Fills a need in the marketplace because most task managers cannot categorize data well enough to prevent power users from being overwhelmed
- ✔ Uses a proven task-management methodology rather than just a standard to-do list format

Weaknesses

- ✔ May be too complicated for casual users who don't want to invest in learning how to use the app

Purpose

The purpose of OmniFocus is to extend the full-featured task management environment of the desktop app to the iPhone. You can manage multiple tasks across multiple projects and view them in sophisticated ways that are intended to allow you to focus only on tasks you need to finish in a given moment while still keeping track of everything on your plate.

Strengths

- ✔ Can keep lots of tasks organized by category, rather than in one huge list
- ✔ Can sync with the desktop and other team members
- ✔ Can sort on context, by grouping tasks from various projects if they have something in common

Weaknesses

- ✔ Drilling through layers of projects and categories can be overwhelming on the iPhone.
- ✔ Organizing tasks into the OmniFocus pattern can be somewhat daunting.

User interface

The OmniFocus user interface is based on lists arranged hierarchically so that users drill down into a project or context by pressing successive list items. Users can, at the project level, select check boxes to mark completed tasks. Each task has a view that displays details such as notes, associated photos and audio files, and start and completion dates.

A tab bar at the bottom lets users move to the top of the hierarchy (home), see tasks based on their geolocations, refresh the view, add miscellaneous tasks, and specify settings.

Strengths

- ✔ Users can simply and directly navigate a large set of data.
- ✔ Users can relatively easily add new tasks.

Weaknesses

- ✔ Users must click multiple times to access tasks that are grouped into projects.
- ✔ Users might have difficulty understanding the Details pane in projects.

Design

The OmniFocus design is straightforward and utilitarian. No gorgeous or flashy graphics are used. Transitions are simple horizontal page slides, and global functions are housed on a standard tab bar. This app focuses on functionality over style.

Strengths

- ✔ Fancy transitions don't delay you being able to see your data.
- ✔ Users can easily see what buttons do and figure out how to use them.

Weaknesses

- ✔ OmniFocus does not have a visually stimulating or "exciting" interface to use.
- ✔ Users receive no graphical "payoff" for completing tasks such as setting goals. Although attractive graphics that accompany certain app functions can make the experience more fun and rewarding, this app doesn't have any.

Usability

OmniFocus is a power-user app, not meant for casual users to just pop open and gain everything they can by just poking around inside the app. To truly get the most benefit from the app, users must read the book and follow the task-management philosophy that it's based on.

The process of putting information into the app and working with it is relatively straightforward. If you want a more powerful task manager, learning to use the app is worth your time.

Strengths

Users can

- ✔ Easily navigate to even a complex set of tasks
- ✔ Quickly enter new tasks and assign attributes to them
- ✔ Use audio and photo options to add depth to tasks
- ✔ Sort tasks by geolocation
- ✔ Sync with desktop data

Weaknesses

- ✔ Syncing with the server can take a long time, and users can be blocked from using the app while it updates.
- ✔ Setting up both a context and a project for a task can be tedious.
- ✔ Geolocation works only per context, so you can't set a geolocation for a certain task individually.

Interoperability

OmniFocus can easily synchronize with other iPhone and desktop implementations of the software. It checks its current data against a file that exists on a WebDAV server (a type of server that acts more like a computer hard drive) such as MobileMe. If the local copy is more recent, it updates the server. If the server data is more recent, it updates the app.

Strengths

- ✔ OmniFocus is an effective way to keep tasks up-to-date across computing environments.
- ✔ It features one-button updating of information.
- ✔ You can assign your own Web server for the files if it supports WebDAV (one example being Dreamhost).

Weaknesses

> ✔ OmniFocus doesn't allow multiple users to select which specific tasks they hide and share with each other.
>
> ✔ If you have a lot of tasks to complete, even one change can incur a long download or upload time when you sync.
>
> ✔ To sync with your desktop, you need to buy the full version of OmniFocus (about $80).

Take some time to create this kind of analysis document for a few apps in an area that interests you. The categories you'll want to write about are:

> ✔ Concept
>
> ✔ Purpose
>
> ✔ User Interface
>
> ✔ Design
>
> ✔ Usability
>
> ✔ Interoperability

Start by writing a short paragraph about each section, the write some bullet points covering strengths and weaknesses in each area, just as we did for Omnifocus.

Comparing similar apps

The iPhone is by nature a communications device. Its ability to communicate across many mediums and platforms makes it a terrific device to use for a variety of communications tasks. Therefore, we use the Communications category in the next example to compare two existing applications and gauge their strengths and weaknesses, especially against each other. Our example compares two instant messaging apps, AOL's AIM application, shown in Figure 4-3, and the Palringo Instant Messenger Lite application, shown in Figure 4-4.

Concepts

AOL Instant Messenger is one of the most popular formats for desktop chatting. The iPhone version allows users to log in to their standard accounts to see and interact with all their existing buddies.

Figure 4-3:
The AOL
AIM
application.

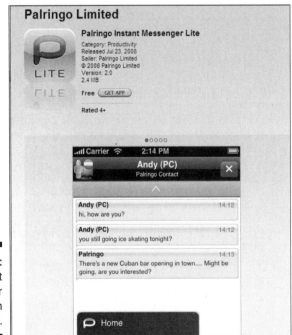

Figure 4-4:
Instant
Messenger
Lite, from
Palringo.

Palringo is designed to be an instant messaging client for a wide variety of services, including AIM, Facebook, Gadu-Gadu, Google Talk, iChat, ICQ, Jabber, MSN, and Yahoo Messenger chat. It boasts not only text chat but also the ability to send messages and one-way voice messages. Users can set up groups so that they can send the same text to multiple contacts at the same time.

Strengths

- ✔ AIM already has a huge user base that can use the iPhone app easily.
- ✔ Palringo expands on the features of larger companies' chat clients.
- ✔ Palringo has novel features, such as the ability to send voice messages and pictures.
- ✔ Palringo allows group texting.

Weaknesses

- ✔ Because users cannot add new buddies from the AIM iPhone app, the application is limited from becoming a desktop replacement.
- ✔ Users have to configure each of their accounts on the Palringo app, extending the setup time.

Purpose

AIM for the iPhone lets users maintain their AIM presence while mobile.

The Palringo app expands the services that can be used in one chat application and gives them more functionality for chatting.

Strengths

- ✔ The AIM app keeps users engaged with the AIM platform.
- ✔ Users of the AIM app appear to other users as though they're at their desks.
- ✔ The Palringo app support for all the chat services is helpful for users with multiple chat accounts.
- ✔ The Palringo app adds some functionality missing in other apps.

Weaknesses

- ✔ The AIM app doesn't support AIM users who may have other chat accounts.
- ✔ The Palringo app may provide too much complex functionality for users who rely on only one or two chat accounts.

User interface

The familiar AIM list-and-tab-bar-style user interface allows quick access to buddies and chats. After a chat begins, you can flick across the screen to tab between active chats so you can easily have several chats going at one time.

The Palringo application UI also uses a list and tab bar interface. The tab bar uses a More button that opens the Settings screen. The Palringo home screen groups Services, Location, and Help sections.

Strengths

✓ The AIM app is familiar and easy to use.

✓ The AIM app cleverly uses pages to tab between active chats.

✓ General navigation in the Palringo app is intuitive.

Weaknesses

✓ The AIM app user interface isn't very original.

✓ The Palringo app user interface can be annoying and difficult just to add a service such as AIM because the Details screen isn't clear about how to save new settings.

✓ On the Palringo app, figuring out how to modify account settings, such as changing a password, is difficult.

✓ Buttons at the bottom of the screen in the Palringo app are sometimes obscured by the status bar, as shown in Figure 4-5.

✓ The More button in the Palringo app should be labeled Settings.

Figure 4-5: Sometimes, Palringo obscures its own buttons.

Design

The AIM iPhone app design uses standard UI toolkit elements that are used in many apps. The only custom elements for AIM are its buddy icons.

The Palringo app design is standard for this type of app, relying mostly on the UI toolkit. Palringo has some custom icons and its company logo, but the font size used on the Settings screen is nonstandard.

Strengths

- ✔ The AIM app looks familiar and "legitimate."
- ✔ The Palringo app is fairly clean and easy to look at.

Weaknesses

- ✔ The AIM app is uninspired, design-wise.
- ✔ The AIM app has no audio or visual "payoffs."
- ✔ The Palringo app logo isn't well executed, and its icons are plain and uninteresting.
- ✔ The nonstandard text size in the Palringo app cheapens its look.

Usability

AIM for iPhone is quite easy to use, and anyone who has used its desktop app will find it familiar. For beginners, the AIM app presents an easy-to-master standard user interface.

Although users can easily access the basic functions on the Palringo app, many of its functions are flawed.

Strengths

- ✔ The AIM app is easy to learn and use.
- ✔ The Palringo app has standard navigation elements to make it easy to move around.

Weaknesses

- ✔ The Palringo application's new account setup is unnecessarily confusing.
- ✔ The process for editing the existing account process in the Palringo app is even more confusing.
- ✔ The Palringo app's bottom status bar suffers from bad placement.

✔ The Palringo app displays unnecessary and annoying messages, such as "Will try to reconnect shortly." (The reconnection process should happen in the background without reminding the user that this is happening.)

✔ After you press a button in the Palringo app, it often responds slowly, and sometimes doesn't even work.

Interoperability

AIM communicates with any other AIM client on any device. AIM also supports AOL, ICQ, .mac, and MobileMe accounts.

Palringo, on the other hand, claims to operate with a wider variety of instant messaging providers. However, its setup and usage flaws may prevent users from enjoying its interoperability advantage.

Strengths

✔ The AIM app is quite flexible as far as interacting with other supported participants across platforms and account types.

✔ The Palringo app provides a wider variety of providers than does the AIM app.

✔ The Palringo app provides more ways to communicate (for example, by sending pictures or sound) than do other apps.

Weaknesses

✔ The AIM app doesn't support certain other account types, such as MSN.

✔ The Palringo app exhibits flaws when trying to set up and use multiple accounts.

Generating Ideas

The process of generating ideas is part science and part intuition. A number of philosophies and techniques have been developed for this process over the years in both the business and software sectors. In this section, we explore some of these techniques and describe how you can use them as an individual or as a team to start the flow of ideas and flesh them out. Also, in the following sidebar, we take a look at innovation styles so that you can have a framework on which to understand your own process.

Specific idea-generation techniques

The four everyday approaches described in the following sections can stimulate your mind and your thought process to flesh out your initial idea and turn it into a viable proposal and blueprint from which you can build your own iPhone application.

Surveying

After you have an idea of what kind of app you want to create, you can take your idea to the people — specifically, people who will spend a few minutes talking with you. Ask family members, friends, co-workers, or anybody else who isn't a potential competitor to imagine what kind of app they want to use, in the area you thought of, and to then pretend that they just purchased the app on their iPhones and are preparing to use it. Have the people on your list answer these questions:

- How does the app look?
- How would you interact with it?
- What are its specific features?
- What benefits would you expect to get from using it?
- How do you think using the app would make you feel? (You might feel productive, entertained, or surprised, for example.)

Prompt your list of reviewers with some information if they need help imagining characteristics, but provide as little information as possible. Even if the ideas in their responses aren't technically possible, their insights and expectations are always valid. As you're recording thorough replies to these questions, feel free to ask any other questions you can think of. Don't worry about how your notes might read to someone else. Just write down everything that comes to mind. You can organize and edit your notes later.

Brainstorming

By now, you've already sat down and done some thinking and brainstorming. If you want to widen your list of ideas or bullet points for a specific idea, you can continue to brainstorm in order to have a long list of concepts and ideas to work with.

Innovation styles: A formal approach to idea generation

Global Creativity Corporation has researched and pioneered the concept of *innovation styles,* which helps individuals and team members understand how they're naturally inclined to approach the process of generating ideas. Based on the notion that everyone can be innovative, the approach breaks innovation types into four groups based on a matrix (or grid) composed of answers to the questions "What stimulates and inspires this style's innovativeness?" (facts or intuition) and "How does this style approach the innovation process?" (focused or broad). Answers to these questions create a grid on which a person's ideation approach can be identified. The grid is composed of Visioning, Exploring, Experimenting, and Modifying styles. Individuals and companies can take a test to help place them in this grid, but just understanding the various styles of innovation is valuable in its own right.

GENERATING INNOVATIVE SOLUTIONS

Often the hardest part of generating new innovative solutions is knowing where and how to begin looking for them. Whether you are wanting to inspire your staff or facilitate an idea-generation session, you'll benefit greatly by knowing which techniques belong to which Innovation Style. You can better select the techniques that will work for a particular mix of people, or which tools to introduce first and last. For example, a group of people who strongly prefer Modifying will not start well with Exploring techniques, but could use them well if they were introduced later.

Modifying and *Experimenting* idea-generation techniques begin by gathering facts, details and other data. *Modifying* builds on what is known, while *Experimenting* combines the components in new ways. These techniques are more linear than intuitive in their approach to generating ideas. They take advantage of different ways of organizing known information so as to approach problems from new and more comprehensive angles. Using a logical pattern or a sequence of steps, they help focus the attention on where to look for innovations.

Visioning and *Exploring* idea-generation techniques start with an intuitive insight, hunch or hypothesis; then they gather information to confirm and fill out the intuition. The difference between these two techniques is that *Visioning* searches for a clear mental picture of the future, while *Exploring* often employs symbols to sense what is metaphorically possible. These techniques take advantage of the right-brain capability to perceive whole solutions in sudden leaps of logic.

Here are some typical characteristics of someone from each style group:

- ✔ **Visioning:** Inspired by intuition and has a focused approach

- ✔ **Exploring:** Inspired by intuition and has a broad approach

- ✔ **Experimenting:** Inspired by facts and has a broad approach

- ✔ **Modifying:** Inspired by facts and has a focused approach.

All these approaches are good and necessary for an optimal app idea. On one hand is the concept of pure creativity, and on the other is the concept of context. Understanding the context of the App Store and injecting pure creativity into that context can be a winning combination. If you can identify yourself in one of the innovation styles we just listed (or if you take the test, for a fee, at `http://innovationstyles.com`) and you and your development group are looking for a highly structured approach, you can focus on innovation techniques that support your natural style. Then you can broaden your horizons by using techniques made for the other three styles.

TIP

Here are some ways to keep your thoughts flowing:

✔ **Research, research, research.** After you identify an area of interest by using the techniques outlined in Chapter 1, start researching the area more widely. If you're interested in creating a role-playing game, for example, study the history of this type of game all the way back to Dungeons & Dragons (and further), and be sure to write down any insights that come to mind. If you need more information to draw connections between the items you discover, use Internet research, library research, interviews with friends and family members, or whatever other methods you can think of.

✔ **Daydream.** Take some time to relax in your chair with paper and pencil in hand, and simply imagine yourself in various scenarios that pertain to the type of app you're interested in creating. Write narratives about these situations and how your app can solve them or make life more enjoyable. Don't worry about the details until later.

✔ **Role-play.** Try to put yourself in real-life situations that would pertain to the use of your app. Imagine that you have in your hand an app that would perfectly fit the given situation. Write down your insights. Just hold your imaginary iPhone and think about the results.

✔ **Think differently.** As a fun way to mix it up, you can download an app such as Idea Generator (see Figure 4-6), which gives you a random set of words for creating lists. Make these three lists from each word:

• How the word resembles your idea.

• How the word doesn't resemble your idea.

• How your idea can incorporate the concept found in that word. You'll find some interesting combinations!

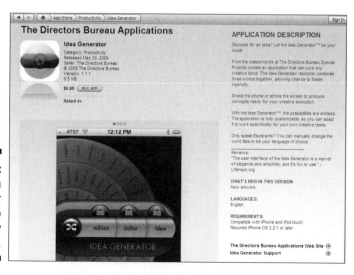

Figure 4-6:
Use Idea Generator to come up with a new idea.

Mash-ups

The mash-up approach involves combining, or "mashing up," two or more known elements to create a new one. Follow these steps:

1. **Identify an area in the App Store that interests you.**

   You might be interested in cars, for example.

2. **Find an app within that area that you think is very useful or has an excellent design, such as Dynolicious.**

3. **List apps from completely different areas of the App Store, such as sports, games, and finance.**

4. **Imagine what would happen if each app in your list were combined with the app you started with.**

   Break down the apps by concept, purpose, user interface, design, usability, and interoperability.

5. **Mash up the two apps to create a brand-new app.**

6. **Read all the analysis for your newly created app and ask yourself whether it's an app that you personally would want to buy (or sell).**

   For example, we mashed up Dynolicious with the popular game *Flight Control*. Table 4-1 shows our analysis for the new app named Dyno-Control.

Table 4-1	Feature Comparison of the New App Combination Dyno-Control		
Feature	*Dynolicious*	*Flight Control*	*Dyno-Control*
Concept	A glossy app for measuring various aspects of a car's performance, such as acceleration, horsepower, or g-force.	A retro-style game about steering aircraft onto a runway without letting them run into each other.	A retro-style game that uses the motion of a real car to determine game action.
Purpose	To give car aficionados a fun way to interact with their iPhones and measure their cars' performance.	To keep lots of random items on track to their destination without colliding.	To merge the fun of driving and playing video games and to bring together real-world and digital challenges.

Feature	Dynolicious	Flight Control	Dyno-Control
User Interface	Real-world-style buttons are combined with graphs that can be saved to the photo library by tapping them. Users navigate sections by using a tab bar.	Press on a plane and drag it to create a line that describes its flight path. The plane follows the flight path to its destination.	Use real-world-style buttons to make moves in the game by driving your car to activate the iPhone's accelerometer.
Design	Features slick, glossy, authentic-looking car dash instruments and bright, colorful, glowing graphs.	Features retro-style pastels and muted colors, a cartoonish illustration style, and a 1940s-style music bed. Slogans such as "Good Show" appear whenever a user scores points.	Photorealistic and designed like the dashboard in an old-fashioned car.
Usability (Playability)	The app is easy and intuitive to use and fun to play. Buttons behave like they do in the real world.	Press and drag the planes to set their course. New levels present more planes and a different landing strip layout.	Play is engaging because it interacts with the real world. Buttons do what their equivalents do in real life.
Interoperability	Charts are saved as images for sharing with others or using on a home computer.	No multiplayer support.	Users can challenge friends to multiplayer games or compare scores.

Evolution

The evolutionary approach simply improves the ideas and concepts that are already in the App Store. Rather than come up with a brand-new (or revolutionary) idea, we simply improve, or evolve, the ideas being downloaded and used by Apple iPhone users.

Identify every weakness you can find in an app from your competitive analysis efforts (which we discuss earlier in this chapter, in the section "Studying an app's strengths and weaknesses"). Look at the other apps you've analyzed and see whether any of them solve each of those weaknesses particularly well. If so, write down which app fills the weakness and how it appears to do so.

If some weaknesses aren't filled by other apps in that category, look to apps outside it. If the weakness still isn't filled, think of some ways that it could be overcome.

Identify the strongest app in that category and repeat this process by listing the app's strong points. Do the same for each of the other apps you listed. If two apps are strong in the same area, identify the stronger of the two and eliminate the other one.

Now that you have a list of weak points that have been overcome and you highlighted the strong points, combine your lists to describe your "super app" — a combination of the strongest points of all existing apps in that category with none (or few) of the weak points. Then you have a specific road map, ready to be developed.

If you work with multiple people, consider leaving a common area available for brainstorming and note gathering. For example, the makers of iSamurai put a white board in a hallway in an office they shared. Anytime someone had an idea, they put it on the white board. After a few weeks, they got together to analyze and consider the ideas together.

Creating Barriers to Competition

Coming up with an idea for an iPhone application is like coming up with an idea for any new business. The specter of competition always looms large. Is someone else coming up with this idea simultaneously somewhere else? With the amount of excitement about the iPhone and mobile development in general, chances are good that they are.

The challenges facing a new iPhone business are similar to the challenges facing any new business. A conventional way of sizing up the difficulty in entering a new business is to analyze barriers to entry. A *barrier to entry* is any difficulty experienced by a new business: Regulation, existing competition, unproven technology, and high start-up costs are just a few examples of barriers that challenge new enterprises.

The number of barriers to entry for the iPhone business is low. It costs only $99 to create a developer account. A person with nothing but an idea can usually find engineers who can convert their ideas into reality after just a few months of development. Perhaps $10,000 to $50,000 is all it takes to launch an iPhone application — a relatively small investment.

As an entrepreneur, you want barriers to entry for your competitors. In a dream scenario, you would have these benefits:

✔ A unique idea that no one has thought of yet

✔ A worldwide monopoly on that idea and the only reasonable way to implement it

✔ Tremendous regulations that weed out anyone else who tries to compete

✔ The best brand-name recognition, synonymous with the idea

✔ The world beating a path to your door

In the business world we live in, the challenge is to find ways to "stake a claim" in your chosen idea's category or market of the iPhone App Store and defend it.

Anyone can register to be an iPhone developer, and someone else is probably thinking of your idea right now. (In fact, if no one else is thinking of your idea, are you sure that it's a good one?) So the issue is what you can do to have or maintain a competitive advantage.

You can differentiate yourself from the rest of the market in a number of ways, either through marketing, protecting the idea, or sheer execution.

Your marketing techniques early on in the development phase can also be different, or "outside the box" of what most people might recommend. For example, the makers of iSamurai wanted to promote their new upcoming app without giving away what it was to other potential developers. So they created a "Guess Our App" contest on Touch Arcade (an iPhone games review site). Since their game lets players use their iPhone like a samurai sword, they posted a 3D image their designer made of the inside of a martial arts dojo to spark people's imagination without actually tipping them off. The contest got them lots of attention with power gamers in the community and was the start of a clever PR campaign — all starting with *not* giving away their idea too soon.

Time to market and first to market

The old saying "Look before you leap" is contrasted by the saying "He who hesitates is lost." There's truth in both sayings: If you spend time in endless deliberation and vacillation, unsure whether you should enter a market, you may miss out on one of the easiest available barriers to entry — being first to market.

If your intelligence (and your research) tells you that the idea you're pursuing will take between four and six months to prepare, and the only competitor you know about is just starting and you're a few months into it, you probably should carry through and be first to market with your product.

The first entrant in a market space, assuming that it's backed by some marketing effort and decent execution (the product works), has a chance to become the market leader by simply being first. The first product that has an interesting story behind it ("the first iPhone-controlled blender") is most likely to be novel enough to attract press coverage (positive newspaper stories are the same as free advertising) and "link love" (Web links) from all the iPhone fan sites. With some marketing support pressing the novelty of the product into the consciousness of the buying public, you have lots of opportunity to create a market-leading perception in the eyes of the public.

In addition to marketing and PR advantages, the "first mover" inherently has the advantage of market feedback and a customer base that later entrants lack. Assuming that the burden of supporting user requests doesn't slow down new features, the first product can reach version 1.1, 1.2, or even 2.0 before competitors leave the gate, satisfying all new consumer preferences and needs that pop up in the meantime.

If you can get ahead of the pack and stay there, and then organize well enough to ensure that your product's features, stability, and customer support are better than the competition, you have a good shot at maintaining the top position in your product category.

You don't have to be technically first — just first to be noticed. If early entrants haven't invested in marketing their apps, and if product searches show no true market traction yet, you still have a good chance of creating a "first" perception for your product. If you've been working on your product longer than your newest competition, you can even claim the "first" banner through some marketing-speak, such as "first to develop," and if you're the first to be noticed by a clear majority of users, no one will successfully argue the point.

Better product and execution

Perhaps you're in the middle of developing when you find out that a competitor is beating you to the punch. Or, maybe three competitors are already selling iPhone apps in your chosen category, but you still feel like you have something unique to add.

Never fear, because early entrants can run out of steam. In fact, you can take heart in knowing that Apple is consistently late — even years late — to its product categories, such as with the iPod and iPhone. Like hated "campers" in a first-person shooter game, your product team can figuratively crouch behind a rock and then snipe the competition when they noisily reveal themselves.

Assuming that your competitor has gained any market traction, you now have a great potential marketing position: underdog, number two, and, of course, better than the other app. Even if the competition has already won an Apple Design Award and been featured on the company's home page, you can still pry away part of the user base. For one thing, your application category is now well popularized, and you can say "Try ours instead." There is always some angle of attack on the product in the number-one position: price, features, nagging bugs, speed, compatibility with other services, or reliability, for example. Whatever the angle, you can now define yourself positively against the competition.

Execution is everything in a follow-up strategy. You have some catching up to do, but your competitor just played its hand and doesn't know yours. Now is your chance to do your homework (quickly) and find out what your competitor is doing wrong. Find out why people are deciding not to buy. And, because almost no one earns a five-star rating at the App Store, why aren't they buying? If you can cull those complaints into a product plan and then develop it and respond with an even marginally superior product at a marginally more attractive price, you have a chance to wrest control of the market from the incumbent.

If multiple players are in the market, especially if the product category is well-established, you still have angles of attack. Perhaps existing products haven't been updated for a while and they aren't earning enough money to justify the funding to write their next product update. Or, perhaps the existing product developers have moved on to their next project, leaving their current product, your competition, needing maintenance. You might be able to find a way to develop your app more cost effectively — if only because, by studying the market landscape, you have less design work to do. Newer is better in many people's minds, and if you're competing at the 99-cent level, people may try out your new version just to "kick the tires." Outdo the competition and you'll bring more customers over to your side.

Another tried-and-true tactic is to "preannounce" your product along with the launch of your competitors'. Assuming that you'll execute better, create a wait-and-see attitude on the part of potential buyers. It's a bold move — best played when you know that you can deliver on time. But, if you can broadcast the message that your product is better — and, perhaps, cheaper — the fear of buyer's remorse may allow you to swipe customers from your competitors before you even launch a product. Apply some aggressive pre-marketing where people "sign up to be notified," and you might just build a better list than the first entrants to market.

Exclusive content

A surefire barrier that you can use to block entry into your chosen iPhone application category is exclusive content. *Content,* in this case, can mean anything from movies to music and from books to maps. Even the simple act of having a skilled artist create a unique graphical design for your application can qualify as having enough content to attract people to your unique offering, as shown in many e-book applications, such as Eucalyptus (see Figure 4-7) and Classics. But offering anything in your app that people can't find elsewhere is a way to ensure that you maintain a strong customer base.

You can get exclusive content in several ways. The simplest, albeit most difficult, way is to create it. For example, a game idea is yours, so unless someone clones it, you're the only one who has that offering. If you have created or own a series of games, novels, characters, artwork, songs, or anything else, you have exclusive content.

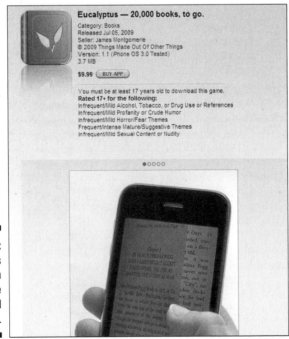

Figure 4-7:
Eucalyptus
gives you
a unique
way to read
books.

If you can get a license to distribute some particular content, even for a limited time, you can establish yourself as the iPhone-based distributor of that content. Millions of brands and products, ripe for licensing, are well established in consumer minds. Dedicated teams in most large, brand-based organizations even actively seek out people to license their products, characters, logos, and experiences. You can call a music act, a movie property, a studio, or a publisher of any type of content and pitch an idea. Even someone who doesn't want to be part of your plan might simply set a rate at which you can rent their content — and then offer it up. If someone isn't already playing in the mobile application market, your offer probably will intrigue them, and the marketing advantages of having a product "on the iPhone" may be enough to get them to grant a license.

Licenses don't have to be purely exclusive; a "performance-based exclusivity" agreement can be negotiated that guarantees exclusive rights as long as the app is performing according to the agreed-on success measurement. Even without an exclusive agreement, the simple "execution-based" exclusive applies: If no one else is doing anything useful with the content in question, your app can effectively be the exclusive source of that content.

Sometimes, content is exclusive simply because the licensing cost is a barrier. Internet-based mapping and consumer navigation have been dominated by big players in part because getting a license to display street maps and satellite imagery can cost hundreds of thousands of dollars. Many other content categories exist, especially in vertical markets such as professional, medical, engineering, and industrial, where training and certification costs are high. Even if the eventual market of the app is limited, you can command a higher price for a sleek translation of much-needed information to an iPhone-accessible format. If your budget lets you license a product that no one else has, you can create a barrier to competition immediately.

Online properties are a good source of exclusive, or at least unique, content. Assuming that a site doesn't already have its iPhone strategy in place — or even if it does — you may be able to write an application that works with the application programming interface (API) of that Web site and provides its content for mobile users.

The amount of exclusive content that's available is practically endless; by doing some inventive thinking, you should be able to find or create a product that no one else can.

Proprietary technology

Having exclusive content is only one part of differentiating your app from the competition. The other part is exclusive technology, sometimes called "secret sauce." If you can make the iPhone do something clever that no one else has been able to figure out, you can sell your applications with that unique feature. For example, if you can code well, perhaps you can write a graphical utility, sound utility, or other program that runs faster than all competing solutions. If you manufacture a device and you're writing a program to work with it from the iPhone, you have exclusive technology.

If you're the first to invent a novel product, you may be able to achieve a different kind of exclusivity — a patent. Many software and hardware innovations are protected by patents, even systems you wouldn't suspect. Perhaps you have a method of solving a problem that you know it's going to be *big*. You may be able to file a patent on it, implement your solution on the iPhone, and then enjoy some patent protection, courtesy of your government. For more on patents, see the later section "Protecting your intellectual property," later in this chapter.

Large companies have one or more dedicated research-and-development (R&D) departments, filled with scientists and researchers inventing new products and improving on old ones. They fill lab notebooks with ideas and test out innovations and patent them as they go. Even if you have a small company or are a one-person operation, you can dedicate some time to R&D: Just put on your research hat and then figure out what you can improve and how you can add high-tech features to your application.

User experience is one big key to success on the iPhone. When you look at user reviews and public reviews and even Apple's own guidelines, you can see that an exceptional user experience is one of the key criteria of a successful application. If you can reengineer your application so that it has the best user interface, and especially if you can optimize your code so that it has the fastest, snappiest user experience, your competition will have trouble keeping up.

Strategic partnerships

No matter what size of operation you are, making alliances can make you stronger. And, especially if you're small, a big friend is a huge help. One common way that small companies find their way is by befriending big companies.

For example, the solution you're creating or offering might do a helpful demonstration of another company's technology. Perhaps you made a utility that allows people to more easily access a large Web service. Or, maybe you're creating solutions in a niche market (education or medical, for example) and you can convince one of the bigger players in that market to use and promote your application. If you're writing a recipe app that focuses on healthy food, for example, you might partner with a major grocer, such as Whole Foods Market, to create the Whole Foods Market Recipes app, as shown in Figure 4-8.

Figure 4-8:
A strategic
partnership
can come
with lots of
advantages.

A distribution agreement is another common barrier to entry, but it's less applicable to the iPhone market, where the Apple App Store is the sole distributor. The agreement applies primarily when Apple decides to highlight your app in its App Store, in a top ten list, in a featured app exhibit, or by giving an Apple Design Award.

An effective use of strategic partnerships can allow you to essentially scare off competition ("Darn! They partnered with BigCo, so maybe we shouldn't even try.") And, a partnership can help you with introductions: Whenever your larger partner introduces you, it helps you move through most of the vetting process directly to the "Let's get to know them" stage. This concept is even more applicable if you're a design house creating iPhone applications for another company and BigCo is making the introduction. But if you can get BigCo's general endorsement, perhaps riding its coattails in marketing literature or, ideally, participating in one of its keynote addresses, trade shows, or PR initiatives, you'll be way ahead of your competitors.

Cheaper supplies

If you can build the same product cheaper than your competition can, you can outspend them on marketing and win. The costs involved in developing an iPhone app (we discuss budgeting in Chapter 13) come from software development and design and graphics; ongoing supplies can involve maintaining an online back-end service or paying for ongoing access to content. A creative entrepreneur can find ways to shave down all these costs.

For example, perhaps you can find good engineers to give you a development discount in exchange for application royalties or the right to reuse the code they develop or another nonmonetary benefit that's available to you. Perhaps you're a designer, coder, or graphics artist who can avoid paying yourself initially and thus save development costs. If you're running an online service to support your application or you're paying ongoing fees for the content that serves it, you might be able to negotiate with your providers: Try to prepay for longer discounts or just persuade someone there to give you the prepaid rate because you're writing an app for the iPhone and that's the only way you can "make the numbers work" for your business. Let them know what constraints you are working with. Software developers often want to help their clients reach their objectives enough to bend on the finances to a certain extent.

Many successful businesses deliver only acceptable quality, but cheaper than the rest. Figure out how you can lower your own cost of doing business.

More expensive ingredients

On the other side of the coin from cheaper supplies are expensive ingredients. A barrier to entry can be created by essentially "gold-plating" your application when your competition is using bronze, copper, and tin.

Expensive ingredients aren't always superficial. Gold *is* a superior conductor, and it corrodes less than other metals. It's often used in high-reliability circuit design because of its performance characteristics. When you then add marketing and branding to the equation, perhaps the benefits of gold become overinflated, but if profits also inflate, who's to complain?

For example, we found two iPhone apps that let you send physical postcards made from pictures taken on your iPhone. One charges $2, and the prints are of good quality. The other app charges only $1, and the prints are mediocre and have obvious flaws. Sadly, both apps have poor user interfaces, according to reviews. The most popular postcard app in the app store doesn't have this snail mail feature; it sends only e-cards, yet it receives glowing reviews.

So here's a potential opportunity to spend more on developing your app and truly satisfying the needs of your potential customers. Spend more on the postcards so that they look great (charging $2 and up for them). Spend enough money, time, and effort on designing and implementing the user interface so that people are delighted to use it. Expand the app so that you can send other types of more expensive mail — first-class letters, for example. Spend some more on a Web site that links with social networks and imports people's address books so that you can remember everyone's birthdays and holidays. You can also send out push messages, to remind people to send thoughtful cards, for example, and you can add the ability to send flowers for $10 and more.

Your iPhone app doesn't have to undersell its competitors. Why target the value-obsessed customer who's content to pay you next to nothing for your hard work and still give you a bad review? Solve a problem for someone who has money to spend and charge them a bit more. Use fresh, high-quality, healthy ingredients for your application; Focus on overall quality and efficacy, and even a bit of luxury, and take the royal road to App Store riches.

Products under regulation

You can create a barrier to entry by developing an iPhone product that requires regulation. This approach isn't available to everyone, but it can be a formidable barrier.

Certain professions must operate under certain regulations and acquire the certifications required in order to practice these professions. For example, you can't practice law or medicine without the proper license. But if you're a lawyer or a doctor, you may be able to develop applications with a natural monopoly. You can create an application that enables real-time access to your legal or medical advice, for example.

Another related example of regulation is product certification. For example, some types of medical devices require FDA certification. On a more general level, devices that use radio frequency transmission require FCC certification, and any device that connects to the iPhone requires Apple certification. If you're developing hardware for the iPhone platform, you have a natural advantage — because it isn't easy.

Each of these certification steps adds extra hurdles to the product development cycle. The steps are hard to navigate without specialized knowledge, training, and experience, but that's good because, for those hardware and software developers savvy enough to overcome these obstacles, their competition will be left behind, tangled in red tape or simply puzzled and stuck.

The global scene

Many of the most successful companies are global operations. By either extending manufacturing overseas to reduce costs or finding new customers from the billions of people around the world, a global viewpoint is a key to 21st century business success. This statement is true for iPhone applications, also.

About half the sales opportunity for an iPhone app lies outside the primary U.S. market. Localizing your application — by translating the language, graphics, and cultural cues — can open the door to vastly increased sales. NSC Partners, LLC, has localized its Kids Math Fun app to other languages, such as Portuguese, Spanish, and Filipino, as you can see in Figure 4-9.

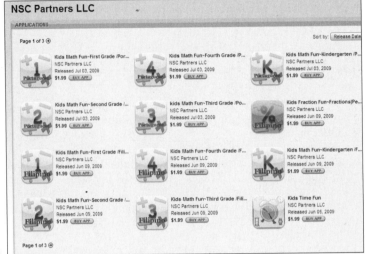

Figure 4-9:
Make versions of your app for a global market.

Although the U.S. and English-speaking markets are substantial, specific country markets may be easier nuts to crack, from a marketing perspective. If you create an excellent Italian, French, or German version of an application, you can conquer a good chunk of Europe. Make an outstanding Spanish version and you can target Spain and Latin America *and* a tasty portion of the Spanish-speaking United States. Because there's less focus on these markets by Anglocentric iPhone developers, there's less competition as well.

Going global isn't easy. You have to care. If you aren't bilingual, have your app professionally translated. You have to understand the culture you're targeting enough to ensure that your application is relevant and translated correctly and with cultural sensitivity, and that it works the way users expect. In fact, if you have a particular intuition about another culture or you're a member of that culture, you may be able to craft an application experience that works *only* for that culture.

Many a performing artist has learned this trick well. You might hear puzzled Americans say "They're big in Japan" or "I guess he's famous in Germany" as they try to explain to themselves why the band that seemingly broke up in the late 1980s just went platinum with its 18th album.

Going global can give you a big advantage over your competitors who only focus on their own domestic market.

Undercutting

Undercutting, or offering a price that's less than your competitors', is a dangerous but sometimes rewarding tactic for creating formidable competitive barriers in your chosen product category.

The iPhone industry has seen somewhat of a "race to the bottom" as developers have complained about the challenges of profiting from a 99-cent application that cost $30,000 to create.

Many industries are confronting the challenge of the "free" business model, and numerous business books are being written about it. And, it's almost the standard technique of a disruptive Web start-up to give away for free something that another Web site now charges for.

The 99-cent price point is here, and it's real. For the masses who have already been trained to buy music for 99 cents per song, changing their habits is difficult. But if you have to sell so cheaply, the challenge is how *else* can you monetize the application?

Other revenue models — advertising, sponsorship, co-branding, in-application purchases, subscriptions, upselling, cross-selling, and user-base monetization strategies — can be used to cleverly minimize the sticker shock on your application and *still* make a lot of money. For example, you can give away a version of your app that requires users to register — and then use that newly formed communication line with your enthusiastic audience to upsell them on other goods and services. You might support your application with advertising alone — and by gaining market share for your application, have the largest audience on your topic, which raises the value of your advertising space. We've covered a lot of models for doing this in Chapter 1.

And, don't forget the good old-fashioned way of being able to cut prices — lower your costs! If you can truly make your app more cheaply, then you can sell it more cheaply, too.

So, if you have strong competition in your market, look for a creative way to practically or actually give away your app — and still get paid.

Switching costs

A switching cost creates a barrier to entry for competitors by creating a *barrier to exit* for consumers. Maybe you decided not to switch to a different computer or phone model because you didn't want to confront the headache of moving all your information — or reentering it. If so, you've experienced switching costs — the tangible delay and expense involved in acquiring something new.

Part of the penalty for people who want to ditch their iPhones and buy the Pre or Android models instead is that the new phone

✔ May not work with iTunes

✔ Probably won't play all their music

✔ May not transfer over their calendars and address books

If you're technically minded, these switching costs are hardly visible; for common users, however, merely backing up an iPhone to get a replacement can be a nightmarish ordeal fraught with the fear of data loss.

Learning to use a new device is another cost of switching, and unfamiliarity can be a deterrent for consumers trying to buy a new device or even learn a new program. "Well, I know how to use this one" or "This is working for me — thanks" are the refrains of the content consumer who just doesn't have a need for the latest and greatest.

Switching costs can be exploited on both the defense and offense of your market position. If you've put out the first version of an application, your best strategy is to create a way to lock your customers in to using your app. Back up their data to a Web site automatically. Create a seamless registration process. Perhaps you can mix up their data and present it to them using a method other than their phones, such as sending them e-mail messages to let them know that the data is safe and sound. If the data in your app doesn't quite fit the cloud-computing mold, figure out ways to personalize it so that users don't want to remove it from their phones. Also, be sure to offer them an app they'll miss if they switch to another solution.

On the offensive side, you're playing catch-up — someone else is the market leader — and you're trying to penetrate their defenses and steal their users. If you can find a way to seamlessly import their data, do so. "Works great with [whatever you already use]" is a useful marketing line that calms the switch-averse consumer. If you're just head-to-head with the other application, though, and you have no practical way to import *its* information, study the weaknesses of the competitive applications and find out where they aren't creating switching costs.

Perhaps your app is just as easy to launch as the competitor's and does much the same thing. You have to find a way to defeat any resistance to switching. Make your app faster or improve it in another way by using better technology, and then entice users to taste the experience with you. Promote to their customers and tell them how easily they can switch. You can even exploit the crowd mentality with marketing leads such as "Everyone is switching to OurApp" or even the classic faux mystery "Why are so many people switching to OurApp?"

You may find, fortunately, that your competitor has done nothing to create a switching cost. That situation works well for you — just lure their customers over in herds to your application, and create a walled garden that they won't even consider leaving.

Network effects

Network effects appear when more people use your product and it becomes more valuable. The fax machine is the classic example: If just you and I have a fax machine, we can send contracts to each other and that's about it. After *every* office has a fax machine, however, the machines become much more useful.

Social networking and new take-over-the-world trends such as microblogging (Twitter is an example) benefit from and rely on network effects: The bigger the network of people that use a given function, the more valuable that function becomes, until a second entrant into the space can topple the giant. Imagine, for example, that you create a better fax machine. You would have an uphill battle in trying to sell it to all the people who already have the old kind.

So how do you exploit network effects in your application? Well, assuming that you won't create the next microblogging revolution, all you need to do is figure out a reason why two people having your application is far better than one. For example, the Bump application, shown in Figure 4-10, enables two phones to swap contact information by simply bumping the phones together. If you have Bump and the other person doesn't, you can just say "Download Bump so that I can give you my contact info" and the other person will likely recommend it to other users, who recommend it to others, and so on.

The Ocarina application created a real instrument based on blowing into the iPhone microphone. But when your music traveled to Ocarina's servers and users around the world could listen to it — and even plot the music on a gorgeous virtual globe — the global network effects that were created made the application even more of a success.

Since Apple launched its version 3.0 firmware update, the iPhone has some useful peer-to-peer (phone-to-phone) communication capabilities. They combine with the iPhone's network connectivity and location awareness to make amazing new phone-to-phone applications possible. What's needed now are *your* bright ideas on how to turn your app into a the-more-the-merrier proposition.

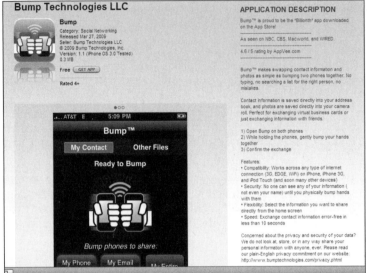

Figure 4-10:
The more
people who
have Bump,
the more
useful it
becomes.

Figure out why two people having your app is far more fun than just one person having it and you'll be on your way to creating and exploiting network effects that make *yours* the application to get.

Advertising and marketing

The best form of marketing is word of mouth. But you have to get the word out yourself during the period between no one knowing about your application and getting bought by BigCo for billions of dollars.

Even if you don't spend a dime (or don't have a dime to spend) on marketing, you still have to participate in it: You can, for example, spend dozens of hours a day on the Web, promoting your app in the blogosphere, sending tweets (short messages sent from Twitter) and messages, and sending a free copy of your app to every mom-and-pop iPhone review site.

If you're at your local Apple store wearing a pastel shirt and posing as an employee to steer unsuspecting customers to your application, you may have gone a bit too far. Simply going to venues or events where iPhone users congregate and proudly recommending your useful application doesn't hurt a bit.

If you had a cure for cancer and didn't market it right, no one would buy it. Well, considering the number of lives that can be saved by early detection and prevention, and how much marketing is done on these issues, you can see that marketing truly is an essential part of product success.

Almost every site that reviews applications can sell you advertising for your app. Google, Yahoo!, Microsoft, and countless advertising networks let you bid for spots online. If your application fits a niche in any way, you may get great results from running an old-tech magazine or newsletter ad or simply sponsoring a blog related to your target market. Is it any surprise that you can find a prominent ad for iBird on the Birdwatcher's Digest Web site?

Journalism can be your ticket to incredibly valuable free advertising. If your application has any sort of new angle — maybe it's the first of its kind or you have a unique approach — blogging sites are usually delighted to pick up on it. You can use sites such as PR Wire (www.prwire.com) to produce a professional press release if the story is good, and you can and should assemble your own list of key iPhone application reviewers or "tastemakers" to announce your application to. If the story behind your app is interesting enough, it may get picked up by the mainstream media (MSM) and wind up in newspapers or on television, all of which should skyrocket the number of times your iPhone app is downloaded.

The sky's the limit on creatively advertising your application, and after your app is complete, you can dedicate a good deal of your time to promoting it.

Protecting Your Intellectual Property

The term *IP* is part of the lingo of today's technology, and we aren't referring to Internet Protocol. *Intellectual property,* or IP, consists of ideas and creations that, although they aren't physical, can still be legally protected.

These three major types of intellectual property are usually discussed in relation to business:

✔ Copyright

✔ Trademark

✔ Patent

Each type has its own characteristics. And, of course, because laws are involved, each has its own, dizzying array of complexities that can be deciphered only by a lawyer. We give you enough information to know when you need to go hire a lawyer.

Copyright

Copyright is a fairly simple concept, in principle. When you write a book or a song or software in the United States, your work is automatically protected by copyright. Other people can't simply copy what you wrote and make money from it, without your permission. In other words, you have the *right* to prevent *copying*. However, if someone rewrites your work — substantially — you may not be protected.

Think about this concept in the real world: People clone items all the time. (How many copies of *Tetris* or *Pac-Man* have you played?) But when your work is copied fairly closely — with the same graphics, same words, or same title, for example — someone usually runs into trouble. And, don't forget about plagiarism — copying words and even specific ideas from other works without giving credit. Copyrighting helps fight some of these problems.

Where copyrighting clearly *doesn't* help you is in protecting the core idea of your application. For example, you may want to write an application that helps businesspeople use the iPhone to track their sales numbers. It's an excellent idea, but you can't stop other developers from thinking about creating the same product or from writing an app that does it, with copyright. The only thing you might be able to stop is the wholesale copying of the graphics, video, code, and text you used in your app.

Copyrights are time-limited, in theory, but that period keeps getting extended in practice; nonetheless, copyrighted information eventually enters the public domain (where everyone can use it), though that usually takes place a while after you're dead, so it isn't your problem.

If you're trying to prevent your video, graphics, and text from being directly and literally copied, copyright protection may be the IP defense for you.

Trademarks

A trademark lets a company that has created a product protect its name, and the various names of its products, so that new entrants can't just copy the logo, colors, and other elements to trick consumers into buying a substitute product or knockoff.

A *trademark* reserves a mark (such as a word, a symbol, or a combination of symbols and colors) to identify a business, or *trade*. For example, you're probably familiar with the "swoosh," fancy lettering, and various other marks and symbols used to promote Coca-Cola. The Coca-Cola company even uses polar bears to advertise Coke during the winter months. If you tried to make a beverage — or *anything,* in the case of Coke — and name it Coke, you would probably quickly receive a letter from a lawyer telling you that you're likely to confuse consumers into thinking that your product was made by or endorsed by the Coca-Cola company.

Service marks provide similar protection, but are aimed toward services rather than products. The letters *TM* or *SM* near a name or logo indicate the owner is using that name as a trademark or service mark. If you see ®, it means that the mark is registered with the government.

If you're trying to identify your iPhone application or associated products or services to your consumers and you want to prevent other people from copying those names and logos or even using similar ones, trademark protection might be the IP defense for you.

Patents

A *patent* is a government-granted monopoly, in the country where the product is sold, that gives the patent owner a right to prevent others from making or selling a certain invention. A patent is the hardest intellectual property to gain: You file for a patent and then wait (often, years) for the patent office to

✔ Inspect the *prior art* (items in the same field that were invented before yours)

✔ See whether your invention is *novel* (new or original)

✔ Grant your patent, if the first two bullets apply

If you don't have the tens of thousands of dollars it can cost for a law firm to draft your patent, you can, with the help of a lawyer, buy some initial protection for your invention: For about $1,000, you can file a *provisional patent* (in the United States) that gives you a year to file the real one and provides some evidence of your *priority date,* or the date on which you invented your item.

If you've come up with a novel combination of hardware and software, it might be worth protecting with a patent. Many relatively simple but new ideas are protectable, and the only reason that they aren't patented is that the inventor didn't think they were creative enough.

Because a great deal of innovation is now happening in the mobile space, it stands to reason that just as much IP protection will be sought. The powerful aspect of patents in an IP arsenal is that, after they're granted, they protect the invention itself, not the name of it (as with trademarks) or the specific software code, text, or graphics used in it (as with copyrights). The hard part, of course, is that if you write a lousy patent on something that no one else wanted to do anyway, you wind up spending a lot of money and time on something that provides very little protection.

One of the biggest patent settlements of all time was in the mobile space. A company had invented an elaborate method of delivering *push* e-mail — e-mail that's moved, or "pushed," out to the phone almost instantly after it's received. RIM — the company that makes the Blackberry — apparently infringed on the patents covering this invention. After years in court, RIM paid up, showing how powerful a mobile invention can be.

Perhaps the idea you have for an iPhone application is protectable IP. If you're trying to keep other developers from duplicating your specific, new invention, patent protection might be the right form of IP defense for you.

For a specific look into these areas, check out *Patents, Copyrights & Trademarks For Dummies,* 2nd Edition, by Henri J. A. Charmasson and John Buchaca (Wiley Publishing).

Chapter 5

Leveraging Brand, Skills, and Content

*A*fter you have a pool of great ideas for your iPhone app, step back and take a look at your environment from a business perspective. (We get into the specifics of designing and staffing your team in Chapter 10.) Your immediate goal is to assess your current company's strengths and weaknesses, if you already have one, or to envision your company from a high-level perspective, if you don't already have one. To succeed in the marketplace over the long term, you need to craft your corporate identity — not just your company's brand image but also your corporate culture, your daily operating basis, and the goals you're building toward with your business. All these elements can then be organized and mapped out using a business plan to help you reach the next level of launching your business.

Looking at the Big Picture

Since the advent of the App Store only a short time ago, a number of companies have built a strong identity for themselves as iPhone developers. Some of these include ngmoco, Smule, and PosiMotion. Although thousands of iPhone app developers and development companies exist, these three companies, and others like them, rise above the crowd because they have developed strong branding for themselves based on the iPhone or mobile computing platform. They have also delivered a series of products that are related to each other and their brands. This strength and cohesion is based on an explicit company vision that has been articulated throughout the company. As new projects and strategic directions are contemplated by the company, they are held up against the light of this company vision. By and large, if these product ideas don't contribute to the established motion of the company or lead it in a direction that further enhances the brand, they don't get done, even if they were "good" ideas. There's no better example of this type of thinking than Apple itself, which has pushed the envelope of brand integration so far that it's practically redefined it.

Brand integration doesn't just have to do with a company's vision or its products. The corporate culture is also integral to how well the brand is integrated into the business and (eventually) the marketplace. Google is a great example of brand integration in corporate culture. The Google corporate campus (or "Googleplex") is a large-scale development in Mountain View, California that has been designed to provide an all-encompassing lifestyle environment for its employees ("Googlers"), as shown in Figure 5-1. Bikes to get around the campus, plug-in hybrid cars attached to solar panels, 19 cafes plus "micro-kitchens" spread throughout the complex, and green building techniques and materials provide an environment that provides context for the company's corporate principles. Company slogans such as "You can make money without doing evil," "You can be serious without a suit," and "Work should be challenging and the challenge should be fun" articulate to Google employees and the world what the company is trying to be about. The Google practice of including employees in company earnings — and its executives' insistence on being compensated entirely by their Google stock portfolios rather than by salaries — further creates a spirit of camaraderie at the level of the pocketbook. Google also allots one full day a week to each employee in the organization to work on his or her pet projects, a practice that has yielded some of the most successful Google projects — an institutionalized "skunk works," if you will.

The fun, innovative, collaborative, spirit that Google fosters in its work environment is evident in its products. On the flip side, some reports of the intense committee-oriented control structure that Google exerts on its employees (taking several days in committee to decide a particular line width in a design, for example) also comprise part of the Google corporate culture. The total environment of the company creates a flow of activity and ways of doing things that new employees are swept into. As the company expands, the power of that flow increases. If a company has loose or nonexistent principles that are guiding its growth, it will develop into an environment that's hard to qualify and quantify — and that makes it hard for employees to know the "right thing" to do to help the company. This limits expansion of the company because nobody really knows where the company is supposed to be going, so they're not striving to get there. People begin to "just do their jobs" without any direction to guide them, provide inspiration, and let them know when they're doing a good job or going off the rails.

About the Googleplex

Our world headquarters building (aka the Googleplex) is located in Mountain View, California, a stone's throw from the Shoreline Regional Park wetlands. While not all Google offices around the globe are identical, they share some essential elements. Here are some things you might find in a Google workspace:

- Local flavor, from a mural in Buenos Aires to ski gondolas in Zurich, expressing each office's unique location and personality.
- Bicycles for efficient travel between meetings, dogs, lava lamps, and massage chairs.
- Googlers sharing cubes, yurts, and huddle rooms (few single offices!) with three or four team members.
- Laptops in every employee's hand (or bike basket), for mobile coding and note-taking.
- Foosball, pool tables, volleyball courts, assorted video games, pianos, ping pong tables, lap pools, gyms that include yoga and dance classes.
- Grassroots employee organizations of all kinds, such as meditation classes, film clubs, wine tasting groups, and salsa dance clubs.
- Healthy lunches and dinners for all staff at a wide variety of cafés, and outdoor seating for sunshine brainstorming.
- Snack rooms packed with various snacks and drinks to keep Googlers going throughout the day.

Here's a look at life at the Googleplex:

Life at the Googleplex
★ ★ ★ ★ ★

Figure 5-1:
The Google corporate campus adheres to the company's vision.

As you're starting out, having an idea of what principles and visions are guiding what you're creating and how you're creating it are going to be key as you move beyond releasing your first iPhone app and creating a reputation for yourself. Even before you start your first app, having a clear vision for the type of company you're creating and making that specific is going to go a long way in terms of gaining support from partners, investors, employees, media, advertisers and consumers. It gives people

✔ Something to know you by

✔ A storyline to get excited about

✔ A shared picture to work together toward creating

Defining your corporate vision

To get started, we're going to walk step by step through crafting your company's vision statement. Your have to back up your vision statement by identifying attainable goals that you can put into action with your company. When we've defined those, we're going to refine the vision further to get a look at *how* your company accomplishes its goals. This will be the seed of your company's corporate culture. Then we're going to break those goals down into actionable items that you can integrate into your daily operations. When you have a strong corporate vision, you can take a look at branding.

If you already have a company, and you want to use this chapter to help you set a new direction for it to include your iPhone endeavors, involve the people who are working for and with you in this process. You and your executive team are in charge of setting the overall course, but input and feedback from the various personnel in your organization will not only make your new vision for your company stronger, they will also help you dramatically in getting them to buy in to implementing your new vision.

Writing your vision statement

To craft a vision that people can get interested in, get behind, and act upon, you need to get specific about what you want to offer. PosiMotion, for example, has based most of its early product line on the concept of creating software tools that utilize the GPS and motion sensing systems in the iPhone. The PosiMotion name and logo also reinforce this orientation, as you can see from the company Web site in Figure 5-2. The original PosiMotion vision statement might have been something along the lines of "To create top-quality geolocation and motion-sensing applications that emphasize design elegance, ease of use, and specificity of purpose that make iPhone users' day-to-day lives more navigable."

To find the heart of your vision statement, start with what your best product does best.

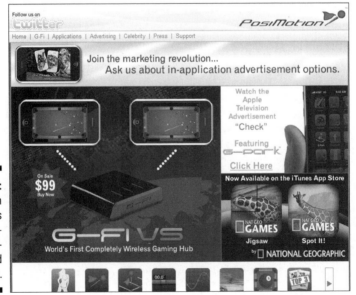

Figure 5-2: PosiMotion emphasizes wireless- and GPS- related apps.

The PosiMotion vision

A good portion of PosiMotion applications (and all its early apps) are consistent with our hypothetical vision statement in terms of design and functionality. It has even moved this concept into hardware design with its G-Fi Mobile GPS Network Routers. A look at the PosiMotion Web site, however, reveals a number of application titles that don't quite fit our hypothetical vision statement (nor the company name and logo), such as Bikini Hunt, Pool, and Solitaire. These products, although successful in their own right, weaken the PosiMotion brand and make it harder for the company to answer the question "What are you all about?" without simply reverting to the generic answer, "We make iPhone apps." The authors sense that this is going to make it harder for PosiMotion to differentiate itself in the marketplace and maintain its relevance as a company. This difficulty won't have a short-term effect on app sales — consumers in the App Store rarely think about who made a given app — but the company's reputation in the iPhone business community can easily fall off as it becomes less specialized and more like "just another development house with some interesting products."

Today, the PosiMotion About page has a more generic vision statement: "An innovative technology leader, PosiMotion develops, designs, and engineers breakthrough applications, programs, and devices. The first set of edgy brands that the Company has released include G-Spot, G-Park, G-Minds, G-Fi and G-Life. PosiMotion stays ahead of the curve by bringing to market applications that are cutting-edge, original, and ultimately enhance the end-user experience." If we were to advise PosiMotion (and trust us, we don't), we'd suggest that it brand its non-GPS/motion-sensing-related apps under another brand with its own identity — and exhibit a more specific vision statement for each brand.

We use our made-up corporate vision for PosiMotion to identify some key characteristics of a vision statement.

1. The offering ("what it is")

Because this is a book about the iPhone, we're assuming you're going to be offering iPhone applications, hardware, consulting, or some combination. But your real offering might be something that the iPhone is only part of. If (for example) your company makes medical devices or creates software for them, the iPhone might be only one of the many hardware platforms that you utilize. Alternately, you might start by wanting to create an iPhone app and realize that what you're *really* trying to do is provide solutions for a problem that might use desktop software and non-computing resources as well.

Getting clear about exactly what you're offering is an important first step; in exploring it, you might be surprised to find that the iPhone is only a part of what you want to offer.

PosiMotion, for example, has branched out into offering hardware networking products that connect a variety of computing devices for mobile collaboration and gaming (see Figure 5-3). By adding these devices, PosiMotion moved from being an "iPhone app creator" to being a "mobile computing solutions provider." This is an important difference that it can use to help tell the story of its company.

Figure 5-3:
PosiMotion expands its offering with hardware devices.

2. Specific market differentiators ("how we are different")

PosiMotion's main market differentiator is that it makes geolocation and motion-sensing applications. It also has created a design look that sets it apart from the pack; you can use nearly anything as a market differentiator as long as it's specific. One very prolific app maker makes only apps that showcase Jewish content; another innovative app company, Smule, uses several factors:

- A unique, simple, and beautiful design aesthetic

- Apps that turn the iPhone into a musical instrument

- Real-time, worldwide viewing of other users' content (seeing drawings done by others with Zephyr, songs being played by others with Ocarina, other people's virtual lighters around the globe with Sonic Lighter)

- Inter-device collaboration (playing together with Leaf Trombone, "lighting" another iPhone with Sonic Lighter)

You don't have to stick with only product features as a differentiator. You can use many categories to make your company stand out in the eyes of the market. These include

- Design style

- Technologies used

- Type of content

- Demographic served (the type of person your apps appeal to)

- Genre of application (games, productivity, e-books, and so on)

- Specific problem-solving methodology

- Unique design for a user interface (the way the user interacts with your apps)

- Social purpose (promoting a certain philosophy or way of life)

After you define what differentiates your company from the rest of the companies out there making apps, try to stick with it. This doesn't mean you have to reject any app ideas that don't fit perfectly into the vision you already have. If appropriate, you can expand or redefine your vision (a classic example: Apple rebranded itself as a "digital lifestyle" company rather than just a "computer and software manufacturer"). But try not to revise your vision radically at the drop of a hat. We don't suggest changing course unless you can identify a strategic direction that offers a future for your company beyond that one new app.

If you want to keep your brand identity intact, but still do a project or series of projects that don't align with it, another option is to create a separate brand identity to support those projects. For example, Toyota is the owner of both Lexus and Scion cars. Lexus is the Toyota "up-market" brand that competes with BMW, Audi, and Mercedes; Scion is the Toyota "down-market" brand that competes with other economy vehicle manufacturers. Each company has its own brand identity and brand integration that keeps its products and its image all aligned so they tell a consistent story to the consumer. Almost all large automakers segment their brands this way. Take a look at who owns some of your favorite car brands and you see that a very small number of companies actually operate a large number of the world's car brands. But each brand is separate and unique, with its own product line and message to the consumer.

3. **Qualities that the company values ("how it is done")**

After you define *what* you're offering, now you need to define *how* you're going to offer it. In our imaginary vision statement, this is in the line "emphasize design elegance, ease of use, and specificity of purpose". Are your apps going to be hard-nosed business software that emphasizes functionality over fun features? Are you going to put a premium on eye-candy that captivates people with the imagery in your apps? Is ease of use your primary value, or are you more interested in offering a large set of features?

These qualities represent another level of differentiation to the market. Not only does your company create social-networking apps, for example, it does so by integrating with standard online social networks such as Facebook.

- The "what" is creating social-networking apps.

- The "how" is making them integrate with existing social networks.

  You could go further into the "how" part of this by specifying that your apps use the geolocation features of the iPhone so each user can connect with people in the local vicinity.

Suppose this social-networking dimension applies not only to your products, but also to your corporate culture. Okay, why not acknowledge that? Here's what we'd add to our original made-up vision statement: "Company X is a company that grants employees the opportunity to integrate work into their daily lives in such a way that creates harmony between work and home life."

This part of a vision statement deals with how your company is going to get things done and what kind of work environment that will create. Even if the sample description given here doesn't work for your company (you might prefer an office with a geographical address that everybody comes to daily to collaborate in person, and set hours that end at 5:00 p.m.), other elements of your operations that have more significance to you may find a place in your vision statement. At this point, we're sketching a general direction for what kind of company you want to operate, not sorting out every detail. If you make it something that brings a smile to your face and gets you excited about running such a company, you've got a great start.

4. Value to the consumer ("why you are doing it")

When you've defined what you're offering and how you're offering it, the next order of business is to define what your product's value is to your customers. How is someone better off as a result of using your product? In our example, we state that we want to make applications "that make iPhone users' day-to-day lives more navigable." This is a simple but powerful statement — that still leaves room for growth. If you had a company like this and did really well at meeting this goal, you would have a very strong platform from which to promote your products.

People think in categories. As any artist knows, "pigeonholing" yourself into a particular category can be somewhat painful. Most of us know that we can do basically anything we put our minds to, so the idea of limiting ourselves to one category seems rather cramped. As a consumer, however, we're constantly being inundated with information. The way we cope with the daily deluge of advertising, entertainment, news, education, and mundane data is to put things in categories. By and large, if something isn't tucked into a category in the consumer's mind, it's rapidly forgotten. It's as though the context of a category gives a particular piece of information something to "stick to" so that associations can bring that item back to light later. Without a context to stick to, new information is often filed in the "miscellaneous" category — and we all know what happens to that miscellaneous folder on our computer: One day, you just have to empty everything out because you forgot it was there.

In order to not get filed as "miscellaneous" — and to give your products an end goal that connects with the consumer — identify exactly what your product is going to do for them. If you make games, you could say you make apps that "provide hours of excitement and enjoyment." But if your statement is moving in a direction like this, step back and get more specific; almost every game has that same basic purpose. What are you going to provide that is unique? "Giving users a way to play games that operate in both the digital and physical worlds simultaneously" is much more specific. "Giving users a way to explore their creativity" is also specific. As you zero in on these special qualities, you should be able to find (or make up) a picture of your customers — the identities of specific people whose needs or wants would be met by your company. You should be able to see how finding the apps you offer would be a breath of fresh air for these people because they see themselves or some aspect of their lives reflected in what you're offering them, and in who you are as a company. Perhaps you're opening a new possibility for your customers. Perhaps you're filling a need they already have in their lives. In either case, when they think of that area of their lives, you should come to the top of their minds — because you're the one who creates the things that fit into that spot in their day.

These four components: your offering, market differentiators, qualities of your company and product, and your value to the consumer, will give you a good base for seeding and growing your company. In all, your corporate vision amounts to an "elevator pitch" you can use to represent your company to the media, prospective employees, potential investors, partners, and others in no more time than it takes to ride an elevator several floors. After the initial phases of getting your company going, you refer to your vision to determine whether you're still on track with what you set out to do — and whether the reality of your company fits the vision you had for it. If it doesn't, you have a guide you can use to adjust things.

So — to get started writing your own corporate vision — plan on writing about each of these four elements. If you're ready to do that, we've got some bullet points to offer you some starting points. If you're not feeling ready yet, skip to the next paragraph. Here are the starting points:

- ✔ What exactly are you offering?
- ✔ What will differentiate you and your products in the marketplace?
- ✔ What qualities will your products and company exhibit that give depth to what you're offering?
- ✔ What is the specific value to the consumer that your company fulfills with its products?

If you weren't quite ready to answer these questions yet, take a step back and look at who you are, what you want to do, and what effect you want to have on your environment. If you haven't yet done so, refer to the "Sensing How to Enter the Marketplace with a New Application" section in Chapter 1 — and take a thorough look at that process. It includes identifying needs in the marketplace, assessing the environment around you, and taking an inventory of what you have to offer. These items are applied to generating an idea for a specific app, but the same questions apply to creating a vision for your business. To be successful, your business will need to encompass those elements and fulfill the four elements of a vision statement we discussed previously. But you don't have to jump from here to there all in one leap. Creating a new business can require some gestation. Feel free to take some time to formulate your approach by researching the App Store market; observing your surroundings; identifying needs around you; and deepening your understanding of your own capabilities, talents, and interests.

If you're ready to answer the questions that will help generate your vision statement, take a moment to write thoroughly about each one, not worrying about how your sentences are formed or about keeping it concise. Just write about each one until you don't have anything left to say about it, and then move on to the next. When you're done writing on the last question, go back to the first one and write anything else that comes to mind. After you've gone through a couple of times and really feel that you've written everything you want to say about each question, go back and read through what you've written.

- ✔ If you created a company like this, would it be something you'd be excited about creating — every day of your work week?
- ✔ If you were a consumer and encountered such a company, would you get excited about its products and image?

If you're unsure, go back and write more or revise what you've written. You can also go back to Chapter 1 and delve deeper into the "Entering the Marketplace with a New Application" section.

When you're happy with what you've written, go through and organize your writing into a concise vision statement that you can easily tell to someone within 30 seconds or so. If you have a lot of material, you can write two versions of your statement, a longer-form detailed vision and a shorter-form "elevator pitch" version. Use the longer one on printed material; commit the shorter one to memory for rattling off any time someone asks what you're up to. This single vision statement is going to provide the intellectual seed for growing your company. The shared vision that you create with it will attract and keep collaborators, interest investors, give the media something to know you by, and allow you to create a consistent experience for your consumers.

You also need to develop — and state clearly — the goals you have for your company, from the perspective of what you and your partners get out of it and what kind of an effect you want to have on the consumer.

Letting your goals motivate you

Having goals is a straightforward concept, but goals are too often never fully conceived or forgotten in the day-to-day fray of keeping things going. Just as your vision statement is the light that is guiding you through the wilderness of starting and crafting your company, goals keep you motivated to get there — and let you know when you're sidetracked or stuck.

Take a few moments to consider these categories and write down your goals:

- ✔ **Your personal income goals:** This isn't just what you want your company to make, but what you personally take home from it. Of course, everyone wants to make as much as possible, but what would be an attainable-but-still-exciting goal that you can aim for first? After you attain that, you can and should set a new, even higher income goal. Remember: If you're conscientious, as your income increases, so does the income of those around you. So don't be shy about wanting to make money!

- ✔ **Your ideal day:** Start with a piece of paper and put the time you get up at the top and the time you go to bed at the bottom. Or you can do this with a one-day organizer page. Map out your perfect day from start to finish, including your work and personal-life activities. Get as detailed and specific as you can. What kind of day would make you go to bed with a smile, happy and satisfied with yourself and what you've been able to accomplish, but not stressed and stretched?

- ✔ **Your ideal role in your company:** Just because you're starting it doesn't mean you have to be CEO, unless you want to be (and feel you are) the best person for the job. You could be founder and Creative Director. You could hire a CEO and oversee that person on a more general basis. Or, of course, you could *be* CEO. You might start out as chief cook and bottle-washer. But what roles and responsibilities would you be happy to have responsibility for — and which ones would you prefer to hire (or partner with) other people to do?

✔ **The number of products you want to release per year:** Tap Tap Tap, an independent iPhone development house, releases about 6 apps a year, a number it finds profitable and sustainable for a company its size (see Figure 5-4). In one of their colorful blogs they complain about a venture capitalist taunting them to accept money so they could release 100 apps a year, an offer that they politely declined because they value quality over quantity (a value the authors endorse). Releasing 6 apps a year might seem daunting to you, or you might be even more ambitious than that. Of course, the practicality of finding funding and talent to produce all these projects will be a real-world factor you have to deal with. But we're not thinking about that for now. Just think about — and state — your ideal goal for a product lineup so you have something to work toward. If you don't know how many you'd like to do yet, and don't feel you have enough context to do an accurate estimate, that's okay. Just keep this question in mind and keep moving. At some point along the way, it will become clear to you.

Figure 5-4:
Tap Tap Tap
releases a
manageable
list of apps
per year.

✔ **The size of the company you want to own:** Some people dream of just getting out from under the thumb of their boss by freelancing. Running your own show is certainly a lot more freeing than having a day job, but it can also get stressful and lonely to keep all those balls in the air yourself. Others want to create a vast empire such as Google, Apple, or Microsoft. But being responsible for generating that much income and managing that many people can be as daunting as it is thrilling. What size company would be a thrill for you to own and run, but not bowl you under the table with responsibility? As you grow as a business owner, this number will probably change. Just write down what seems a good size to you now.

✔ **The amount of revenue you want your company to make per year:** This is related to your company size. You'll need enough revenue to support your payroll and overhead, of course, but what about profit? Do you want to have a company that issues stock and becomes a profit center for investors and employees? Or would you rather have a private company that pays everyone (including you) and leaves you with a profit? How much profit do you want? Again, everyone wants as much as possible. But if you don't reinvest in your own company, it will have trouble maintaining profits in the long haul. Twenty percent reinvestment is a conservative number. Many entrepreneurs reinvest 50% or more. Some don't take any profit until their company is very far along and has become a power in its field. There are many good business books written on this subject. Take some time to further educate yourself on this point; get a basic idea of your financial goals for your company.

✔ **The effect you want to have on your customers:** This is related to the "value to the consumer" that we put in our vision statement, but it's more about how you want them to see you, what effect you want to have on them, and what you want their response to be. For example, if your vision statement says you want to make apps that "make iPhone users' day-to-day lives more navigable," you might end up with customers who see you as their source for navigation assistance. They might be affected by having some everyday hassles alleviated — finding their cars in vast parking lots, measuring things on the spot (say, the width of a drive-way), and getting around in an unfamiliar city. And they might respond by enthusiastically recommending you to their friends and taking an interest in every app that you make. You don't have to limit yourself to these three types of effects. Write what is exciting and interesting to you.

Take a moment to think of other types of goals you might have — and write about them, too. After you've written up your goals, separate them into *quantitative* goals (ones you could measure with a number, such as income or time commitment) and *qualitative* goals (ones that can't be given a measurement with numbers but have to do with the quality of life, such as your ideal day). The quantitative goals will become a basis for tracking your progress with statistics. The qualitative goals are ones that you can refer to — along with your vision statement — to make sure you're headed in the direction you want to go.

Understanding Your Corporate Culture

Every company has a corporate culture, from the most basic freelance opera-tion to the largest industrial enterprise. *Corporate culture* simply means the attitudes, beliefs, thoughts, myths, and rituals that a company and its employees develop and promote while working together. It's the company's "way of doing business." A culture will develop by default in any company, but the best companies don't let it "just happen." They get in and shape the culture of their organization to promote the values they want their company to hold, shape the attitudes employees have about working there, and form the impressions customers have of the company.

Corporate culture may seem a "fluffy" topic. But in today's saturated business environment, the way your customers feel about doing business with your company can be just as important to them as the product you provide. The experience your employees have working with you will sculpt attitudes that certainly spill over into their customer interactions (ever been served by a waitperson who obviously doesn't like the job?) and even their desire to stay with you or move on. Great iPhone designers, developers, project managers, and support personnel aren't a dime a dozen. Companies that have the best employees will create the best products and win out over the competition. Your corporate culture will be integral to your ability to attract and keep great people — and to having those people represent you well.

Starbucks is a terrific example of a well-cultivated corporate culture. Love them or hate them, Starbucks has done a terrific job of creating an interesting, successful way of doing business that is both internal and external (that is, apparent to the customer). Every employee of Starbucks goes to Starbucks University, where they not only learn the ins and outs of how to make and serve coffee; they're infused with the attitudes of fun, individuality, and personal service that the company has found important to making a winning customer experience. Cashiers are called "partners" in order to foster a sense of ownership. Coffee makers are called "baristas" to give their job flair. Managers are promoted to the position only if they exhibit a fun, positive attitude to customers and employees consistently. In other words, no jerks are allowed in management; managers bring the mood of the stores up rather than pushing stress down on other employees. All employees are given stock options to encourage the partnership metaphor — and each is entitled to one pound of free coffee each week. Training videos specifically illustrate to employees how to give exceptional service by getting to know their customers by name, having personal interactions with individual customers, and making sure that customers get exactly what they want — with a smile — every time.

What's more, the décor of Starbucks has been crafted and selected to be homey, interesting, and high-end without being snobby. Each Starbucks is decorated slightly differently, but with a very similar theme, as shown in Figure 5-5.

The kind of detailed attention that has gone into shaping attitudes, environments, and interactions at Starbucks has led to a global company that you can walk into and expect the same level of service and quality of product anywhere you go. What Starbucks is really selling is an *experience*. This kind of high-quality consistency allows positive word of mouth to spread — because people can feel safe referring their friends if they're confident that their friends will have the same quality experience they had. Starbucks may not rely on word of mouth now that it's a huge company, but it certainly took off that way, and those personal interactions (and addictive coffee-drink recipes) keep people coming back for more.

Figure 5-5:
Starbucks stores have a particular look and feel.

Other successful companies have very different corporate cultures. (We already illustrated something about Google in the beginning of this chapter.) Think of some of the companies you interact with as a consumer; try to iden-tify some elements of their corporate culture. How do they handle customer service? How do employees treat each other? What kind of environment do you find yourself in when you interact with the company? If you work for a corporation currently, analyze its corporate culture. Is it a "cubicles and water coolers" type of culture, or a "boss's door is always open" kind of culture? How do employees treat each other and their customers? Get specific and write a few paragraphs about two or three corporate cultures you can observe.

Now turn your attention to your own corporate culture. Your vision state-ment and your goals lay the groundwork for this perspective. But now we're going to make it concrete in terms of how things go from day to day:

✔ How should executives, management, and employees treat each other in your company?

✔ What is the physical environment of your company like? If you're planning on running a virtual company, what are the communications systems and protocols of your company like? Is it "business only" or are you going to create ways for people to get to know each other personally?

✔ What level of service do you provide your customers? How are your customers treated when they have sales or support issues? What can you do to make them feel special?

✔ What is your Web presence like? What kind of image do you want to project? Is it going to be a hip, clean "Web 2.0"–style site like that of ngmoco (see Figure 5-6), or a cute, thematic site like the one belonging to Tap Tap Tap?

Figure 5-6: ngmoco has a deliberate Web presence to match its company culture.

After you get going on these questions, keep riffing on what you want your company to be like to work for and do business with. Write a story (or series of stories) about customers and other businesses interacting with your company and how people in your company get their jobs done, how they feel, and what they experience while doing it.

When you've thoroughly defined your corporate culture for yourself, think of some policies that you can put in place to give your ideas legs. For example, if you want a work environment that provides lots of natural light to employees and allows them to get snacks without taking a break from work, you could create a policy about what type of office space is acceptable for you to consider leasing and another one about how many on-site snack options you're going to provide. If your company is just you and a few partners, it's still a good idea to get specific about what kind of interactions you want to have and how you're going to conduct your business day. This is going to be your life! Create it in such a way that you enjoy living it!

As you can see, your vision for your corporate culture is going to color the writing of actual company policy. If you're ready to start writing a policy document or two, go for it. We're not going to get deep into that here, but, again, some great resources are available to help you do that.

Putting Goals into Practice

Okay, after all this visioning and writing comes the real world: putting some of those principles into practice. We do this by getting specific about the things we've put into our vision statement, goals, and corporate-culture documents. The magic question: How do they get implemented on the ground?

Defining your operation

In the "qualities" section of our hypothetical vision statement, we added a brief description of how we wanted work life to affect employees: "Company X is a company that grants employees the opportunity to integrate work into their daily lives in such a way that creates harmony between work and home life." This is a very strong ideal for the company — but it doesn't really tell us what this principle looks like in the real world. In order to get to something we can put into practice, we need to describe this in terms of something that can be done in the physical world.

Here's one approach: "Company X will use telecommunication and online management tools to bring together designers and developers from around the globe to produce our applications. We won't have set working hours, but instead will operate to meet specific goals and timelines. This will allow Company X employees to create a work schedule that integrates well with their personal lives. As long as employees are hitting their deadlines, doing solid work, and attending virtual meetings on time, they're free to manage their own schedules."

This is an example of getting more specific, allowing enough room for you to be somewhat flexible about how you implement it. As you get into actually setting up your communications infrastructure, writing policy documents, and instructing employees about how to operate, you can develop the nitty-gritty details of how this idealism goes into place. The previous paragraph is intended as an example to guide you and your team so you know whether you're actually implementing your vision. You can also refer to the general statement of principle that you gave in your vision statement to make sure you're accomplishing the kind of vision that you had in mind.

Take some time to parse out each item that you've put into your vision statement, goals, and corporate-culture documents — and write a more specific paragraph or two about how those things get implemented in the real world.

When you're done with this detailed examination, go back over everything and turn it into a more polished document that you can go over with partners, investors, and employees. You'll be well on your way to putting your visions into practice just by getting the feedback and buy-in of the people you're working with to create your company.

Introducing branding

As with any vague subject matter, *branding* is a subject that has many experts and gurus. There's a stack of references you can refer for a more detailed view of this subject, but keep a basic rule in mind: Although there's no one "best" approach to branding, there are some principles that can guide you toward a successful brand.

Many people think of branding only in terms of a company's logo and design look. Although these are vital to a successful company (as described in the first half of this chapter), branding really starts with thoroughly defining who and what you want your company to be — and then implementing that vision. *Implementation* is following through with tangible activities that support your vision. When you have this strong vision for your company in place, you can begin the process of creating your company's look by distilling what it is that makes your company unique and working with a designer to translate that quality into a graphical language.

Here are some principles that should guide you and your designer:

✔ **Great logos are simple and easy to recognize from a distance.** This is far more important than how "pretty" your logo is, though beautiful design is increasingly important, particularly when your product is related to the Apple brand. If you drive down a street populated by a lot of retail stores and restaurants or cruise the mall, you see that the logos most familiar to you are ones that you could pick out from a long way away. Some of them, such as FedEx, aren't terribly artistic or interesting, but they say something to your eye that creates immediate recognition.

The fastest way to mess up a logo is to use fine lines and small type. Such nuances turn into a blur at a distance — and they don't create a lasting impression from close up. Also, using small details alongside large details might look good as you're designing them, but the small parts will get lost in the contrast of their size to the larger parts in a quick glance or at a distance. Photos are usually not a good component of logos for this reason.

Simplify the artwork in your logo into the most distilled form you can while still maintaining the flavor of what you're after. Smule and ngmoco have done a good job of this, as shown in Figure 5-7.

Of course, most people aren't going to see your logo on an outdoor sign because their interactions with your brand are going to happen mostly over the iPhone or the Internet. For this reason, some software companies create logos that are more detailed than might be acceptable for a retail business. This is perfectly acceptable to a certain extent, but the same principles still apply — because a logo that can be recognized from far away will also be the most recognizable when viewed up close. Also, sometimes you have to use your logo in very small places, which is equivalent to viewing it from far away; even if the detail gets lost, the recognition should still be there.

Figure 5-7:
Smule and
ngmoco
have
simplified
logos that
work!

Although Tap Tap Tap and PosiMotion have used finer details in their logos, the overall shape of the logos doesn't *depend* on these details. So logo shape is still contributing some degree of recognizability. The PosiMotion concept for its icon of a flying map pin is particularly strong and overcomes the drawbacks of its finer line art to an extent. Tap Tap Tap has a similarly strong concept of using fingerprints to convey the touchable nature of its product.

✔ **Great logos use a limited set of colors that appeal to the target demographic of the brand's intended audience.** Food chains often use the colors red and yellow because these colors have been found to make people hungry. They're also bold, fun colors, which works well with many fast-food chains' brand images and corporate cultures.

• Many technology services companies use blue (that is, IBM blue) because blue conveys a sense of trustworthiness, technology, and intelligence.

• Green gives a sense of liveliness, nature, and futurism.

• Bright colors connote fun, strength, boldness, and excitement.

• Muted colors connote seriousness, softness, warmth, and calmness.

You should use colors to convey a specific message about your company that reinforces the vision that you have crafted for it.

More than three colors are too many for your logo. Two is strong. One color can be very strong as well.

✔ **Great logos can have an icon associated with them, or not.** Okay, we're operating in the software space, so having an icon associated with your brand is a pretty natural fit. Some very recognizable icons include the Nike swoosh, the McDonald's arches, and the Apple apple illustration. But many companies have a successful logo with only text. FedEx, CNN, Microsoft, and Oracle are great examples of text logos that don't have a pictorial icon. In each of these cases, the text itself has been treated so it's unique and not just a typeface.

If you use an icon, try to use something simple that conveys your company's image or reinforces the name of your company. The Nike swoosh conveys speed and flight; the Apple apple simply repeats the word "Apple" in graphic form. The General Motors' iconic "GM" square is simply the initials of the company. Each of these examples varies in its artfulness, but each brand has achieved legendary status in its own right in terms of recognizability.

In the iPhone market, cute sells — and that pertains as much to icons and designs as it does to products. Not all winning designs have a cuteness factor, but many do. As you're creating your brand identity, you may want to take this into consideration.

✔ **Great brands have a consistent style guide to govern their design.** You shouldn't have your designer stop with creating a logo for you. Your company also needs a document called a *style guide* to help make sure that all your print and graphical communications have a look and feel consistent with your logo and your overall brand. Physically, a style guide is a small reference booklet that spells out the dos and don'ts of laying out anything from a company letter to your Web site, advertisements, and anything in between that are part of your company's visual impression. When evaluating potential designers, make sure that the one you select can also provide you with a good style guide to help you implement your look company-wide.

Writing Your Business Plan

Often, a "great idea for an iPhone app" is actually the start of an entirely new business. People may not fully realize the amount of work that goes into supporting the creation of a new idea. Although sometimes the "fun" part of a new idea is its conception, it is the subsequent planning and execution — through hard work — that brings an idea to fruition and success.

Ideas, large and small, require planning to be a success. For every exception — every so-called "overnight success" — there are dozens of examples that prove the rule that planning is a necessity.

If you're inside an organization and promoting the idea of — or already designing — an iPhone application for your company, a customary stage of this process is writing a *business case* — a document that explains how this new initiative will benefit your business. If you're creating a brand-new business around the application — even if it's a part-time business, then you're at a different (and more elaborate) stage: writing a business plan.

The purpose of writing a business case (or, for that matter, a business plan) is twofold:

- ✔ Convince others that you have a good idea.
- ✔ Convince yourself that you're really on to something.

Recognizing that cynicism doesn't work

Sometimes people approach the development of business plans cynically. They're "only" trying to get funding or resources — but don't really believe in the idea, and don't really DO the planning necessary to make the project happen. But the most effective fundraising documents will be those that present a rock-solid plan that describes the opportunity, paints a realistic picture of potential success, and shows the steps that will achieve that success. A great business plan will tell the convincing story "If you would just add money and resources to this plan, it's going to succeed."

Writing a business plan can be a daunting, even overwhelming, experience. As with a term paper, small novel, or other Big Document, you should expect a convincing business plan to take some work. But before you decide that "writing a business plan is a waste of time," that "it's a distraction from the real work of creating a business," or (worst of all) that you're "no good at writing," realize that you may have already done most of the work that has to go into your plan.

Incorporating business plans into the culture

Human beings have been creating business plans since the dawn of time. Our entrepreneurial instincts surfaced when one of our distant ancestors realized he could trade one of the extra sharp rocks he collected for some meat. He may have thought to himself "Hey if I just collect all the sharp rocks around I can trade them for food and avoid all that hunting and getting-bit-by-wild-animals."

Much, much later, a clever herder figured out how many byproducts could be made from the flock — candles, sausage, clothing — and figured out how many animals were needed to make *somebody* a great living. Perhaps he realized if he asked that rich guy to help him get a bit more land and feed, the business would grow faster. The rich guy invested in the herder's (live)stock and received a nice return on his investment, and voilá the herd doubled, the herder got a big house in the hills, and the "rich guy" got paid back.

That's all a business plan is: a plan. The more thorough you want to be about your plan, the more convincing you can be to yourself and others that you've thought your idea through and know what's going to happen.

Inspecting the ingredients of a business plan

Having a business plan means two things:

- ✔ The plan itself — what you're going to do to succeed
- ✔ A formal or informal document that helps you communicate the plan to others

You can find free information on writing business plans from sources such as the U.S. Small Business Administration, (`www.sba.gov/smallbusiness planner/plan/writeabusinessplan`), as shown in Figure 5-8.

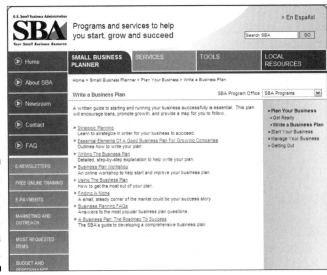

Figure 5-8: SBA can help you write a business plan.

In fact, business plan information abounds online, and it's fairly well agreed upon what the basic pattern is. Essentially, a business plan is all the ingredients of running a business. And if you have any business sense, you probably already know them. So all a business plan asks you to do is write down what you're planning. It doesn't have to be in formal language; just write what you know. If you need to spruce up the plan to impress an investor or in-company stakeholder, you can do that as a second pass; the first thing to do is simply document the plan, so you can look at it and see if you agree that it *is* the plan.

The following outline presents some of the usual headings found in a business plan, along with typical questions that you want to answer — both for yourself *and* in your business plan. Really, the most fundamental question for business planning is, "How do we make this business succeed?" All the other questions flow from the thousands of details necessary to make a successful project.

- ✔ Product

  - What's the business?

  - What product or service are you creating and selling?

  - Who is going to build it?

  - How will you ensure its quality?

  - Will you be able to make it good enough?

- ✔ Customers

  - What is your "market"? That is, how big is the potential group of people who will buy your product?

  - Out of this vast number, how many of them will you really be able to convince to buy your product? Ten percent? Five percent? One percent?

- ✔ Surveys and statistics

  - Do people really want your product?

  - How do you know this?

  - Have you looked at the size of the market?

  - Have you looked at comparable products and found out what they made?

  - Have you studied any other companies with similar approaches to your market?

  - Are your estimates of actual buyers realistic and based on comparable results of other companies?

  - Do you really understand the needs of your customers?

  - Do you have "market proxies" (people who represent your customers) that you can interview for needs?

- Have you done more comprehensive surveys on (dozens, hundreds) of people representing your market?

- Have you really verified your assumptions?

✔ Pricing

- How much will you charge?

- Is that enough to cover costs?

- Will you be undersold?

- Have you done a pricing survey?

- Will you be able to charge what you need to for the application when it's complete? If not, will you be able to sustain service?

✔ Competitors

- Who else is doing it?

- Won't a bigger company outdo you?

- Won't a smaller company be more agile and beat you to the punch? Why not? Who else is providing similar or substitute or alternative products to yours?

- Will people have to switch from some other product to yours? Why will they?

- If no one else is doing your idea yet, why not?

- Are you in a "green field"? If so, are there enough people who even want your product yet?

- Is your product better/cheaper/cleaner/quicker/nicer/sexier/fuller-featured/simpler/easier to use/better integrated than the competition? Is that enough?

✔ Barriers to entry

- What are the "Barriers to entry"; that is, is it hard to do your product?

- Do you have any unique advantages?

- Are you well ahead of the competition (faster time to market?)

- Do you have any patents (temporary monopoly) or any exclusive content that your competitors don't have access to?

✔ Team

- Do you have the staff you need?

- Is your team especially talented in this?

- Do you have the resources of another division, company to help?

- Do you have the roles technology, budgets, sales, marketing, and quality covered?

- Do you have access to the right people to create your product on time and within budget?

- Will it be high-quality enough to sell?

- Do you have access to people who know exactly how to make your product sell in high volume that will support the project or company?

✔ Sales, marketing, public relations

- How are you going to let the world know about your app?

- Do you have a list of marketing initiatives and their costs worked out?

- Do you have a press release and PR strategy?

- Are you relying only on word-of-mouth?

- If one strategy isn't delivering results, do you have alternate plans?

- Do you have enough budget to sustain a marketing campaign as long as it will take?

- Do you have a conference budget?

- Do you have a book, magazines, speaking engagements that tie in to promotion?

- Are you purchasing online ads?

- For vertical applications, are you promoting in the appropriate trade magazines or periodicals?

- Are you submitting your app to competitions?

- Do you have beta testers who can provide case studies or testimonials?

✔ Finance and budget

- How many units of your product will you sell every day/week/ month/quarter?

- How many will you sell in the first year?

- How do you know this, that is, what assumptions are your sales projections made from?

- How much does it cost you (in marketing, advertising, and so on) to acquire a customer?

- What are your worst-case, best-case, average-case sales projections?

- Are they real or something you made up to greenlight your project?

- Do you really believe them?

- Can you deliver them?

✔ Funding

- Are you self-funding?

- Are you funding through "sweat equity?" Are you keeping your day job?

- Have you estimated the costs thoroughly?

- Have you chased up every potential cost?

- Have you put real costs in for development as well as promotion and marketing?

- Do you have sources of money?

- Are you raising "Angel investment"? Are you financing on credit cards?

- Are you raising venture capital?

- What will you do if the money runs out?

- If you're bootstrapping, do you have enough resources to at least get the first version of your product out?

If you're building your iPhone application within a division of an existing company, you may already have good answers to the majority of these questions. But even then, you may have to rationalize all of these issues in your business case. Even if your application is a pure marketing effort — designed to bring attention to some other product, service, or idea — you still need a PR and marketing plan to ensure that your application really delivers the value you intend it to.

If you're a developer writing an application in your spare time, or an entrepreneur with a great idea for an application, you're going to need to answer all these questions, if only for yourself, to ensure success. And if your plans and dreams are big enough that you're going to need help and money to achieve them, then a well-written business plan is probably the most important document you need to write to communicate those dreams.

If you want additional information regarding how to build your own business plan, you should consult other books and guides, such as *Business Plans Kit For Dummies,* Second Edition, by Steven D. Peterson, Peter E. Jaret, and Barbara Findlay Schenck (Wiley).

Seeing the forest and the trees

In looking at all the tiny questions that can come up, you may have gotten a bit overwhelmed. "I can't answer half these questions!" But never fear — and here's why — the essentials are quite simple:

1. Make a quality product that fills an actual need.

2. Price the product so you can profit nicely (or make it cheaply enough to fit in the price you can charge).

3. Sell it!

If you do your homework, chances are you can figure out something people want. Pricing it right is just a matter of either charging a fair price for it, or finding a way to make it dirt cheap. (We talked more about pricing your application in Chapter 3.) And selling it is simply figuring out how you're going to make sure everyone who could possibly want your program finds out about it and is encouraged — repeatedly — to buy it. Commit those sections to paper (or your favorite word-processing program) to make up your business plan, which can help you with funding, support, or even provide a guide to follow as you develop and market your app to the world.

Chapter 6

Collaborating Internally and Externally

*H*opefully, you are getting the sense by now that creating an iPhone application is rarely a one-person job from start to finish. You will need to collaborate with various people about different aspects of creating, developing, and ultimately promoting and selling your iPhone application. While you may do all the actual coding yourself, brainstorming and evaluating your idea are tasks that greatly benefit from other input, even if you simply read other people's thoughts and comments without talking to them. Your application will exist with tens of thousands of other applications, it's important to get a sense of where and how your application will exist within the larger community. Thankfully, you are never alone in this arena, as there are many voices looking for collaboration.

In this chapter, we take a look at how you can interact with other members of the community in terms of your application, and you as the developer or creator. In the first part, we will walk through how to get a sense of your current competition in the marketplace and how you should try to study or sense any potential new developments that could compete with or complement your idea for an iPhone application. In the second part of the chapter, we will review various mechanisms, both online and in person, that can help you find the specific answers you are looking for before you start developing your application and give you a sense of the direction, focus, and trends in your niche of the iPhone application market.

Getting an Idea of What is in the Marketplace

When you build and publish your iPhone application, keep in mind that you will not be application #1 hitting the App Store. (More likely, it's 40,001 or 50,001.) Therefore, it's important to see what your current competition is in the marketplace. Not only can you get a sense from the beginning if this is a crowded or wide-open space, but you might get some ideas from other apps that will or will not play a role in your app.

The information you find today may not be the same as when your app launches in the store, but everyone needs a baseline. So start now and check back often as you are developing your iPhone application.

Surveying the marketplace

Now it's time to look at the marketplace, but with your iPhone app idea in your head, ready to analyze. From the moment you open up the iTunes store and pull up the App Store on your desktop screen (this is probably something you want to do on your computer instead of using your iPhone), you should be paying attention to the applications already available for sale or download, and how other applications may impact a customer's decision to buy or download your app.

As you look around the marketplace, here are some questions to ask that may guide you in the right direction:

✓ **What competition exists for my app today?** The easiest way to initially get a list of competitors is by using the Power Search function. When you click Power Search, enter a keyword or two that would describe the core functionality of your app into the Title/Description box and click Search. For example, let's say that you want to create an Expenses Tracker app. If you do a Power Search for Expenses, you will get a list of apps like in Figure 6-1. You can click each application to learn more about each app's functionality, price, and reviews.

✓ **What types of apps are selling well?** You can start by browsing the Top Paid Apps section to see the current list of the 100 Top Paid applications at that moment. As we discussed earlier, you will probably see a lot of games on that list, but keep track of the position on that list of any apps similar to your idea, and check every few days or every week to see if that position goes up or down.

Figure 6-1:
Do a search
to find any
competitors.

You can also click the New and Noteworthy section to see what apps are gaining attention or the What's Hot section to see apps with rising downloads and/or sales numbers.

✔ **What's hot in my category?** If you are pretty sure you know which category best represents your app idea, then you should click that category from the App Store home page to learn more. Not only can you go through the Top Paid (and Top Free) Apps for that specific category, you can see how many apps currently exist in the category.

✔ **What developers should I keep my eye on?** You can search for both types of applications and the developers who write those apps. If you see an application that you want to study, do a Power Search and put the name of the developer in the Developer Name box. This will give you an idea of how many applications they have recently launched and whether there are any niches or categories in which they specialize.

Utilizing Resources to Help You

As you get a sense of where your application will fit into the larger market, it's important to know that there is a wealth of resources available to help you throughout the entire process. Not only can you benefit from other people's advice of avoiding traps and pitfalls, you can get answers to burning questions, bounce ideas off like-minded individuals, and stay up to date with all the new and exciting changes that affect this market.

Navigating the Apple Developer Forum

The first place to start is the Apple-owned Developer Forum, which you will have access to as a registered iPhone developer. This forum is designed for developers to be able to converse with each other and Apple personnel on the technical aspects of developing iPhone applications. These forums are moderated by members of Apple's Technology Evangelism team so you know you're getting the authorities on the subject.

You can get started by going directly to the forums at this Web address: `http://devforums.apple.com/community/iphone`.

You will have to log in with your Apple ID and agree to the Developer Forum Terms and Conditions. Once you do, you should see the Developer Forum home page, like in Figure 6-2. You will see that the forum is divided into a number of topics, such as Getting Started, Core OS, System and Device Features, and Distribution.

Keep a few aspects of the Developer Forums in mind:

✔ **Search function:** At the top-right corner of every page within the Developer Forums, there is a window to enter search terms. Simply enter your query into the space provided and hit Enter to read through hundreds of past threads and discussions that could lend some insight into your question. The thousands of previous posts make up an database for you to find a specific and topical answer to your question.

Figure 6-2:
Take advantage of Apple's Developer Forums!

✔ **E-mail updates:** Within each specific topic, you should see an option that says E-mail Updates. When you click the option so the light next to E-mail Updates is green, you will receive e-mail updates on the new threads being posted to that topic. This way, you will receive automatic updates on the newest conversations happening within your chosen topic without having to visit the forum! Each topic has its own e-mail update option, so if you want to monitor multiple topics, you will need to turn on e-mail updates in each topic.

✔ **Getting Started topic:** When you are unsure which topic to pose a question, it's typically safest to ask your question in the Getting Started topic, especially if it's a question in the beginning phases of your application development.

These forums do not only have to revolve around programming questions. There are questions in this forum regarding the approval process, iTunes connect, and even requests for tutorials (which we will discuss in the online resources section later on in this chapter).

✔ **Responses from Apple:** While you can benefit from interactions and answers from your fellow iPhone developers, you also get the benefit of having direct answers from a member of Apple's team. When reading through a particular thread, if you see someone's answer with the dark blue shading, an Apple icon in place of the silhouette picture, and the location of Cupertino, CA, you know that you are reading an answer directly from someone at Apple.

Topics within the Developer Forums may be Apple Confidential, like discussions of upcoming OS releases. Don't repeat or post any information from these forums in another online forum or Internet Web site.

Meeting people in this space

While you can read up on the iPhone application development process through Apple–provided resources and books like this one, sometimes the best education comes from physically meeting other people who work in this field. There are avenues where you can connect and network with other like-minded individuals, as well as the staff from Apple, to learn about the latest updates and ongoing education.

Apple's Worldwide Developer's Conference

The most popular and well-attended live event related to iPhone application development has become the Apple World Wide Developer's Conference (WWDC). Every year, Apple brings together developers and IT professionals to give out the latest technical information about the iPhone (and Apple's other products) and provide hands-on learning experiences to the attending developers that are led by Apple's engineers.

One of the most valuable aspects of the WWDC is the comprehensive set of sessions and labs available to discuss the technical aspects of the iPhone and how to write applications to take advantage of all the current and new features. Apple provides a general overview of new announcements and technology, along with dozens of different sessions and labs over the five-day event (see Figure 6-3) that you can attend to learn and ask questions about virtually every feature available.

Sessions & Labs

At the heart of your WWDC experience are technical sessions and hands-on labs presented by Apple engineers. Get in-depth information on the technologies that power iPhone OS, Mac OS X Snow Leopard and Mac OS X Server Snow Leopard, gain insight into new development techniques, and learn best practices on integrating features that will define your product's success.

View the first set of sessions and labs to get a preview of your five days exploring Apple technologies at WWDC.

Descriptions: ⊙ off ○ on

Title	Focus	Type
Accessing the iPod Library	iPhone	Session
Apple Push Notification Service	iPhone	Session
Cut, Copy, Paste, and Undo on iPhone	iPhone	Session
Effective iPhone App Architecture	iPhone	Session
Embedding Maps in iPhone Applications	iPhone	Session
Game Kit Lab	iPhone	Lab
Getting Started with Graphics for iPhone	iPhone	Session
In App Purchase on iPhone	iPhone	Session
Introduction to Core Data on iPhone	iPhone	Session
Introduction to iPhone Development Tools	iPhone	Session
iPhone Application Design Using Interface Builder	iPhone	Session
iPhone Apps Communicating with Accessories	iPhone	Session
iPhone Interface Design Consulting Lab	iPhone	Lab

Figure 6-3:
Attend one of the many sessions or labs at WWDC.

Equally important to the technical sessions and labs is the incredible access to Apple engineers to look at your specific situation and provide valuable one-on-one advice and answers. You can actually bring your iPhone application code to a developer to get answers. Apple brings its human interface designers who can work with you on a one-on-one session to help you with the visual design and usability of your iPhone application.

Finally, you get to connect with thousands of your fellow peers who are at all stages of the process, but share a serious desire to create and distribute their iPhone application. You'll hear daily presentations from developers with real examples of how they used Apple's technology, like the iPhone OS and SDK, to solve problems and create solutions. You can network with fellow attendees to get ideas or inspiration from their development process.

If you are interested in WWDC, sign up early. Tickets can sell out in advance. Typically, this conference is held in the San Francisco Bay Area in June. You can find out more by going to its Web site: http://developer.apple.com/wwdc/.

Other live events

WWDC is not your only chance to meet other iPhone developers and entre-preneurs. There are a number of other events throughout the year that pro-vide the opportunity to network and share information:

- ✓ **iPhoneDevCamp:** One of the newer trends in the conference arena is the idea of the "un-conference" or "BarCamp style," where people interested in a certain topic will gather and create their own agenda and sessions, and attendees will generate the content by presenting their particular specialty or expertise to the crowd, instead of the conference organizers bringing in special guests.

    The iPhone crowd is no exception to this concept, as the iPhoneDev Camp has developed its own session, held annually. It offers you a chance to hear from experts and write code throughout the event. You can find out more details at its Web site: www.iphonedevcamp.org.

- ✓ **Local developer groups:** Typically, these are known as user groups or get-togethers where developers in the area meet to talk about their goals and experiences. You can use a Web site such as Meetup.com (see Figure 6-4) to find whether there's a developer or user group in your area.

Figure 6-4: Find a local user group in your area.

Online Resources

The growing community of iPhone application developers and vendors has created their own set of online resources that is growing every day, and can provide invaluable assistance or ideas to anyone going through this process.

Outside Developer forums

If you're interested in answering questions and learning from other developers, here are some additional forums outside Apple that you can use:

✔ **iPhoneDevSDK.com:** Started by Chris Stewart several years ago, iPhone DevSDK.com runs several forums dedicated to discussing all facets of the iPhone application process using the Apple SDK. This forum has threads on specific development issues facing gaming applications, for example; and threads about business, legal, and promotion issues facing iPhone application developers. As of this writing, this site has over 12,000 members and 16,000 threads of lively and helpful discussions.

✔ **iPhoneDevForums.com:** Similar to iPhoneDevSDK, iPhoneDevForums maintains a number of topics and threads related to application development with the SDK, as well as threads about developing iPhone Web applications, bouncing ideas around for applications, and even a "Rent-a-Coder" thread where you can go look for a developer to write the code for you. (We discuss hiring a developer in depth in Chapter 10.)

Keeping up with the commentariat

We recommend some ongoing light (or heavy, depending on your interest) reading about the iPhone app market through various information sources:

✔ **Blogging:** Blogs can be ever-changing, here are a few that seem to be on the cutting edge and provide quality information:

  • www.theappleblog.com (not affiliated with Apple Computer)

  • www.iphoneatlas.com (now a part of CNet)

  • www.mobileorchard.com

  • www.furbo.org

✔ **Tutorials:** While Apple's Developer Center provides a wealth of tutorials, there are other sites that provide user-generated. One of particular note is iPhoneDevCentral.org, which has organized an entire library of video tutorials that are grouped by experience level, from beginner to intermediate to advanced, and were created by fellow developers and entrepreneurs.

✔ **The World Wide Web:** There are new resources and information being added to the Internet on a second-by-second basis. Use search engines like Google and Yahoo to do searches with the words *iPhone App* and your question or pertinent keywords. Search in your social networks on sites like LinkedIn or Facebook to find friends or experts who can help you with your app. You can search discussions being broadcast on micro-blogging sites like Twitter to find experts, thoughts, and trends that apply to your situation.

Chapter 7

Sizing Up the Competition

● ●

In This Chapter

▶ Using competitive analysis tools

▶ Analyzing the competition

▶ Creating a spreadsheet to make feature comparison charts

▶ Reading free information sources

▶ Finding paid research

▶ Listening to the buzz

● ●

*A*fter you've spent some time to think of the idea behind your iPhone application and you've formulated your thoughts into a concrete document, while surveying the marketplace and your own strengths, it is now time to combine everything you're doing. Imagine that your iPhone app is created, approved, and ready to enter the App Store. Ask yourself what kind of competition your app will face in the already-well-established App Store — and what welter of products your prospective customers may have to wade through as they try to decide whether to buy your app or go with a competitor's product. Since you're the new player in the Apple world, you need to do something called *competitive analysis* to figure out how and where you can go after and attract customers. Don't worry — we're not going to suggest using supercomputers, highly complex formulas, or tens of thousands of dollars in focus groups and research. Your computer, your wits, a little spending cash, and this book should guide you just fine.

This chapter gives you a look at different methods you should use to perform competitive analysis, pitting your iPhone app against any potential competitor currently in the App Store or (to the best of your knowledge) in development by someone else. We encourage you to dig a little to quantify the features of existing apps, and offer tips on using a spreadsheet to map out the features of each competitor's product so you can easily compare them — to each other, and to yours. You may even find what marketers call the "sweet spot" — a combination of features that no one is currently offering to the public that could make your app sales soar. We will also put in a word for good old-fashioned research — whether it's reading up on free information sources or accessing paid research. Finally, we point out the usefulness of getting to know the "buzz" in the market — going beyond the specific Web sites discussed in the previous chapter to get an idea of whether your most important competitors have actually *launched* competing apps yet (maybe they haven't).

Using Competitive-Analysis Tools to Analyze the Competition

When we talk about "tools" for competitive analysis, we're not talking about expensive computer programs that require a lot of inputs and setup. We're talking about using your eyes and ears to survey the current marketplace — and about being aware of what the current entrants in the market are offering that will compete with your application (and, hopefully, what those products can do better — or worse — compared to yours).

If there's no direct competitor (yet) for your idea, we recommend that you still worry about competitive analysis to see whether there's a *similar* app or something close to your idea that people are using as a substitute to solve the problem your app will handle.

Believe it or not, the moment you start on this process, you're *already* analyzing the competition — by going through the App Store, examining current apps for ideas on your app, installing apps on your phone to get a feel for how these products actually work with the iPhone, and reading up on the various Web sites about iPhone applications. At this point, though, we want to offer a step-by-step, focused approach so you can do an appropriate analysis of the situation before you even start developing your application:

1. **Identify your competitors.** Run a search on the App Store for keywords identifying what your app is about. (For example, if you search for "tip calculator," you see a results screen like the one in Figure 7-1.) Go through the search-results list, and read through the description of each app. Make a list that includes each application that could be considered a competitor.

2. **Identify the price points**. For each application on the list from Step 1, write down the price of each app next to the app name. Even if the application is free, make a note of it, so you'll know later how many competitors' products are free versus how many are offered for a price.

3. **Identify the common features.** As you click the name of an application to bring up its description window (as in Figure 7-2), write out a list of the most common features for that app.

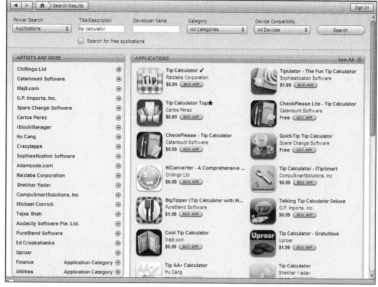

Figure 7-1:
Pull up a
list of your
potential
competitors
on the App
Store.

As you continue to go through the list of competitors, keep an eye out for features that most (or all) of your competitors have put into their products. For example, in the realm of tip calculators, you will find that virtually every calculator offers similar features — such as a big numeric keypad for entering the bill amount, variable sliders to allow the user to choose the gratuity percentage and the number of people sharing the bill, and a total per person — as shown in Figure 7-3.

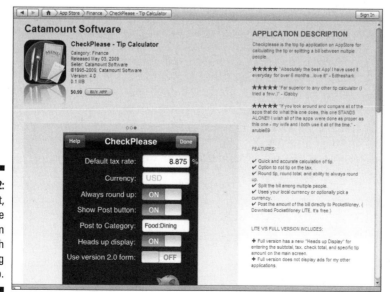

Figure 7-2:
First,
read the
description
of each
competing
app.

Figure 7-3:
Then you
can see
which
features are
common
among
these apps.

4. **Identify the unique features**. As you're working on Step 3, and are taking an inventory of what each application offers, make a note of any features you would think are valuable or important that only show up in one or a handful of competitors' applications. Pay attention to the comments found in customer reviews to see other people's opinions and impressions of these features.

Even if an application describes a certain feature as being unique, you will only know for sure by going through your list of competitors and seeing whether any other apps have adopted that feature.

5. **Experiment with the apps**. Depending on the price, you should consider buying or downloading the app, to test all the features the author describes and determine whether the description is accurate. Update your lists according to what you discover; include any features not mentioned that are present in the app that you're considering for your application.

6. **Study the update pattern**. When you know what a particular application offers, you may want to know where this app is headed, and the best way to predict that future is to anticipate the competing product's next release. Get an idea of how many updates the authors have issued for their application. Try to determine from that cycle when the next update may be released.

One great Web site that tracks the updates, price changes, and other important releases of an iPhone app is AppShopper.com; Figure 7-4 shows the site's page on tip calculators.

Use a Spreadsheet to Make Feature-Comparison Charts

By now, you probably have a lot of notes, and making sense of all that info could seem a little overwhelming. You could be wondering, "Okay, I've looked around the marketplace, now what?" One method that we've found helpful is to use a spreadsheet program, such as Microsoft Excel, to pull together all our findings into one spreadsheet that we can sort and manipulate to do a better analysis of the situation.

If there are very few competitors for your idea, this process is not necessary. On the other hand, if you have hundreds of competitors, you may simply want to pick 10 or 20 of them to analyze instead of trying to capture everything about everybody.

We'll assume you have access to a spreadsheet program and know how to use it. When you've walked through all your applications and generated your notes, and you have your spreadsheet open and ready to fill, here are a few steps to follow:

1. **Create and head your columns.**

   Along the top row of your spreadsheet, assign header names to each column you plan to fill. Examples of header names include: Name of the Application, Price, Feature 1, Feature 2, etc.

2. Fill out your rows.

After you've assigned your column headers, create a row for each app you consider a competitor, filling in the appropriate information.

When you fill out the price for an application, put $0.00 instead of FREE in the field, so you can sort all applications in the list numerically. If some fields have a numeric price, and others have the text word FREE, a sort on the Price column won't work properly. To sort everything, simply highlight all your columns, select the Data menu from the top of the screen, and then select the Sort option. Excel will ask you which column (or columns, up to 3) you wish to sort by, either ascending or descending. When sorting by price, pick the column that holds the price, select Ascending, and click Ok to sort by price.

3. Start sorting.

After the data entry comes the analysis. You can sort by the Price of the app (low to high, or high to low) or by a certain feature. You can even sort by multiple columns, to group together apps with similar features.

4. Do the math.

You can perform some simple calculations using the information you entered to give yourself some benchmarks for comparison. For example, if most of your competitors offer applications that the consumer pays for, you can calculate the average price of an app by adding up all the prices and dividing by the number of applications. You can even calculate an average with a mixture of free and paid applications. In addition, you can calculate the percentage of competing apps that have a certain function. So, for example, if you have 20 apps in your list, and 19 have Feature 1, then 95% of your competition has that feature, which is a good reason for you to have that feature as well. We started a basic analysis of tip calculator programs as an example; a sample spreadsheet is shown in Figure 7-5.

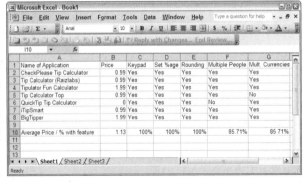

Figure 7-5:
Put all your data in a spreadsheet for easier analysis.

5. **Insert a new row to represent your app.**

   Fill in the proposed name of your app; then examine the other columns to create values for what your app should have to become competitive and/or desirable. Use the benchmarks or averages you created in Step 4 to help you estimate or fill in target values.

Finding Information Sources

The App Store's offerings are by no means the only information you can use for competitive analysis. A lot more sources of free information are available for your research: Web sites, forums, blogs, and other information sources that you should monitor and look up when you're trying to learn more about your niche and how that niche operates as part of the larger market. Here are some examples of information sources you should consider:

✔ **iPhone App Review sites**: If you want to know more about the performance and perception of a competing app, see what the various app review sites have to say about it. Sometimes these review sites will even compare a host of leading apps in a given area (say, the weather applications shown in Figure 7-6), and do some of the work for you.

   You can find a list of Influential App Review sites in Chapter 20.

Figure 7-6:
Learn about competing iPhone apps from review sites.

✔ **iPhone- or tech-related blogs**: If you want information that's current and recently updated, it's hard to beat the postings on various blogs, whether it's the TechCrunch blog evaluating a new category of iPhone applications, or a specific application developer relaying his or her experience throughout the app-creation process. You can use a blog search engine such as Technorati to search for postings related to your specific target area or category, or follow your favorite tech blogs such as furbo.org, Engadget, or Macrumors to stay up to date on the entire field.

✔ **AppShopper**: As mentioned earlier in this chapter, AppShopper has been set up to track the progress and update patterns of many applications currently on the App Store. Not only does AppShopper track price changes and new updates, it also monitors the top 100 paid and free applications on a daily basis, so you can see how long a particular app stays on the top 100 list, check the peak slot on the list, sample some customer reviews, and compare prices, as shown in Figure 7-7.

✔ **Do a Google (or Yahoo) search**: When all else fails, a few targeted searches on your favorite search engine couldn't hurt. Do a search on the category or segment of the market you're thinking of entering, plus the words "iPhone app" (or "iPhone application"), and see what sources pop up.

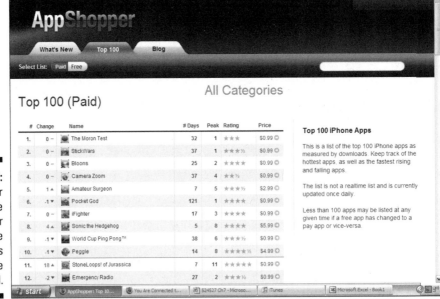

Figure 7-7:
AppShopper lets you see how other iPhone applications have progressed.

Finding Paid Research

Depending on the size and scope of your application, you may find yourself in need of more specific information, and on a higher level than what you can find by browsing the Internet. If that is the case, then getting some paid research reports may be what you need to complete a proper competitive analysis. Because the iPhone itself, and the App Store, are relatively new concepts as of the writing of this book, there are not a lot of archived or historical reports in the area of paid research. Thankfully, there is a high level of interest and a growing market from iPhone apps that are generating the paid research reports that you can order and use.

If some paid research is the way to go, here are a few ways to get started:

✔ **Do searches on sites such as comScore**: While the iPhone may be a relatively new product, the Internet has been around for a while, and there are firms that are set up to monitor areas such as traffic, usage, popularity, and other key statistics of technology companies. One such company is comScore, which is often quoted and referenced by other sources for its reports, such as its study of penetration of apps among iPhone app users, as seen in Figure 7-8.

comScore Apple App Store Report Enables Digital Marketers to Understand Audience Size, Demographics and Online Behavior of iTunes App Installers

RESTON, VA, April 7, 2009 – comScore, Inc. (NASDAQ: SCOR), a leader in measuring the digital world, today reported that Tapulous's Tap Tap Revenge has the largest installed base among applications downloaded from the Apple App Store, with 32 percent of Apple App users having installed the game by February 2009, according to the comScore Apple App Store Report. The new report, which observes the cumulative installed base of applications downloaded via iTunes, is the first tool enabling digital marketers to understand the audience size, demographic profile and online behaviors of Apple app users.

"It's impressive that a game like Tapulous's Tap Tap Revenge can attract a higher penetration among Apple app users than apps for larger and more established brands," said Brian Jurutka, vice president, comScore. "Tap Tap's success demonstrates that there is ample opportunity in the app space for any publisher to obtain significant distribution with a product that engages users. Since the number of app users is growing nearly ten percent each month, that opportunity will only continue to grow for both existing and emerging app developers."

Top 25 Apple Apps

A review of the top 25 most heavily penetrated apps illustrates the importance of gaming to devices like the iPod Touch and the iPhone. Twelve out of the 25 most popular mobile apps were games, including classics like Hangman and Pac-man, and more non-conventional titles like Cube Runner and Crazy Penguin Catapult. Among non-gaming applications, Stylem Media's "Backgrounds" applications had the highest installed base, followed closely by the top social networking applications: Facebook and MySpace Mobile.

Top 25 Apps by Penetration of Apple App Users
February 2009
Total U.S. – Home/Work/University Locations
Source: comScore Apple App Store Report

Application	Penetration of Installs	Category	Developer
Tap Tap Revenge	32%	Games	Tapulous, Inc.
Backgrounds	27%	Entertainment	Stylem Media
Touch Hockey: FS5	26%	Games	FlipSide5, Inc.
Facebook	26%	Social Networking	Facebook, Inc.
Pac-Man	24%	Games	Namco
iBowl	24%	Games	SGN
MySpace Mobile	23%	Social Networking	MySpace.com

Figure 7-8:
Pay attention to reports from sites such as comScore.

✔ **Read mainstream articles to look for quotes/statistics from paid research; then follow the source.** When you read about the iPhone or the iPhone app market from a source like *The New York Times* or *USA Today*, typically there will be some quotes attributed to a research firm. When you see that, do an Internet search to find out more about the report the article was quoting. If that research report pertains to what you're trying to accomplish, see if there is more information publicly available, or find out how much it would cost to buy the report for yourself.

✔ **Look for specific reports.** Distimo, for example, is a company that distributes and monitors mobile applications; it's trying to expand its reach, and one method is to publish a combination of free and paid research reports on markets such as the iPhone (see Figure 7-9).

Listening to the Buzz

The best competitive analysis doesn't stop with the initial research; it's ongoing. Therefore it's important to set aside some time — on a regular basis — for following the iPhone application market. Get to know the different companies, personalities, and trends that have an impact on this growing market. Of course, it wouldn't hurt to follow some of the larger markets, such as the iPhone and mobile computing in general, but you don't want to spend all your time listening. (After all, you have at least one iPhone app of your own to develop, right?)

Figure 7-9:
Look for targeted reports that can help your analysis.

Beyond all the sources we've mentioned so far, here are a few extra tips to help you stay in touch with the buzz out there:

✔ **Set up Google Alerts**. Why do all the surfing on the Internet when the information can come to you? Currently, Google has a great feature called Alerts, which can send you a collection of links that are new to the Google database and match the search terms you're looking for. So, if you go to Google Alerts (www.google.com/alerts) you could set up an automatic alert to look for, let's say, "iPhone tip calculator application" or even "iPhone gaming apps" and get a daily update of new Web pages and blog posts that you can click and read more about.

✔ **Subscribe to targeted blogs**. As you check out all the resources available online, you'll probably come across some blogs that talk (at least partially) about the area of the iPhone application market you're researching. Perhaps a developer of a potentially competing app is blogging about his or her experiences and tribulations — or maybe a blog of a popular app-review site is comparing different applications. As you find blogs that you think will be useful on an ongoing basis, subscribe to their RSS feeds or bookmark them on your Web browser so you can check back often and stay up to date. For example, if you go to the iPhoneBlog's Web site (www.theiphoneblog.com), it gives you several options for subscribing to its blog, as seen in Figure 7-10.

✔ **Follow iPhone App Developers on Twitter**. If you want a medium that gets updated even more frequently than a blog or discussion forum, check out Twitter, the micro-blogging site. All sorts of professionals post their status and updates on Twitter all day long, which can add up to a lot of interesting, timely information. You can "follow" someone who is on Twitter, which basically means you will be notified of every tweet, or status/update message, that he or she posts to Twitter.

Figure 7-10:
Subscribe to blogs to stay informed!

✔ **Do Searches on Twitter conversations**: Twitter allows you to do searches on everyone's tweets, or status messages. This gives you the ability to get the most current discussions, Web site links, and information about what people are doing that could relate to your market within the iPhone application space. Let's say, for example, you're writing a game and want to see what people are twittering about regarding iPhone games. You could search "iPhone games" on Twitter and get a whole host of messages that are talking about that subject right now (Figure 7-11 shows what that looks like).

✔ **Participate in the conversation.** At the end of the day, you can either *watch* what's being said or reported, or you can become part of the conversation. After all the research and digging, often you can find the best information by meeting other people who work in this market, getting to know them, and exchanging information directly, on a frequent or infrequent basis.

One way to start participating is to start replying or adding comments to the blog postings, discussion-board postings, and news articles that you find online. You can use social-networking sites such as LinkedIn to find other iPhone application developers or entrepreneurs in your space. The key is to stay involved, provide honest feedback or information, and be willing to give a little (without revealing all your plans) in order to get information that can help your efforts.

Figure 7-11:
Search
Twitter con-
versations
to see who's
talking
about your
market!

Part III
Lay the Groundwork

The 5th Wave   By Rich Tennant

In this part . . .

The excitement is building, your idea for an iPhone application feels more and more like a reality, and perhaps you're lying awake at night wondering what to do next. (Don't worry — staying up at night fretting is not a requirement here.)

In this part, we go through some of the necessary steps to get you started on creating your iPhone application. We cover the registration process with Apple to become an iPhone developer and then detail the parts of the Software Development Kit your developer will need to create the app. Then we describe some extra tools that other folks have created that can speed up or smooth out your programming efforts. Once you've got all the software, it's time for the physical stuff — namely, the team of people you plan to use in order to create your app.

It doesn't require a village to write an app, but the more help and skills you can get, the better.

Chapter 8

Registering with Apple

. . . .

In This Chapter

▶ Understanding the relationship between you and Apple

▶ Preparing your company and financial data

▶ How to sign up with Apple as an iPhone app developer

▶ Navigating the sign-up process

▶ Registering your iTunes Connect account

▶ Submitting the necessary contact, bank, and tax information

▶ Lining up your requirements as an iPhone app developer

. . . .

As we start Part III of the book, it's time to start preparing all the necessary registration to allow you to start developing (and selling) your iPhone application. Of course, the first step is to formalize your relationship with Apple so you can create and submit iPhone applications to be sold on the Apple iTunes store and be paid when people buy your application. Since the Apple iTunes store is the only way that you can sell an iPhone application directly to the user community, then registering yourself with Apple is a simple, one-stop method to gaining entrance into this community.

In this chapter, we are going to examine the structure of the agreement, or relationship, that you (as an iPhone application developer) have with Apple and what information you should have ready before you log on to Apple's site. We will walk through all the various screens and steps necessary to register with Apple as a developer, and talk about what items need to be submitted to Apple before you start uploading applications to be sold in its store.

Your Relationship with Apple

When you want to start creating, selling, and distributing an iPhone application to the public, you will first need to create a relationship with the iPhone's creator, namely Apple Computer. Don't worry, there's no romantic courtship or awkward silences to worry about, but rather a legal structure that sets you up as a qualified iPhone application developer that will not damage or negatively affect one of Apple's most important brands and product. Because Apple has chosen to centralize the sale and distribution of applications to run on its iPhone (and iPod Touch) products, it allows them to control and monitor the types of applications available. It also allows you, the developer, to benefit from a suite of development tools and code that can help you build an application quicker than other types of computer products or platforms.

This centralization of power also means that you need to treat your relationship with Apple very seriously and studiously, since it is your sole gateway to providing authorized iPhone applications to the user base. Thankfully, Apple's goal is to provide a large and diverse set of applications for its users, so the requirements are not overly burdensome or lengthy. Instead, its system is designed for you to get up and running as quickly as you can, so you can focus your efforts on building, testing, and promoting your iPhone application instead of worrying about tests and certification.

Preparing Your Data

Apple is very flexible about the types of developers it approves to provide iPhone applications. You do not need to be a Fortune 500 company with thousands of employees to qualify as an iPhone application developer. In fact, many of the developers are independent contractors who work for themselves, either as a full- or part-time endeavor. Apple welcomes the range of interested developers, from one-person shop to cutting-edge corporation.

One of the things to keep in mind when registering with Apple is the name that will be associated as the seller of your iPhone application. In other words, when people decide to buy your application, do you want them to see the Seller as "John Doe" or "JD Enterprises?" If you sign up with Apple as an individual, then Apple will display your name as the seller, whereas you sign up under your own company (or your current employer) and Apple will show your applications as being sold by the company name. There is no right or wrong answer here. Simply consider what your goals are for this application, as we discussed in earlier chapters. If this app is meant to promote you or give you a portfolio, you should register as an individual. If the app is meant to be an authorized product of your company, register as that company.

Regardless of company structure, here are some of the pieces of information you should have ready before you decide to sign up for the program:

> ✔ **EIN (or TIN):** Otherwise known as the Employer Identification Number, or Tax Identification Number, this nine-digit number is what is used to identify you with the U.S. government, when Apple reports your monstrous earnings year after year. For those of you living in the U.S. who are working on your own, whether it's self-employment, as an independent contractor, or working after hours from your day job, your choice can be

simple: your Social Security number, which is also (conveniently enough) nine digits long. If you set up your own small business, you can register to get your own EIN so you're not giving out your Social Security number for all your business needs, a wise move in today's world of identity theft.

You can go online to get your own EIN for your small business by going to this link: `www.irs.gov/businesses/small/article/0,,id=102767,00.html`.

- ✓ **W8-BEN form:** For those of you who live outside the U.S., Apple requires a different form known as the W8-BEN form, which you will fill out online, as well as mail in a paper version of the completed form to Apple's offices.

- ✓ **Bank information:** Once you start selling paid applications, Apple needs a way to deposit your earnings directly into a bank account; so you should decide whether to establish a business checking account or use your personal bank account to set up your earnings disbursements. You can always update this in the future, but you should have an account ready when you complete the sign-up process. Be sure to have the bank information, branch information (such as address and branch number) and the ABA routing number and account number.

- ✓ **Contact information:** Like most other accounts that you establish, Apple will want contact information on file for information like new updates or other information. Decide which set of contact information you wish to put on file here. For example, do you want to provide your work or day job information; your home information; or a separate set of information, such as a PO Box or mailbox, mobile phone number, and Internet fax number?

Signing Up with Apple As an iPhone App Developer

Once you've got your information ready to go, it's time to go online and make the process official by becoming an iPhone app developer.

Navigating the sign-up process

When you're ready to enroll in Apple's iPhone Developer program, follow these steps:

1. **Navigate your Web browser to Apple's Developer Program Web site at** `http://developer.apple.com`.

You should see some information about the iPhone Developer program. Click that link to bring up more information about the program, like in Figure 8-1.

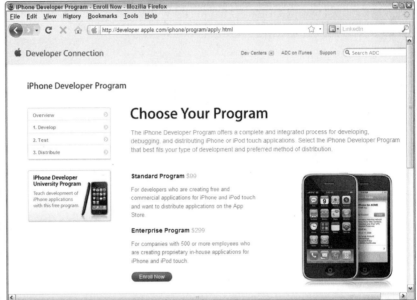

Figure 8-1:
Start at
Apple's
Developer
program
Web site.

2. **Click the Enroll Now button from the iPhone Developer Program screen to start the process.**

   You'll be asked to choose between its Standard Program and Enterprise Program. If you are working on an application on behalf of a company with 500 or more employees that you plan to distribute to your employees, then choose the Enterprise Program. Otherwise, you should be fine going with the Standard Program, which is what we're choosing for the purpose of this process. If you are asked to click another Enroll Now button, please do so to start its three-step process, as seen in Figure 8-2.

3. **Register as an iPhone Developer by associating an Apple ID as an iPhone application developer.**

   You will be taken to a Program Enrollment screen, where you will need to log in with your Apple ID or create a new one to be associated with the iPhone developer program. If you do not yet have an Apple ID, you definitely need to follow the prompts and create a new ID, which you can use throughout Apple's sites.

   If you already have an Apple ID for your personal enjoyment and you are planning to write your iPhone apps as part of a business, you may want to create a new Apple ID for your iPhone development needs that will stay separate from your personal needs.

Figure 8-2:
Follow its
three-step
process to
become a
developer.

4. **After you provide your personal information, complete the screens that build your professional profile as an iPhone developer.**

   Apple will prompt you with some questions, wanting to get an idea of how many applications you hope to write in the next year, what categories you plan to develop for, and what you plan to be your primary market. You are not locked into any answers you give here, but rather Apple will use that information to guide you in the right direction. Fill in the questions, like those in Figure 8-3, and click the Continue button to move to the next step.

5. **Review the Terms and Conditions of the iPhone Developer Program and click Continue to proceed.**

   You will see the agreement, which you should read through and then click the check box to confirm that you read and agree to be bound by this agreement and that you are of a legal age to go into this agreement.

6. **Watch for a verification code to be sent to your e-mail address, and click the link inside that e-mail or provide the code on the next screen to confirm your e-mail address.**

   You should get an e-mail from Apple's Developer program. Click the activation link or use the verification code on the Developer Web site to continue with the process.

7. **In part 2 of the process, pick from the three choices of iPhone Developer program that match your goals and click the appropriate Select button to continue.**

   You can either choose to enroll as a Standard Individual, which only requires your basic contact and banking information, as well as Social Security number; a Standard Company, which will require some documents proving that you are properly set up as a company (like registration, DBA, or incorporation documents); or an Enterprise, where you will distribute your iPhone applications in-house to your own employees or clients. Once you make your selection onscreen (like in Figure 8-4), click the appropriate Select button.

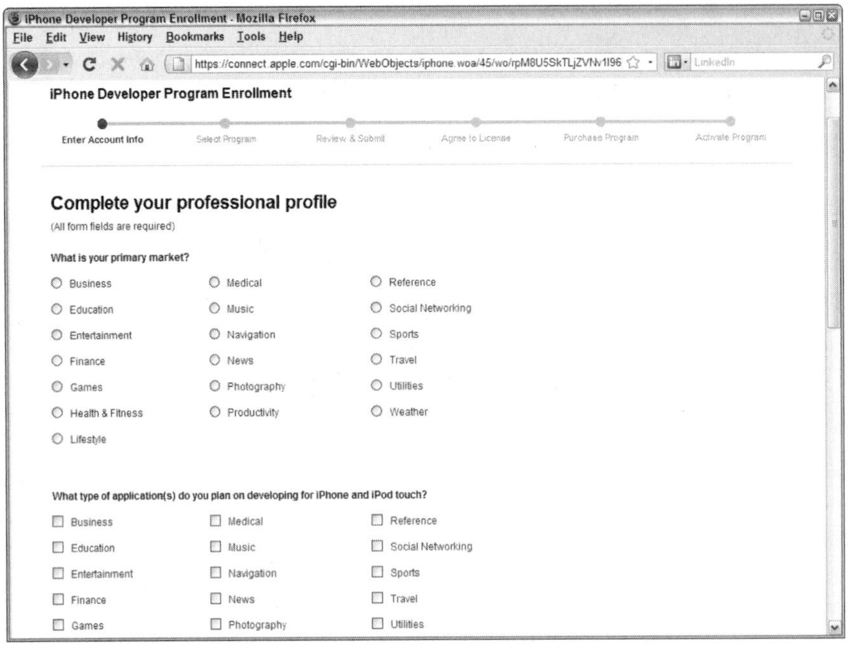

Figure 8-3:
Decide on your primary market and categories.

8. **Review the information you have given so far and submit it to Apple. Then, review the iPhone Developer Program License Agreement and agree to those terms.**

   By this point, you should be prompted with the License Agreement, which talks about how you can use Apple's software to develop and distribute your iPhone application. Click the appropriate check box and the I Agree button to continue.

9. **In part 3 of the process, you will then be taken to the Apple Store for your particular country to buy the Apple Developer Program, like you would buy any other product or media from the Apple Store.**

   You can do a search for *Apple Developer* to find the right item. Simply add that item to your shopping cart and check out to pay for the item. This will allow you to enroll in the Developer program, because you will receive an activation code in your e-mail after your payment is processed. Once you get that e-mail, log back in to the Apple Developer Program, and you will be prompted for your activation code like in Figure 8-5.

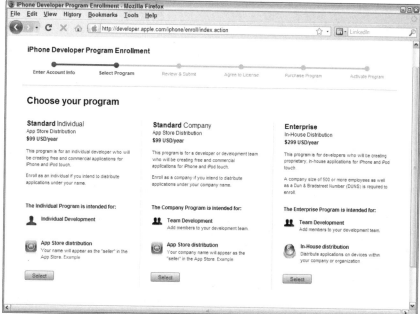

Figure 8-4:
Review the different types of programs available.

10. **Enter your activation code in the box provided to start your enrollment in the iPhone Developer program.**

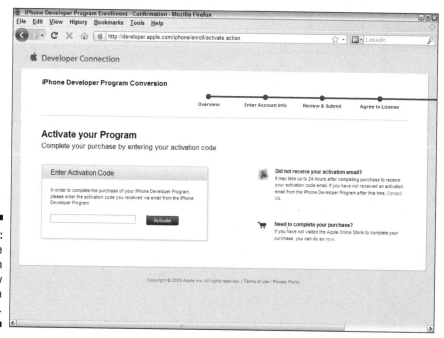

Figure 8-5:
Provide Apple with your new activation code.

Registration information

If you enrolled as an Individual, your activation code would have arrived in your e-mail inbox in approximately 1–24 hours from the time of purchase. If you enrolled as a Standard Company or Enterprise, then Apple would have asked you to mail in appropriate business documents, such as your Articles of Incorporation, Doing Business As form, or a Partnership or LLC agreement. Apple would then work to verify your company and make sure you are an authorized representative of the company so you can agree to the program on the company's behalf. To this end, Apple will ask for a legal representative for your company so they can ask that person the same question.

Once you are enrolled in the program, you should be taken to the Apple iPhone Dev Center, like in Figure 8-6. This is your central hub for accessing software updates, documents, and other critical information. Your registration is not complete, however, because you will need to have access to iTunes Connect to manage your application delivery, access sales information, and monitor your financial reports and payments into your bank account.

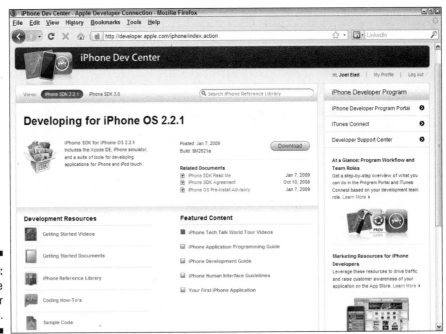

Figure 8-6:
Your iPhone
Dev Center
home page.

When you are ready to set up your iTunes Connect account, just follow these steps:

1. **Click the iTunes Connect link from the top-right corner of your iPhone Dev Center home page.**

   This should take you to the iTunes Connect Terms of Service page. Review the document by scrolling through the text presented, click the check box next to "I have read and agree to the Terms of Service" statement; then click the Accept Terms button to continue.

2. **When you get to the iTunes Connect home page, click the Contracts, Tax and Banking Information link to set up your financial information.**

   After you have signed up for the iPhone Developer Program, you will probably see a contracts page similar to Figure 8-7, where an initial contract has been created and you have to submit an agreement to sell paid applications in the iTunes store.

3. **Click the check box next to Request Contract and click the Submit button to create and submit a Paid Application Agreement.**

   You will be taken to the Paid Applications Schedule 2 Agreement page to review the agreement for paid applications, which includes Apple's fair use of your application and the payment schedule. When you have reviewed the agreement, click the check box next to "I agree" and click the Submit button to send in your Paid Application agreement. Apple will e-mail you a copy of the agreement, in PDF form, for your records.

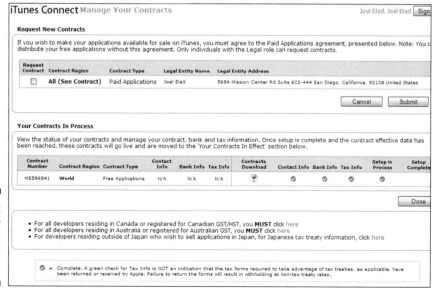

Figure 8-7:
Set up your contracts and banking information.

4. Once you have submitted your Paid Application Agreement, you will need to set up your Contact Info, Bank Info, and Tax Info for this agreement. Click Edit under Contact Info (see Figure 8-8) to set up this information.

While Apple already has the contact information for your legal entity, now it is requesting the contact info for various roles within your company, including Senior Management, Finance, Technical Issues, Legal, and Promotions. Once you get to the Contact Info screen, simply click Create New Person and define the contact info for each position, even if you handle every role in your company. For each person, Apple requires having its first and last name, e-mail address, phone number, and official title.

5. Once your contact info has been defined, click Edit under Bank Info to define your banking information.

The first thing that Apple is going to ask for is the Bank Address, so unless your bank resides at the same place as your company, you will need to click Add Address and define your bank address. Once you define this address, click the drop-down list and pick that address, and then click Next. Now, you will be asked to provide the specific bank name, account holder, type, and number, as well as the bank's branch id, routing transit code, and SWIFT code in the boxes provided, like in Figure 8-9. Once you've entered everything, Apple will prompt you to review all this information and confirm it by clicking the Submit button.

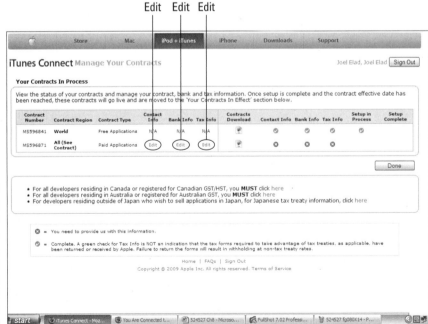

Figure 8-8: From your Contracts screen, define the contacts in your company.

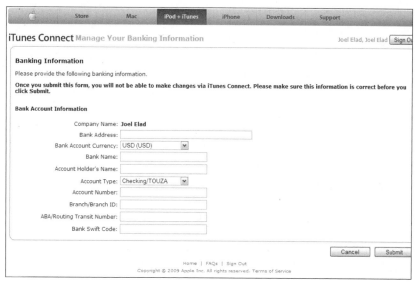

Figure 8-9:
Provide
the bank's
address,
then
provide
all the
important
banking
information.

Enter this information as precisely as possible. You will not be able to fix it online if you make a mistake. Any changes after this point have to be made in writing to Apple.

SWIFT stands for The Society for Worldwide Interbank Financial Telecommunication, an industry-owned co-operative supplying secure, standardized messaging services and interface software to nearly 8,100 financial institutions in 207 countries and territories. SWIFT members include banks, broker-dealers, and investment managers.

6. **Once your banking information is inputted, click Edit under Tax Info to provide your tax information.**

    You will be earning money by selling paid applications, so Apple has to report your earnings to the U.S. government for tax reasons. Therefore, you have to fill out a virtual W-9 form online by providing tax-related information about you and/or your company. Specifically, you will be prompted for your Name, Business Name, Type of Business, Exemption Status, Address, and either your Social Security or EIN number, as seen in Figure 8-10. Once you provide that information, click the check box next to the certification statement and click the Submit button.

7. **You're done!**

    Apple will review the information you've provided, and if there are any questions or concerns, it will contact you about it.

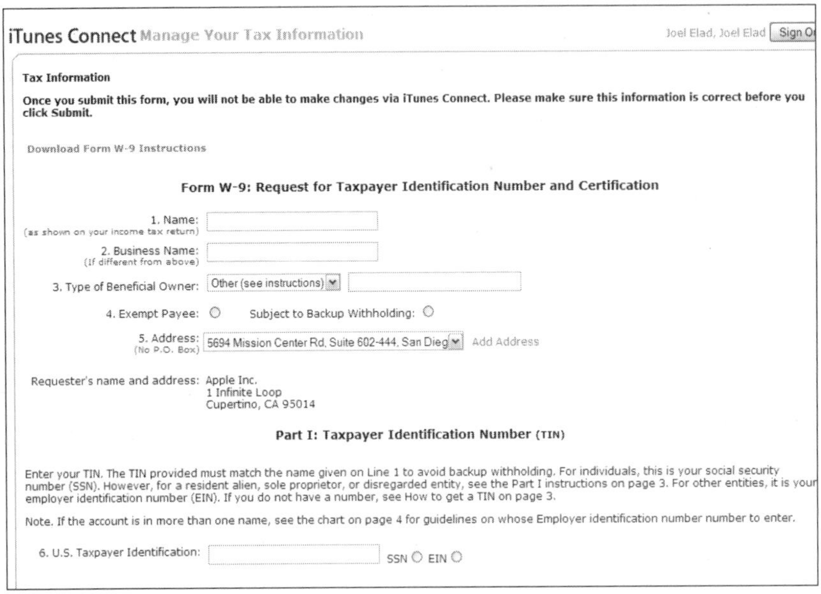

iTunes Connect Manage Your Tax Information   Joel Elad, Joel Elad Sign Or

Tax Information

Once you submit this form, you will not be able to make changes via iTunes Connect. Please make sure this information is correct before you click Submit.

Download Form W-9 Instructions

Form W-9: Request for Taxpayer Identification Number and Certification

1. Name: [   ]
(as shown on your income tax return)

2. Business Name: [   ]
(if different from above)

3. Type of Beneficial Owner: [Other (see instructions) ▼] [   ]

4. Exempt Payee: ○   Subject to Backup Withholding: ○

5. Address: [5694 Mission Center Rd, Suite 602-444, San Dieg ▼] Add Address
(No P.O. Box)

Requester's name and address: Apple Inc.
                               1 Infinite Loop
                               Cupertino, CA 95014

Part I: Taxpayer Identification Number (TIN)

Enter your TIN. The TIN provided must match the name given on Line 1 to avoid backup withholding. For individuals, this is your social security number (SSN). However, for a resident alien, sole proprietor, or disregarded entity, see the Part I instructions on page 3. For other entities, it is your employer identification number (EIN). If you do not have a number, see How to get a TIN on page 3.

Note. If the account is in more than one name, see the chart on page 4 for guidelines on whose Employer identification number number to enter.

6. U.S. Taxpayer Identification: [   ]   SSN ○ EIN ○

Figure 8-10:
Provide your
important
tax
information.

Lining Up Your Requirements

Once you are signed up as an iPhone developer, you will have access to download the necessary software, such as the Software Development Kit (SDK), the digital certificates necessary to authenticate your iPhone application code, and the simulators you can use to test your iPhone app before you submit the application to Apple for approval.

In Chapter 9, we discuss additional items you should have in place to properly start your development cycle for your iPhone application.

Chapter 9

Understanding the Development Tools

*O*ne of the many beauties of developing for the iPhone is the fact that Apple has made it quite easy to jump in at any level and get started. Though we recommend that you have some object-oriented programming experience before getting into iPhone development, some folks have been known to figure out how to develop for the iPhone without any prior programming experience (though the learning curve would be quite steep).

Robert and Doug Hogg, who created iSamurai, had object-oriented programming experience but had never programmed in Objective-C (the programming language of the iPhone) before they began to code their game. The same is true of Ben Satterfield's team, which created Gigotron. While Robert and Doug supplemented the help Apple provides with some third-party reference books, Ben's team used the Apple help and documentation exclusively from start through completion.

Because Apple invented the Objective-C language and continues to be the language's main developer, Apple is the prime resource about the language and how to use the tools it provides to work with the language. And Apple does a very thorough job of educating iPhone developers about Objective-C. So we are simply going to get you oriented to the help resources and some third-party resources you might find useful.

Getting Set Up as a Developer

You can join the Developer Program for $99 a year. However, if you want to start with just getting the Software Development Toolkit (SDK) set up to begin building and testing apps, you can simply register on the developer site to gain access to the SDK and help libraries without joining the Developer Program. (You won't be able to distribute any apps nor ask for direct help.)

To do this, click the Register link in the upper-right corner (see Figure 9-1) of the iPhone Dev Center home page at `http://developer.apple.com/iphone`. When you're ready to get serious, you can join the Developer Program.

Register

Figure 9-1:
You can register as a developer and gain access to the SDK without fully signing up for the Developer Program.

After you've either joined or registered, download the newest version of the SDK from the Downloads section of the main page. When the SDK is downloaded, run its installer just like any other app. Even if you aren't going to code your own iPhone software, gaining basic familiarity with the tools and language your developers will be using will make you more capable and effective at running your project, simply by virtue of basically understanding what everyone is talking about.

After you've installed the SDK, go back to the Dev Center site and work your way through the Getting Started Documents. You can get to them by either

✔ Clicking the Getting Started Documents link (see Figure 9-1)

✔ Clicking the iPhone Reference Library link and clicking Getting Started in the Resource Types section of the table of contents at the left

When you reach the Getting Started section, click the link for the document labeled Getting Started with iPhone (see Figure 9-2). From this document, you can start off knowing nothing and expand your knowledge all the way through the basics of creating your first iPhone app. At that point, you should be well enough oriented with the documentation to find your way to the resources you need.

The best start depends on your experience with object-oriented programming:

✔ If you're somewhat familiar with object-oriented programming but haven't developed with Objective-C, start with the document called Learning Objective C: A Primer.

✔ If you are familiar with programming, but have never programmed in an object-oriented language, you'll want to check out the document Object-Oriented Programming with Objective-C, which is linked to in the first page of the Learning Objective C: A Primer document.

✔ If you have *no* programming experience at all, start with *Beginning Programming* by Adrian and Kathie Kingsley-Hughes (Wiley).

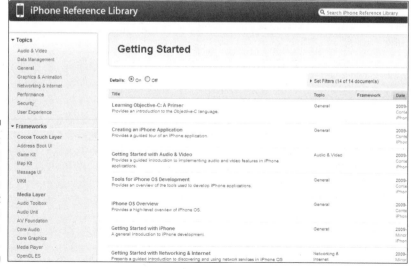

Figure 9-2:
The Getting Started with iPhone document can help explain everything.

When you start to get a feel for the platform through the text documents, go back to the Dev Center main page and click the Getting Started Videos link. This link brings you to iTunes, which gives you access to an array of help videos, as shown in Figure 9-3. Checking out the text before watching the videos is best because the videos can get a bit deep right away. If you watch the videos after getting a ways into the documentation, you will have put your hands on the SDK a bit and have a better understanding of what the videos are getting across. Moving back and forth between the videos and the text documents will give you the best balance:

✔ Watch a video and then read the sections of the Reference Library that correspond to that topic.

✔ Try things out yourself with the coding how-to's and sample code.

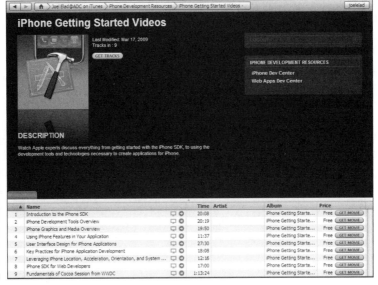

Figure 9-3:
Apple
provides
a wealth
of helpful
videos on
iTunes for
developers.

The introductory help videos

To give you a preview of what you can expect when you view the Apple videos, we've assembled the following outlines of the video content for the first two Apple videos you'll want to watch.

Introduction to the iPhone SDK

The Introduction to the iPhone SDK video is a fast overview of all the tools and technologies contained in the SDK. It explains that the SDK is the exact same toolset that Apple uses for its development, and it examines each piece of the SDK. The video is divided into two sections: Tools and Technologies.

In the Tools section, the video explores the following tools within the iPhone developer SDK (see Figure 9-4):

✔ **Xcode:** Xcode is an integrated development environment for project management, source editing, and graphical debugging, in addition to containing templates and sample code.

✔ **Instruments:** The Instruments software tool allows you to see exactly where to tune your programming code for efficiency and performance.

✔ **Dashcode:** This tool puts user interface layout (Interface Builder), code writing, testing, and debugging under one simple-to-use application.

✔ **iPhone Simulator:** This tool lets you run and debug applications without connecting to an iPhone. The Simulator is a program that runs on your Mac and resembles the actual iPhone runtime environment; it even lets you simulate finger gestures used on the iPhone with your Mac's mouse and keyboard.

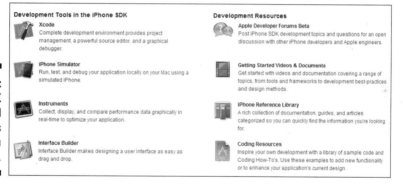

Figure 9-4: The SDK has several resources for you to use.

Development Tools in the iPhone SDK

Xcode
Complete development environment provides project management, a powerful source editor, and a graphical debugger.

iPhone Simulator
Run, test, and debug your application locally on your Mac using a simulated iPhone.

Instruments
Collect, display, and compare performance data graphically in real-time to optimize your application.

Interface Builder
Interface Builder makes designing a user interface as easy as drag and drop.

Development Resources

Apple Developer Forums Beta
Post iPhone SDK development topics and questions for an open discussion with other iPhone developers and Apple engineers.

Getting Started Videos & Documents
Get started with videos and documentation covering a range of topics, from tools and frameworks to development best-practices and design methods.

iPhone Reference Library
A rich collection of documentation, guides, and articles categorized so you can quickly find the information you're looking for.

Coding Resources
Inspire your own development with a library of sample code and Coding How-To's. Use these examples to add new functionality or to enhance your application's current design.

The Introduction video also shows you how to get up and running quickly with a sample project that utilizes the different parts of the SDK. In addition, the video gives a brief overview of the technology behind the iPhone operating system, which is based on Mac OS X. It describes the operating system as a layered architecture composed of four different layers (see Figure 9-5) that work together:

✔ **Core OS** is the bedrock of the operating system where the low-level features of the system operate. Most programmers don't really interact with this level of the system.

✔ **Core Services** is the layer where the Core Foundation Framework, CF Network Framework, Security Framework, SQLite library, and XML libraries reside. These services allow you to store, manipulate, communicate, and secure data.

✔ **Media** is the layer that contains a lot of the fun stuff, including the graphics engines for both 2D and 3D drawing and animation, the audio engines that allow you to play and record sounds, and the video engine, which supports a number of top video formats.

✔ **Cocoa Touch** is the layer of the operating system that allows you to implement a user interface. It contains primary classes for windowing, standard views and controls, event handling, text management, and more. It also contains frameworks for working with addresses and the Address Book and measuring the geolocation of the iPhone through Core Location.

Figure 9-5:
The iPhone
OS is
broken up
into four
distinct
layers.

iPhone OS Technologies

The implementation of iPhone OS technologies can be viewed as a set of layers, which are shown in Figure 2-1. At the lower layers of the system are the fundamental services on which all applications rely, while higher-level layers contain more sophisticated services and technologies.

Figure 2-1 Layers of iPhone OS

Cocoa Touch
Media
Core Services
Core OS

As you write your code, you should prefer the use of higher-level frameworks over lower-level frameworks whenever possible. The higher-level frameworks are there to provide object-oriented abstractions for lower-level constructs. These abstractions generally make it much easier to write code because they reduce the number of lines of code you have to write and encapsulate potentially complex features, such as sockets and threads. Although they abstract out lower-level technologies, they do not mask those technologies from you. The lower-level frameworks are still available for developers who prefer using them or who want to use aspects of those frameworks that are not exposed at the higher level.

The following sections provide more detail about what is in each of the exposed layers of iPhone OS, starting with the topmost layers and working downward.

iPhone Development Tools Overview

The iPhone Development Tools Overview video goes deeper into the Xcode development environment, describes the four stages of iPhone development, and shows off the power of the Instruments tool for testing and debugging.

Xcode is a full-featured development toolset that features code editing, debugging, performance tools, and other features for efficiency and productivity. It's described as a refined, mature development environment that's based on seven versions of OS X and nearly two decades of history and refinement. It contains out-of-the-box templates to jump start your process and was used to develop Mac OS X, OS X Server, and the iPhone OS.

The video then walks through creating a sample project and shows how the Xcode Build and Go feature is used to compile the application and launch it in the Simulator. The video also describes the four stages of iPhone development:

✔ **iPhone management:** This stage has to do with provisioning your iPhone as a development device so you can install your developing applications on it, managing software and firmware updates on the iPhone, viewing logging information and crash logs, and capturing screenshots of apps running on your iPhone.

✔ **Coding:** This stage covers using the Xcode IDE (integrated development environment) to actually develop your applications. The simple, straightforward project management capabilities of Xcode are described along with some basics about code editing. The video covers the snapshots feature, which lets you capture the complete state of a project so you can move forward with risky or large-scale changes and be able to go back to a working version of your app at any time. The video also talks about support of source code management applications such as SVN, Subversion, and Perforce. Then the video covers the Xcode Research Assistant, a tool for quickly getting to the help and documentation you need about the specific feature you're implementing at the time, and the built-in Xcode documentation that can be kept up-to-date with the online documentation. Some focus is given to Interface Builder, which allows you to lay out graphical interface elements and link them with your code in an efficient way.

✔ **Building and debugging:** This stage covers rich debugging experience in Xcode, which allows you to stay directly in the source code editor for debugging. It highlights data tips that give you contextual information as you mouse over elements of your code and showcases the single window interface of Xcode. After debugging comes the build and deployment process, in which apps are compiled on the host machine and pushed to the iPhone with a single click.

✔ **Analysis:** You tackle this stage by thoroughly using the Instruments tool, which the video calls a *meta-analysis tool* — a bird's-eye view of how your app is behaving in real time. The Instruments tool allows you to set up multiple measuring tools that let you track data points that are mapped live in graphs in the track view. This allows you to see data as it varies over time to see how processes and actions correlate. You can use the Instruments tool to answer tricky questions by using various combinations of measurement tools. Some instruments are appropriate for the iPhone Simulator, but others are effective only on the iPhone.

Apple offers many other videos to help you get familiar with the development tools. You can access all of them from the iPhone Dev Center site, and iTunes delivers them.

Stanford University iPhone development classes on iTunes

Stanford University's iPhone Application Programming class (CS 193P) is a great video resource for learning iPhone development. This class is taught by Apple engineers at Stanford, and its lectures are posted for free in the iTunes U section of iTunes. Because the class takes place over the course of a semester, the pace of the videos is much more relaxed, and detailed concepts are explained more thoroughly by the lecturers than you generally find on Apple videos. You can even download and follow along with the assignments at www.stanford.edu/class/cs193p. (See Figure 9-6.)

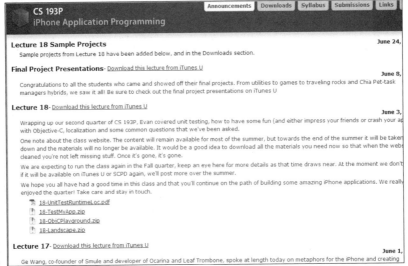

Figure 9-6:
Follow Stanford's iPhone Application Program-ming class online.

The class requires a basic level of programming experience. At Stanford, its prerequisites for this class were CS 106a and CS 106b or CS 106x. (CS 106b is also available on iTunes from Stanford.) If this class seems to be a bit over your head, start with the other resources we discuss in the earlier section, "Getting Set Up as a Developer."

Stanford's iPhone Application Programming class covers these topics:

- ✔ Real-world software engineering
- ✔ Object-oriented architecture and design
- ✔ Cocoa Touch and iPhone SDK
- ✔ Object-oriented design patterns
- ✔ The development tools Xcode and Interface Builder
- ✔ The frameworks Foundation and UIKit
- ✔ The Objective-C language
- ✔ View controllers
- ✔ Displaying data
- ✔ Dealing with local and remote data
- ✔ Text input

> ✔ Multithreading
>
> ✔ Address Book and other system integration

You can download the class slides, as well as the handouts for various class projects the students had to complete, from the Downloads section of the class Web site, as shown in Figure 9-7. You don't have anyone to submit any completed projects to, but the project assignments have some helpful hints and reminders that could come in handy if you plan on writing something similar. (See Figure 9-8.) Projects they worked on included a basic Hello World app, a basic GUI app, a Twitter client, and a variety of final projects that the students chose.

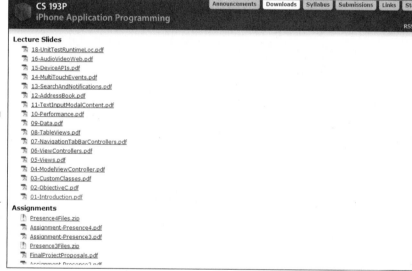

Figure 9-7:
You can download the class notes and project assignments to your computer.

Further resources

As Apple continues to enhance its iPhone OS and update its development tools, you may be interested in more help or information from other sources besides Apple. If you're interested in using the development tools, we recommend these titles (all from Wiley):

> ✔ *iPhone Application Development For Dummies* by Neal Goldstein
>
> ✔ *iPhone SDK Programming: Developing Mobile Applications for Apple iPhone and iPod touch* by Mr. Maher Ali
>
> ✔ *iPhone Game Development For Apple Developers* by Chris Craft and Jamey McElveen

✔ *Cocoa Touch for iPhone OS 3.0 For Apple Developers* by Jiva DeVoe

✔ *iPhone SDK 3 Programming: Advanced Mobile Development for Apple iPhone and iPod touch* by Mr. Maher Ali

Figure 9-8:
You can find hints and reminders about different programming exercises.

Third-Party Tools

There are a few third-party applications you can use to develop iPhone applications. Many are for games, but there are tools out there for a number of applications. These range from full independent SDKs that compile to iPhone–native Objective-C, to prebuilt code libraries that you can integrate with your project in the Apple SDK.

Game SDKs

Currently, games represent a large number of iPhone applications available for purchase or download from the App Store. Not only are games popular, but they also require a lot of programming to handle everything from the rich graphics usually displayed in an iPhone game to the programming interfaces to iPhone features like the accelerometer and multitouch interface. Therefore, there has been a rise in the development of game-specific Software Development Kits that aid iPhone game developers in writing their newest games.

One popular SDK provider is called GarageGames, and you can find its Web site at www.garagegames.com. Besides providing software tools for other gaming tools like the Nintendo Wii, GarageGames offers two flavors of its Torque Game software for the iPhone, Torque Game Builder (iTGB) and Torque Game Engine (iTGE). iTGB is designed for 2D games and iTGE is designed for 3D (see Figure 9-9).

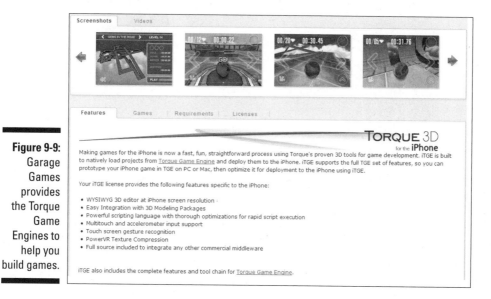

Figure 9-9: Garage Games provides the Torque Game Engines to help you build games.

Another SDK provider is called Unity, and you can find its Web site at www. unity3d.com. Unity makes tools and applications for the PC and Mac, as well as the Web and the iPhone. Unity offers a game SDK that supports iPhone deployment and pioneered the field of offering developers the opportunity to deploy one project to multiple platforms seamlessly. (Figure 9-10 shows the SDK.) As an example, the popular *Zombieville USA* iPhone game was developed with Unity.

Using a third-party SDK to develop for the iPhone has advantages and disadvantages:

- ✔ **The upside:** These software packages make many difficult tasks much easier and provide you with a graphical interface that's geared for game building.

- ✔ **The downside:** You may not have fine-grained control over the resulting Objective-C code and will rely on the software you're working with to make any changes. This lack of fine control can limit your ability to fine-tune, optimize performance, and use low-level software interfaces.

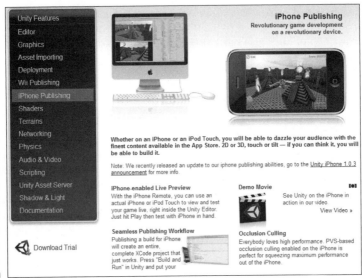

Figure 9-10: Use the Unity game SDK to develop for the iPhone and multiple platforms.

The Torque Game Builder user interface is designed so that you can set up a 2D scrolling game easily with no code. As your game interactions get more interesting and complex, you can create custom code for them. Torque Game Engine and Unity have interfaces that will be familiar to any 3D designer. You can import 3D resources directly from a wide variety of formats and manipulate them in what-you-see-is-what-you-get (WYSIWYG) fashion in the editor. You can assign behaviors to objects, and your coding can range from nonexistent to complex. When coding in third-party SDKs such as these, you often can't code in Objective-C, but rather the application's native language (which often resembles JavaScript). This could be a benefit or a distraction depending on your background.

Frameworks and code libraries

Code libraries and *frameworks* are sets of developed code structures that you can use to speed up your development because their creators have done a lot of the grunt work and heavy lifting for you.

- ✔ **A code library** is a set of classes that you can drop into your project and use however you like.

- ✔ **A framework** is an almost fully developed application that you can bend to achieve your goals.

  A framework has a more developed logic system and behaves almost as an extension of the API (Application Programming Interface, the component set you use to create programs). Because it has its own logic system in place, a framework can be both very

- *Powerful:* It lets you do complex things easily and quickly.

- *Limiting:* You need to learn and use the prebuilt logic system.

Many programmers prefer not to use third-party frameworks whenever possible because they want to intimately understand everything that happens in their applications. However, a framework used wisely can save you huge amounts of time and money and give you a stronger coding foundation than you might otherwise develop.

One way is to use a framework but learn it very thoroughly. The only problem with that approach can be that in the same time it takes you to learn a framework, you might have been able to develop your own custom solution that might be even better tailored to what you're trying to accomplish.

Beginning developers can benefit from learning a framework in order to understand better how to structure code and to be exposed to ways of doing things that they might not otherwise. If that's the approach you're taking, make sure you're using a framework that has been built by a respected developer using best practices, so your developers don't pick up bad habits.

In most cases, you should insist that your developers either use frameworks that they could fully take apart and put back together again on their own, or none at all! One possible exception would be if you were using a resource from a company that provided strong, fast tech support for your coding. Then the support technicians are essentially acting as a safety net for you. Just make sure up front that the company support *your* code and not just their own.

Here are a couple of frameworks out there that you can consider using:

- **Three20 (`http://joehewitt.com`):** Joe Hewitt developed the Facebook iPhone app under the stipulation that he could release its framework as open source software, which he has named Three20 (it stands for the 320-pixel-wide iPhone screen). Now you can leverage the photo viewer, message composer, Web image viewer, table view controllers, and more that Joe used for the Facebook app.

  You can download the code (see Figure 9-11) by going to `http://github.com/joehewitt/three20/tree/master`.

- **Cocos2D-iphone, a 2D game framework:** This is an example of a typical code framework deployed on Google Code. You can download it from `http://code.google.com/p/cocos2d-iphone`. (See Figure 9-12.)

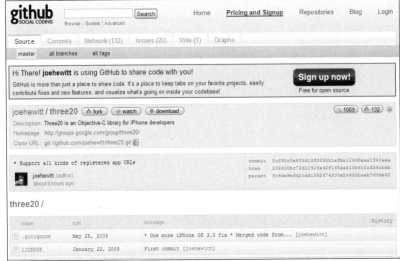

Figure 9-11:
Use the underlying technology behind Facebook's iPhone application.

If you're interested in finding more frameworks, you can search iPhone frameworks by going to either of these sites:

✔ Google Code (http://code.google.com)

✔ GitHub (http://github.com)

Figure 9-12:
You can find code on Google Code like this 2D game framework.

Chapter 10

Staffing Your Team

*B*efore you can start creating any iPhone application, you have to know that you have a team in place that can handle all of the various tasks. Many of those people on your team may be the same person, actually . . . you! (Just don't have too many arguments with your teammates.) Or building a team will require gathering bids and conducting interviews — or applying a little finesse to requisition somebody's hours (or *lots* of somebody's hours) to work on this project.

Help is at hand: This chapter reviews the elements of why you need critical (and even a few not-so-critical) members on your team, and what to keep in mind as you go out and find the people necessary to pull off a world-class (and/or profitable) iPhone application. You get a look at the basic skills you need to have available full time, and then round out your team with specialized skills (such as legal or accounting) that could possibly be handled by part-time help. Finally, when you get to the stage when it's time to sell your application, you need people to go out and *sell, sell, sell* while you're busy making sure the next update is coming out.

Identifying the Team Positions

After you have your idea mapped out and you're ready to see it implemented, you need to find the right team of people that can make your idea into a reality. As you read through these sections, decide which pieces of the development process should be handled by you and which parts will have to be outsourced. Don't worry if you're not a tech genius. As the holder of the idea, you can outsource everything and just be the ringleader of everything.

Every great iPhone application needs a ringleader or coordinator to make sure everything gets done properly. Beyond the leader role, the major roles fall into in three distinct categories:

1. Write the computer code so your application actually does something.

2. Add the useful icons, graphics, and screen displays so your customers will see what is going on and be able to use your application.

3. Integrate all the computer files generated from your programmer, and all the graphics files from your designer, into one package so you can send your app to Apple for approval to be sold in the App Store.

If you're like most folks, you'll probably need help in the other elements of making your own business. In some cases, one person (perhaps you) will be handling one or more of these "secondary" skills. In many cases, you may never meet face to face with members of your team. Thanks to the power of the Internet, you may never even have to meet in person — but can still get the work done and delivered.

Getting the application programming skills

There's one skill area that most people think of when they think about developing an iPhone application: programming. After all, every iPhone app is a computer program that runs on the Apple iPhone (or iPod Touch) and cannot exist unless a computer programmer puts together the lines of computer code that makes the application start up and function correctly. (There's more to it, but focusing on one element at a time saves headaches.)

Your first inclination may be to simply type in a query to your favorite search engine to see if you can hire someone. We typed in "hire iPhone application developer" into Google, and got over 80 million possible search results, as shown in Figure 10-1. So you can tell that this is a *very* popular category — and (obviously) you'll have to narrow down your search.

The first decision to make is what kind of application programmer you're looking to hire to complete this project. Some of your options include

✔ Asking a friend, co-worker, or local college kid who has computer programming skills to develop your app.

✔ Soliciting bids for an iPhone app developer from freelance Web sites such as eLance or guru.com.

✔ Hiring an iPhone Application Development consultancy or firm to handle your application programming needs (and the other aspects of your app)

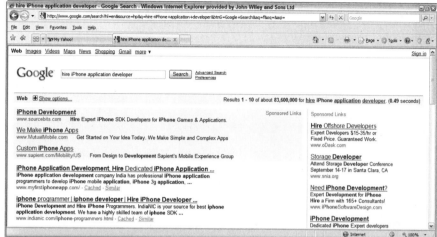

Figure 10-1:
If you want
to hire a
developer,
you have
a lot of
choices!

Whichever route you take, whoever provides the application programming skills needs to have a few skills or equipment to finish the job. Specifically, make sure that whoever you choose has the following:

✔ Knowledge of how to write programs using a programming language called Cocoa Touch

✔ Owns or has access to an Intel-based Macintosh computer for writing and testing the computer code

✔ Preferably, has written iPhone applications in the past or is launching at least one application, whether for themselves or another client

Chapter 12 details how to hire an application programmer for your project, from writing up the project request to evaluating the different people or companies you'll have bidding on your project.

Understanding the importance of a great designer

When it comes to iPhone applications, style is just as important as substance. Your app has to stand out and look exciting and professional to your customers, whether it's free or a paid application. Therefore your computer efforts don't stop with the application's programming code. Unless you are a professional designer yourself (and often, even if you are), strongly consider hiring a graphic designer to help you come up with the visual elements of your application, from the icon and buttons to your overall screen designs and background graphics. Design also encompasses

- ✔ User interface design (how the user interacts with your app)
- ✔ User experience (the type and quality of experience the user has)
- ✔ Sound design (possibly)

Why hire a graphic designer? Here are a few good reasons:

- ✔ **Make a great first impression.** Your application's icon is the first impression your app makes on your customer base. The icon is the first thing those folks see when they consider buying or downloading your app, and it's a visual that will always crop up on their iPhone screens after they acquire your app. Although it's a cliché to say that you only get one chance to make a first impression, there is merit to that saying. If you're in a crowded field of competitors, you need an icon that grabs people's attention and gives your app the visual appeal to make a *great* first impression. Let's say you're writing a Sudoku-puzzle game application. Your brainchild is competing with many other similar apps, most of which have professional graphics to attract a player's attention (like those in Figure 10-2).

Figure 10-2: Professional graphics and icons make even a simple puzzle game stand out.

- ✔ **Pictures convey your app's quality.** The screenshots within your application speak volumes about the quality of your work. Those screens are visible to potential customers in your application description on the App Store, and are visible to customers as they acquire and use your application. Part of the "X factor" behind the incredible popularity of the iPhone is the high quality of design, which customers expect to extend to any *application* running on the iPhone.

✔ **Your app has to "look the price" to justify a fee.** If you're creating a paid application, your iPhone app has to "look the price" if you hope your customers will pay any amount for your app, even $0.99. Customers expect a return on their investment, and the first measurable quality they have for that return is the visual appeal of the application — the first thing they see after they pay and download it. If they paid $9.99 for something that looks like it's barely worth a quarter, the customers will feel robbed before they even start using your app!

✔ **Apple's Human Interface Guidelines.** One of the requirements that Apple puts on every application before that app can be sold in the App Store is something called the Human Interface Guidelines. It's a set of guidelines that allows iPhone users to use applications on the iPhone with the limited set of input options — mainly the touch screen and accelerometer. There is no standard keyboard or mouse that comes with the iPhone, so your app has to interact with the user in certain ways that are intuitive to human beings using the iPhone. Having a graphic designer on board your team will help ensure that your app has the clean and intuitive interface necessary for Apple to approve your application.

✔ **Design builds your brand image.** Your iPhone app will help develop your brand image to the outside world, regardless of the purpose your iPhone application serves. Therefore, if you want to promote a positive and consistent brand image, your iPhone app visuals should match the rest of your identity — your Web site, business cards, company logo, and any other visual items attached to your company. A graphic designer can help ensure a consistent brand image.

Don't just hire the first designer you can find. Try to find a *great* designer. If you don't know what you are looking at, enlist someone who is artistic to help you evaluate designers and survey various designers' portfolios with everyone you can. The best designer for you will get the strongest positive reaction from those who would be potential buyers of your app (they fit your other requirements, such as budget and personal rapport).

IT skills to tie it all together

Okay, it's no big revelation that information technology — and the skills to use it right — are part and parcel of app development. To put together an iPhone application, you have to collect a variety of different computer files into one virtual bundle — along with your graphics, application information, and any other pieces of information that are a part of your application (or that Apple requests). There are also some steps at the very end of the process (covered in Chapter 14) that require the touch of someone who knows the iPhone app submission process — for example, to certify your application with your Apple Developer Certificate.

Many iPhone application developers could be paid to "go the extra mile" and prepare all the files for you, on top of doing the actual programming, but there are some benefits to having your own IT person or IT staff available to handle your app's non-coding needs:

- **Don't overpay someone for a simpler task.** If you're paying your developers to handle all the prep work for submitting your app, typically you're "overpaying" the person (based on the skill level of the tasks required). This is not to suggest that the IT skills required to prepare your app are basic or cheap. However, the actual application-coding skill is more specialized (therefore more expensive) than the IT skills you need at this particular stage.

- **IT staff handles smaller but more frequent tasks.** Typically, your application coders are given a large chunk of work, and hand in pieces (or achieve goals) of the program until they are done. The finishing steps of preparing an app for launch or updating your application files after launch may require a lot of smaller steps that require quicker turnaround time than your application coder can provide.

- **Too much work in one person's hands can create a bottleneck.** If you heap too many responsibilities on one owner, you increase the risk of delays or problems because so much of the process is controlled by one person (or company). By having your own IT person or staff available, you can partition assignments: The coder can work on the coding part of the process, and your IT staff can handle their part, as pieces of the application come together.

- **Minor changes after launch are easier to make with an available IT person.** After you launch your application, if its files happen to need minor changes done, you might not be able to get your application coder back to do them; the coder could be working on several new projects. Having someone available or on call in IT can help you answer a need for minor changes in your app in a timely way.

If you can handle processes such as "building" your application and attaching your developer certificate, then perhaps you can act as the IT person to tie everything together. If you're part of a larger company, check to see whether someone on staff has enough familiarity with Macintosh OS X and Macintosh development languages to help you with your IT needs.

Rounding out the team with business skills

Whether you're selling hot dogs or hot rods, any business requires basic business skills and resources. Here's how to apply those skills in iPhone application development.

Legal skills

At some point, you will need to consult with a lawyer regarding at least one aspect of what you're trying to accomplish with your iPhone application.

Regardless of the need, most people can agree on the following: It's *much* better to have obtained the legal advice or work *before* a problem or concern crops up, because the problem is usually much worse (and much more expensive) to fix after the fact.

Your need of a lawyer will vary, depending on the size and scope of your business (and those of your application), but here are some of the most common concerns that an iPhone-application business has to deal with:

✔ **Who owns the software code?** If you're hiring programmers, make sure that *you* own the code, not them. This is basically called a "work-for-hire" situation, where you're hiring an independent contractor (namely the programmer) to create a work for you. At the end of the process, after getting paid for such efforts, all rights associated with the "work-for-hire" belong to the owner, or employer, namely you. The last thing you want your coder to do is to take the code and

  • Resell it to your competitors.

  • Launch a competing application that's virtually identical to yours and cuts into your profit or download statistics.

✔ **How is your business structured?** If you want to go into business for yourself, at least in the United States, it is known as a *sole proprietorship*, and you simply file your business income as part of your personal income tax return.

If you want to set up a more sophisticated business entity, such as a partnership, Limited Liability Corporation (LLC), or a (fully incorporated) Corporation, then you'll need some help in filing the right documents to form your business entity. There are a lot of companies that specialize in this sort of work, from `www.incorporate.com` (see Figure 10-3) to filing firms such as `bizfilings.com` and `legalzoom.com`.

✔ **Are there any copyright or trademark issues?** If you're using any brands, trademarks, copyrights, and such in your application (or you're displaying a graphic that's very similar to one with a known copyright or trademark), then you need to know whether you're legally allowed to use them, and whether you're displaying them correctly. You'd better have someone on your side who can check those legal issues, before someone sees the image in your launched app and starts asking thorny questions. There are even some questions regarding use of celebrities' names, images, or work — and whether your usage falls under the definition of parody or could be seen as defamation.

Figure 10-3: Companies such as this can help you form your business and file its documents.

✔ **Are there any user-privacy issues?** If you're using or reselling your customer's data as part of your iPhone app, then you need to mask some of the data you provide — or advise your customers accordingly, depending on the privacy laws in your state or country.

Apple's Software Development Kit User Agreement states that you have to comply with all state, federal, and international privacy laws. If you're unsure, pull up all the privacy laws and consult an attorney.

Accounting skills

Even if you are offering a free app, your development effort probably will incur some expenses along the way; you may need help managing your budget and making sure that everything is documented correctly and everyone gets paid properly. If you plan to finance your project with someone else's money, they'll most likely demand having someone "watch the books" as it were.

If you're planning on creating a paid iPhone application, then you're doubly in need of some accounting help — not only to manage your development budget, but also to account for the incoming app revenue so you're not penalized or creating a tax liability.

✔ If you're a CPA or come with years of accounting experience, then you can check this box and move on.

✔ If you're developing this application as part of an existing company's efforts, then chances are the accounting expertise you need is already working in your company, and you would simply coordinate with those folks to handle details of bank accounts, disbursements, and payments.

✔ If this is your own new business and you aren't a trained accountant, it's time to hire someone, either on a temporary or (in some cases) permanent basis. When you interview for a CPA or accountant in this area, you might want to ask the following questions:

- Have you ever dealt with similar clients before (similar size, similar type of business)?

- What systems would you use to log recurring sales of my application?

- How do you calculate your fees?

- How much interaction or data will you need from me on a monthly, quarterly, and yearly basis?

Marketing skills

Part V of this book explores a variety of marketing initiatives you can do in order to promote your book. The question you have to ask just now is, *Are you going to coordinate these efforts or do you need a marketer (or someone with more marketing experience) to handle them?*

Regardless of the price of your iPhone application, here's some food for thought regarding the marketing of your app:

✔ **The app will not sell itself.** Even if you know how to write the programming code for an iPhone app, do you really know how to sell it? As with hiring a specialist for other skilled activities, you may want to hire an experienced marketer — especially if you're dealing with a big-budget or high-profile investment. If your natural inclination is not marketing, then perhaps you could benefit from an expert here.

✔ **There's more to the app success than gross revenue.** Even if your app is being given away for free, you're still trying to gain something — at the least, a sense of accomplishment or recognition — and marketing will help you achieve your goal. You need to announce your iPhone app as loudly and clearly as possible, whether you're after paid revenue, a large user base, or notoriety to use on a future project.

✔ **There are only 24 hours in a day.** Do you really have the time to handle the marketing tasks yourself? There is the inclination to save the money and take on the extra tasks yourself (see the later section, "Cost Considerations," for more discussion of this issue) but you run the risk of these tasks being delegated or relegated to the bottom of your list and possibly not happening — which could have negative influences on the overall success of your iPhone app and your business in general.

Project-management skills

With all the various people working on their parts of the application, it's useful to have someone whose primary responsibility is to make sure that everything is on track and everyone is providing their work on a more-or-less timely basis. Now, if you're developing a small application yourself, then perhaps you can act as your own project manager. However, the more people involved in the project, the more you need someone who stays focused on the "big picture" of your entire application and can manage the schedules and delivery dates of your various programmers, designers, and other skilled professionals. That's especially true if some team members' work is dependent on someone *else's* delivered work. Why do I need thee, Project Manager (PM)? Let me count the ways:

✔ **There are always multiple parts to developing an application.** Someone has got to keep track of all the different deadlines and milestones, especially if there are pieces of the program that are dependent on something else being completed first, or multiple pieces of the application being designed in parallel.

There are programs, such as Microsoft Project and @task, that can map all the steps in your project, track dependencies and milestones, and help stay on the road to completion.

✔ **Nothing always goes according to plan.** (That's probably a clause in Murphy's Law.) You need someone who can estimate a problem and predict each person's effect on the team effort. It's not just about how long it takes a particular programmer to write a function; it's about building in the time to test the function, do integration testing with other functions, and incorporate the function into the larger application.

✔ **One person is your focal point.** If you're bringing a diverse team together to get the project done, then each person will need a contact person to gather requirements and deliver his or her specific results. It helps if one Project Manager (or a PM team) acts as the focal point to talk to everyone and help the whole crew understand the big picture.

Filling the Gaps on your Team

You may have some of the pieces already in place, but you probably don't have them all. If you have to go out to get one or two, or even a small team of people, how do you integrate them smoothly with the rest of the operation? There are a lot of different considerations to keep in mind as you bring in new people — or (for that matter) outsource various efforts within your project. Usually, there will be at least one additional perspective for you to consider. This section walks you through some of the most common situations you may encounter while you're developing your iPhone applications.

Adding business sense

Even the best programmers can easily write computer functions without understanding the business sense of whether that function is needed in the final product, whether that function can produce (or hinder) revenue, or whether that function will make sense to the customer who has to use it. Therefore it's important to inject some "business sense" into the discussion of which functions and features become a part of your application.

This starts with the development of your application features list and the requirements you will give to your application programmer(s). Sometimes the programming team may tell you they can add Function X for a certain amount of money and it will make your app "really cool." Although that can add buzz to your application, which *could* lead to a more successful sales cycle, you should be asking whether that investment — to design, write, test, and integrate the function — will *really* pay for itself in terms of greater sales or more loyal and happy customers.

You can also ask yourself these questions along the way:

- ✔ If I don't add a recommended feature, will I lose sales to competing apps that have the feature? Does every major competitor have this feature?

- ✔ Will my marketing campaign be greatly aided (or affected) by implementing a certain new function or feature?

- ✔ Does my application offer so many functions that it could be confusing to my customers?

The key is to balance the gee-whiz factor with practical needs. That's not to say your app can't bristle with technological prowess and the newest exciting features. Just keep any discussion about "pushing the envelope" in perspective: How should the technical capabilities or "bells and whistles" of your iPhone app be balanced against the impact those functions have on your revenue, bottom line, or other real-world goals?

Applying technology

There are some readers of this book who have an idea, or will come up with an idea, and have absolutely no idea how to make that idea occur, technologically speaking. The point of hiring targeted tech help, with extensive planning beforehand, is to allow you, the entrepreneur, to lay the path — and have specific technology gurus provide the pieces to make that happen.

The key to adding technology to your idea is this:

How can technology, namely the iPhone and the Software Development Kit (SDK) that allows me to create an iPhone application, help me solve the problem behind my idea?

As you turn your idea into a list of application requirements and functions — and as you have your application programmers turn that list into an iPhone app — you should always be talking out your reasoning in plain English. For that matter, always have someone available who understands the technology but can *also* put those ideas across in plain English — who can help you take each idea or step and "translate" it into a specific task or goal that a programmer can readily understand.

You don't have to know exactly "how it works" beneath the sleek shiny case, you just have to know whether your idea is possible, reasonable, and something a programmer and/or designer can create to run on an iPhone. Some people would say that you can think of the iPhone as a "black box" (in this case, a silver-and-black box): Never mind the innards; all you need to worry about is what someone would do (or input) and what would show up on the screen as a result (what would be the output) — and then hire someone to handle the rest.

However, you do need to be aware of exactly how you want your app to function. That means understanding how you collect information from your users (through the touch screen, pop-up keyboard, accelerometer, whatever) and what the users can do with your function. The best way to figure that out is by scrutinizing some examples:

> ✔ **Looking at existing applications within the App Store.** By now, you've been studying the existing applications for your idea to figure out where and how your app will compete. You may want to take an extra pass

through the list, just to study how different applications tackle the tasks you want your app to perform. Screenshots and application descriptions can tell you how certain inputs and outputs are handled, and that information can demonstrate some of the possibilities available in an iPhone app. When you see those possibilities, you're that much better informed to discuss app features with your application programmers. For example, if you were thinking of implementing a Wi-Fi Finder app, your best bet would be to search the existing apps (see Figure 10-4), noting that many of them use the GPS functions of the iPhone in conjunction with an internal database of WiFi Hotspots.

✔ **Reading the reviews.** Instead of looking at which apps are delighting the customer, you can look for the ones that aren't. Make a list of "things to improve" and find out what limitations the current applications have. Typically, reviewers acknowledge when an app's shortcoming is due to the app itself or to the fact that the iPhone platform cannot handle a particular user request. You can also study the positives, of course, but look for comments that mention how an application is really utilizing the iPhone to the best of its ability.

✔ **Look at other platforms.** Sometimes the answer to your request is already available, but in another form, such as a PC desktop computer's operating system. Although a regular desktop or laptop PC may not be as sleek and inviting as the iPhone, the PC market has been around a lot longer — which means a lot of different applications have been written over the years, and many problems have found solutions through the computer or computer-accessory market.

Now that the iPhone is building in support for accessories, you may need to find your solution in an existing platform — and have your technology experts find a way to *port to* the iPhone (that is, develop the same solution using the language of the Apple iPhone SDK, so the solution makes the leap to the new platform).

Figure 10-4:
See how existing applications take advantage of the iPhone technology.

Borrowing skills within your company

Sure, you may be able to cobble together a solution on your timetable, but if this app is meant to represent your company, your company may have a ready-made pool of talent available. If the company has dedicated programmers, graphic designers who know the brand image, IT folks who will have to support this app anyway after it's launched, and so on, then it makes sense to bring in those folks into your app's development as much as you can. Potentially that can make the whole process better on everyone.

However, unless you're the CEO of the company, there will be protocols to follow and requests to be made in order to have these people work *officially* on the company iPhone application. Depending on the size of your company, you may be able to simply ask your boss for the necessary support, fill out a requisition form, or even make a formal presentation or request to the head of a certain department.

Before you go through all the forms and headaches, do a little research first to find out if this is the right track to acquire those skills. Here are three questions you should ask your potential new teammate or the management:

 ✔ **Does this person have the skills that I need?**

 Sometimes, people just ask their management, "I need a programmer for 20 hours to code this project." Well, not every application programmer may have the correct skills to handle an iPhone application. Your programmer needs to have experience with object-oriented programming languages like Objective-C and Cocoa Touch, plus be able to write code on a Macintosh system, not a PC. Make sure the person you ask for has at least the basic capabilities, and hey, if he or she has written an iPhone app before, even better!

 ✔ Can this qualified person afford to spend time on the iPhone app project?

 When we say *afford*, there are multiple meanings:

 • Perhaps the priority of this key person is tied to another critical project for the company.

 • Perhaps the company makes more money by having this person work on outside jobs than the value this iPhone app can bring to the company.

 A frazzled, overworked person is not going to be too much help if this project just gets piled on top of everything else that has to be completed "yesterday."

✔ **Is the company prepared to make alternative arrangements if in-house help isn't available?**

This is a very polite way of asking whether the company will fund the outsourcing effort of bringing in somebody qualified to do the job if nobody inside the company has the skills or time to help on the project. This is especially important to ask if management's first thought — upon hearing that the right help isn't instantly available — is to delay the iPhone app project until that help *is* readily available. Things that help your case here include showing the benefit of having the iPhone app ready to go — hopefully ahead of your direct competition — or (say) to complement an already-scheduled marketing or launch promotion of a company product.

Your other alternative is to look for the skills you need regardless of the position the person holds in the company. Maybe some non-programmers can write code in their spare time, or someone in marketing happens to be a graphic design whiz but spends every day doing marketing plans. The benefit is that hopefully, the ability to do something different would appeal enough to that person to take on the extra work. The downside is that this person really doesn't have the "extra" time and management gets worried that you're diverting someone from his or her main responsibility.

These questions are worth asking about graphic designers, IT personnel, or people handling other aspects of the project. Make sure that whomever you're asking for has the correct skills to handle the job.

The key here is to ask around, borrow when you can, and always be ready to explain or quantify the benefits of this iPhone app to the company at large. We will leave all the internal negotiations and request ability up to you.

Effective Outsourcing

Every time you have to hire someone outside your core team to perform a task, there are certain issues you have to anticipate and plan for in order to succeed. Unfortunately, people are not as "plug-and-play" when it comes to their efforts. You can't just say, "Person 1 will handle X," gather up Person 1's work, try to "plug" those efforts into the project, and expect that things will "play nice together." Tasks done by various hands almost never mesh perfectly with the rest of the project without delay, mistakes, or implications.

That said, this section's goal is to help anticipate some of the classic trade-offs you may face while designing and building your iPhone application. Remember, in all these situations, your specific needs and situation will (hopefully) just about make the decision for you, at least in terms of which course to take. There isn't always an absolutely "right" or "wrong" answer; just as many times, the valid answer will be, "It depends."

Staying within your budget

This is probably one of the top concerns that most iPhone app developers have at some point in the process: How much do they take on personally, and how much leeway is in the budget to outsource tasks to someone else? When you come to that point, ask yourself a few questions:

- ✔ **Do I spend the money for someone else to do it, or do I try to do it myself?** This is one of the classic considerations, especially when you're trying to keep your budget very low.

  One very common trap is that the person behind the application takes on as much of the work as possible to keep the outsourcing bill as low as possible. Although this may be you, and you simply do not have the budget, you should ask yourself whether all that extra work is delaying you from launching and selling your application — and whether that delay in revenue may cost you more than hiring someone to speed up the process!

- ✔ **Am I having the right person do the right job for the right cost?** You don't want to waste (for example) a programmer — whom you're paying $100 per hour to code your app — on $10-per-hour routine jobs. Although you may think those are your responsibility, you should ask yourself, "Is my time best spent doing $10-per-hour routine tasks?" You may want to hire specific people and pay them according to the complexity of the task.

- ✔ **Am I only focusing on the hourly rate?** Some people think they're getting a deal because they have someone who bills at a rate at 25 percent lower than the competition. Then again, you have to ask yourself a practical question: If this person is taking more *time* to complete the task than the competition, are you actually saving any money? Keep your competitive bids and "clock" the hired gun on some simple, early tasks. If your worker is taking much longer to get the first few tasks done, and billing you for all those hours, you may want to consider paying for the "pricier" help, provided that person can get the job done efficiently.

Streamlining the integration

Let's say you've determined it will take 100 "man-hours" to complete your iPhone application development. One question a project manager might have is this: *Do you have 5 people working 20 hours each, or 20 people working*

5 hours each? Usually it's never that simple. Trying to coordinate the work of 20 different people takes additional time for integration. The question is whether you gain anything from having lots of people work in parallel with each other to tackle one piece of the problem.

If you're bringing on a second person to help someone finish a tricky part, remember to allow some time for the two people to integrate each other's work and/or comments. Unless they work in two different parts of the world, the best scenario looks like this: When one person hands off a finished piece, Person 2 has to see what Person 1 has completed, and vice versa. Sometimes paying one person more to handle more tasks on a solo basis can save you some integration costs.

There is the misconception among some managers that you can simply "throw more people at the problem to get it fixed quicker." It isn't necessarily so; every time you add another staff member, that person's work probably has to be checked or verified before it gets absorbed into the larger project. Each verification step can add up to bigger and bigger delays, especially if another part of your team is depending on work from this newer member.

Making sure everything is solid and robust

It's easy — and common — to fall into the misperception that everything will be performed at the quality level of your best team member. This may not be the case. The quality of each part of your app depends primarily on the specific person performing that task, and the more you spread out development — perhaps hiring someone more on the basis of cost than qualifications — you risk the quality of the application.

When different people write and test their own pieces, there is a risk of not doing tests to make sure those pieces all work with each other. Without such tests, you may not find a system-failure error until the end of the process — when the person who should fix it may be reassigned on another project or be completely unavailable. Test each piece on its own, but *also* test each piece as it talks to every *other* piece.

To preserve your app's quality as you go through the development cycle, keep these things in mind:

✔ **Test for quality as early as possible.** Try to validate someone's work as soon as you can by having an initial milestone or project piece completed near the beginning of that team member's work cycle. You or someone else within the team should check the person's submission for quality and functionality, and use that first submission (or wait until a couple of small projects are completed) to gauge attention to quality.

✔ **Allow for some "fudge" time.** Budget some extra time for the developer, or team member, to have a little extra time (if needed) to finish their tasks. That way, if you know you need something by Friday, ask initially to have it submitted by Thursday. If the team member is struggling to get it done on time, or you sense some slacking off on quality, now you have an extra day to offer — and to invest in getting it done right.

Don't hold too much time back for the last-minute considerations. If you're pushing too hard in the initial development phase, all that extra time won't fix declining quality as the person gets burned out.

✔ **Set the proper example.** It's true that team members take their cues from project leaders, even if the team members are unaware that they're doing so. Set the best example you can for quality effort, even if it's through timely meetings, quality communications (clear, professional, no mistakes, and so on), and a sense of urgency without sacrificing quality. If you set a bad example, your team is sure to follow you; if you set a good one, you can create an engaged, inspired team.

Part IV
Assemble Your iPhone Application

"Russell! Do you remember last month when I told you to order 150 SMART phones for the sales department?"

In this part . . .

*I*t's time for some heavy lifting — the kind where you start building your iPhone application turning your ideas on paper into a clickable, functioning, downloadable application in the App Store.

In this part, we walk you through the application development process necessary to build an outstanding iPhone application. We start by helping you lay out detailed specifications that you can give to your developer. Then we cover what a developer needs to get going and how you can find one who can write the code you need. Of course, you must first understand and create a budget for your project, and hopefully even find an investor or a client to back your efforts. Finally, we detail what to expect as the development process is underway, and how you can steer the ship if things get rocky. No Dramamine needed — just a clear head and a clear direction.

Let's get into it!

Chapter 11

Building Your Application Specifications

*M*uch like an architect's blueprints are used when building a new home, when it's time to start building your iPhone application, you should focus on creating your own set of "blueprints" based on your *application specifications*. These "specs" describe and outline how your application should look and operate. After you have the specs, you can hand them to any iPhone app developer, as well as to a graphic designer, so that the person can start building your app.

In this chapter, we offer several suggestions to help you create your application specs. We illustrate (pun intended) how sketches of your app help you verify its basic functionality. After you draw your basic operations, you can draw for users mock-up versions of different screens in your app and create a comprehensive list of the features you want to include. After you have your sketches, mock-ups, and list, you can decide what your app will look like, in terms of graphic design, so that the app is easy to use. You then need a specific testing plan to ensure that your developed application is tested thoroughly so that it works and looks the way you specified.

Creating an Application Blueprint

When you're ready to start drawing the blueprint of your iPhone application, you should consider several factors, which we describe in the following sections. You need to see your app in its entirety (the "big picture"), and you need to understand how the pieces of the application flow together to make one whole application.

As you work through the process of creating the apps, don't be surprised if these two different views of the project cause you to update or revise your initial plans, especially if looking at the application in this way helps you identify problems with your initial idea.

Documenting your app's basic functionality

When movie directors put together motion pictures, they often create *storyboards,* or drawings of what they want each scene to look like on film, from the script. These storyboards contain representations of the people in the film and, often, some key props or scenery details, in specific poses and angles. These storyboards may look like rudimentary comic strips, but they're collections of the scenes and angles of the cameras within the film and they allow the director (and the crew) to prepare for the making of the film.

When it comes to making iPhone apps, much with the storyboards, making sketches or rough drawings of what your app will do is a helpful way to get started. You can represent the different functions within your app as boxes and create something akin to a flowchart or sequence of events to represent the logic behind the application and the flow between functions within it. It needn't be as complex as a fully rendered flowchart, as shown in Figure 11-1, but you should start to put the pieces together on paper to give yourself a visual representation of the idea in your head, describing how the parts of the application connect and "talk" with each other.

Don't take the simplest actions for granted. If you need to connect with an Internet server or a Web page, the connection itself is an action, receiving the information is another action, and so on. Even figuring whether the iPhone should display information horizontally or vertically is a separate action.

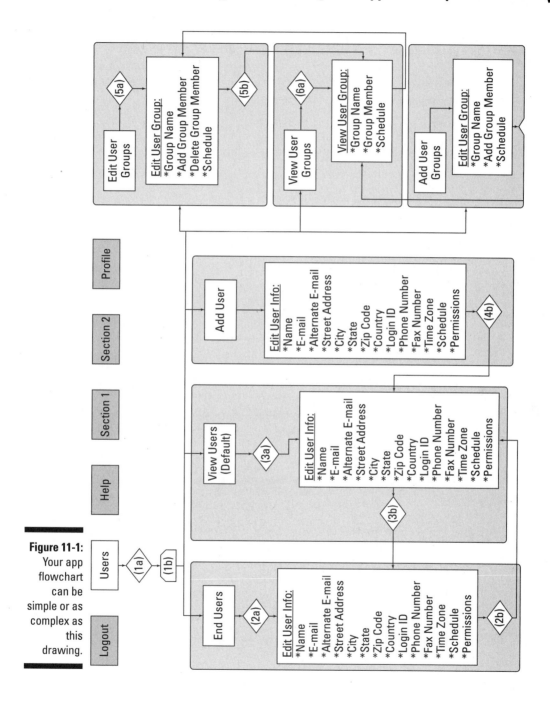

Figure 11-1:
Your app flowchart can be simple or as complex as this drawing.

We start with a basic example. Suppose that your User List application displays a list of names that are saved in a database and you can

✔ Add a name to the list

✔ Remove a name from the list

✔ Search for a name on the list

Therefore, you need to document the following actions in your sketches, like this:

User List application steps

1. Load your application.

2. Main screen — the list might already be displayed.

3. If the Add button is pressed, go to the Add User screen.

   3a. **Add User screen:** You can enter your first and last names and fill in additional fields.

   3b. **Add User screen:** When you click the Save button, information is sent to the database and the main screen is displayed.

4. If the Delete button is pressed, go to the Delete User screen.

   4a. **Delete User screen:** Display the list of names, but with buttons next to each name. You click buttons to select names.

   4b. **Delete User screen:** Clicking the Delete button sends instructions to the database to delete the names where a button is selected and load the main screen.

5. When you click the Search button, the Search User screen appears.

   5a. **Search User screen:** Display the search box and keyboard at the bottom of the screen. Allow for input in the search field.

   5b. **Search User screen:** When you click the button, send the search command to the database with the terms entered in the search box. Wait for the results to be sent back.

   5c. **Search results user screen:** Display the search results screen with the information returned from the database. When the menu button is clicked, load the main screen.

After you map out this as a flowchart, it looks similar to the one shown in Figure 11-2.

After you create your flowchart, study it by thinking of the basic scenarios and ensuring that all options within the application are represented in the flowchart. It's much easier and less expensive to add steps, functions, and screens at this stage than to add them during development.

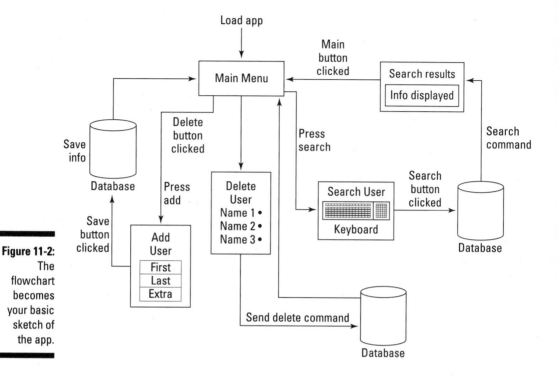

Figure 11-2:
The flowchart becomes your basic sketch of the app.

Creating mock-ups

After you depict the basic flow of your application in your sketches, you specify exactly what the user will see by creating mock-ups of the screens to be displayed. Then you can think about these issues:

- The information you need to capture
- The point in the process where you need to ask or display the information

As you're making your mock-ups (such as Figure 11-3 and Figure 11-4), keep this advice in mind:

- **Don't overload the page:** Simplicity is a key element of usable design on the iPhone, so don't jam every available pixel with a button or a text field or another request for information.

  Space your input fields appropriately, and use an extra screen, if necessary, to capture or display the information. Too much information can overwhelm your eyes.

✔ **Remember how people will use the app:** In your mock-up, try to use elements such as sliders, scrollable lists, and other touch-friendly elements that don't require the pop-up keyboard so that users don't have to peck away at a keyboard that occupies half the screen area.

The arrangement of elements should lead users through the elements on the screen intuitively. In the United States, for example, elements should be ordered from left to right and from top to bottom. In other countries, the order might be reversed.

✔ **Highlight the button labeled Action or Next:** Make sure that whichever button or action is necessary to move forward in your application is obvious and highlighted on the screen. There are a couple of methods:

- Make this button or element a little bigger than the other elements.

- Create enough white space around the element to draw attention.

When you draw screen mock-ups, size them consistently in one of these modes:

✔ **Portrait:** Vertical size is 320 x 480 pixels.

✔ **Landscape:** Wide-screen size is 480 x 320 pixels. If one of your app's functions is to search your database, you see a screen mock-up of the search page and then a screen mock-up of the search results page *after* you complete the search. Consider both screens as you create your mock-up.

For a typical User List application, you might need to draw mock-ups of the following user screens:

✔ Main

✔ Add User

✔ Delete User

✔ Search User

✔ Search Results

In Figure 11-5, we provide examples of what these screens might look like.

Creating a full feature list

People always seem to be making lists, whether they're grocery lists or to-do lists or lists of goals to reach in the next year, in the next five years, or in their lifetimes. But when you're making your iPhone application, you need to make another list: the features you plan to implement in the application.

Figure 11-3:
Finding the elements for your mock-ups.

Figure 11-4:
Using the iPhone stencil kit to draw your own mock-ups on paper.

Figure 11-5:
Mock-ups
of the User
List app
screens.

You should create this list before development begins, for several reasons.
You can

✔ Better estimate the development cost and time schedule for writing the
code if you know beforehand which functions you want to include.

✔ Choose developers with the right skill sets for your project, based on
the functions in your list.

✔ Chart your progress and, ultimately, the successful development of your
app against a measurable set of action items for your development team.
Your developers can know that after they include every feature you
specify, the app is ready for testing.

✔ Develop your application documentation and use the features list to
start crafting your marketing message, even while your application is
still being developed.

After you research your app's feature list, you should review the list of features and make your final choices to include in your iPhone app.

You may decide to delay the release of some features or schedule them for a future update or release.

This finalization process helps you mentally prepare for the specific iPhone app you will coordinate through development, testing, and launch.

After you decide what to implement now and what to implement later, stick to your feature list as much as possible so that other features don't creep onto the list later and add time and expense to your project.

Prove your concept with rapid prototyping

One software development concept that has particular appeal within the iPhone application community is *rapid prototyping,* which helps iPhone application developers smooth out, and prove the concept of, what they want their iPhone application to accomplish. Rapid prototyping consists of these tasks:

✔ Quickly designing the basic screens of the application

✔ Assigning programming so that when a mouse click is registered over a button inside a screenshot, the corresponding screenshot is displayed onscreen, making it seem that the application is working.

Suppose that you develop a database application and you design the main screen to hold the Add User, Delete User, and Search User buttons. You're using rapid prototyping if you design each of those three function screens and add some programming so that the Add User screen loads only if someone clicks the Add Button area of the main screen, simulating how the application works.

This concept is already being used by several iPhone app developers, who even load the rapid prototypes on their iPhones so that they can develop a sense of how the screens will look and act on the device itself. We discuss

rapid prototyping in other chapters, but you can start at this stage in your app's development.

If you've already designed your app's screens and defined its functions, you have a couple of ways to simulate a rapid prototype with different sheets of paper, each one representing a different screen.

✔ Display the first screen for a test user, and manually change the piece of paper in the user's view when she says she wants to click a button or enter data.

✔ Tape the paper prototype screens to a wall and examine the data flow that way, as shown in this figure.

You can get instant feedback without yet having to sink any money into programming costs using this method.

Defining the look and feel

After you know which features your app will include and how it will work, and which screens are necessary to code, you have to consider one last element: how your application will look and feel to users. Discuss these questions with your graphical designer:

- ✔ **Buttons:** Will you use existing button designs or make your own?
- ✔ **Color palette:** Which colors will you use for the app's text, buttons, and background?
- ✔ **Input method:** Will you rely on elements such as sliders, scrollable lists, and keyboard entry, or another method?
- ✔ **Consistency:** If your application exists elsewhere (on a PC or a Web site, for example), will your iPhone app look similar to its other versions, or will you create another look and feel in your application?

Looking at the Role of Quality Assurance

Regardless of who develops your iPhone application, you might be tempted to assume that the code is written correctly and everything works as planned. Anyone who works in software development can tell you that, unfortunately, computer programs don't always work as planned. Thankfully, for this reason, all computer software requires quality assurance.

Quality assurance, or *QA,* consists of testing your software and ensuring that it is of high quality. The process involves someone — either a dedicated software tester or anyone other than the developer — trying out your application. The quality assurance tester works through a list of test cases, or *use cases,* to see whether the application works as you intended.

We discuss this process now because, as you create application specifications, you can easily turn those specs into your test case scenarios, letting this list become ready when development is almost complete. Be sure to test your application before releasing its developer from active duty, in case the testers find a bug or a problem that the developer has to go in and fix.

In an ideal setting, you would have the budget and capability to hire specific, dedicated testers to verify that your application works as designed, or you would have the resources to buy a testing application, such as the Squish GUI tester from Froglogic, shown in Figure 11-6. In the real world, though, you or members of your team might have to act as the testers. The key to working through these test cases successfully is to pretend to be an ordinary user who is using this application for the first time. As someone who designed or developed the application, you likely already know what to do in each scenario that users might encounter. The test of an excellent application is that anyone can run the app without experiencing problems along the way.

froglogic's Squish Supports Automated GUI Testing on Apple's iPhone™ and iPod touch®

Hamburg, Germany April 28, 2009—froglogic has announced that Squish, its leading, automated GUI testing tool, will support the testing of Cocoa Touch™ based applications on iPhone and iPod touch devices and simulators.

Cocoa Touch provides an abstraction layer over iPhone OS, the operating system used by the iPhone and iPod touch. Cocoa Touch is based on the Cocoa® API and toolset used for building software for Mac OS X computers.

Squish is a professional, cross-platform GUI and regression testing tool that enables testers to create and execute automated GUI tests for applications based on a variety of different GUI technologies. This includes applications based on Nokia's Qt, Mac OS X Carbon and Cocoa, Java SWT/Eclipse RCP, Java AWT/Swing, Web/HTML/AJAX, and many other UI technologies. Squish stands out from other GUI test tools thanks to its close integration with each supported GUI technology—a feature which helps ensure that tests created with Squish are very robust and stable.

Figure 11-6: You can use apps such as Squish to help test your iPhone apps.

Writing your test plan

After you lay out your specifications, you can create a separate document that lists all the use cases that you want to check when your app is developed.

Have your app specifications in front of you when writing this plan, and keep these guidelines in mind:

✔ **Think of every possible scenario.** If an input calls for a number, try entering a text answer instead. If you need a number between 1 and 8, try entering the number 9. If an input field is required, try leaving it empty. The goal is to test for any potential scenarios in processing user input.

Never assume that users will automatically do the right thing every time. Whether it's intentional or not, they may enter information that the field can't accept and you need to know that your app can handle the error without crashing.

In case there's simply too much incorrect information that users can enter into your app, determine the most likely scenarios and work from there.

✔ **Test for all levels of data, even missing data.** What happens if a user is looking for something that isn't in the database? Make sure that the correct error message or system message is displayed, one that makes sense to an average person (not necessarily a developer) so that users don't become frustrated and close your application.

✔ **Test for different sequences of actions.** Suppose that on one screen, users must enter five pieces of information. Though you should definitely test for the normal scenario of the user filling out each field in order, you can also test for the fields being out of order. Though doing so shouldn't have an adverse effect, make sure that no stray command can cause a problem when the app is running in the real world.

✔ **Try to "break" the application.** If you want to thoroughly test your application, have your testers do whatever they can to cause it to crash.

Be sure that whoever does this type of testing documents his deliberate mistakes so that he can repeat the steps if he finds a sequence or chain of events that causes the application to fail.

When you're ready to write your test plan, focus on the following:

1. **Write the base case scenario of starting your application from an iPhone (or an iPhone simulator, based on your testing capabilities).**

   In your first test case, you should familiarize the tester with starting the application and any initial actions that are required. Here's an example of what that use case might look like:

   Use case 1: Starting the application

   a. *Click the application icon from your iPhone.*

   b. *Verify that the start-up screen matches the screen in your documentation.*

   c. *After the initial screen appears, verify that it matches the screen mentioned in your notes.*

   d. *Click the Home or Power button to close the application.*

2. **After the base case, write at least one scenario that tests for the basic usage of your application.**

   For example, if your app reads the news from CNN, write a use case that has a user select an article from the main page and read it and then return to the main menu (perhaps to read a second article). Here's an example:

Use case 2: Reading a news article

Procedure:

a. *Click the application icon from your iPhone.*

b. *After the initial screen loads, select the first article from the list and tap it to select it.*

   Wait for the article to be displayed on the screen.

   Scroll down the page to make sure.

c. *Click the Menu button to return to the initial screen and repeat Step 2 and 3 for the second article on the list.*

You can write several use cases based on the number of core functions within your application. (Step 2, click Function A from the main menu; Step 3, return to the main menu; Step 4, click Function B from the main menu; and so on.)

3. **Write specific scenarios that test for incorrect input on each screen.**

   After you have tested to ensure that your application works, check to ensure that it still works even if a user makes incorrect entries while using your app. So, every time you ask the user to enter something, write a use case where the tester has to enter incorrect input in the input field.

4. **Write specific scenarios that test for input errors on screens that have input.**

   • **Incorrect:** Entering the numeral 9 when the range for a number is 0 through 8, for example

   • **Invalid:** A letter in a field that accepts only numbers, for example

5. **Make sure that every screen within the application has been displayed at least once.**

   You can write one long use case that loads the app and tests every single function within it, to ensure that you visit every possible page.

Defining success criteria

Though your concept of success for your application may change throughout its development (success in terms of revenue or gaining attention, for example), success in the quality assurance part of the development process means achieving the milestones or occurrences you need in order to know that this app is ready to be submitted to Apple to be sold or downloaded from the App Store. In other words, what does your app need to do to be ready for sale? Your app may not be perfect, but at some point, you should be satisfied enough to say, "Let's just roll it out."

No single correct answer exists. (Well, we hope that your answer includes a set of criteria where nothing is visibly broken or crashes the app.) That's why you should think about what you want to see, guaranteed, before you submit the app to Apple. It's easier to do this now so that you know what to measure and look for, rather than just assume that you will know the signs of success when you see them.

Chapter 12

Assembling Your Development Team

*O*ne of the most challenging and time-consuming parts of creating your own iPhone application has to be the development process. Many people are scared away by the thought, "Well, I don't know how to program. How can I get this idea to work?" Thankfully, in today's interconnected global economy, it's possible for anyone to pull together a development team to write an app. Whether that team has one software programmer or a whole firm working toward your idea, a successful project will have you acting as the coordinator or guide for the team.

In this chapter, we look at the process of building your development team from two angles. If you (or someone you know and can hire) already have some programming knowledge, we review the different tools and skills you need to become an iPhone application developer. Otherwise, we discuss the process of hiring the right developer, the initial steps of looking, collecting different bids on your project, and completing the agreement for them to write the software code to make your iPhone app a reality.

Tooling Around with Your Programming Skills

You may already possess the proper programming tools and software skills to develop an iPhone application. Perhaps you're a whiz at coding C applications or you've worked with Java/JavaScript applications for the Web. Your question might be, "What tools and skills do I need to code for the iPhone?" Here are the basics:

✔ **You need access to a Macintosh computer running OS X.** No way around this: There's no Windows equivalent, and no port available to other operating systems. You have to create all the different files and code bundles on a Mac, and do your compiling and app preparation on a Mac.

If you have access to only Windows or other non-Mac machines, then you need to find, buy, or borrow a Mac and get familiar with using OS X.

✔ **You need to download the Apple Software Development Kit (SDK).** Apple provides a rich set of tools and all the software you need to create, test, and package your iPhone app before submitting it to Apple. *Note:* To receive the Apple SDK, you must join the Apple iPhone Developer program for $99 per year.

We discuss how to register with Apple in Chapter 8. In Chapter 9, we discuss the different parts of the SDK.

✔ **You need to know how to write the software code that makes up your application.** You should know these languages:

- *Objective-C:* Think of Objective-C as an object-oriented superset of the C programming language. Instead of the structured programming language that you might be used to with C, Objective-C works with instances of objects and events that happen to these object instances. In the 1980s, Objective-C got a lot of its syntax from the Smalltalk programming language, especially in terms of the messaging syntax.

  When programming with Objective-C, you need to separate the user interface from the implementation of the classes you use to create objects. A number of books written about Objective-C can take you through the steps of learning and implementing this language in your programming.

- *Cocoa:* If you're thinking of the powdery stuff used in hot chocolate, you're a wee bit off. Cocoa — one of the Apple-specialized object-oriented programming environments — works with the Mac OS X operating system. A series of Cocoa APIs, or Application

Programming Interfaces, allow developers to write programs for the Mac. You can also utilize the programming environment using other languages, such as Python, Perl, and Ruby, but this usually requires something called a "bridging mechanism" that allows the different languages to work together and the Cocoa commands to translate properly.

- *Cocoa Touch:* Within the Cocoa API framework is a set of API commands specifically geared for developers writing programs for the iPhone (or iPod touch). You or your developer will use this specific language to write your application. Cocoa Touch acts like a bridge between the instructions found in the software code of your application and the iPhone Operating System itself, which allows the software to display all the screens and access all the functions that make up your application.

  As an example, Cocoa Touch gives you specific commands to access these iPhone features:

  Multitouch events and controls

  Accelerometer support

  Camera support

  Ability to localize your application

- *XCode:* When you hear XCode, it actually can refer to several things. XCode is a set of tools that allows a developer to write programs for the Mac OS X operating system. Within that set is an integrated development environment, also called XCode, which can be used for Mac or iPhone programs. The XCode toolset also comes with a compiler and debugger, which are used to help finalize the software development of your iPhone application, as the compiler turns your code into byte-sized language the iPhone can understand and the debugger finds any potential mistakes in your software code.

For more information on writing code for an iPhone application, pick up *iPhone Application Development For Dummies,* by Neil Goldstein (Wiley).

Hiring an iPhone App Developer

If you're not a programming whiz, don't worry. Help is not impossible to find. In fact, legions of programmers have the right programming skills and are looking for projects like yours to implement.

Depending on the size and scope of your iPhone application idea, you will have to spend some time finding and hiring the right person (or firm) to handle the development.

Where to find an app developer

You can choose to collect your bids from one developer or from multiple developers. You can choose from a number of freelance sites, such as:

- ✔ Elance (www.elance.com)
- ✔ Guru.com (www.Guru.com)
- ✔ oDesk.com (www.odesk.com)
- ✔ Rent A Coder (www.rentacoder.com)
- ✔ Craigslist (www.craigslist.org)
- ✔ Get A Freelancer (www.getafreelancer.com)

Entire software consultancy firms dedicate themselves to coding your iPhone application (see Figure 12-1) as well. The author's firm, Perceptive Development, is just such a company. Do a simple Google search for a firm or a developer, and then do your homework, which we discuss in the upcoming sections.

Figure 12-1: You can use firms like My First iPhone App to develop your app.

What to look for

When you search for *iPhone application developer* in Google, the search engine returns more than 1 billion hits. We doubt more than 1 billion iPhone developers exist; however, we acknowledge that there are many application developers out there. If you're wondering how to choose the developer that is right for you and your project, seek these qualities:

- ✔ **Documented experience:** Can they point to a completed project, an application in the App Store with their credentials, or any kind of experience that shows they have programmed for the iPhone before?

- ✔ **Specific experience:** Consider the developer with experience specific to your needs. For example, if you're creating a new iPhone game and trying to decide between two app developers, choose the one who has gaming experience over the one who has only app development experience.

- ✔ **Attention to detail:** Did they take the time to answer your request for a proposal properly? Did they complete what you asked them to complete, or did they just send in their cookie-cutter, basic proposal?

- ✔ **Competitive bid:** Unless you have a blank check to develop your app, you must consider the cost. If the right developer costs a little more, it is usually worth it. That said, when evaluating a developer, if the hourly rate or project rate is above (especially *way* above) the average you find, then you have to determine if this particular person has the skills or benefits to justify the higher rate. Conversely, we would challenge you to seriously consider someone's qualifications if their rate is too low. One reason why their rate could be so low is because of their inexperience. You may end up paying this person for more hours to accomplish simple tasks. We discuss billing arrangements in the upcoming section, "What Your Contract Should Cover."

References and a portfolio

Getting a developer's name and number (that is, the bid price) is not enough to tell you whether this developer is worth hiring. You need to ask for references that can answer questions about the developer's past projects, and look over a portfolio of completed work to gauge the abilities of the developer you're considering.

Follow these guidelines to evaluate a developer:

- ✔ **Try to get at least three references.** The more references you get, the better chance you receive an honest, well-rounded opinion of the developer. Remember, not everyone takes the time to respond, so if you count on one reference to provide an answer, you might be asking for issues.

✔ **Ask about the results the developer delivered.** Most of the time, a developer will not give out a reference if the person will say negative things. Therefore, you need to push past the expected glowing comments to ascertain what kinds of results were delivered when the developer worked for this person. Hopefully, you will get a clear idea of how the developer performs in a work-for-hire situation and whether that developer was able to deliver on their promise.

✔ **Ask about the developer's communication.** Chances are, the references won't know too much about specific programming skills, but every reference should have good information about the communication skill of the developer, which is critical to a successful project. Ask about specific ways the developer kept the person informed, the frequency and tone the developer used, and how accommodating the developer was to the reference's questions.

✔ **Follow up on any trends you discover.** If the first reference brings up a point about the developer, such as a style or habit, then ask the second reference to elaborate on that point as well. Talking to references is an investigation, so capitalize on any tidbits you discover.

✔ **Always ask, "Why?"** After you get the facts from a reference, try to add some of the reference's impressions and reactions to your information. Your goal is to get an honest opinion from the reference.

For example, you could ask, "Why do you think the developer would be a good fit?" Anybody can say, "Oh, John was a great programmer." The more details you have as to why John was so great (or not so great), the more you'll feel you're making an honest assessment.

When it comes to evaluating the portfolio, you are mainly looking for depth and breadth in the developer's application experience. Look for someone who has written other applications for the iPhone. Given that this is a relatively new market, if the developer has other examples, such as Web applications or Blackberry, Palm, or Pocket PC applications that appeal to a mobile audience, then consider those, too.

When looking at the iPhone applications that are part of the developer's portfolio:

✔ Does the developer have multiple apps to his credit, showing a deep list of accomplishments?

✔ Does the developer have a broad range of experience with various kinds of applications, or has the developer built an expertise in a certain niche of applications? Is that niche related to the area you wish to go with your application?

The easiest way to pull a developer's portfolio list of iPhone applications is to search the developer's name in the iTunes App Store to see what apps have that developer's name on it (like we did for Mitch Waite in Figure 12-2). However, if the developer did work for hire, you would have to pull up the application by title based on the portfolio the developer gives you.

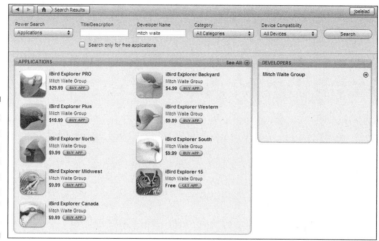

Figure 12-2:
Pull a
list of a
developer's
iPhone apps
to get an
idea of their
portfolio.

Download and use some of the applications within the developer's portfolio to get a sense of the quality and style you could expect if you hire this particular developer. After all, past work is not a guarantee of future performance, but it can serve as a general idea of how the developer could operate with you.

Terms of engagement

When you look for a developer to write your iPhone application, many questions can come up from each party about exactly how the process is going to work. In other words, you need to have an idea of the terms of engagement, or the rules and expectations of how this project is to work between you and the developer.

Have some answers to these questions in mind when you start soliciting a developer:

- Is this the developer's only project or one of many projects?
- When will the developer be working on the project? (Time per day, days per week, and so on.)
- When is the developer available for discussion?

✔ What is the developer's target date for completion?

✔ How often will the developer provide status reports?

✔ What is the payment schedule?

The developer might have a system — a Web site or a freelance agency back-end system — that helps regulate the terms of engagement. Be aware of any restrictions or preconditions the developer's system might impose on you. Be ready to use the developer's payment and tracking systems, too.

Estimating Development Costs

When you collect bids for a development proposal, the first thing you need to think about is the estimated cost. You can study the bids to get an idea of what people are charging for development, but then you have to compare what they are asking versus what you will be asking.

Bids give you useful information:

✔ The hourly rate for a range of iPhone application developers

✔ The general price range for projects like yours

iPhone consultancy firms will give you a free quote, often via their Web site. (See Figure 12-3.) You can submit a few requests to see whether you get a consistent range of responses, and to decide whether that firm is appropriate or if you need to keep looking for a better fit and price.

Figure 12-3: Use the Web to get free quotes to help estimate your dev costs.

Getting competitive bids

When looking for a developer, you always want to get more than one bid. As far as how many you should collect, there is no right answer. You can keep your proposal open for either a fixed period, like one week, or until you get X proposals. (X can be 3, 5, 10, or whatever number you think will give you a wide range of proposals to consider.) You can always extend the period, or X, based on initial submissions, but hopefully, at some point, you will see similarities and know immediately whether the bid is too low, too high, or close to the mark.

When writing your request for a bid, you can arrange it into the following sections:

- ✔ **I'm looking for:** Provide a basic overview of the project you want completed.

- ✔ **I have:** Describe the elements you already have in place.

  - Do you have a full specification, or are you still developing it?

  - Will you be handling the design, or will the app developer need to network with your graphic designer?

- ✔ **I want:** Detail the skills the developer needs to have. In addition to any basic iPhone app programming skills, specify how much experience they should have, whether they need to have access to the necessary equipment already, and what other skills they should possess.

- ✔ **How to apply:** The end of your proposal should detail what the developer needs to do to place a bid. In some cases, you may just want a basic overview of their capabilities and thoughts about the project. In other cases, you may be asking for a full written proposal. You should always ask for examples of their portfolio.

If there's one core skill that you want the developer to have (for example, if you're building an iPhone game, you want someone who has gaming development experience), make it clear in the last section. Something similar to, "Please apply only if you have iPhone gaming development experience" will work.

Comparing developer capabilities

After you receive bids from different people, you need to decide which developer has the best set of abilities and capabilities to hire for your project.

Ask yourself these questions as you are reviewing each applicant's proposal and portfolio:

✔ **Has the developer worked on similar projects?** If you have to decide between two developers and one of them has experience that is more relevant, then that person would get more consideration. You want to evaluate each candidate and look for experiences on projects similar to yours.

✔ **Has the developer worked on similar sized projects?** Look at the quantity and quality of the developer's projects to see whether they match up with your project's size. Has the developer worked on mostly small applications, or focused and contributed to a number of larger applications?

You are looking for someone that will understand the pace and demands of your project's size, especially if you are building a large application.

✔ **Is the developer working solo or part of a team?** Sometimes, you will be hiring a firm instead of a solo developer.

- The upside is that you get the experience and range of the team.

- The downside is that you hope the project isn't shuttled around the team and generally ignored.

  Look at the skills of the team. Look at the team's Web site, if they created one, and if possible, ask the team which member will be assigned to your project (before you pay) so you can evaluate the specific team lead who is focusing on your project.

✔ **What certifications does the developer have?** There is no iPhone App Dev Certification like there is for Microsoft or Cisco products; however, you can look to see if the developer has earned any credentials in the skills he or she needs to code your project. Additionally, some outsourcing firms, like oDesk, administer tests to their freelancers, so that you can get a better idea of who is more qualified. For example, oDesk has an iPhone Programming OS 2.1 Test (see Figure 12-4) that only 46% of its applicants pass, which helps narrow your list.

✔ **Is there information about the developer on the Web?** Sometimes, you can verify the employment history of a developer by doing a search for that person online. You can see whether the person has a profile on a site, such as LinkedIn, to see how many years they've been developing and what skills they list. You can see if they have a profile on job search sites, such as Dice.com or Monster, to help measure their skills as well. Finally, you can verify any Web sites that are listed in the portfolio as being created by the developer.

Qualification Tests » iPhone Programming OS 2.1 Test

Start Test

Read instructions and FAQ for taking the tests before you hit the Start Test button.

iPhone Programming OS 2.1 Test

Syllabus of the Test

Threads
Memory Management
Event Handling
Graphics
Network
Application Architecture
Views
Xcode
Objective-C
Human Interface Guidelines
Internationalization
Audio
UIKit Framework
Address Book

Rules for taking the test

| Duration: | 50 minutes |
| # of Questions: | 50 Multiple Choice questions. Each question has between 1 and 8 options of which 1 or more may be correct |

Test Statistics ⑦

# of Tests taken:	323
# of Providers that have taken this test:	289
# of Qualified Providers:	135
Pass rate:	46%

Hourly Rate, minimum:	-
Hourly Rate, average:	$14.56
Hourly Rate, maximum:	$35.00
Avg # of qualifications:	3.81
Avg oDesk Hours:	470
% working as independents:	40%

Figure 12-4:
To help you decide, see what tests or certifications a developer has.

In-house or outsource?

You may have access to developers within your company or network who can help you develop your iPhone application. In fact, you may have a staff of programmers within your company who are supposed to code any software your company needs, which could include a company iPhone app. In other cases, you may be serving as your "in-house" developer because of your programming skills. Regardless, when you're trying to put together an iPhone app, you might have to ask yourself, "Use an in-house developer or outsource it?"

If the answer is really simple or obvious, then there's nothing to worry about here, right? If the answer isn't so clear, then you need to do a little analysis. Here are some points to consider:

✔ **Are your in-house developers really qualified?** It's very easy for someone to think, "We have a programmer on staff. He can handle it." The truth could be that the programmer in question, while very talented, simply does not have the hardware or specific skills needed to write this application. You will need to speak to anybody who feels this way and explain how the programmer on staff might not be able to do the job, even with some extra funding.

✔ **What extra costs could you incur doing it in-house?** If your in-house programmers have to start buying extra hardware, attend the Worldwide Developers Conference, and take training classes to get up to speed on iPhone development, then you (and your company) are spending more than hours developing the project; you're spending real cash.

✔ **What opportunities is your in-house talent missing to do this app?** You have to factor in what the person could work on if he weren't working on your project. Sometimes, the in-house talent is needed somewhere else for the good of the company, or because the in-house talent's skills allow the company to receive a higher benefit for each of the in-house talent's work hours than the amount you'd spend to outsource the iPhone app development to someone else.

✔ **What are your budget and cost considerations?** In the end, we recognize that budget and cost considerations might force you to "work with what you have" and utilize in-house talent. If that is the case, perhaps you can consider an alternate plan where the truly vital or hardest part of the app can be given to an expert, while the meat of the project stays in-house.

Getting Contracts in Place

After you choose a developer (or development company) to handle the programming for your app, it is time to formalize the deal with a contract. It is very important to lay the proper foundation here and get a valid working contract so both parties can move forward with their interests protected.

If you're using a site, say oDesk or Elance, it will have standard terms to agree to before the work begins. If you're hiring a firm or an independent contractor, you might want to consult a lawyer to help you draw up the necessary paperwork. Other sites, such as Rent A Coder, will build your contract by "interviewing" you, the buyer, and including those interview answers (see Figure 12-5) as terms of your contract.

When you're ready to draft your agreement with a developer to create your iPhone application, there are many things to keep in mind. Here are some key points for your overall agreement:

✔ **Document as much as possible in the agreement.** Do not wait until a problem arises during the development process and then try to decide (between you and the developer) how it is going to be solved. If there are any special arrangements or deals at any phase in the project, document them in the initial agreement.

You should have a clause about what to do if there is a disagreement, such as whether you both agree to arbitration. Include any discussions you've had with the developer, whether by phone or e-mail, in the contract.

✔ **Be as clear as possible.** If there are any vague terms or confusing language in the contract, you could be facing problems down the road. Try to make the contract as clear and easy to read as possible so everyone understands the terms without any doubts or preconceptions. Never assume anything! Make sure they are spelled out in the contract.

✔ **Be consistent.** Refer to the name of your application consistently throughout the document. Do not change wording or use synonyms throughout the contract. Even if you feel like you're endlessly repeating yourself, use the same wording throughout the contract.

✔ **Plan for the worst.** Try to cover any scenarios — any sort of delay, problem, or other event that may occur in the process — with a Termination Clause, an Arbitration Clause, or a Remedy Clause (which are three "lawyer-y" ways of saying what you will do if you have to terminate, or fire, the developer; whether you and the developer will have to use Arbitration in case of a disagreement; and whether you or the developer have to provide a specific Remedy if the contract isn't fulfilled). You probably don't have to plan for natural disasters, but don't hesitate to include something if you think it's remotely possible that it could occur. It's much better to discuss your options before you start than to have this problem down the road with no clear options.

Requirements Interview Answers: NEW

To help you bid more accurately, the buyer was interviewed about the requirements for this project. Below are their answers.

Project Type: What kind of work do you need done?
Software related (Includes desktop applications and internet websites)

Project Parts: What do you want the seller to do on this project?

Requirements: The seller will analyze the problem and propose a software-based solution to the problem.

Programming: The programmer will take the requirements and translate them into the language of the computer (and test it).

User installation: The installer will move the software from the place it was created (which is called the development or QC environment) to where you will use it (which is called the production environment). The installer then tests the installation was done properly and completely.

Req. Doc. Type: What kind of documentation do you want for this project?
Informal documentation - As the buyer talks back and forth about the project with the seller, those conversations become the requirements. Remember to communicate ALL of the details of your project on the Rent A Coder site. If you don't, and there is a dispute, then important details of the contract will not be documented and cannot be taken into account in arbitration. If you feel you MUST go offsite (for example, using the phone or IM) then afterwards post everything onsite and get the other party to post that they agree to those contractual terms.

Program Type: What kind of software should the seller create (and/or install)?

• Other:iphone

Legal: 1) I require complete and fully-functional working program(s) in executable form as well as complete source code of all work done (so that I may modify it in the future).
2) Deliverables must be in ready-to-run condition as follows (depending on the nature of the deliverables):
2a) If there are any server-side deliverables (intended to only exist in one place in the Buyer's environment) then they must be installed by the Seller in ready-to-run condition (unless specified elsewhere by the Buyer).
2b) All other software (including but not limited to any desktop software or software the buyer intends to distribute) must include a software installation package that will install the software in ready-to-run condition on the platform(s) specified in this bid request (unless specified elsewhere by the Buyer).
3) All deliverables will be considered "work made for hire" under U.S. Copyright law. Buyer will receive exclusive and complete copyrights to all work purchased.
3b) No part of the deliverable may contain any copyright restricted 3rd party components (including GPL, GNU, Copyleft, etc.) unless all copyright ramifications are explained AND AGREED TO by the buyer on the site per the seller's Seller Legal Agreement.

Other Requirements:

Figure 12-5:
Sites like Rent A Coder work with you to build terms.

Bid rate versus an hourly rate

Deciding whether to pay a fixed bid or an hourly rate involves looking at a number of differences.

With an hourly payment system:

- ✔ Developers know that they're going to be paid for every hour they spend on development.
- ✔ There is more flexibility to handle adding changes to the program.
- ✔ Client could fear that the developer will be taking longer than necessary to complete the project, so the developer can bill as much as possible.
- ✔ Clients run the risk that by the time they realize the project is over budget with the developer, they've already invested most of their budget and have to accept a higher cost or end the project early.

With a fixed bid payment system:

- ✔ Clients know the final price tag for the development; therefore, they can plan and budget more accurately.
- ✔ Developers could make more per hour with a fixed bid if they are able to complete the project in less time than projected.
- ✔ Developers run the risk of underbidding on the project and being stuck developing for more hours than projected.
- ✔ Clients run the risk of the developer doing "quick work" at the end to fulfill the contract and providing a potentially substandard product.

When deciding which system you want to use, your consideration should include the quality of communication and documentation:

- ✔ If the project specifications and proposal are worded clearly, the developer knows exactly what to do and can estimate the development time better. Additionally, you reduce the amount of confusion and investigation that typically leads to a bigger bill from the developer.
- ✔ If you need the developer to provide more input and direction to the project, find a developer who will include that perspective, factor it into his rate (and subsequently your budget), and guide you and the project to completion.

In an hourly payment situation, offer a bonus or incentive to the developer for a speedy or faster-than-expected solution delivery. It encourages the developer to stay on track, provides a quality solution ahead of schedule, and reduces the risk the development effort will be delayed or drawn out.

If you decide to pay your developer on an hourly basis, you will need an estimate for the hours they plan to work on this project. If possible, try to get detailed breakdowns for the specific tasks they need to accomplish. This is helpful when you compare bids to see whether different developers quote the same amount of time to complete the same task. A detailed quote is also helpful after the developer has started the work. You can measure progress based on initial estimates and get an idea whether the developer's estimates were accurate or way off, and take action before thousands of dollars are spent. Many of the freelancer sites like Elance allow you to track the progress of your job online (see Figure 12-6) so you can see how the developer's progress matches their estimates.

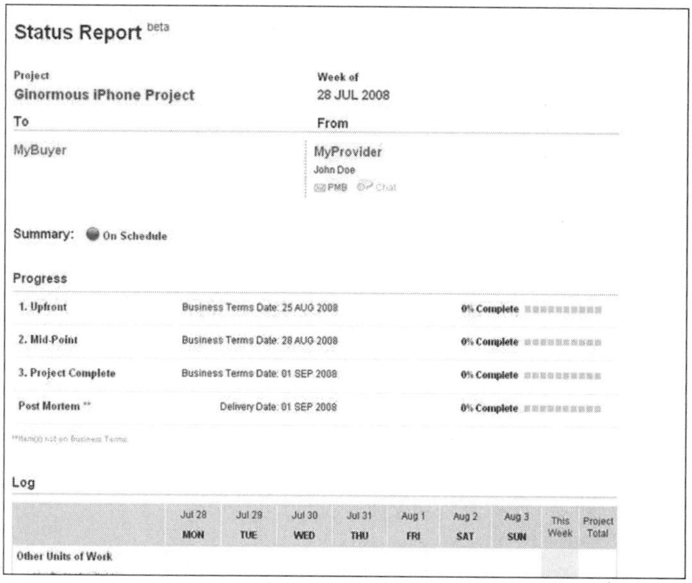

Figure 12-6:
Keep track of an hourly developer's progress on the tasks at hand.

Change management and billing

After the developer starts work on your application, you may run into a scenario where you want to change the specifications and add, change, or delete a function within your application. Perhaps early testing demonstrated that your specs had not accounted for a certain situation, or you discover that your competitors are rapidly adding a new function to their apps that you feel you have to incorporate into yours.

In software development, *change management* defines the way changes are considered, approved, and handled by the developer. Without a change management process, the client could ask for small updates or changes infinitely and the project is never completed.

The simplest way to handle change management is to create a "mini process" where changes are handled as "mini projects." Here's how:

1. Someone (either you or the developer) writes up the summary of the change requested, an overview of the development work needed to implement the change, and an estimate of the monetary cost and the hours necessary to complete and test the change.

2. You and the developer have a meeting where this change request is reviewed and discussed.

3. If both parties agree to the change, then the developer will work on the duties stated, the budget is updated to include the cost of the change, and the timeline/deadline is updated to include the work necessary to complete the change.

If you discover a change needs to be made, and the developer estimates it will take several minutes to complete, the preceding process may be unnecessary or "overkill" to implement. However, your agreement should include a clause that states that any additional changes to the specifications and functions agreed upon will be considered and agreed to by both parties and some sort of consideration should be made that could extend the monetary budget and deadline if necessary.

Licensing and ownership

If you're hiring someone to write the code for your iPhone application and you can pay the rate, then you should definitely consider work-for-hire where you, as the project owner, have a full license to the product that is developed *and* you receive ownership of the code that is created. If you do not receive ownership, the developer could theoretically license out the code for your competitors to create very similar applications.

To find more information about work-for-hire under the 1976 Copyright Act, download a paper from the U.S. Copyright Office (see Figure 12-7) at www. copyright.gov/circs/circ09.pdf.

In some cases, you could work with the developer and receive a particular kind of license to use and sell the created application, but the developer retains the right to adapt and sell the work to another interested party. Because the developer now has more ways to earn money from this work, the client should pay less for the development. This is how many entrepreneurs cut the costs of development although it makes it potentially easier for their competition to offer a competing product to yours.

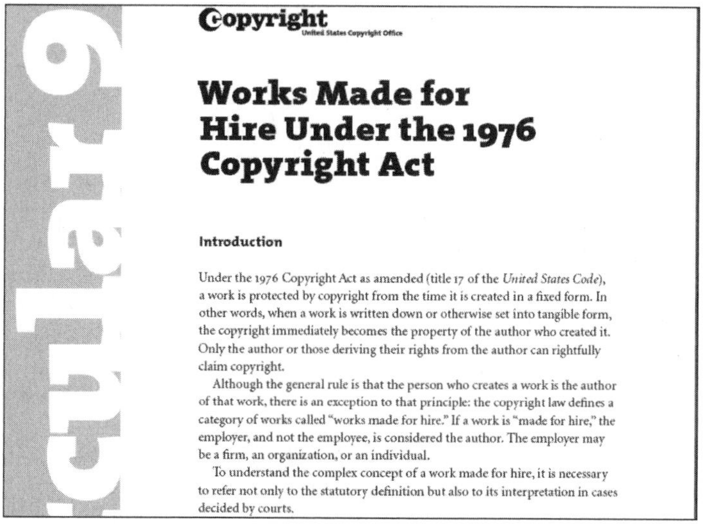

Copyright
United States Copyright Office

Works Made for Hire Under the 1976 Copyright Act

Introduction

Under the 1976 Copyright Act as amended (title 17 of the *United States Code*), a work is protected by copyright from the time it is created in a fixed form. In other words, when a work is written down or otherwise set into tangible form, the copyright immediately becomes the property of the author who created it. Only the author or those deriving their rights from the author can rightfully claim copyright.

Although the general rule is that the person who creates a work is the author of that work, there is an exception to that principle: the copyright law defines a category of works called "works made for hire." If a work is "made for hire," the employer, and not the employee, is considered the author. The employer may be a firm, an organization, or an individual.

To understand the complex concept of a work made for hire, it is necessary to refer not only to the statutory definition but also to its interpretation in cases decided by courts.

Figure 12-7: Ownership of work-for-hire deals from the U.S. Copyright Office.

If you need to create an arrangement where your developer retains some rights in exchange for a lower amount of compensation, it's important to ask for the right kind of license:

- **Exclusive License:** Grants the client a set of rights over the developed application for exclusive exploitation, and the developer retains the ownership rights to the underlying software code. You and the developer would need to agree to a set of terms of how long your license would last and how you could renew your agreement. Asking for an exclusive license restricts your competition from gaining any rights to the code and creates a nice preventative measure against quick competition.
- **Non-Exclusive License:** Gives the client predetermined rights over the application, but allows the developer to sell non-exclusive licenses to other parties for the same application. The developer retains the ownership of the software code, and your competitors have one more way to enter your market.
- **Usage License:** The client can use the software product that the developer created, but cannot modify, repurpose, or resell the software to anybody else. Because the goal of writing an iPhone application is to sell it in the App Store or make it available for download, you do not want this license from your developer. Rather, you make this license available to your customers who buy or download the app.

Source code

Even if you never plan to write one line of computer code, you should always be aware of and ensure that your source code is safely stored and protected. If you ever plan to update your application (which almost every iPhone application requires at some point), you need to give access to your source code to somebody to make the changes. If something needs fixed within your application, a developer will have to look through the source code, make changes, and test those changes to see whether they fixed the problem.

One way that clients can ensure access to their software code is by having an escrow agreement with the developer. In an escrow agreement, the developer agrees to keep an up-to-date copy of all the source code, any dependent code or functions, and all the documentation created for the client. In exchange, the client agrees to certain ongoing maintenance terms and a specific process for receiving a copy of the code when necessary.

Any escrow agreement should include a clause that covers the final distribution of source code, documentation, and other files to the client in case the developer goes out of business or the maintenance agreement ends.

You can create this agreement directly with your developer, or use a third-party escrow service, such as Iron Mountain (see Figure 12-8), to handle your source code. You definitely want to make sure that your source code is backed up and protected in case something happens to your computer or your developer's computer.

Figure 12-8:
You can use an escrow service to protect your source code.

Chapter 13

Greenlighting the Budget

. . . .

. . . .

*A*mazing, exciting opportunities abound all over the App Store as evidenced by the tens of thousands of applications (and app developers) in existence. And folks who want to seize these opportunities have to contend with at least one barrier to entry: the cost of development. An exciting idea needs to have a specific budget so that funding can be obtained and the idea can become a reality. This planning is done to convince someone — you, an investor, or a client — that this application deserves the funding. Creating a budget also helps you plan the development phase before you spend a dollar, which hopefully will translate into a better, more efficient product that can save you money and headaches when you start development.

In this chapter, we cover the two sides of finance: developing a budget for your iPhone application and obtaining funding to cover that budget. We discuss all the major elements of goes into a proper iPhone application budget and give you some estimates to consider as you plan. After the planning comes the pitching, or bootstrapping, depending on your course of action. This is a chapter you can read in the early stages of development, or as you're about to move into development. Make no mistake, though: The planning here is valuable in more than just dollars and cents.

Counting Up the Costs of Developing Your App

You can design the most elaborate iPhone application with a pen and piece of paper, but translating that idea into a working iPhone app will take either money or sweat equity, in the form of working in several specialties to make that happen. Therefore, creating some estimates so you have an idea of the approximate budget before you get really invested in the development process is useful.

We don't discuss secondary elements of an iPhone app budget — such as office expenses, laptops, iPhones, computer accessories, and these kinds of expenditures — in this section. By all means, include those costs in your budget when you know that you're going to need them — and if you discover in the planning process that you need to buy something extra, factor that into your budget as well. Because everyone has a different situation and setup, we leave your budget for these other incidental expenses up to you to decide what to include.

Estimating application development costs

The most expensive element of an iPhone application budget is typically the application development cost, or the programming (or coding) cost.

If you're programming the app yourself, value your time as the equity that you bring to the project. After all, you could be earning money in the hours you spend building an application (whether it's overtime at work or moonlighting as a freelance developer). Many developers make the mistake of writing a budget where the application development cost is zero. You should know what your total "cost" to make the app is so that you know who needs to get paid back first when the application starts making money.

Application development costs usually come down to two elements:

✔ Hourly rate of the developer

✔ Number of hours to write all the code

Your cost for development is simply the hourly rate multiplied by the number of hours.

Some developers include any extra costs — such as the cost of packaging the code after development, the use of their equipment, and any overhead costs they incur — into a fixed price budget. If that's the case, simply use the quote that developer gave you as your application development cost in your budget. (We discuss development pricing in Chapter 12.)

If you're using a developer (or you are the developer) who charges an hourly rate, try to estimate or research to find out the going rate for iPhone application developers. Here are some ways you can find this information:

- ✔ **Research the available jobs.** Go to the freelance sites we discuss in Chapter 12 to see what developers are charging for development work. One example, Guru.com, is shown in Figure 13-1.

  Steer clear of the lowest or highest number you find, but look for the median number that you see quoted most often. (We say *median* instead of *average* because depending on the quotes you find, a mathematical average may not be accurate. If 50 percent or higher of developers or consultants are charging within a certain range, that number is often more useful.)

- ✔ **Get initial quotes from development firms.** As we discuss in Chapter 12, some consultant firms offer free quotes. Describe the app you have in mind to a few firms and see what quotes you get. If several firms quote you about the same price, that figure is likely the most realistic price you will find when it comes time to hire someone.

Figure 13-1:
Get an idea of the going rate from freelance Web sites.

✔ **Ask around.** When we interviewed several people for this book, one of the questions we asked was, "What's a going rate for an iPhone app developer?" At the time of writing, we heard consistent numbers in the $100 to $125 per hour range for a good developer. (When it comes to estimating, you're looking for a consistently quoted number, rather than just the highest, lowest, or most recent number you can find.)

After you pin down a consistent range for the hourly rate, get an estimate of the number of hours it will take for a developer to write the code. This figure is a bit trickier to nail down because the developers you talk to will have to take their best guesses based on your specifications and idea. The easiest way to do this is to simply gather quotes from several development firms and see whether they fall within a consistent range. Keep in mind, though, that you may not get the detail you want without giving out too much information or really discussing a contract with the developers.

Don't waste too much of a company's time getting a super-detailed free quote if you're not genuinely interested in hiring them.

Hopefully, you can do some research and come up with a reasonably accurate number on your own. Now, depending on your programming experience, getting an accurate number will entail some discussions with other people. And this isn't a waste of time: Every discussion will help you gain some insight or knowledge that can help you complete the project, find a good member for your team, and develop the most accurate budget possible.

If you want to analyze the situation like an engineer, your estimation process would look something like this:

1. Break down your application into a list of functions that have to be written.

2. Get estimates for how long each function will take to write.

3. Make a total of all those estimates, and add about 15 percent more time to put everything together and check for initial errors — a process also called *integration testing* — when all the functions are combined.

This is where a detailed specification and function list will really come in handy. You can scour the freelance sites and discussion forums to get developers' estimates for the time it will take to complete a given task. If you know any software developers — even if they're not iPhone app developers — you can ask them how long they think it will take to write software code to do a particular function.

You are looking for answers that are reasonable in terms of *order of magnitude.* That is, what is the length of time to write a certain function? Is it a matter of hours, days, weeks, and so on? Obviously, the cost to develop a function that takes 1 to 12 hours is much less than to develop a function that takes multiple days — say, 20 to 40 hours — to complete. A few hours difference should not affect your budget too much. However, if you estimate that the development of a function will take a few hours and it ends up taking a few weeks, your initial estimate becomes meaningless.

At some point, you will have to provide your own estimates to come to a final number, and having a range instead of an exact number is perfectly acceptable. After all, these are estimates, not concrete figures. Say that after your research, you know that it will take at least 100 hours of a developer's time to write most of your application, but there were a few elements you couldn't get a quote for. You can project a final estimate number by adding a percentage of the cost you already know to cover the rest:

100 hours + (10–15% × 100 hours for unknown)

+ 10–20% × (110–115 hours) for integration × $100/hour

$12,100–$13,800

You could then round your answer to $12–14,000.

This will give you a good estimate. There is a truism in the development community, however, that states that development will almost always take exactly twice as long as you estimate it will take. We find this to be often but not always true. And many developers have internalized this equation into the estimates they give. On a practical level, this simply means that you should prepare for your project to take longer and cost more than you estimate, so be sure to build a buffer into your budget projections.

Getting graphic design for your artwork

One vital aspect of an iPhone application that might be overlooked at the planning phases is the graphic design, on everything from the logo to the buttons and backgrounds that will make the app distinct.

If you plan to do the graphic design yourself, assign some value to the work you're doing make sure to include that in your budget so that you know the approximate equity value of your contribution.

And because graphic design is more art than science, it is more of an "art" to come with an estimate than to scientifically break down a list of functions and assign estimates to each piece. You will most likely need to ask qualified professionals for quotes to project the costs accurately.

Fortunately for you, some of the basic building blocks of your graphic design needs are priced by the project, not by the hour. This is true of your application logo design. Firms can provide you a logo for your iPhone app for a fixed price, regardless of the amount of phases or hours necessary to finalize your app. Consider the following options for getting your graphic design done:

✔ **Flat rate:** Hire a firm like Iconiza (`www.iconiza.com`) to design an app logo for a flat rate of $75, as shown in Figure 13-2.

✔ **Hourly:** Order a quote from a design firm like OrderMakeWork for your logo, at $50 per hour.

✔ **Bidding war:** Post a job request on a freelance site to get graphic designers to bid for the job. An example job request form for these sites is shown in Figure 13-3.

When picking a firm to make your application logo, make sure that firm or designer knows the exact specifications required by Apple to submit your app. Currently, you need two versions of the logo:

✔ 57 x 57 PNG file

✔ 512 x 512 JPG file

Your logo is only part of the equation, however. You can either

✔ Use the standard visual elements available to you through Apple's software development kits (SDK).

✔ Hire a designer or design firm to create an entire set of graphics files to be used throughout your app, including matching buttons, backgrounds, color choices, and other graphics, as well as the matching graphics for your Web site and the application description within iTunes.

There are no great rules for deciding on your logo or graphics. Choosing a route for the graphics in your app is a matter of your priorities. Do you want custom designs that are different from everyone else? Do you want to buy pre-made graphics that are already in use? Or do you want to create your graphics or logo using the tools and resources that anyone can use? If you want one more way to differentiate your application, then investing in graphic design could be the way to go.

Since your options vary so widely, so does the pricing. Hiring a solid designer for a relatively involved iPhone app will probably cost you between $1000 and $5000. For a very simple app, you can probably find someone for about $500. Design is one thing you generally don't want to offshore because of cultural differences, but there are some offshore outfits that do good design for much less. We condone buying American (or whatever your native country is), however.

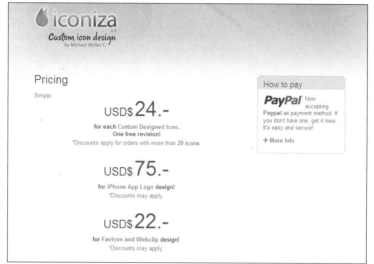

Figure 13-2:
Pay a flat
rate for logo
design.

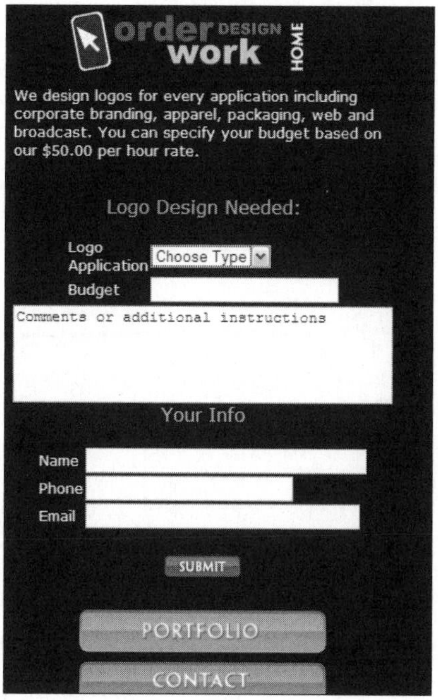

Figure 13-3:
You can also
hire a firm
to design a
logo at an
hourly rate.

If you want to simply use Apple's UI toolkit, you might be able to get away with no designer at all, except perhaps for custom tab bar icons, which can be obtained for between $25 and $100 each. This is best for utility-oriented apps, however, as it won't do anything to give graphic buzz-potential to your app.

One thing is for sure; strong design in your app will go a very long way in terms of differentiating you from the competition. In a category that has a lot of competition already, you may not even be able to compete without a compelling design.

Putting more energy into this area than you might immediately think necessary will often pay off well in the end.

Budgeting for marketing expenses

After you build your application, you need to sell it — or promote it if it's free. Promotion takes time, effort, and in most cases, some money.

Check out Part V of this book for information on various marketing initiatives you can use to generate public awareness and build the buzz, as well as some paid marketing strategies you can use.

Some people may need a marketing professional to help manage and execute a marketing plan. If you work for a company that's launching its own iPhone app, hopefully the marketing department within your company will absorb the efforts and responsibility, which means you don't need to worry about the cost.

As you might guess, the expense for your marketing and promotion efforts can vary widely. For those folks without an in-house, available marketing department, allocating some money in the budget to cover marketing expenses is usually a wise move. Remember that this budgeting exercise is just an estimate. If Apple latches onto your app on the first day of release and does tons of free publicity for you, maybe your estimate never actually is spent — and that's what we call a good problem to have.

You have many options for estimating your marketing expenses. Here are a few of the most popular:

> ✔ **Percentage of your total budget:** Add up your entire development budget, including graphic design, and assign a portion of that total as your marketing budget. Say, for example, that you determine it will cost $25,000 to build your application. You could add an extra $5,000 (20%), $12,500 (50%), or go for a really big push and allocate $25,000 (100%) for your marketing expenses.

✔ **Per specific job:** You can decide which marketing campaigns you want to do and come up with estimates per job either by doing it yourself or hiring a marketing professional. For example, say that you decide to run a quarter-page ad in *Macworld* magazine. (Figure 13-4 shows an example of a price list for magazine ads.) You also send out three e-mail marketing messages, purchase keyword advertising, and purchase banner advertising. Assign totals to each specific campaign and total those to calculate your total marketing expenses.

Figure 13-4: Get prices for specific marketing costs, like a magazine ad.

✔ **A "self-sufficient" marketing budget:** You could allocate an initial budget for a paid keyword advertising campaign — say, on Google AdWords — but continue the campaign only if the sales achieved through the campaign are greater than the marketing expense of bringing in the customer. (See Chapter 17 for specific instructions on how to set up a paid keyword advertising campaign.) For example, if paying 20 cents per click brings in $10 of revenue for $5 worth of clicks, your budget for continuing the campaign comes directly from new sales — not the original budget.

Many "free" initiatives still require someone (that could be you) to implement them: You can write a blog, "Twitter" your app status, or send in app review requests to different review sites on the Internet. In your budget, you should account for ongoing time to market your application.

There are also lots of free publicity options available to you. Blogging, Twittering and review requests are some of them. The creators of iSamurai created a "Guess Our App" promotion that only cost them a few iTunes gift certificates for the winners, and generated lots of buzz for almost no cost at all. They also staged iPhone sword fights outside of the WWDC and Apple Stores and handed out cards when people walked up to find out what was going on.

Pricing the legal costs

At some point in the app development process, you will likely need a lawyer. Just as in any business, creating an iPhone company requires you and those who work for you to sign contracts and can open you up to certain liabilities Therefore, consider including potential legal costs into your overall iPhone application development budget. You may incur legal expenses because of the following factors:

- The size of the application
- The size of the business you wish to create to sell the application
- The number and type of investors that you plan to seek
- The functionality of your app

Some of the activities you might need legal assistance with are:

- Deciding what type of corporate structure to create (Sole Proprietor, LLC, S-Corp, C-Corp, etc.)
- Researching intellectual property issues
- Reviewing contracts you are asked to sign
- Helping to write and/or reviewing contracts you create for others to sign
- Crafting consumer-facing policies such as a privacy policy and terms of use agreement

You can do upfront research on your own with online resources, like the United States Patent and Trademark Office (USPTO; www.uspto.gov). The home page for the patent and trademark office is shown in Figure 13-5. Or check out the Legal section of the Small Business Administration Web site (as shown in Figure 13-6) for more information. A lawyer can cost as much as $500 per hour, so the more time you can spend doing research and figuring out exactly what to ask, the less you may have to pony up for a lawyer.

Your legal costs will also depend upon the types of issues that arise, whether you choose to use one lawyer to coordinate everything or hire specialists for each issue, you do some of the work yourself, or you outsource everything.

Figure 13-5:
The U.S.
Patent and
Trademark
Office has
a wealth of
information.

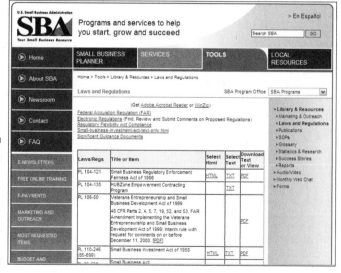

Figure 13-6:
The Small
Business
Adminis-
tration also
has many
answers.

Some of the most common issues developers often factor into their legal budgets include

- ✔ **Trademarking your product visuals:** If you want to create a unique trademark or logo to distinguish your product from anyone else, you will need to register that visual as a trademark with the United States Patent and Trademark Office.

- ✔ **Copyrighting your application:** As we discuss in Chapter 4, if you want to protect your actual code, graphics, or text from being copied by another application or developer, you can file a copyright for your work. You should also include a copyright statement in your text, but consult a lawyer for additional information.

  Technically, your work is copyrighted the moment you create it. Should you need to defend it, however, you'll need to prove when you created it. This can be done by registering it with the Copyright Office at the Library of Congress. While it is not necessary for you to state that your app or designs are copyrighted to make them so, affixing the © mark to an info page in your app will remind potential plagiarists that you intend to defend your copyright. You can learn more about copyright at the USPTO's website or consult your lawyer.

- ✔ **Drafting a terms of use statement:** If you're going to provide an ongoing function or application and you need to show your users of the proper use of your application, you may want a lawyer to help you draft a terms of use statement so you can legally enforce that agreement in the future if necessary.

- ✔ **Coping with liability and infringement issues:** If your application relies on other applications or company functions, if it uses someone else's intellectual property (like a previously created game, someone else's music, or the image of a celebrity), or if it violates users' privacy, you may face liability and infringement issues. Discuss any potential threats with a lawyer now before you launch a potentially hazardous or contentious application into the App Store.

- ✔ **Business incorporation and organizational bylaws:** If you're developing this application independently but want to organize your efforts into a corporation or limited liability company (LLC) so that you are seen as a legitimate business, you need to file the appropriate paperwork with your government. File this paperwork before you start making money; otherwise, you'll have to pay personal income tax on that money (instead of through your company). You can incorporate yourself using documents from sites like LegalZoom.com (www.legalzoom.com) or from firms like the Company Corporation. (See Figure 13-7.)

If you're planning to get investors to fund your business, consider some form of legal structure for your business. A legally structured business — like an LLC or corporation — will help you assign equity to your investors, which they may require before you receive any money from them.

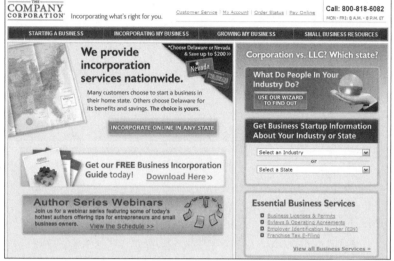

Figure 13-7: The Company Corporation can help you incorporate.

Funding Your Project

You have got a great idea, complete with specifications, a budget, a feature list — everything you need to get started. Now the question becomes, "How do I pay for it?" Thankfully, the entrepreneurial nature of iPhone applications gives you several options for obtaining the necessary funding. You have several options to help you make your iPhone application into a reality.

Self-funding

Many great businesses were started on the backs of the founders . . . and their credit cards. This is true of iPhone applications because self-funding is still one of the most popular ways of funding an application. Perhaps you have to volunteer your time, write the code yourself, buy the elements you need to finish the job, launch the app into the App Store, and then wait for the revenue to fill up your bank account again. This is a perfectly acceptable method, especially if your budget projections are less than your available credit.

Of course, there are other ways to secure your own financing. Traditionally, a small business might pay for a new venture by obtaining a business loan from a bank with backing from the Small Business Administration (SBA). (You can find the information about these loans on the SBA Web site.) If you've written a business plan, app specifications, and a budget, you will have plenty of documentation to accompany your loan application.

A recent trend in loans — enabled by endeavors such as social networks and the Internet — is *peer-to-peer lending*. In this model, you borrow money from other people who pool their money and decide which loans to fund based on the loan requestor's application and credit score. Sites such as Prosper.com (`www.proper.com`) and Lending Club (`www.lendingclub.com`; shown in Figure 13-8) connect people who wish to invest directly with people or small businesses that need a loan.

Figure 13-8:
Check our peer-to-peer lending.

If you're interested in obtaining a loan to finance your iPhone app development by using peer-to-peer lending, here's how the process works:

1. Register with the site you wish to use and create a profile on that site. This profile explains who you are and what your goals are.

2. The lending site runs a credit check on you, and assigns a credit or letter score to your profile so that investors get an idea of your credit and risk potential.

3. You create a lending request — just like filing a loan application — detailing how much money you are looking to borrow and the purpose for the loan. Items such as a business plan or app details can be supplied here, so people can decide whether to invest with you or not.

4. Investors in the lending site see your proposal and profile with your credit information, and decide whether they want to invest in your loan or not. In some cases, there is bidding available as to the percentage of interest they can receive by investing in your loan.

5. When enough investors have agreed to support your loan, the terms and interest rate of the loan are set, and you are approved. An equal amount

of money is deducted from each of the investor's accounts and given to you as your loan.

6. You are given payment terms, which you need to follow by sending in your payments directly to the lending site's accounts. (This information will be provided when you receive the loan.) The lending site redistributes the payments into each of the investor's accounts.

7. When the loan is complete, the parties can sometimes leave feedback about their experience, and you can likely pursue another loan with an improved history thanks to the loan you just completed.

Getting investors

Say that self-funding isn't an option for you right now. Perhaps your iPhone app idea requires more money than you can raise, or you're not in the position to make the investment right now. There's always another option: Other People's Money (OPM). Entrepreneurs and idea holders have long gone out to get investors to back them to build their new idea, and the iPhone application world is no different.

Many investors are eager to participate in the burgeoning iPhone application field because they see the growth and adoption of the iPhone into the market and the success of early iPhone application developers. For example, H-FARM, a European venture capital firm, launched an iPhone seed funding program in 2008, offering $250,000 in prize money to interested app builders, and iMapper was one of the ones who won and got launched in 2009 (see Figure 13-9).

Figure 13-9: Venture Capital firms around the world are funding iPhone app development

Of course, getting an investment means that you have other people's concerns to consider as you grow your business:

- ✔ **Nothing is free.** Typically, you have to give up some equity or revenue in your business in exchange for the early funding, but at least you don't have to max out your credit cards and file for bankruptcy if the idea does not work.

- ✔ **Compromise, compromise.** Your investors may decide that at some point, they want a different managing team in place, especially if your business begins to grow beyond your expectations. Understand that you will have to accommodate some compromise in exchange for the infusion of cash and connections.

Business planning

During the dot-com boom, entrepreneurs would sometimes receive a check from investors based on a good idea or a strong management team. Today, however, investors are looking for a little more — okay, a lot more — in terms of business planning and strategy. You need to demonstrate that you have thought this idea through and that you understand its potential in terms of revenue, promotion, or whatever the end goal of the application is for you. Be sure to do some business planning before you go to potential investors with your hand out for funding.

How to put together a proposal

We discuss how to write a business plan in Chapter 5, so refer to it for any information about creating the important sections of a business plan.

When it comes to investors, make sure you have the following elements in place (in addition to the suggestions we make about business plans in Chapter 5) for the proposal you plan to hand over:

- ✔ **Executive summary**: This is your one-page overall description of your iPhone application idea and execution.

  Avoid using industry-specific jargon or get into minute, technical details on this page. Investors will quickly read this page to decide whether they want to keep reading, so it's got to be simple, compelling, and clear. You don't have to dumb it down, but it's safe to assume that your potential investors should not require a master's degree to understand your executive summary.

- ✔ **Management team:** Many times, investors aren't just betting on an idea; they're betting on the team that is going to make the idea a reality. They may want to get to know the people behind the idea to get an idea of what kind of managers, founders, and leaders you will be if iPhone app is successful, and your new business takes off.

Prepare biographies of all your management team, focusing on your accomplishments in the industry, experience, education, and any other awards, certifications, or achievements that are relevant to your business and help distinguish you and your company from the competition.

✔ **Exit strategy**: We're not talking about how to leave the building, but rather how the investors will be paid back for their investment, allowing them to "exit" the investment. When you're just a small business making money, this is not usually an issue. As a small business seeking an investment, though, your investors will want to know how they can cash out on their investment. There are several types of exit strategies for a small business:

- Have an initial public offering of stock, where the investor's equity turns into stocks that can be bought and sold on the open market, thereby having monetary value.

- Build up enough market share to become attractive to an acquiring company, which will pay the investors for their equity share.

- The management or initial owners of the company earn enough throughout the years that they can do a management buy-out of the company from the investors.

Types of investors

All sorts of investors are out there, but we focus on the four main types of investors you can approach for funding:

✔ **Angel investors:** If you're thinking wings and halos, think again. *Angel investors* refer to wealthy individuals (or small clubs) made up of businesspeople who decide to invest their money directly into new companies.

Typically, angel investors invest anywhere from $100,000 to $2 million to $5 million into a company, and normally they invest in the early stages, from the company founding to the successful launch of the company's first product. These investors fill a void between self-funded entrepreneurs and the venture capital firms, which typically look only at investment opportunities of $5 million or more. One example of an angel investor network is the Tech Coast Angels, which provides funding to technology-focused startups, primarily in the Southern California area. See Figure 13-10 for the home page of the Tech Coast Angels' Web site, www.techcoastangels.com.

✔ **Venture capital (VC):** *Venture capital* firms are companies or funds specifically designed to make large investments in new companies in exchange for a portion of the company's equity or the ability to buy publicly traded stock in the new company. These funds or firms typically look for the large investment opportunities (usually $5 million or more), but they can bring more than money to the arrangement.

Figure 13-10:
Angel
investor
networks
like Tech
Coast
Angels can
provide vital
funding.

These firms are typically well connected within their industries, so they can help recommend new managers and support personnel — and, in some cases, help connect a new company with marketing and publicity opportunities. VC firms can be "hands-on" in coordinating strategy and business with the founders for the day-to-day operations of a firm. Some VC firms are superstars in their industry, and getting funded by one of them can help ensure the success of their new investments.

✔ **Managing investor:** The role of a managing investor is pretty much what it sounds like: This person not only brings an investment to the new firm but also manages the new firm.

Managing investors are typically wealthy business people who want to have a direct hand in guiding their investment. So, unlike other investors who want an equity share of the company in exchange for their investment, managing investors want the equity and control.

✔ **Silent investor:** A silent partner is rarely mute, and is the opposite of a managing investor. Typically, the silent investor can offer one thing: money. The silent investor generally puts up the money and steps back, allowing the company founders to run and build the company.

Silent investors do expect updates, as well as some sort of return on their investment. They're not as concerned with the day-to-day operations, and they rarely provide direct advice or connections.

Finding a client

Sometimes, the answer to your funding woes doesn't come from your credit cards or investors. Perhaps your iPhone application idea is best suited with one particular partner or a set of companies. Some iPhone developers have found particular clients to pay for the development of the iPhone app in exchange for some specific benefit, such as branding of the app or the revenue potential that the app could bring. If you're a developer looking for a financial backer to pay for your development work, perhaps finding a client is your best option.

Of course, finding a client isn't as simple as looking at a wanted ad. Your clients might not know why they need your application, understand the power and potential of the application, or see the necessity for to be involved. Increasingly, companies are seeing the benefit and importance of extending their brand with some form of iPhone application and partnering with a knowledgeable developer can help speed them to market. Here's how to find them:

1. Identify a potential list of clients or companies that could sponsor your development.

   Think about the app idea you've come up with and then brainstorm a list of companies that would benefit from having an app like yours in the marketplace that's either branded with their name or integrated into their company's outreach for customers.

2. Find companies or clients on the list that already have a presence in the App Store. Furthermore, see what online presence these companies have and also whether they have any other applications, Web pages, or functions specifically geared for mobile clients.

When you find companies that have no presence (or you feel their current presence needs to be improved), locate the decision makers within those companies so you can pitch them your idea.

Pitching your idea

Pitching to a client is much like pitching to your investors. You need to be able to explain the following:

- How the application operates
- What kind of return the application is expected to make
- Why you and your team are the people able to develop and launch the application

When you want to pitch a client, though, be ready to answer these specific questions:

- **What is the specific benefit can I (the client) expect to get from this application?** Typically, if the only benefit of your iPhone application is to make money, you would be looking for investors rather than a client. In these cases, you need to quantify what the company can expect to gain from sponsoring this application. For example

- *An increase in sales* of their main product by providing some sort of availability or access through the iPhone

- *An increased customer base* or improved customer retention because the application offers something new and user-friendly

- *A level playing field* with their competitors that may already have iPhone applications, and therefore relevance for their customers

- *A competitive advantage* by offering something new or novel to existing and new customers

✔ **Why did you approach me (the client) specifically?** This question really has to do with the potential fit between you and the client. In other words, you could've pitched this idea to competitors, so why did you choose this company?

Your answer should include a discussion about the company's current strengths and how your idea for an iPhone application fits with the company's presence in the market and its offerings. This is a chance to explain exactly how your iPhone app is what the client needs.

✔ **Why should we (the client) hire you to create this app for us?** Of course, you never want the situation where you get the client all excited about an iPhone application, and then have the client turn around and find some other way to get it done.

After you sell the client on the idea that the company needs this iPhone app, now (in the same pitch meeting) you need to sell yourself (or your team) as the perfect person to implement the idea. In other words, you have to sell yourself. Here is where you talk about your qualifications, some elements of how you came up with the specifics of the application (after all, don't give everything away before they say yes), and how your research and initial efforts have positioned you as the perfect person to handle the development and any unexpected issues that might arise. After all, the client is busy doing its main business, so if the company hires you, you can focus on your specialty, and the client can focus on running the business.

Of course, you need to do as much research as you can on the client before you get an appointment and walk through the door. If the company already has IT or programming staff on hand, you may have a challenge providing the development effort yourself. Then again, if you planned on outsourcing the development effort, you may have found your programmers. The key to this pitch meeting is to present a strong case, listen to comments, objections — and most importantly, questions — to try to find a fit that works for both parties. If you're pitching to a client that has no presence in the App Store, you may have to explain the concepts in a way that's exciting but not scary, and in a way that reminds the client that the reward is worth the risk.

Looking for money? Try the iFund

Kleiner Perkins Caufield and Byers is one of the top venture capital firms in the United States, and it funded many of the popular dot-com companies during the Silicon Valley Internet boom in the late 1990s. It has continued to fund excellent companies and has turned its attention to the iPhone. Specifically, it has created a $100 million fund simply called the iFund. (The iFund Web site is shown in the figure here.)

This venture capital investment initiative is designed to fund innovators who are writing applications and services for the iPhone and iPod Touch markets. The fund is managed by the partners of the firm, with some market insight and support from Apple.

The iFund is open to requests from entrepreneurs and companies at any stage of the process, granting anywhere from $100,000 in seed money to $15 million in expansion capital.

The fund managers are open to products and ideas throughout the iPhone space, but they acknowledge that they have five focus areas:

- Communication

- Entertainment

- Location-based services

- Social networking

- mCommerce, also called mobile commerce, including mobile advertising and mobile payments

You can file an application online at KPCB's Web site by going to www.kpcb.com/initiatives/ifund/apply.php and filling out the Web form or you can contact the fund via e-mail at ifund@kpcb.com for more information.

Chapter 14

Managing the Development Process

So you have your team in place, and you've agreed on the scope of the project. You've paid your deposit, and now you've started the clock — development is in motion!

But unless you're a seasoned software developer, you're going to find out that managing software development is far trickier than, say, having your house remodeled. And if you're not attentive, you may find yourself waiting . . . and waiting . . . for a process that never seems to end.

Building software is a compromise between features, quality, time, and price. The art of software development is balancing these factors in a commercially successful way.

Setting Up Hierarchy and Roles

If you have a small project with just one or two people doing the implementation, project management is pretty easy. For instance, a simple game might require an artist, a software developer, and some friends as testers. You can see the artwork and the storyboards, so that's easy to track, and you can at any time ask the developer "where are we at?"

But once you get more than a few people on the team, you need some *hierarchy.* A developer won't get anything done if they're taking meetings and status calls. And artists, designers, developers, and testers may be working on multiple projects, requiring project management to keep it all straight.

For most software development projects, the primary point of contact between the customer and the people doing the development is a project manager or customer representative. And even if you're developing an iPhone app using a team that's internal to your company, it's always a good idea to sharply define the points of contact so you don't contaminate the process with unintended changes to the plan.

Although some iPhone apps are developed using internal teams or by development teams already familiar with the process, many iPhone app projects are initiated by people who don't have prior experience in iPhone development or even software development for that matter. In these cases, the relationship may be between a stakeholder who has money and an idea, with or without a graphic designer. In these cases, it's very important for the stakeholder to understand what's going on with the developers.

Software development firms tend to work on more than one project at once. To keep a steady flow of work and money, it is necessary to balance resources (iPhone developers, designers, quality assurance, and project managers) with the amount of money (revenue, royalties) being provided by that work.

Often, a customer wants to have a direct line to the developer or designer. "If I could just get the developer's cell phone number, I could tell him exactly what I want." This is a great idea, but it rarely works out that way due to the following reasons:

- **Scope creep:** Offhand, verbal conversations usually result in added features that increase the size of the project beyond what was agreed upon — and paid for.

- **Cross-orders with the project manager:** Talking directly with the engineer may put him in the awkward situation of explaining why he was working on the other project for the last 24 hours. It can also result in the customer asking to just put a feature back in that was formally cut from the spec.

- **Bypassing the user interface designer:** Unless the customer is a user interface designer and is taking full responsibility for documenting, prototyping, and testing out the design, little "improvements" can often be harmful to the full project. For instance, a customer's desired feature may make him happy but be inconsistent when viewed from the perspective of the full application.

- **Slowing things down:** Phone calls take time — time that the engineers, designers, and PMs are not implementing the software. The best way to get an iPhone app built is to find the right team, establish a shared vision, define success, provide the necessary resources, and then get out of the way.

Establishing a Timeline

When you have the right team assembled, you want to watch the game and cheer on the team members. To keep score, you need to establish timelines and milestones as part of the software development process.

If you did your job in building your application specifications (see Chapter 11 for more details on app specs), estimating time is easy. The problem is that rarely is the specification, or *spec,* complete enough to fully estimate the job. The simpler and less sophisticated the application is, the easier it is to estimate. And the closest an application is to an existing application, the easier it is to estimate. However, you're probably not going to win any awards or get rich by making something that's already out there the same way it was already done. Thus, there is always an inherent risk in your timelines.

There's a general guideline in software development, and it's frustratingly consistent: Projects often take twice the time you think they will. Why is software so hard to estimate? Here are the major reasons:

- ✓ **Innovation:** There's always a bit of invention, a bit of creativity, and what's called *engineering risk* — something new or not yet developed. The risky portions of the project — "oh, and integrate bar code scanning through the camera" or "and integrate with Facebook and Twitter" — may seem easy at first. The risky portions of your project may even turn out to require other projects. But unless you know for sure that there's a drop-in piece of software that your developers won't have to write, it's anyone's guess as to how long the risky portion of the project will take. The risky portion may not be new to the industry, but if it's at all new to your engineering team, estimation is just that.

- ✓ **Testing:** Once the application is built, you still need to test it. And debug it. And if it relies on an online service, test integration with that. And make sure it's running. And get the Web site up. And get the promotional materials in place. And get the app approved through the App Store. (Getting an app approved through the App Store is a one-week process sometimes, but it becomes a grueling, patience-testing ordeal when an app has that extra, unidentified something that sets off Apple's approval process alarms.)

When developing an iPhone app, you need to work backward from the goal, list every time-consuming task, add up the times of all the development and non-development related tasks, and string them together in their sequence. You can even map out your tasks and projected time into a project management program like Microsoft Project, or you can draw your own timeline, like the example in Figure 14-1.

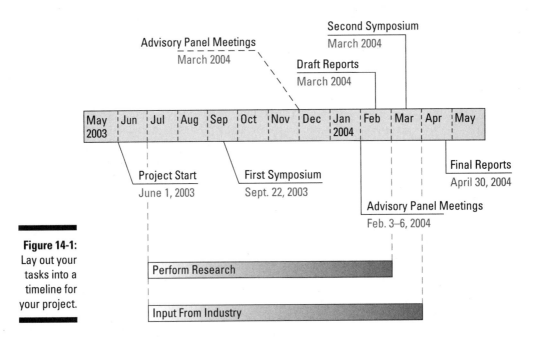

Company
Project Title
Project Schedule

Second Symposium
March 2004

Advisory Panel Meetings
March 2004

Draft Reports
March 2004

| May 2003 | Jun | Jul | Aug | Sep | Oct | Nov | Dec | Jan 2004 | Feb | Mar | Apr | May |

Final Reports
April 30, 2004

Project Start
June 1, 2003

First Symposium
Sept. 22, 2003

Advisory Panel Meetings
Feb. 3–6, 2004

Figure 14-1: Lay out your tasks into a timeline for your project.

Perform Research

Input From Industry

The Software Development Process

You can choose from several methods of managing a software development process, depending on the size, scope, complexity, and purpose of an application. However, the Apple lumps all iPhone software under the term *app,* blurring the distinction. Thus, someone may erroneously try to apply a project management technique that works fine for a marketing Web site to a complex client-server app.

Creating the specification

You can achieve a good specification for your project in different ways:

> ✔ **Build a specification based on specs for another, similar app.** If you're duplicating an existing application or porting an application from another platform, building a spec based on the specs for the original application can help you a lot. You can obtain (or reverse-engineer) a feature list from the existing application. This alone saves a lot of time,

and shortens the communication between the stakeholders (including the people writing the checks) and the people implementing the app. If you can point and say "it's done when it does what that other app does, but on an iPhone," that can sometimes be enough of a spec.

✔ **Build an original specification.** A more formal spec is better. In the situation where the customer is or has an artist capable of user interface design, the spec can and should include mock-ups (either the exact screen shots, mocked up on Photoshop, or *wireframes,* schematic stick-figure renderings of each screen in the app). By flowcharting the entire application, you can eliminate the majority of confusion between the customer and the developers. For example, when the designers of iSamurai were going to build their app, they created a detailed flowchart (see Figure 14-2) as their guide to development.

If you're relying on the iPhone developer to provide the specification, that's fine — but you'll need to pay for this, too, and if you skimp on it, any ambiguity in the spec may not be decided in the customer's favor. The spec should reflect the agreement on what the app is going to do and should be just detailed enough to provide something that, if completed, would be successful.

That doesn't mean that the spec has to be never changed. In the course of developing the application, things invariably change or get improved, or plans that worked out on paper just don't work in practice. This is natural.

Also, routine details don't have to be painstakingly described. For instance, the spec may simply say "a config screen will let you set most parameters for the app, including timeout values, name, and password." That sentence alone may be enough to get the results needed.

The key in all of this is to have a fairly complete spec agreed upon before you start development.

Building the application

When you have your specification nailed down, getting the application developed is just a matter of time. The engineer or team that's doing the programming will translate the spec into code that runs on the device.

Because of the critical nature of iPhone user interface, some development is done collaboratively with the specification process. For instance, a programmer may take screenshots — mocked up in Photoshop — and then put them into a sort of dummy application that responds to clicks. The app doesn't do anything, but a tester can fully run through it on the phone to see whether the interface design is holding up to scrutiny.

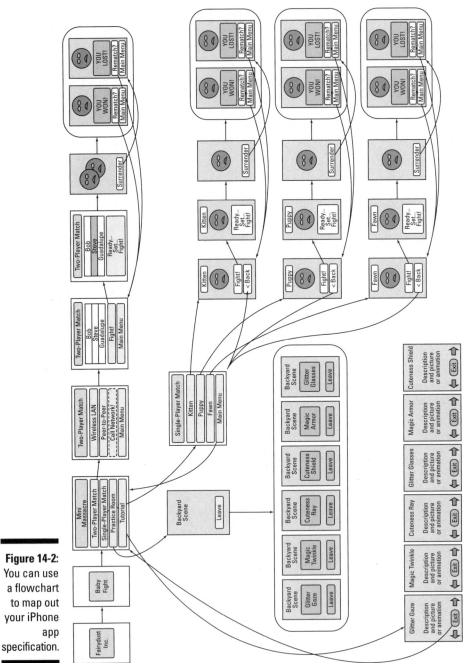

Figure 14-2:
You can use
a flowchart
to map out
your iPhone
app
specification.

Software development at a glance

Although many software management techniques and methodologies are available, they
all boil down to a similar set of tasks, as shown
in the following figure.

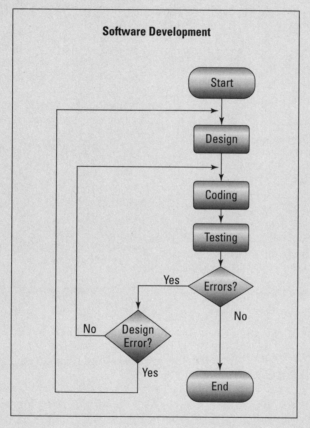

Spec, Build, Test, Fix, Ship

1. You have to specify, or define, what the
   product is going to be and what requirements the software has. The specifications
   need to be pulled together in one or more
   coherent and agreed-upon documents.
   These become the agreement (and possibly part of the contract) between the
   people developing the application and the
   customer or department.

2. When a spec has been more or less agreed
   upon, it's time to build the application. If the
   spec was well done and correct, the engineers can simply implement every feature
   in the spec, one by one.

   Sooner or later, the engineers will have
   an *alpha* build, something without all the
   features that can be looked at. Then they'll
   arrive at a *beta,* a term usually used to
   describe a feature-complete but not-fully-
   debugged version of the app.

(continued)

(continued)

3. When a beta stage is reached, it's time to test. One of the biggest problems with resource and time allocation in development is that people forget that finishing the software is only the beginning of a long test-and-repair cycle. Now it's time to get quality assurance (QA) testing in place, test the application yourself, and get it out to your beta testers. (You've signed up dozens of them, right?) Then you have to collect all the feedback from these testers and ensure that the feedback gets back to your developers.

4. When you start fixing bugs, here's where you really learn how complicated it can get. You have to perform *triage,* sorting bugs just like an emergency room sorts patients. You need to decide whether a bug is a show-stopper that must be fixed before you can ship or whether it's just an annoyance you can leave in. Also, you have to carefully sift through new feature requests masquerading as bugs or software defects — and curb your own impulse to keep tinkering with the application before you ship it.

5. Depending on how long it took you to get to testing or how well you did the specification, you may find that you have to add or change features toward the end of the project, or that while you were in development, external factors have changed the scope of what you must now accomplish. Working to keep up with such external factors can be like trying to hit a moving target.

Depending on your team members, their training, and the type of project, you might be using different software development methodologies, but the basic elements remain. The basic waterfall technique follows the preceding pattern. Some techniques loop around the spec-build-test cycle many times during the process, so you always have a fairly stable, working, if feature-lean, product.

But once the application is really being built, it needs to be understood that this early effort is essentially thrown away, and the real development begins, connecting the graphics to the actual code that will make the application come to life.

Estimating the time it's going to take to finish the development is completely possible. It simply depends on the experience of the engineer and the absence or elimination of unknown factors. Or in other words, experienced iPhone developers know how much time they need to implement certain features, and the only elements that will throw off their estimates are things they've never done before and can only guess at in terms of time estimates.

Milestones

After you start, how do you know at any given time whether you're on schedule? To track your project status, you should use milestones.

In project management, *milestones* are the markers that are used to establish how things are proceeding on a weekly, monthly, or even yearly basis. It's not practical (and it can destroy productivity) to ask for constant or random updates on a project. Milestones are also used as synchronization points, when multiple subgroups working on the same project, such as artists and engineers, can integrate their work.

Here's a simplified example set of project and development milestones for a hypothetical iPhone game:

- ✔ MS1: Contract signed
- ✔ MS2: Spec agreed upon and signed
- ✔ MS3: Mock-up application and major artwork signoff
- ✔ MS4: Implementation of basic game motion and mechanics (no enemies, one level)
- ✔ MS5: Implementation of AI enemy engine
- ✔ MS6: Implementation of peer-to-peer feature
- ✔ MS7: Implementation of all ten levels
- ✔ MS8: Final graphics implemented
- ✔ MS9: Feature complete, to QA for testing
- ✔ MS10: QA signoff, submitted to apple
- ✔ MS11: Apple approved, ship date set
- ✔ MS12: Launch site, marketing, and PR launch

In practice, the engineering team may have good reasons to carve up the milestones in a different order, to implement full gameplay before levels, to implement final graphics at the beginning, and so on. The key is to figure out a realistic set of roughly equal chunks of work that can be objectively declared complete. With these milestones, progress on the project can be tracked and monitored, and production targets and goals can be set. You can chart your progress with milestones and tasks by laying them out in one project file.

Keeping on track

The *stakeholders* (check writers and other important people with something to say about the project) should agree with the timeline containing the estimates of when each milestone will be complete. After these milestones and dates are set, the key is to stay attentive.

Many, many of the delays in software development are communication-based. This is especially true during the testing phases, but it comes up frequently in the development phase as well. Some customers wander off, checking in after a month only to find that the engineers have been legitimately stopped by the lack of artwork or other inputs to the process. Before you curse them as helpless lemmings, you may want to review your e-mail and their impassioned pleadings that they get the final artwork, or your sign-off for a design, or an answer to a key question without which they can't move on.

Communication delays add up, just like traffic on a freeway. The engineers send an e-mail on Thursday asking for a clarification. An incomplete answer is sent back mid-day Friday by an inattentive customer. The weekend passes by; next Tuesday, a key milestone is missed. The answer to a simple-but-showstopper question can completely pause software development. Software specs aren't perfect blueprints, and there isn't always something else that an engineer can work on while awaiting an answer.

Thus, keeping on track has a lot to do with making sure that all dependent elements of the process — artwork, specification, feedback, design work, corrections, bug fixes, and most of all, decisions — are supplied to the development team in a timely and unambiguous manner.

The art of being a software customer, after a good team is in place, is to watch the process and make sure that you're holding up your end of the bargain. Make sure you provide everything you've committed to — not to cover yourself in case of a dispute, but because that's what's necessary to get software done. Also, make sure you check in frequently enough to know whether the process has stalled, so you can unstick it.

Even if you're not the project manager, you can monitor and repair the process if you've agreed on good milestones.

Testing the application

Many modern development strategies emphasize a test-as-you-go strategy, avoiding an overwhelming test stage at the end by testing throughout. Even if your development group is using one of these methodologies, there will still need to be beta testing at the end to ensure the product works as finally built.

Time spent testing your application is time saved in the submission process to Apple. When you submit an app with a noticeable bug to the app store, you could add weeks of delay as your app falls out of the approval queue for you to fix it.

As a customer, you should clarify what testing responsibilities are held by the developers and by you. Developers by the nature of their role are not the right people to find bugs. Their job is to make an application work correctly; a tester's job is to break it. Developers may unconsciously avoid buggy behavior by simply always clicking the correct buttons correctly. A tester will click the wrong buttons, click them multiple times, make random gestures on the screen, click too fast, and perform other such acts of punishment on the application. They will use it in ways it was not designed to be used, just like the mass of critical end users will do when they get their paws on your inno-cent application.

If the group or firm you contract to develop your application provides the testing service as well, ask them these questions:

✔ How many testers will be used?

✔ How extensive will the beta testing be?

If the secrecy of the application is especially critical, you may need to handle this internally with only trusted testers. If you want to set up testing profiles with Apple so your testers can install the application (see Figure 14-3), you can request the proper codes by going through the iPhone Dev Center.

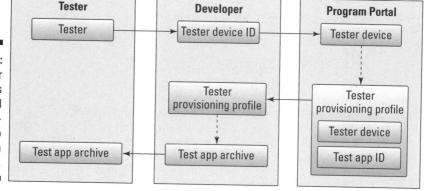

Figure 14-3:
Have your testers download the appli-cation to test it on an iPhone.

Untrained testers may not be good enough. While you can get some superficial testing done by installing it on some friends' iPhones, without a commitment on the part of the testers to spend a certain amount of time with the app and to go to a Web site and write up their experience, you may not get sufficient feedback. (We discuss writing test cases, which can help ensure a smooth test-ing cycle, back in Chapter 11.)

The key to bug fixing is *repeatability:*

✔ If you can repeat a bug, in almost all cases it can be fixed by the engi-neer, often quickly.

✔ If you can't provide steps to repeat a bug, no matter how furiously you insist that the bug comes up all the time, the engineer won't be able to fix it.

When you have a working flow of bugs being reported, with steps on how to reproduce them, you have another responsibility: deciding what to fix.

Software is never done; it simply gets shipped. You have to decide, in collaboration and negotiation with your development partner, which bugs have to be fixed and which bugs the users can tolerate. You may assume that as a customer, any bug you report should be fixed, but this is rarely the case. Rather, most development contracts state that all bugs you report *before signing off the contract* will be fixed, and for a certain time after that additional bugs will be fixed as part of software maintenance. Because bugs are a fact of life, it's very good policy to talk openly and frankly with your development team about how you will deal with pre-ship bugs, beta testing, post-ship bugs and software maintenance.

Thus, as a customer, it's important that you work out the following details with the developers regarding the testing process:

✔ Who is going to run the beta testing?

✔ How many people will be involved?

✔ How are bugs going to be reported?

✔ What constitutes shippable quality?

✔ How will post-ship bugs be handled?

In the process of testing, many times you can discover that the design of the application wasn't perfect. But changing the design of the application, even a little, is often not bug fixing but, more properly, adding features. If a proposed "bug fix" adds new features to the application, which themselves need to be beta tested, this can create an interminable cycle that prevents the application from ever shipping.

Iterating (repeating) the build-test process

In many modern development strategies, the phases of spec-develop-test-fix are looped, so that it goes spec-develop-test-fix-develop-test-fix, or even spec-develop-test-fix-spec-develop-test-fix, over and over until the application is finished. This hand-crafted approach is better in many ways at providing visibility to customers because there's always *something* to show at any stage of the process. These iterative design approaches are also good because after the minimum set of features have been implemented, the application can be shipped if time is critical.

An iterative process isn't always the best choice. If you have a hard deadline, it may make sense to stick with a traditional approach where the developers work to get the basic set of features implemented, and one big test-fix cycle gets the app in good enough shape to ship. But this decision rests with the development manager, and it's the responsibility of the customer to communicate the goal, including the dynamics of the ship dates, how critical marketing and other deadlines may rely on the ship date, and so on. Armed with all the data and customer trade-offs, the engineering team can best decide which approach to take in developing the app on time and, with any luck, under budget.

Incorporating needed changes into your application

A major benefit of an iterative approach is that it allows late modification of the design. Many times, no matter how much work goes into the user interface design during the spec stage, it's all theoretical until someone actually runs the app. Ideas that seemed great at the time can turn out to be duds, either because they're too slow, because they couldn't really be implemented, or because they just didn't make sense to end users.

In any of these cases, an iterative process will not only allow them to be tested sooner (because testing is integrated into a weekly or monthly cycle, not three months after development starts) and thus the feedback from end users can be quickly integrated into a design meeting early into the project.

Handling unexpected cases

Sometimes, factors external to the project change the requirements midstream. Competitive project launches, new or changed stakeholders, a change in funding situation, or the addition of new strategic partners are just a few of the situations that could lead to changes in the middle of a project.

Even if a straight-through, non-iterative approach was being taken to develop the software, changes such as these may make it necessary to press "reset" and reevaluate priorities. Do you still need those extra levels? Do you have to connect to all three online services today? Can you take out the ads and make a pay version? All of these questions may lead to the answer that it's time to go back to the drawing board and see what's going to change and what's going to stay the same.

A key part of iterating design is to document the process. It's such a common occurrence for companies to perform a beautiful specification ritual at the beginning of a project and then let the project morph throughout and never look back at the spec. In the interest of time, sometimes this is necessary. But it's possible that the new ideas were already considered — and thrown out for good reason — at the beginning of the design process.

Any changes to the spec should be treated with suspicion as a matter of practice. An iterative process may provide a time to look again at the spec and see what needs to change, but if changes are made, they need to be documented, if not formally, at least agreed upon. If all relevant stakeholders are engaged in the process and getting new builds of the application and delighted by the changes they're seeing, a formal process may not be necessary. But to prevent misunderstandings and disagreements, especially over a customer/developer boundary, it's always best to put it in writing.

Submitting Your Completed App

After you've built your app, tested it, and have it working to your satisfaction, you can submit it to the App Store. (See Figure 14-4.) But you're not out of the woods yet, because the App Store is another testing and qualification milestone that has to be passed:

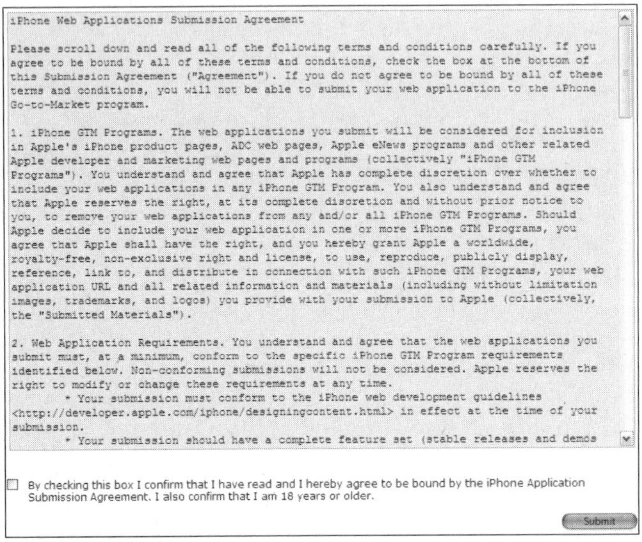

iPhone Web Applications Submission Agreement

Please scroll down and read all of the following terms and conditions carefully. If you agree to be bound by all of these terms and conditions, check the box at the bottom of this Submission Agreement ("Agreement"). If you do not agree to be bound by all of these terms and conditions, you will not be able to submit your web application to the iPhone Go-to-Market program.

1. iPhone GTM Programs. The web applications you submit will be considered for inclusion in Apple's iPhone product pages, ADC web pages, Apple eNews programs and other related Apple developer and marketing web pages and programs (collectively "iPhone GTM Programs"). You understand and agree that Apple has complete discretion over whether to include your web applications in any iPhone GTM Program. You also understand and agree that Apple reserves the right, at its complete discretion and without prior notice to you, to remove your web applications from any and/or all iPhone GTM Programs. Should Apple decide to include your web application in one or more iPhone GTM Programs, you agree that Apple shall have the right, and you hereby grant Apple a worldwide, royalty-free, non-exclusive right and license, to use, reproduce, publicly display, reference, link to, and distribute in connection with such iPhone GTM Programs, your web application URL and all related information and materials (including without limitation images, trademarks, and logos) you provide with your submission to Apple (collectively, the "Submitted Materials").

2. Web Application Requirements. You understand and agree that the web applications you submit must, at a minimum, conform to the specific iPhone GTM Program requirements identified below. Non-conforming submissions will not be considered. Apple reserves the right to modify or change these requirements at any time.

* Your submission must conform to the iPhone web development guidelines <http://developer.apple.com/iphone/designingcontent.html> in effect at the time of your submission.

* Your submission should have a complete feature set (stable releases and demos

By checking this box I confirm that I have read and I hereby agree to be bound by the iPhone Application Submission Agreement. I also confirm that I am 18 years or older.

Submit

Figure 14-4: Submitting your app to Apple via the Dev Center is only the beginning.

- Some applications get approved in less than a week.
- Some applications are rejected because of a bug.
- Some applications are rejected with a short statement that they've violated App Store guidelines, such as by containing objectionable content, or by duplicating functionality. The App Store will sometimes approve risqué apps or apps with advanced functionality that was rejected in another app. The Apple approval process is a crossover to the entertainment industry, similar to approvals for console game platform. The Apple emphasis on being "fashion police" to iPhone apps is probably one of the reasons for the recent renaissance of mobile application development.

The basic intention of Apple is to keep application quality high, to prevent problems due to poorly running or potentially harmful applications, to create a chain of accountability so that if an application does start misbehaving, it can be deleted from the App Store. But in the process of carrying out those benign intentions, other factors come in:

✔ An ever-present issue is *objectionable content,* where interest groups create PR discomfort for companies that endorse or even permit what they view as objectionable.

✔ Apple doesn't want you to replace the core features of the iPhone such as e-mail, media playback, and so on. We've seen Apple reject a podcasting application (see Figure 14-5) for "duplicate functionality" and then come out with its own podcasting feature.

✔ Testing whether the application crashes, but even this test can add weeks and weeks when several loops have to be done and when, as in any testing, Apple can duplicate the error but the engineers who developed the application cannot.

✔ Approval standards change over time. There was tremendous pressure on Apple to approve a line of flatulence-based applications that were not lewd but more distasteful. Now, these noisemaking applications are prolific and acclaimed. So if your application isn't getting approved right away, have heart, for you may be a vanguard, and after yours gets approved, an entire subeconomy of similar apps may follow.

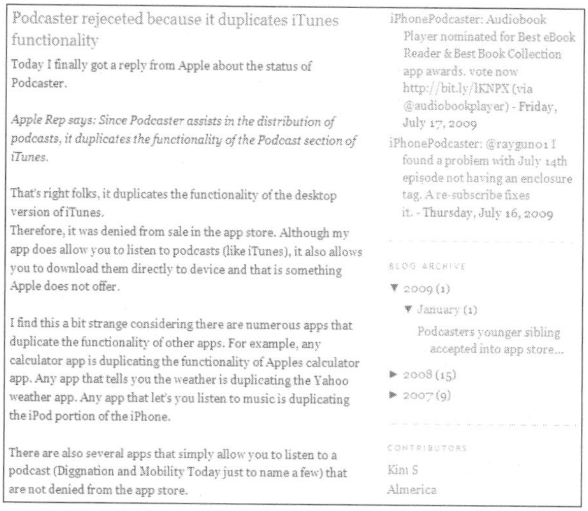

Figure 14-5:
Your app can be rejected if Apple senses duplicate functionality.

Podcaster rejeceted because it duplicates iTunes functionality

Today I finally got a reply from Apple about the status of Podcaster.

Apple Rep says: Since Podcaster assists in the distribution of podcasts, it duplicates the functionality of the Podcast section of iTunes.

That's right folks, it duplicates the functionality of the desktop version of iTunes.

Therefore, it was denied from sale in the app store. Although my app does allow you to listen to podcasts (like iTunes), it also allows you to download them directly to device and that is something Apple does not offer.

I find this a bit strange considering there are numerous apps that duplicate the functionality of other apps. For example, any calculator app is duplicating the functionality of Apples calculator app. Any app that tells you the weather is duplicating the Yahoo weather app. Any app that let's you listen to music is duplicating the iPod portion of the iPhone.

There are also several apps that simply allow you to listen to a podcast (Diggnation and Mobility Today just to name a few) that are not denied from the app store.

iPhonePodcaster: Audiobook Player nominated for Best eBook Reader & Best Book Collection app awards. vote now http://bit.ly/1KNPX (via @audiobookplayer) - Friday, July 17, 2009

iPhonePodcaster: @raygun01 I found a problem with July 14th episode not having an enclosure tag. A re-subscribe fixes it. - Thursday, July 16, 2009

BLOG ARCHIVE

▼ 2009 (1)
  ▼ January (1)
    Podcasters younger sibling accepted into app store...

► 2008 (15)
► 2007 (9)

CONTRIBUTORS
Kim S
Almerica

Factor these app-approval guidelines into your schedule:

✔ If your app is similar to something in the store already and doesn't do anything technically new, you should sail through quickly if it works.

✔ If your app has anything that you think involves a higher content rating, many weeks may be required to work through the approval issues.

✔ If you're breaking ground technically, expect delays. New features require more testing.

   • If the feature makes clever use of Apple's APIs and shows the phone in a good light, it may actually speed things up.

   • If the feature creates questions of whether you used unreleased API features or it doesn't look like you should be able to do that based on the public API, you can expect additional scrutiny as your tester checks with his manager.

✔ If you're running close to features that could be interpreted as duplicate functionality, expect delays (even if it's very clear to you how different it is).

✔ If your application works with external hardware that plugs into the iPhone, you won't want to advertise that feature unless that hardware is properly licensed in the Apple "Works with iPhone" hardware programs.

✔ If you aren't getting your way after many tries, it can be hard to escalate within the Apple communication framework, and you may feel like you're trapped in a black box with no way out.

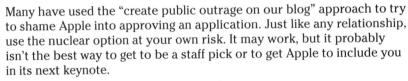

Many have used the "create public outrage on our blog" approach to try to shame Apple into approving an application. Just like any relationship, use the nuclear option at your own risk. It may work, but it probably isn't the best way to get to be a staff pick or to get Apple to include you in its next keynote.

The key to hitting your release dates is to plan ahead. You have to factor in the Apple QA process just as you might factor in your own. Factor in several weeks for the app approval process.

You don't have to ship as soon as it's approved; you can get that out of the way, get the marketing and Web site in order, and then launch the application when you're ready.

Part V
Market to the Masses

In this part . . .

An ethereal voice might promote a baseball field in the middle of a farm, but it doesn't quite hold true about your iPhone application once it launches into the App Store.

In this part, we take a look at the different ways you can market yourself and your application to the buying public so they can be aware of, buy, and use your iPhone app. We go through the basics of generating publicity, whether it's writing press releases or getting reviews. We cover a lot of the ways you can build buzz for little or no money — just some of your time and ingenuity. If you have more money for promotion, we detail some of the paid advertising options; they may be cheaper than you think.

The whole goal is to get you into an online conversation and presence with the public so they can learn about you, your application, and your future.

Chapter 15

Capturing Free Publicity

· ·

· ·

Some people think the development job is done the moment Apple approves the application and the new app is available for sale in the App Store. After all, Apple runs TV commercials, places the magazine and newspaper ads, and funnels all traffic through iTunes to the App Store for the tens of thousands of apps out there.

The good news is that Apple iPhone users are very loyal and eager to download new apps to their phones; they rely on the different lists from the App Store, such as New and Noteworthy, Staff Picks, and the Top 100 list. There is one slight problem – okay, not a *slight* problem, since it's measured in tens of thousands. Namely, tens of thousands of applications are *already* in the App Store, and the number grows every day! Unless Apple picks your app for its next TV commercial, you will need some other way to rise above the noise and make a name for yourself (and your app) in the iPhone app community.

The first step is let people know that your application is available — and that it serves a particular function. The best way to do that (just now, anyway) is through reviews. Although Apple lets users review the apps they download, there are *also* lots of Web sites that constantly review the newest apps out there. These reviews give potential customers a better sense of what the app can deliver, and whether it's worth their money (or time) to go get it. Because recommendations are still one of the most powerful ways to encourage a sale, we're going to discuss how to approach these sites and get your app reviewed, as well as other techniques you can employ — such as writing articles — to let people know about your iPhone application.

The Importance of Getting Reviewed

An iPhone owner can choose from tens of thousands of applications to download to his or her phone. Naturally, a quick browse of the App Store is nowhere near thorough enough to give users a good working sense of what's out there, so they need help and information. These users are looking to know why they should pick a certain app and what they can expect from using the app. From that need, a host of iPhone application review sites sprang up, along with regular features found in places like *The New York Times*, *The Wall Street Journal*, *USA Today*, and other publications — in both their hard-copy and online versions.

Every review you can get of your application is another way to visibly promote your app and attract attention to it (and, from that attention, generate sales of your paid app or downloads of your free app). It's an available way to rise above the noise of so many applications. Each review gives your potential customers insight into how your application works, briefs them on what its strengths are, and could even get them into the mindset of *wanting* the benefits they would receive from getting your particular application.

Specifically, what you're looking for are positive reviews of your application. If your app keeps getting negative reviews, it's a pretty clear picture of what you need to fix. When you get positive reviews, you also get more links to your promotional Web site, as the review will point people to your app, and potentially to some testimonials you can use in your future advertising.

If you have received negative reviews about your app, and you've launched an update to your app that corrects the problems mentioned, contact the app review sites just as soon as the fix is out there; let them know that you've fixed the situation and ask for another review or an update to the original review.

Overview of iPhone app-review sites

As more and more applications became available, Web sites that catered to Mac or iPod news had to expand their coverage to start discussing and reviewing all the applications now available on the iPhone. Entire Web sites appeared almost overnight, dedicated solely to offering reviews of different iPhone applications:

- Some review sites are highly specialized, covering only a category of applications (such as Games).
- Some review sites allow you to compare applications, see video reviews, or download reviews as a podcast.
- Some review sites are part of a larger entity that may cover the iPhone, Apple products, technology products, or even general news.

Chapter 20 profiles important review sites — be sure to check those out, and when you've done that, submit your application to be reviewed on those sites. Hopefully you identified a number of sites when you did your initial research into the market, but you can follow up readily: Search for "iPhone app review sites" on Google or Yahoo. You can even add some keywords referring to your niche to get the most targeted sites.

How to write a press release

The most uniform way to get publicity about your new iPhone application is to send out a press release to the media. A press release announces all the facts about your new iPhone application launch, or whatever event you are coordinating in conjunction with or associated with your new app. Journalists, bloggers, and Web sites receive press releases every day that help influence what stories are developed and published.

Therefore you need to write a well-formatted press release that not only meets the expectations of its readers, but also helps get journalists interested in your story. That means your release should include reasons, facts, and quotes that would be of interest to the audience that the journalists you have in mind like to reach. Your release has to stand out from the pile so as many people as possible will want to cover your story.

Follow these style conventions when preparing your press release:

- ✔ If you're printing and mailing a press release, put each contact's name and address in the top-right corner.

- ✔ Make sure that your text is double-spaced and does not exceed two pages.

- ✔ Your own contact information should be at the bottom of the release.

Breaking down the sections of a press release

Your press release should conform to some basic sections, in the following order:

1. **Write a compelling headline that grabs the reader's attention.** Public-relations professionals will tell you that the headline is the single most important part of your press release. Why? Because there are so many press releases and so many potential stories that journalists and reviewers typically scan the headlines first; if they're not interested, they may toss the release before reading the first paragraph. Your headline needs to have a "hook" or unique message that might intrigue, grab, or otherwise stop a potential reader from moving on. Now, writing that perfect headline is easier said than done, it's true. You can come up with a headline and look at it again before you send it out, but ask yourself *what*

you'd like to see as a potential iPhone app customer. What features make your app stand out? If you could only tell someone one sentence about your app, what would it be? Those questions may help you pick an effective headline.

After you've written your headline, put your dateline right below in the second line of the press release. The *dateline* contains your location and the date you sending the release, such as "San Diego, CA, January 1, 2010."

2. **Write the first paragraph of your press release.** Most news articles answer the "five Ws and 1 H" in the first paragraph of the story, specifically Who, What, When, Where, Why, and How. There's a reason for that: Many readers never go past the first paragraph. The same is EXACTLY true for people reading press releases. Make sure that all the critical details are included in the first paragraph, about *who* you are, *what* the application is, *when* is it available (hint: the best answer is "now"), *where* they can learn more, and *how* your app works. The *where* is mostly obvious, but the other questions are valid.

3. **Write the next few paragraphs of your press release.** Typically, your second paragraph should offer more details about your application — including the features a user can expect. By the second or third paragraph, you are expected to put in a quote from someone affiliated with the application. This quote can come from you, a member of your development team, or your client. The purpose of the quote is to allow you to relay something important about the application — such as why you developed the app, what early buzz is saying about your app, or some especially striking aspect that would invite a reader to connect with you and your story. Remember, the goal of a press release is to get a reviewer on a Web site to *want* to write more about what you're selling. As much as you can (without going overboard), give that reviewer a reason to care.

4. **Make sure all the important features are listed in the release.** Your press release can be a page or (a little) longer, but no more than two, so make sure it contains all the important features that exist in your application. Many developers accomplish this by putting their apps' features in bulleted lists; the best location for such a list is in the middle of the release.

5. **Write the last paragraph of your release.** Typically, the last paragraph of a press release is where you talk about how and where the reader can get more information. So you'll want to include a mention of your Web site that promotes the application. You can also include personal contact information such as your e-mail address, in case someone wants to request a promotional code, get more information, or to ask some questions.

6. **Write a one-paragraph About the Company (or Developer) section.** After the information-about-the-product part of your press release, you

are expected to put in at least one paragraph containing a description of what you (the app's creator) are about. The idea is for people who read your release to learn more about your company, but stop short of describing the company in detail inside the actual press release. If and when a review is written, the Web site's reviewer can include information about your company from this section.

You can also provide more information than a company bio. For example, when Doug Hogg was promoting his company's first app release of iSamurai, he included several links before the About section (see Figure 15-1) that took the reader to video clips, a media kit, and prepared graphics that could be useful for a Web page containing the game review.

iSamurai 1.0 uses a Wi-Fi connection for two-player mode. iSamurai 2.0 will be a free upgrade for Apple's upcoming iPhone software 3.0, allowing two players to compete anywhere using blue-tooth communication between their iPhones. To schedule an interview with Robert Hogg, please call 323-982-8243 or contact online.

LINKS:

iSamuraiapp.com

Download and Purchase

Video

Screenshot

Application Icon

Media Kit

Headquartered in Los Angeles, California, Toy Kite Software is a privately held company founded in 2008 by robotics engineer Robert Hogg. Robert is a graduate of the Computer Science and Engineering program at UCLA, and works for NASA's Jet Propulsion Lab. Toy Kite's goal is to create exciting software that fully leverages the capabilities of the iPhone platform. The Toy Kite team includes Robert Hogg, Arin Morfopoulos; technical director and lead software engineer, Doug Hogg; research and promotion director, and Ryan Rodriguez; director of design. Copyright 2008-2009 Toy Kite Software. All Rights Reserved. Apple, the Apple logo, iPhone and iPod are registered trademarks of Apple Computer in the U.S. and/or other countries.

Figure 15-1:
Your press release can contain links to valuable information for the reader.

7. **End your press release.** The journalistic standard for a press release is to write 3 #'s (###) on the last line of the document, centered in the line. This signals the end of the press release.

Distributing your press release

You have several options nowadays when you are ready to send out your press releases:

✔ You can use PRMac to send out your press releases for you. For example, Robert and Doug Hogg used PRMac to help announce their first iPhone app, iSamurai. The Web-distribution service has a simple registration process (outlined in Figure 15-2) and offers three distinct services:

- Your free account lets you post press releases on the PRMac site and send it out to your user base while working to get your PR indexed by the search engines.

- You can order Extended Distribution to get next-day distribution, improved placement, and notifications to the RSS-feed aggregators, which collect a lot of live news feeds for subscribers.

- You can pay PRMac to help you write the press release, which it will then distribute with its Extended Distribution plan.

✔ As with PRMac, you can use the PRWeb service to create and send out your press release. The service offers you a number of ways you can link your press releases to your online accounts — such as Twitter, your blog, or any social-networking or bookmarking site you might use. PRWeb also provides tools for tracking the effectiveness of your press release by studying the view rate and the click rate of your document. Furthermore, PRWeb can help you gain attention in search engines' algorithms that recommend the best Web site based on a user search. You can even embed featured video in your press release — sure to catch most people's attention — by selecting the Media Visibility package (itself visible in Figure 15-3).

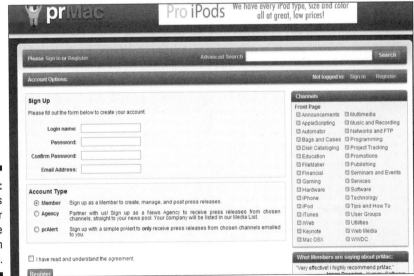

Figure 15-2: PRMac lets you register for a free account on its site.

Figure 15-3:
PRWeb
has several
media-access
packages
to choose
from.

How to submit your app to be reviewed

Most of these review sites post instructions that detail how you should submit your application to be reviewed on the site. Before you start submitting, however, you should take the time to make a list of the sites to which you want to consider submitting your app's press kit for review. In some cases, you may want to target only the review sites that cater to your specific niche. In other cases, you may want to reach as many sites as possible. Take the time to review each site and see whether a review of your application would make sense there. After all, you don't want to submit (for example) a time-management application to a gaming review site.

If you want to get your app into reviewer's hands without asking them to buy it, there are two methods you can use. If you want to prerelease your app to a certain reviewer or other businessperson, you can give them access to an ad hoc distribution of your app, as we describe in Chapter 14. This grants them access on their personal device to a development build of your app, which you can then personally send to them as a file. Use this sparingly, however, because you are allowed only a limited number of distributions this way.

The more standard way of giving an app to reviewers is available only once your app is launched. You can request promo codes through iTunes Connect. You only get 50 promo codes per version, and they are only good for 30 days, so it is best to distribute them only at the time they are needed; at a reviewer's request, for example.

To distribute a promo code for your app, make sure you have the login information for the user in your organization who has been assigned the legal role with Apple. Only this user can access the iTunes Connect account. Follow these steps:

1. **Log in to** `https://itunesconnect.apple.com.`

2. **Click Request Promotional Codes (as seen in Figure 15-4).**

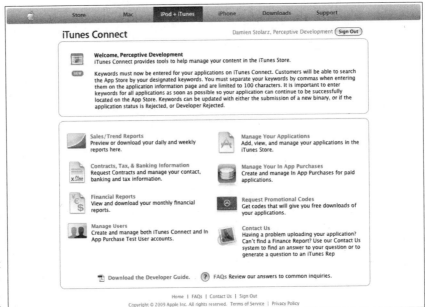

Figure 15-4:
Find the
Request
Promotional
Codes link.

3. **Select the app you want promo codes for and input the number of codes you want into the fields provided, then click Continue.**

4. **Read and agree to the contract Apple provides for giving you these promotional codes, then click Continue.**

   Apple will generate the promotional codes you requested into a file you can download.

5. **Once you see the message that your codes are ready for download, click the Download Codes button on that screen.**

6. **You are prompted to either save the file, or open it with a text editor from your browser (as seen in Figure 15-5).**

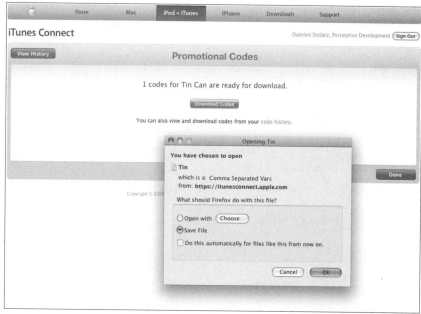

Figure 15-5:
Download
your
promotional
codes to
your
computer.

Once you open the file with a text editor, you should see one or more promo code text strings.

7. **Select one of the text strings, and copy it to your clipboard.**

8. **Paste the code into an email to whomever you want to send the promotional code.**

The recipient only can use the code to download the app from iTunes:

1. **When they receive the code, they can copy it to their clipboard, and then launch iTunes.**

2. **In the iTunes store home page, they will need to click Redeem in the upper right panel to use the code and download your app for free.**

3. **They can paste the code into the text area provided and click Redeem.**

   The app will automatically download, ready to be installed on their iPod or iPhone.

Getting reviewed online by *The New York Times*

Roy Furchgott is responsible for writing the App of the Week article for *The New York Times* Gadgetwise blog. As you can imagine, he receives a lot of requests to be reviewed. According to Roy, however, "no one ever asks me what makes a great App of the Week candidate." So he offers some handy advice to anyone planning on submitting a request.

This advice is good in general because you should be highlighting these qualities anyway, no matter whom you want to review your app. Don't worry if your app doesn't have every one of these qualities, as long as it has *several* of them.

Roy's Qualities of a Good App include

- **Appeal to a large national audience.** Let's say you have an app that shows you where bus stops are on a single city route. That's not very helpful to the larger audience unless everybody lives in that particular city, and they don't. An app that can tell you bus schedules in 50 major cities, for example, is good.

- **Addresses an immediate, on-the-go need.** The ability of the iPhone to have access to information when you're out and about can fill a specific need on the spot, such as looking up movie reviews on Flixster while you're standing in a video store, or using Shazzam to tell you the name of a song playing on the radio that instant.

- **Doesn't require much typing on a keyboard.** Given the form factor of an iPhone (compact virtual keyboard and small screen to begin with), having to stop and peck in some information using the keyboard can slow you down and interrupt the experience.

- **Has clear graphics visible on the small screen.** Apparently some app developers forget that their users don't have a laptop-size screen they can use to look at the application when it's in use.

- **Makes the device or service it works with easier to use.** If your iPhone app accesses another service and makes that service easier to navigate, that's a good app. For example, can you program your DirecTV personal video recorder using the DirecTV iPhone app — *and* do it more simply than you could using the DirecTV remote control?

- **Easy to understand, requiring few instructions.** Most iPhone users, after downloading an app to their phones, will start using it right away without reading the instructions or learning more about the app. Therefore, your app should be "ready to go" and intuitive the moment it starts up. Your users shouldn't have to deal with a learning curve to get up to speed.

- **Does something you didn't think a phone could do.** If an app makes your users marvel, "I didn't think you could this with my phone!" and then realize that they can use that app — and do that same task — repeatedly, that's a good thing.

- **The Wild Card.** Furchgott allows that there is always a subjective factor at work: say, that an app can be really fun or give the users something unexpected that makes the app worth covering. Whether it's new and really popular, currently undiscovered, or creatively updated, any application with that Wild Card factor could make a great candidate.

If you think you've got a good candidate, feel free to send Roy an e-mail at `roy.furchgott@nytimes.com`. Make sure you include a high-resolution screen shot of your app (about 1500 pixels wide at 72 dpi, please) for the art department to use.

High-Profile Endorsements

One sure way to gain attention (and maybe even some notoriety) is to have some high-profile people endorse and recommend your iPhone application. You may think that a celebrity endorsement is only good for a consumer product, but it's not so! Today, celebrities and opinion leaders are actively using the Internet and technology to speak directly to their fan bases, so it's credible and likely that the endorsements would ring true.

This method of publicity comes with some drawbacks:

- ✓ You have to deal with the needs and image of high-profile individuals . . . *and* their employees.

- ✓ You may have all sorts of red tape as ten different people (perhaps with some attorneys in that mix) demand pre-approval for any marketing material featuring their client's image or words on it.

- ✓ Your fate also becomes somewhat tied to the person in question, which means your application could suffer some "guilt by association" if the high-profile individual does something unpleasant or unpopular.

Celebrities

The buying public is keenly aware of what their celebrities are up to, thanks to the Internet, video clips, and TV (to name a few sources of information). Heck, we all want to be celebrities so much that Apalon wrote an iPhone app called "iCover" that can superimpose your picture on a fake magazine cover to make you look like a celebrity. (Figure 15-6 shows a typical example.)

Meanwhile, back in the real world (or something like it), celebrity recommendations can be very effective. You can still see the effect that a celebrity recommendation can have by taking note of some of the billboards you might drive by, or on the cover of a magazine you might walk past. This type of effect extends to the iPhone application market as well.

A "celebrity" can be any person who has built up a distinct audience of people who follow what that person is doing and thinking. Some could say that Michael Arrington is a "celebrity" of the startup world because of the TechCrunch blog that he runs, which has millions of readers. Justine Ezarik goes by the name iJustine and has become an Internet "celebrity" with over 600,000 followers on Twitters and hundreds of thousands of downloads of her videos from YouTube.

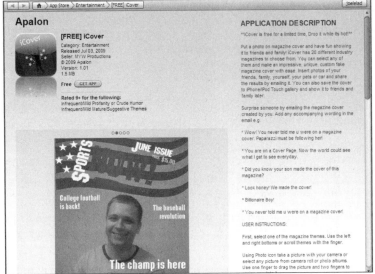

Figure 15-6:
Now you
can be your
own celeb-
rity with the
iCover app.

In some cases, contacting celebrities (or their "people," as in, "have your people call my people") with a request, press release, or note with a promotional code, is enough to get them to try your application and hopefully provide a testimonial or recommendation. In some cases, the celebrity may want compensation. It's up to you to decide whether that recommendation is worth the compensation or not. Here are some things to keep in mind:

- **Pick people who will appeal to your target market.** If you've got a hot new gaming application, you probably won't want to pursue the hosts of Project Runway or any other lifestyle TV show (unless that's what your game is specifically about). Instead, you may want to attempt to recruit folks like Olivia Munn, co-host of the G4 cable network program *Attack of the Show*. Imagine if you got her endorsement and it was included in the broadcast.

- **Be prepared to write up a few quotes and allow them or their team to choose the one you can use in your promotional efforts.** Often those quotes you read endorsing someone's book or product were not uttered by the celebrity, but rather, were drafted by the person seeking the quote — and the celebrity agreed or signed off on the quote (you knew that — right?). Many of these people are very busy and do not have the time to write their own material, even endorsements. You have to get permission, of course; don't put words in anyone's mouth unless you've asked and they've agreed. *First*.

- **Instead of just an endorsement, find out a way to partner with or work directly with a celebrity for their business.** When he's not busy acting in TV shows like *Heroes* or *Lost*, or filming movies like *Cloverfield*, actor

Greg Grunberg has another passion: encouraging people to download Yowza, a new iPhone application that he helped create. Yowza helps you get mobile coupons by tracking your location through the iPhone's built-in GPS and bringing you deals from the network of merchants that Yowza has put together to offer you deals and coupons. The offer shows up on your iPhone, and the merchant can scan the barcode from your iPhone screen to give you the deal. Grunberg uses his blog, Twitter feed, and any other publicity he can generate to help push the app into the hands of new.

✔ **But it's impossible to contact a celebrity right? Wrong.** Many celebrities make a sizable percentage of their income from endorsements. That means that entrepreneurs like you are their customers, not just adoring fans to be flicked away like flies. There are even services which help you make your endorsement pitch. Try these resources to start your search:

- Celeb Brokers (www.celebbrokers.com, 310-268-1476)
- Celebrity Endorsement Network (www.celebrityendorsement.com, 818-225-7090)
- Contact Any Celebrity (www.contactanycelebrity.com)
- Sponsored Tweets (www.sponsoredtweets.com)
- Hollywood Branded (www.hollywoodbranded.com)

Opinion leaders

Most product niches and areas have their own mini-"celebrities" whom people like to follow and listen to for advice and comments. We call these people *opinion leaders* because they establish themselves as experts, or at the very least, extremely informed in a certain area.

Because these opinion leaders (also known as *tastemakers*) are constantly communicating with their following and with the public at large, the things they discuss, review, recommend, or use will receive added attention. Therefore, if you can get your application in front of an opinion leader — and better yet, if they agree to recommend or profile your application — the publicity from that effort could be tremendous.

For example, in June 2009, game developer ngmoco worked with technology celebrities and opinion leaders like iJustine, Digg founder Kevin Rose, and others to promote their new iPhone game Star Defense. Then ngmoco created a Launch Challenge with four celebrities, who played Star Defense against each other. The celebrities promoted the launch challenge on their own Web sites and social networks — writing Tweets about it, for example — and ngmoco awarded $5,000 to the charity of the winner's choice (see Figure 15-7).

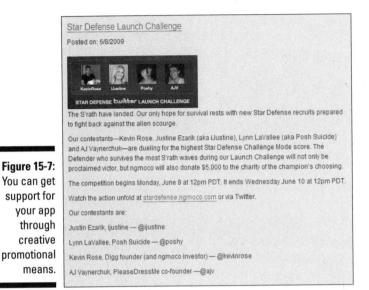

Figure 15-7:
You can get
support for
your app
through
creative
promotional
means.

If you can think of a way to engage an opinion leader to interact with your application, use your application, and even promote your application, then you get instant advertising to that leader's fan base. You should always be looking for the right fit by approaching people whose target audience matches the user demographic you're seeking to attract to your iPhone app.

Writing Articles

When it comes to being noticed on the Internet, search engines value content as one of the highest factors for a Web site to be considered important. Therefore, companies of all sizes are looking to have as many articles and information as possible that relate to what they do, and search engines are indexing new articles every day. If you want to increase exposure for your iPhone application (and for your application business), then you may consider writing articles.

You don't have to be a journalist to write articles. You simply need to have some information to share that other people would want to read. The average Web article is 400–800 words.

Putting together your article

Almost anything can be turned into an article, within reason. When you get started, stick to something you know that relates in some way to your application. For example, your article could be about:

- ✔ Facts or news about your product niche
- ✔ Case studies or user experiences about your application
- ✔ Experiences you are having while building, launching, or distributing your iPhone application
- ✔ Tips and tricks to other people in your situation

The biggest difference you should remember between writing articles and writing other content (such as press releases or requests for a review) is that the focus of your article should *not* directly be your application. In other words, you are not writing an article just for the sake of mentioning your application. You are writing an article that conveys useful information that may or may not contain a reference to your application.

Every article helps establish you as an opinion leader, which can lead to higher trust and a greater likelihood to buy from you. Every article also comes with a biography section of the author, where you can link to your promotional Web site and mention the application directly. Every time that article is republished, those links and information go with the article, which promotes your application further. The more sources you have that point to your Web site, the higher your search-engine results are, which means greater exposure without paid advertising.

For example, as author Joel Elad was writing his e-commerce books, he wrote an article for SmartBiz.com entitled "4 Hidden Ways eBay can Help Your Business" (see Figure 15-8). This article continues to provide referrals to Joel's books years after he wrote the article, plus it continues to be one of the top search-engine results for Joel's name.

The best way to approach article writing is to try and write something brief, but often. If you sit down with the goal of pumping out ten articles at a time, you will probably get so frustrated that you'll abandon the effort. By doing a little at a time, you can achieve a lot. One article per day can lead to 365 different articles after a year's time, for example.

Figure 15-8:
Writing
articles can
help estab-
lish your
presence as
an opinion
leader.

When you're ready to write an article, here are some quick steps to powering through it:

1. **Come up with a catchy title that describes the content of the article.**

   As with a press release, you need a headline that grabs the users' attention and gets them to want to read your article. Using a number in your headline increases the likelihood of being read; that number puts a quantifiable effect on the information. For example, your article title can be something along these lines:

   - "5 Ways Your iPhone Can Help You Improve Your Health"

   - "3 Pitfalls to Avoid When You're Getting a New iPhone"

   - "10 Tips and Tricks to Writing an iPhone Application Faster"

2. **Write your first paragraph that describes the problem.**

   Because your article is giving advice on solving a particular problem, summarize the problem in the first paragraph — and state that the following points in the article will address that problem. Remember to use short sentences that get to the point.

3. **Illustrate each point in your article with its own paragraph or bullet point.**

   White space is your friend when you write articles. You want to use bullets, numbered lists, and short paragraphs to convey your points, with bolded text whenever appropriate. Let's say you're writing about five ways your iPhone can improve your health. After the initial paragraph, you should have five little paragraphs or bullet points, each describing one "way."

4. **Write a concluding paragraph with a call to action or a link.**

   After you've stated the problem and your individual points, you can write a short ending paragraph summarizing everything ("If you follow these points, you should see results in . . . ") and even include a Call to Action or a link for more information ("If you want to learn more about this field, check out my Web site at `www.myWeb sitename.com`").

5. **Include a quick biography of yourself, with a definite Web site link, after the end of the article.**

   This is something you can write once, and simply cut and paste into every article you write. This is a simple one-paragraph biography, consisting of *who* you are, *what* you do, *what* the name is of the application you're promoting, *where* can they find the application ("Available on the App Store", "Coming soon to the App Store", etc.), and the link to your Web site. You can even add the title "About the Author" in front of the paragraph if you like.

After your article is written, you can post it on your Web site, send it in for consideration to a niche Web site that you know is looking for content, or give it to a directory of articles to re-publish over the Internet. Owners of Web sites are looking for articles (as in, fresh content) they can put on their Web sites to attract customers, or articles to include in their newsletters to their customers. Three popular directories of this type are

✔ ezinearticles.com (`www.ezinearticles.com`)

✔ eHow (`www.ehow.com`)

✔ ArticlesBase (www.articlesbase.com)

After you've written and published your article, you can do a few small things to promote your article:

✔ If you have a blog, post your article there, or create an entry in your blog that points to the article.

✔ If you have a Twitter account, you can create a Tweet that directs people to your article.

✔ If you have a social-networking account, you can update your status to include a link to your article.

✔ If you do any e-mail marketing to a new and growing list of customers, you can include your article as content for your next message.

Be an opinion leader

Every time you write an article, you are adding a quick, short boost to your overall status as an information giver on the Internet. If you extend the concept out to a long-term focus — by offering advice, expertise, and perspective on a given topic or subject area — you could become an opinion leader in your given area. Eventually (and hopefully) you may be seen as an expert by people in that niche who want solid, reliable information.

One example that people give from the pre-Internet days is the local hardware store. If you asked the guy behind the counter any question related to home improvement or how to use any of the products in the store, odds were that guy could answer your question. That was part of the appeal of doing business there — not only were you getting products, you were getting the expertise and advice to go along with what you bought. Replicating that sense of advice and authority on the Internet is a great way to build loyalty and status to anything you work on or promote. People like to do business with experts who recommend or endorse something — and know what they're talking about.

Based on what your iPhone application is, we're betting that you've got something to offer the general public that relates to your app. Perhaps you have years of experience in the product niche that your app serves, which is why you chose to build the application in the first place. For example, let's say that you've been following the PC gaming industry for over ten years, which led you to develop a hot new iPhone game application. You can comment on the progression of the gaming industry, either in general or on the iPhone. You can talk about what appeals to gamers, what trends you've observed, what you predict as future trends, and other related topics.

Even if you don't feel like you have expertise or insight into a certain product area, by the time you launch your application, you will have expertise in something — building an iPhone application! Lots of people are interested in this area — hence the publication of this book, for example — so writing about your development experience (even if you're not a programmer), including things you've learned, or even offering a step-by-step discussion of how you put your app together, is likely to build an audience.

To become an opinion leader, get out there and be a part of the conversation that is the Internet. Post information in a variety of places often and consistently. There are lots of ways to establish yourself, such as

✔ Writing a blog or series of articles that demonstrate your expertise or observations.

✔ Participating in discussion forums in your area, posting answers and advice when you can help.

✔ Joining groups in your niche or area (through sites such as Yahoo, LinkedIn, and so on) that discuss a given topic.

✔ Providing comments and links to other articles in your area that people could find useful.

✔ Writing and editing information in any wiki related to your product area.

Being an opinion leader is not something you should pursue if you cannot give some regular time to posting information or answering questions on an ongoing basis. Nothing discredits you faster than a dusty, unused blog or Web site.

As with writing articles, being an opinion leader is *not* about making the sale. That will come indirectly as people start to follow you, take your advice, and listen to your recommendations. Pick an area in which you will genuinely like to be an opinion leader, as sincerity and enthusiasm will help your status become believable and respected.

Chapter 16

Building the Buzz

*B*log is short for *Web log*; essentially a log or diary that you post on the Web. What makes a blog interesting and special for marketing is that it provides you with three of the key ingredients to being found on the Web by search engines, and it allows you to tell your story from your own perspective in an ongoing way that promotes the messages you want to get out there on your own schedule.

Blog content is an important ingredient for search marketing because it is

✔ Fresh

✔ Topical

✔ Educational

Search engines such as Google are geared to favor these types of content because they are seeking to provide timely, relevant, informative search results to their users. By writing a blog rather than (or in addition to) a bunch of ad copy, you are making a stream of information that can serve many purposes for users. Yes, it can advertise your products. But it can also give insight into your company, provide supporting education about your products, and give depth to your entrepreneurial adventure that customers, researchers and reviewers might find more interesting than the surface presentations that are often pitched to them in advertising.

By allowing you to tell your story from your own perspective, a blog lets you drive (or at least contribute to) the narrative of your product and company:

✔ If you are not getting media coverage, a blog can help you get it

✔ Well-promoted blog content can even replace your need for media coverage.

✔ New messages are distributed without having to wait for someone in the media to find you interesting enough to cover.

How to Set Up a Blog

At its core, a blog is simply a Web site that is updated continually with new log-style content. So you can make any Webpage into a blog page simply by updating it with a stream of new text. Several services have been developed, however, that make setting up a blog very easy and give you powerful features for posting, sharing and promoting your blog. Some of the more popular of these services are

✔ Blogger: www.blogger.com (free)

✔ WordPress: en.wordpress.com/signup/ (free; see Figure 16-1)

✔ TypePad: www.typepad.com (free trial)

✔ Squarespace: www.squarespace.com (free trial)

✔ Movable Type: www.movabletype.com (free demo)

Each platform has its angle and style. Some are paid for by you and some are ad supported. Each of these services listed provides strong help and documentation to help you get up and running.

Wordpress, Squarespace, and Movable Type probably offer the most robust software platforms that can be expanded into full-fledged, content-managed Web sites and even hosted on your own server. But that functionality isn't necessary for a basic blog. If you are familiar with Web development, though, they will give you more flexibility down the road.

Identifying your blog audience

The first step is to determine who your core audience for your blog is. This is a matter of the area of interest your app appeals to. The people who read your blog may not be the bulk of your end customers. But they are the ones who, by caring about your process and your app, set the stage for your app to catch on.

Figure 16-1:
You can
set up your
free blog on
Wordpress.

You may have a wide variety of people looking at your blog, but who are most likely to play a role in the promotion or sale of your app? In today's saturated media environment, many PR professionals have found that the best people to target with their messages are *product mavens*. A maven is simply an expert or connoisseur. Product mavens have a particular interest and appetite for a certain product or type of product.

Apple enthusiasts are some of the most well-known product mavens these days. Apple users can be so passionate about Apple products that they take over for sales reps in Apple stores and sell a product for them. Apple supports product mavens by creating high-profile events for product rollouts that nurture a sense of inclusion and being part of the action. Steve Jobs' presenting style has been so effective because of this that it has practically revolutionized the presentation-giving format across many business sectors.

For most app companies, product mavens are the best audience to target with a blog because

- ✔ They care what you have to say.
- ✔ They understand what you are talking about.
- ✔ They want other people to know what they know.

When product mavens get interested in your app, they are likely to

✔ Interject it into conversations they have on other blogs and media

✔ Provide you feedback and commentary

✔ Await the release of your app with anticipation

Get more specific about targeting people who are interested in what your app offers. Defining and discovering your product mavens may take a bit of research. Thankfully, the explosion in magazine publishing in the last few years means that there are probably magazines about the area of interest that your app deals with. If your app lets gardeners know which crops are in season, like Locavore (see Figure 16-2); or helps gardeners know when to plant, feed, water, and harvest their gardens, pick up a copy *of Better Homes and Gardens* or an organic gardening magazine. Most magazines also have Web sites, but the print copy will give you a more complete feel. There are countless magazines targeted at gamers. Try to find a magazine or two that is as specifically related to your app as possible.

To understand how to communicate with your audience, read through the magazines and notice

✔ Topics they cover

✔ The tone they strike with readers

✔ Who their advertisers are

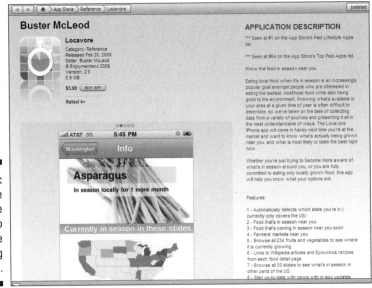

Figure 16-2:
Apps like
Locavore
will want to
target the
gardening
crowd.

Ask the magazines for an information packet for advertisers. All magazines give potential advertisers demographic information about their readership so advertisers can determine if they are hitting the right audience when placing an ad. You can use this data in reverse to determine the type of people that are interested in that type of content. The results may surprise you.

Reach out and find some product mavens to include on your mailing list early. Give them honorary titles (like *board member*) and ask them to communicate with you about your blog. If you were developing the gardening app, for example, get your aunt with a green thumb and your farmer cousin to subscribe and ask them to give you feedback and commentary on each blog post. Their input will help guide you and give you new information that you can include in future blogs. If you can start engaging early, and keep advancing the conversation through each blog entry, you can develop a "sticky" narrative that keeps people coming back to see what you have to say next. These early product mavens are also likely to forward your blog to friends, attracting more potential product mavens.

Search for existing blogs, forums, social networking groups, and Twitter users that relate to the topic of your app. Leave meaningful comments and discussion threads there that lead back to your blog.

These media are generally unfriendly to advertisements, and users quickly mark things that reek of promotion as spam. Postings marked that way are removed quickly and their posters are sometimes blacklisted. This doesn't mean that you can't include a link to your blog in the signature line of a post that has real relevance to the topic at hand. Just don't have your posting read "Check out my blog!" or something similarly obtrusive, and don't slant your posting by saying something like "if you read my blog, you'll find that…"

Just put out a straight comment or answer and have your link in your signature line. You can even write a blog entry about the topic and provide a link to that in your comment.

What to write in your blog entries

The appeal of blogs to their readership is that blogs give them interesting information to follow without being hit over the head with advertising pitches every five minutes. For companies, they fit into the *soft promotion* category of PR because they simply create and perpetuate an environment of interaction with customers. This forwards a collaborative partnership relationship that says "get to know us," not an adversarial sales relationship that says "take it or leave it." Commercially, your blog is like the free Internet at your local coffee shop. It says, "Come in and hang out a while. We don't care if you buy a coffee. Just use our space and make friends with us." Coffee shops know that doing this leads to more coffee sales.

Your blog should essentially do the same. Now that you've identified your product mavens, take a moment to list some things you think they might find interesting in the area of interest your app inhabits. In the case of our gardening app example, blog posts we could write about include

- ✔ Exotic seed varieties
- ✔ Local planting and harvest calendars
- ✔ Origins of various wildflowers

For your first blog topic, take the item that you can most easily write about with the least amount of research. Do any research you require to make an interesting blog post. Write a few paragraphs about the subject. Now, look for ways that your app relates to this subject. Put in a few sentences related to your app that also connect to the subject you are writing about. For each blog post, try to advance the story you are telling about your app one more step, like a page in a book.

Invite your readers to get involved:

- ✔ Ask for comments and feedback in the last line of your blog.
- ✔ Ask what your readers would like to hear about in the future.

Many bloggers find that writing like they speak, rather than like they were forced to write in school, makes the practice of blogging easier. Quantity is more important that quality. If you find yourself blocked, just write whatever is on your mind. You can always edit it before you post it. When you are writing, just let yourself write whatever comes up, then circle back to refine or shorten it.

Keep blog entries to 800 words or fewer:

- ✔ Reading four to six paragraphs every week is much more palatable than being confronted with more than a page.

- ✔ Keeping things short will force you to condense your most interesting thoughts for a more compelling entry. If you can, include a picture or two to make it easier to quickly find something interesting about your blog post.

If you want to go really short, set up a Twitter account and keep people up to date that way. A good Twitter strategy is to first write your blog entry; then twitter an interesting tidbit about the article with a link to the original post (see Figure 16-3).

Figure 16-3:
Use Twitter
to promote
your blog
entries.

Once you've entered your mailing list into your blogging software, post your entry. If you've seeded your mailing list, you should be getting some feedback in a couple of days. You can use any positive feedback and commentary as a starting point for your next blog. As you include the dialogue you've received and mention commenters by screen name where appropriate, you'll engender a sense of participation that will increase enthusiasm for your blog.

Reach Out to Your Social Networks

Social networking is a major buzz term, and businesses are trying to jump on board because they see the potential to create relationships in that space that can turn into buzz and sales. But social networks evolved almost to *spite* marketers. However, social networks are also home to a lot of people trying to be engaged and entertained online. As a marketer, you can use that to your advantage while being conscientious of users' natural desire to avoid advertising.

Take off your marketing hat and just be you. Let your friends know what you are up to! Facebook allows you to link your Facebook status to your Twitter updates. If you are Twittering, your Facebook profile will always be up to date with your latest headline and offer the opportunity to read your blog. Your business is a big part of your life, so this is literally a slice of your life that you should feel proud to share with your friends.

Include the development process in your blog

Don't wait till you are done with your app and in "marketing mode" to start your blog. Start it as soon as you get serious about creating an app. Without giving away information that compromises your unique ideas to your competition, share as much as you can about your process from start through completion of your app.

Use your blog like an ongoing soap opera (without the ugly breakups and characters dying and coming back to life) to get your followers interested in seeing how your story develops. As you near completion of the app, people who have followed you will probably want to get it just to see how the story ends. They may even talk to their friends about your app and increase your followership as you go along.

You can set up your own Facebook page (previously known as a Fan page) for your iPhone app or your overall business/company. When you get to Facebook's home page, click the link that says "Create a page for an artist, band, or business," and follow the prompts, as shown in Figure 16-4, to create your own business page that you can promote to an unlimited amount of friends!

Figure 16-4: Use Facebook to build a following around your app or company.

facebook

Remember Me   Forgot your password?
Email

Login

Sign Up   Facebook helps you connect and share with the people in your life.

Create New Facebook Page
Category:

○ Local

◉ **Brand, Product, or Organization:**
Consumer Product

○ Artist, Band, or Public Figure .

Name of Consumer Product:
Your iPhone App Name or Company

Please certify that you are an official representative of this brand, organization, or person and that you are permitted to create a Facebook Page for that subject.

☐ I am authorized to create this Page

Electronic Signature: enter full name as electronic signature

Create Page

TIP

Become a sponsor

Though users are sensitive to being pitched commercially, they seem to have acquiesced to the fact that companies provide them with interesting things through sponsorship. Sponsorship comes from the same ad category as blogs. Your company can gain awareness simply by being the host of a forum or online activity.

If you sponsor something that users truly find fun or useful, a positive association will be made with your company and you will get an opportunity to ask users to interact with you more directly by following your blog. Your blog will make them even more familiar with your company and when an interest arises in them for the type of product you provide they will think of you first.

Working social networking is an ongoing process:

- ✔ Setting aside at least one hour a day for yourself or a staff member to keep adding and communicating with friends will add up over time to a large base of people who are interested in your message. Each time you release a blog entry, make sure your social networking friends know about it. You can even put promotions out to them if you do it in a way that doesn't come across as too commercial or pushy.

- ✔ Raise interest by participating or generating a larger discussion around the area of your iPhone application, instead of direct publicity for the app itself. You can create a Facebook, LinkedIn, or MySpace group based on the area of interest that your app inhabits. Then you can invite participants to the group. In your group, you can create forum discussions and add blog entries and updates.

If you create and facilitate content that is compelling for your users, they will be compelled to invite their friends, drawing more people into your brand environment.

Quizzes

Cheesy as they may seem, people love little quizzes because they provide something to talk about with friends. Taking the quiz engages people with the topic of your app and gives them multiple opportunities to invite their friends to take the quiz, which spreads your quiz and your brand.

Making a quiz usually involves some programming. But there is a Facebook app that takes all the programming out of the process. It's called Make a Quiz! (see Figure 16-5). The app will guide you through the process of creating and launching your quiz. You can find it by typing in the words "Make a Quiz" into the Facebook search bar.

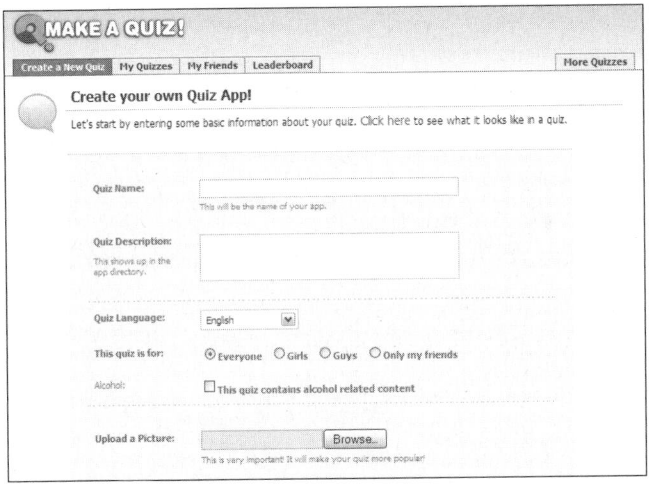

Figure 16-5:
Make a Quiz! allows you to... make your own quiz!

Make a Quiz! doesn't prompt you to add your icon to the Edit Application screen. Be sure to upload an icon for your quiz (like your company logo) in the Edit Application screen.

Before you make your quiz, think of a quiz topic that will be fun for people interested in your app's niche and create a topic question, such as, "What's your favorite food seasonality?" By answering the quiz questions you create, users will be interacting with a ranking system that will answer this question for them.

Now you'll be asked to create some responses. For the preceding question, we would pick

- Spring
- Summer
- Fall
- Winter

Next you'll create at least five questions, the answers to which correspond to one of the responses; for example:

Do you prefer...?

> ✔ Apples (Summer)
>
> ✔ Squash (Fall)
>
> ✔ Oranges (Winter)
>
> ✔ Strawberries (Spring)

The words in parentheses are the responses that will be displayed next to the text fields you enter your answers into.

You'll have to set up at least five questions like that. Then the app will guide you through the rest of the process, which is pretty straightforward.

Be sure to put the name of your company or app in the quiz title and talk about it in the description text areas. Promote the quiz to your existing friends and to each new friend that you make.

Create a new quiz that is directly related to your blog entry each week. Then promote the quiz in your blog, and promote the blog in your quiz description.

You can also make quizzes based on features in your app. This allows you to use the quiz to directly advertise your app while still keeping it fun.

Create a widget

If you have access to more advanced programming skills, you can create a viral marketing piece called a *social networking widget.* This is essentially a small piece of Web software that allows users to play with or utilize something related to your brand.

For example, Bugle Me (see Figure 16-6) is a service that allows fans to get free phone updates from their favorite celebrities. Perceptive Development created a widget that lets users listen to previous messages, sign themselves up for phone calls, sign up friends for a demo phone call, and add the widget to their own Web site or social networking page, which their friends can in turn add to their own. This is called a viral marketing campaign because it is fueled by users spreading it among themselves rather than a top-down ad buy that is pushed to users involuntarily. Users are literally spreading the promo like a virus to each other.

Figure 16-6:
Bugle Me is
getting more
attention
thanks to a
widget.

You can create a similar widget for your own campaign. You can do it on your own, or work with a software developer to develop it for you.

Clearspring (see Figure 16-7) is a company that offers a viral marketing platform that allows the software developer to embed an easy-to-use menu in your widget that allows users to post it to their social networking page or link to it in other ways. Their sister brand AddThis provides an even simpler but less full-featured way to do this.

Figure 16-7:
Clearspring
allows your
widgets to
have clear
menus.

Be sure the company you work with is an expert in marketing, because you'll need to get clever so users really want to forward your stuff to their friends or find it interesting enough to grab for themselves off of a friend's page.

For our fictitious gardening app, we might create a planting calendar widget. Users could encounter it on a friend's page, play with its functionality, and then click the prominent "add this to your page!" button. After a few clicks, they could feature the calendar on their own page. Of course, our calendar widget would also be branded with our gardening app for iPhone.

E-Mail Marketing

The most cost-effective way of communicating with your customers is through e-mail marketing. This allows you to send quick, topical, and trackable messages with offers, information, and other useful sales and marketing news.

Crafting your e-mails

Marketing e-mails may be one of the most derided forms of communication on planet Earth, but they keep being produced for one simple reason: They work. You don't need to become an annoying spammer to use e-mail marketing for your app. If you develop a rapport with your prospects and customers and deliver them something they want or find interesting in your e-mails, e-mail marketing can augment your image, not tarnish it.

Doing this means creating e-mails that emphasize the benefits of your app to your customers concisely in a format that is fun to look at. Letting subscribers know when your app goes on sale or when you've added exciting new features to it can keep you on the top of your customers' mind if you include them in the good news, rather than trying to get them to do something. Imagine your e-mail communications as a way of letting friends know what's happening in the universe of your app. Almost everybody likes (or at least doesn't hate) good and interesting news, and almost everybody hates getting an obvious sales pitch. Here are some concepts to keep in mind when crafting your e-mail marketing messages:

✔ **Be honest and straightforward.**

- Make sure the From: line of your e-mails contains your name or your company's name.

- Have your subject line actually describe the content of your e-mail and mention your company or app name.

- Avoid "sales-y" subject lines or ad copy.

- Use **bold text** to emphasize the most important words in your message, so that the reader who is just skimming your e-mail will get the critical facts or be hooked to learn more.

✔ **Have your app designers design HTML e-mail templates for you.** A design that connects with the look of your app will attract interest. It is much more engaging to look at a well-designed e-mail (see Figure 16-8) than boring text.

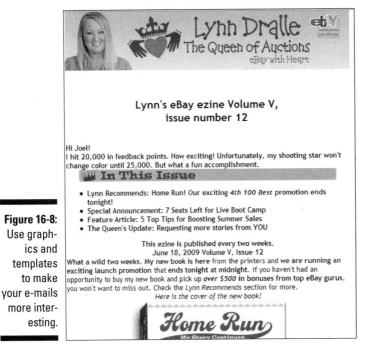

Figure 16-8: Use graphics and templates to make your e-mails more interesting.

To avoid being filtered as spam, make sure that the text that goes in the HTML version of your app matches the text in the plain text version of your app.

✔ **Make your e-mails convey real news.** E-mails that are educational in their character are more interesting than obvious sales e-mails. Educate your customers about the various features in your app; let them know about awards or reviews you've received. Use the content of your e-mail to get them interested to find out more about what you are saying and provide a link to your Web site.

✔ **Use a bulk e-mail service.** Top-notch e-mail services handle all the important aspects of e-mail campaigning for you. Let them. They are good at what they do and have refined the practice over the years. Most of them will guide you step-by-step in creating, sending, and tracking your campaigns. Here are just a few of the e-mail marketing services available:

• Constant Contact: www.constantcontact.com

• Topica: www.topica.com

- A Weber: `www.aweber.com`
- iContact: `www.icontact.com`
- JangoMail: `www.jangomail.com`
- Bronto: `www.bronto.com`
- Cheetah Mail: `www.cheetahmail.com`

Generating and maintaining your list

Many e-mail services make it difficult to just dump in a bunch of e-mail addresses into their system. This is because one of their core offerings is that e-mail originating from them is not likely to be flagged as spam. Systems like Constant Contact prefer that you use a signup form on your Web site that signs subscribers up directly in their system. That way, the service can send them confirmation e-mails that let the user confirm that they want to be on your mailing list. This practice of confirming is called *double opt-in*. It's the best way to generate a list, because you know that people on your list definitely want to be on it. Of course, your e-mails must have an *opt-out* link that allows subscribers to stop getting your messages. Double opt-in helps ensure that the people you are sending e-mails to want them.

Every year or so, send out a new opt-in e-mail to keep your list.

Now that you are geared up to get legitimate subscribers on your mailing list, you'll need to actually attract some. Put your signup form prominently on your Web site, blog, and any other Web presences you have.

An effective way to get people to sign up is to offer them something in exchange. If you are in a business-related category, a *white paper* about your industry is a good lure. You can also offer add-ons and discounts. Simply advertising that your e-mails will provide customers with interesting and useful information to them is a great pitch, but you have to make sure to deliver on that promise by treating your e-mail campaigns similarly to your blog.

You can also send your blog posts as an e-mail to your subscribers. If you are successfully writing your blog regularly, get customers to sign up to receive blog updates.

Buying a list

Building your own list organically is preferable to buying a list because you are getting people who have opted themselves in to get communications from you. Marketing to someone with his or her permission is far more effective than coming out of the blue. But when you start out, your list is probably going to be rather small. There are many sources from which you can purchase a mailing list to get your campaign started.

Several e-mail services are unfriendly to this. If you are going to purchase a list, make sure you have a service you can easily import it into, or use another method for your purchased lists (we'll show you how to get those contacts into your standard list).

The Direct Marketing Association (see Figure 16-9) is an advocacy group that helps ensure that list sellers are using ethical practices. Look for their logo when considering buying a list. You can also use the DMA site as an educational resource by going to `www.the-dma.org/services/`.

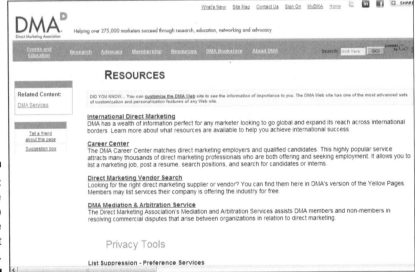

Figure 16-9:
Use the DMA to help you find the right list seller.

When purchasing a list, narrow down the demographic that you target as much as you can. Use what you learned in the blogging section about your product maven audience and target them. You can always purchase more lists, so make your campaigns small at first so you can measure results. Getting a response from one out of 100 on a direct mail campaign is good, so don't be discouraged by slow results. If you are getting significantly less than that, make sure that the lists you are using are fresh and that you've targeted your list to your demographic correctly.

Purchasing a list usually means getting the opportunity to use it only once, so make sure the e-mail that you send them really hits the mark in terms of getting them interested in learning more. Don't go for selling them your app right away. Just get them to sign up for more updates. Getting them to click a link and sign into your standard list turns a cold lead into a warm prospect that you can keep communicating with and gets you that much closer to the sale.

Create a Demo Video for YouTube

Having a demo video for your gives you the opportunity to really show off your app rather than hoping users "get it" by using it themselves.

Of course, your video will go on the Web site that you dedicate to your app, but you can also feature it on your blog, social networking pages, and YouTube.

A demo video fills the following purposes:

✔ Provide a sales pitch for your app.

✔ Educate users about how and why to use your app.

✔ Allow information about your app to spread virally.

✔ Give magazines and bloggers something to link to when describing your app.

Apple is a terrific example to follow when producing a demo video. Apple's videos are simple, straightforward, and informative. They sell the product by explaining its various features. Many of Apple's products feature several videos; some videos provide a product overview and others get more in-depth with individual features.

With some practice, you can produce a similarly polished and well-developed demo video, or set of videos for your app. Producing your video is divided into the following major steps:

1. Concepting

2. Scripting

3. Rehearsing

4. Shooting

5. Editing

Concepting

Concepting is simply the process of deciding what angle you want to take with your video. You could create a step-by-step guide to using your app, or you could wrap your tutorial in a section that provides more background as to how your app fits into a user's life. You could choose to put everything you want to say into one video, or create a series of videos that each covers a different aspect of your app. You can create videos that just feature an image of the iPhone screen, or ones that also have some other footage, such as showing the host of the video.

GardeningApp Video Concept:

Four videos will be created for GardeningApp. The first video will be a product overview that discusses how the app can be used to make gardening easier and goes over the basic features of the app. Each of the other three videos will go more in-depth into a feature of the app. These videos will cover the planting calendar, the seed guide and the weather forecaster.

The videos will be hosted by Tonia (a young energetic woman who knows about gardening) and Jim (a knowledgeable programmer who developed the app). Tonia will talk about the ways the app can be used and give the gardening background info. Jim will do the tutorials about exactly what to do with the app.

Tonia's portions of the video will show her out in a garden with her iPhone. Jim's portions will be screen captures of him using the app.

If your concept for your video gets a bit complex, you can do some basic storyboards to help you put your ideas into reality, as shown in Figure 16-10.

Scripting

Scripting your video could get as detailed as writing and refining every word that your host will say in your video, but we don't recommend scripting your video this tightly. Unless you are going to have a trained actor host your video, it is likely your host will stumble and trip if you ask them to memorize something word for word. Simply write an outline of topics you want to cover in the order you want them covered. For example, this might be an outline for GardeningApp Overview:

1. Why we created an app for gardeners
   a. To help gardeners expand their abilities
   b. To bring gardening resources into one handy package
   c. To let gardeners share and collaborate with each other
2. How GardeningApp works
   a. Consult the planting calendar
   b. Log your plants
   c. Trade with other gardeners
   d. Predict the weather

Storyboard

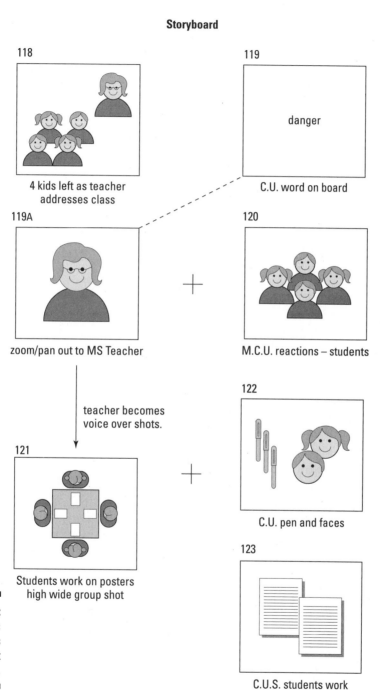

118
4 kids left as teacher
addresses class

119
danger
C.U. word on board

119A
zoom/pan out to MS Teacher

120
M.C.U. reactions – students

teacher becomes
voice over shots.

121
Students work on posters
high wide group shot

122
C.U. pen and faces

123
C.U.S. students work

Figure 16-10:
Use basic
storyboards
to map out
your video.

         e. Water reminders

         f. Order supplies

    3. More resources

         a. Our Web site

         b. Our blog

         c. More videos

Rehearsing

Rehearsing is simply running through each aspect of what you will shoot and taking the time to get the kinks ironed out.

Don't expect perfection right away. Give yourself and your host (which could be the same person) as much patience as it takes to comfortably gain mastery over the material. Getting frustrated will slow you down.

As you rehearse, you may discover areas that your host needs to get more information about. Take the time to get them educated about that aspect; then keep moving through the material. Once your host can fluidly talk about all the topics you want to cover, you are ready to start shooting.

If you are going to video your host, rather than just recording what happens on the screen, make sure that your host is speaking comfortably to the camera and not moving around too much. You'll want to rehearse with the camera so you can go back and review how things are looking before you are officially shooting.

Keeping your host relatively still, but not stiff, will keep you from swinging the camera around which will make your video look unprofessional.

If you are finding that your video just isn't looking good, revert to just recording the screen and using your host as a voice over. That will simplify your shooting and editing, and be easier to get a professional looking video.

Shooting

There are two possible modalities for shooting your video:

- ✔ Screen capture involves recording the computer screen as the host is demonstrating how to use your software.
- ✔ Video recording involves using a video camera to shoot live action such as your host talking or using a hardware device.

Burt Monroy's *Pixel Perfect* podcast is a good example of using screen capture and live action together to create a compelling video. Pixel Perfect is shot with fairly sophisticated equipment and production methods, but you can get good results with a simpler setup.

Screen capture

To see some good examples of screen capture, check out Lynda.com (see Figure 16-11). Lynda.com provides video tutorials for a very wide range of software products. You can access many videos free on a trial basis. By looking at the format of these videos, you can learn a lot about how to conduct a video tutorial with screen capture.

The host speaks very conversationally, and just walks you through the steps of using the software as if you were looking over their shoulder, instructing you about each step as they do it.

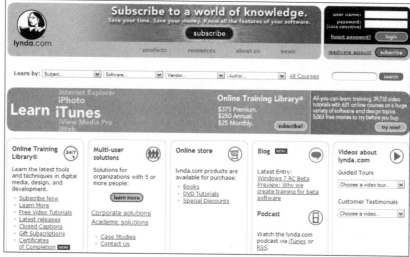

Figure 16-11: Lynda.com is a great place for screen capture examples.

To make a screen capture video of your own, you'll need some software. Some of the more popular software packages for this are

✔ ScreenFlow (recommended)

✔ iShowU

✔ Jing

This type of software allows you to record what you do on your computer screen while recording an audio narration. Jing is designed for short videos, and only allows you to record about 5 minute clips.

We highly recommend using ScreenFlow. It is designed for recording and editing software tutorials, and has such features as

 ✔ Recording video of the host through the iSight camera

 ✔ Changing the shape of the cursor

   The circle setting works particularly well and looks like the setting Apple uses in its own videos.

You'll get a better audio recording with an external microphone. You can purchase a microphone from anywhere between $20 and $300 that will fit your needs, depending on how far you want to go to get the best sound:

 ✔ A microphone company called Blue makes a USB microphone called the Snowball that is designed for podcasting.

 ✔ If you use a higher-end microphone that doesn't plug into your USB port, you'll need a sound adapter to plug it into, such as Protools' M-Box.

In order to record what happens when a user interacts with your app, you'll need to run the app on your desktop or laptop machine in the emulator software bundled with the Apple dev kit. The only drawbacks are that, until recently, most Apple computers don't support Core Location, which allows you to use GPS related services. OS X Snow Leopard ships with core location services using WiFi, and that functionality may be available to the emulator software, but as of this writing this is untested.

Video recording

In some instances, you'll want to record live video of the host or a person using the iPhone in their hand. In our example concept, we are using a mixture of screen capture and live footage. You can use any modern video camera to get a video good enough for YouTube.

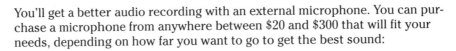

To get the best image, use an HD camcorder.

The main elements to keep in mind to get a professional looking shoot are

 ✔ **Lighting**

   • The main rule in lighting is "use lots of it." You can go too far with this and overexpose your image, but most amateur videographers make the mistake of not having enough light. Enough light for filming often seems far brighter than a person would normally light a scene in real life. You can rent a basic light kit from most places that sell photo equipment, such as B&H and Wolf Camera.

- Use the white balance setting on your camera to make sure that your basic exposure settings are correct.

- Use an antiglare film on your iPhone screen to keep glare from making the screen hard to see in the bright light.

✔ **Sound**

- A muffled or noisy sound track can detract from your video.

- If your camera has an external microphone port, use it with a lapel mic. Your camera may require an adapter.

- If your camera doesn't support an external mic, avoid filming outside if you can. Wind and other noises will make your video seem amateur quickly.

✔ **Set**

- Apple is a big fan of the all-white background. This is because the background can quickly distract from your host. If you film against a white wall, you'll need to throw a lot of light on the wall and use your camera's white balance setting to get a good look that doesn't appear shadowy.

- Things in a room that don't stand out to you in everyday life can start to look pretty annoying on a video. Photographers' backdrops can be purchased at photo stores. These consistent backgrounds can let you film in any room you want without a distracting background.

- If filming in an office, simply tidy up the area that will be in the frame. Film the scene for a few seconds without your host in it and look for things that stick out. Then take those out of the frame, or fix them.

Editing

ScreenFlow has a built-in editor that is geared toward editing screen captures. If you are using a capture-only program such as iShowU, or need to combine screen capture footage with live footage, you can export your video as a Quicktime file, which can be used with any video editing program. Recommended video editing programs include

✔ iMovie: $79 bundled in iLife (recommended)

✔ Final Cut Express: $199

✔ Final Cut Studio: $1299

✔ Adobe Premiere: $799

Unless you want to get into video editing on its own right, you'll be fine with iMovie. You can use editing to cut together your footage. If you can find places to cut, cutting out dead time and covering cuts with transitions can make it more fun to watch.

Communication Is Two-Way!

While you are originating all this communication on the Internet, pay attention to what comes back the other direction. Communication back to you can come in many forms, including

- Comments on your blog
- Reviews in the app store
- Comments on your YouTube page
- Magazine reviews and blogs about your app
- E-mails sent to you

If anything is mentioned in negative feedback that you think you can honestly improve without distorting your own story and objectives, do it. If not, ignore it completely. Shooting back will only poison your image.

While you don't want to dwell on the negative, the feedback you get on your app can be the best source for discovering what you should focus on updating. Even if a customer is frustrated with your first release, making sure you address their concerns in your next update and letting them know about it can turn a heckler into a fan. If they weren't interested in your product, they wouldn't have bothered to comment. If you handle their complaints, they'll appreciate you, even if they were slightly critical at first.

When you've made an update that addresses concerns expressed online, go back to where you first saw the comment and let them. Even before you've made a change, responding by letting them know you heard them will have a positive effect. Then be sure to actually update your app!

Chapter 17

Promoting Your App with Paid Advertising

*W*ith tens of thousands of different applications competing for iPhone owners' attention, it's important to use as many different opportunities as possible to gain attention for your app, especially if you're selling a paid application to earn money. Paid advertising (whether you're a fan or a critic) is still a viable, powerful way to gain attention and earn sales (or downloads) for your app today, and there are lots of types to choose from. The benefit of using forms of electronic paid advertising is that you have access to incredible tracking capabilities that tell you the effectiveness of a given ad campaign.

In the old days, you could run a 30-second spot on TV, put up a billboard by the freeway, or take out a full-page ad in a newspaper, and not really know how many sales were obtained from that ad effort. Today, you can run a keyword or banner ad campaign and know within hours your return on investment and test out multiple campaigns at the same time without the general public realizing it. You can also draw on a wealth of information online that can make your targeting more precise and, therefore, more effective. After all, why put an ad in front of someone who isn't interested in buying? It's like trying to sell aluminum siding to an apartment dweller.

In this chapter, I explore some of the paid advertising strategies you can employ to promote your iPhone application, as well as some of the unintended benefits of building your marketing campaign. I also give you some tips and tricks along the way.

Marketing to Your Niche

If you want to get people interested in your product, start by appealing to people who already demonstrate an interest in your product area. Appealing to existing fans of a given niche is a smart bet for any advertising budget, small or large. You are "preaching to the converted." Most, if not all, of the viewers of your ad will already be predisposed to want to click your ad and find more. At least, they are much more likely to find out more about your product than someone who doesn't actively participate in your app's given niche.

The Internet and other channels like cable TV allow content providers to reach directly to their given niche audience much easier than they have in the past, and this allows you to advertise with those content providers — such as Web sites, specialty magazines, TV networks, and so on — to reach your audience. Typically, these advertising channels run surveys and do studies to provide specific demographic information on who their average reader or customer is, and they can provide those statistics to you before you advertise — so that you have a better idea of the fit between your app and their audience. For example, *Macworld* magazine shares a wealth of demographic information (see Figure 17-1) about its readers, many of whom own iPhones.

Our Audience

PCWorld and Macworld deliver tightly focused, award-winning editorial to a coveted audience of affluent, well educated, technology enthusiasts who use our content for expert purchasing guidance. They wield considerable influence in both home and professional circles.

PC World and Macworld reach almost 14 million tech influencers*** who are actively in the market to gather data, make pivotal brand decisions, and advise others on what products to buy. There are a critical mass of potential buyers across a multitude of computing and CE categories. For example:

Male	65%
Female	35%
Mean Age	44
College†	77%
Own a Home	74%
Median HHI	$73,822
2+ PC's in the home	78%

Data source ***

13.8 Plan to Purchase a technology product in the next 6 Months (74%, index 132)

- 5 million plan to buy a desktop or notebook for personal reasons
- 3.8 million are in the market for a monitor or other display device
- 4.7 million plan to buy a printer
- 4.3 million plan to buy home theatre equipment
- 3.3 million plan to buy a digital camera or digital video camera
- 5.3 million plan to buy storage
- 2.4 million plan to buy security hardware / software

Figure 17-1: See if potential advertisers (like Macworld) match your niche audience.

To find the places that attract your niche audience, get to know your audience! Use the Internet to search out Web sites that discuss and have information that appeal to your niche audience. For example, if you want to appeal to hardcore iPhone gamers, look for Web sites that have reviews, discussions, and news about iPhone game applications. Join their forums, get to know the audiences, and see if they match the niche audience that would like to buy and use your app. Hopefully, you're getting involved in this niche community, as I discuss in Chapter 16. Now, you're simply learning if this outlet offers paid advertising so you can reach the audience even more.

Think about the customers who are interested in your niche and figure out what those customers have in common. To do this,

- ✔ Consider what aspects of your application appeal to this customer set.

- ✔ Think about what other things appeal to this customer set and look for advertising opportunities there.

   For example, iPhone gaming addicts may also be interested in PC games or Nintendo Wii games, so Web sites that cater to those users could be a potential bonanza for your new hot iPhone game.

If you're still having trouble finding sites that cater to your niche, do a Google or Yahoo! search on your niche, and see which Web sites run paid ads in the search results. If these Web sites are paying money to attract people that are using your niche market keywords, these Web sites are worth a little investigation.

Typically, you have several options for buying advertising from one of these niche sites, so when you locate a potential hangout for your audience, see if you can buy one or more of the following from the publisher:

- ✔ Banner advertising on the Web site or print ads in the paper magazine

- ✔ Banner or text advertising in the newsletter or e-zines to readers

- ✔ Sponsorship of a contest or event/conference run by the publisher

- ✔ E-mail marketing partner offer to the publisher's mailing list

In many cases, the publisher is looking to offer advertisers like you some options and will offer a few avenues designed for paid advertising. For example, Macworld created an iPhone Application Guide (see Figure 17-2) and grouped its targeted iPhone content to sell advertising to people who want to reach those readers.

Since you want to get the biggest bang for your buck, you should also ask for more than demographic data. See if the publisher has any statistics on the customer's likelihood to read more, respond to offers, or buy based on an advertisement. If there are any clicks involved in an online advertisement, ask for the ability to track clicks and conversions so you know the effectiveness of the advertisement.

You shouldn't think of your niche marketing investigation efforts as simply a one-time deal. By doing ongoing research and participating over time in various niche Web sites, you'll have a continual list of potential advertising targets that might mirror not only the tastes of your industry but the progression of your app in the App Store as well. As you become more familiar with different user groups, social networks, and friends of friends, be aware of any potential co-marketing initiatives, special advertising events, or other ways to work with these publishers to reach their audiences.

Your paid ad can lead to a lot more

Robert Hogg and the iSamurai development team learned — the enjoyable way — how a simple paid ad can lead to one of the most important advertising vehicles for a new iPhone app. As the iSamurai team researched which Web sites catered to the gaming fans who would like their application, they found Touch Arcade, a review site with information on not just to iPhone apps, but iPhone gaming applications as well.

The iSamurai team used Touch Arcade's forums to build some buzz on and interest in their new app, and they responded often and professionally to the users on that site. They decided to place the minimum-sized ad on Touch Arcade (as shown here), which cost $200, but they wanted to hold the ad until the game was finalized, approved by Apple, and launched into the App Store. While they waited for this to happen, they built relations with Touch Arcade and continued to contribute to their discussion forums, even running a contest on the forums called "Guess this Game!"

Banner ad

Before the iSamurai application launched, the Touch Arcade staff decided to look for unreleased games that they could announce at their first-ever launch party during the yearly Apple Worldwide Developers Conference in San Francisco. Because the iSamurai team had been talking with Touch Arcade and using the site, their app was considered for selection. iSamurai worked tirelessly to provide prerelease information and video, and eventually, their app was selected as one of the six apps launched during the conference launch party.

The iSamurai team got to premiere their application to a who's who of Apple developers and luminaries at the Launch party, including Apple co-founder Steve Wozniak. Based on reviews they got after the party, they were considered one of the top apps shown that night! In addition,

Touch Arcade ran an article about the event on its home page the next day. The article received tens of thousands of hits and created a great launch for the iSamurai app and their team. That publicity helped start the spike of downloads that eventually caught the eye of Apple itself.

While you should never expect extra editorial attention because you become a paid advertiser, there can be some unexpected benefits from doing paid advertising on top of free buzz. By treating your media partners with respect and engaging their customer (or user) base, you present the best picture of you and your app to a group of people who can positively (and negatively) affect your outcome. Do your homework, like iSamurai did, and your uniqueness can be rewarded.

Figure 17-2: Publishers will offer targeted opportunities for you to reach your niche.

Creating a Paid Advertisement Strategy

Because of the ability to drill down and reach individual targeted users (and because you don't have a bottomless budget to run ads) you need to come up with a strategy to use your advertising dollars wisely and effectively. Perhaps your goal is to use paid advertising only on the launch of your app, until you get the buzz from reviews and other marketing efforts to land on Apple's top lists. You could do a slow and steady campaign from development to launch and beyond to drive interest to your Web site and the App Store. Or you could turn to paid advertising when you've reached a certain threshold and want to promote new updates or a major change in your application (or application price), or if you've found a new audience that has interest in your application.

Researching needed keywords

Many people approach their advertising strategy by studying how their customers use the Internet and learning to be in front of the users as they click along. The overwhelming majority of Internet users start their journeys by using search engines to find what they're looking for. Therefore, knowing the right keywords that your potential audience will use is seen as a critical part of your paid advertising strategy.

So, when you want to find the right keywords to reach the biggest relevant audience, it's time to do some research on the most-often-used keywords in the search engines. Thankfully, there are several tools that can help you do that. Google's built-in keyword analyzer is part of its AdWords solution, and you can buy products like Keywords Analyzer and install them on your computer. Here, I profile a subscription Web site called Wordtracker.

Wordtracker (www.wordtracker.com) was built to help advertisers identify keywords and phrases that matter to their business, specifically the keywords and phrases most likely to be used in a search engine. It can also provide information on how many sites competing with yours are using those keywords, and which keywords and phrases have the biggest potential for drawing traffic. Wordtracker accomplishes this through several avenues. Its Researcher tool works like this:

1. **Enter a seed keyword or two into the Research window.**

2. **Pick from various settings that help you get the exact data you're looking for and click Research.**

   As shown in Figure 17-3, Wordtracker displays a list of top keyword phrases and the corresponding number of searches performed on each phrase.

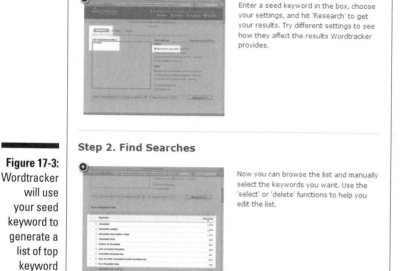

Step 1. Enter Keywords

Enter a seed keyword in the box, choose your settings, and hit 'Research' to get your results. Try different settings to see how they affect the results Wordtracker provides.

Step 2. Find Searches

Now you can browse the list and manually select the keywords you want. Use the 'select' or 'delete' functions to help you edit the list.

Figure 17-3: Wordtracker will use your seed keyword to generate a list of top keyword phrases.

3. **Choose which keyword phrases you wish to analyze further.**

4. **Pick a search engine and click the Evaluate button.**

   Wordtracker tells you how many Web pages compete for those keywords. (See Figure 17-4.) You can click the hyperlink offered to see the search results of the competing pages if you like.

Repeat Steps 1–4 to get more targeted phrases on related keywords. You can also use Wordtracker to export these results to your computer for further analysis.

Wordtracker was designed for companies with search engine optimization strategies, so it's offered as an ongoing subscription. You can subscribe on a monthly or yearly basis, but look for a 7-day free trial on Wordtracker's Web site.

Allocating your budget to multiple campaigns

Don't invest your entire marketing budget to just one campaign. Today, you can quickly test and measure different campaigns and go with the most successful one in a matter of minutes, not days or weeks. When you pin all your hopes on one expensive buy, such as a full-page ad in a magazine, chances are that you'll see very little effectiveness, as customers need to see your product name multiple times before they will remember it.

Step 3. Evaluate Competition

At the bottom of your list, click 'Evaluate'. Then choose the search engine you want and hit 'Evaluate' again. You'll now see the number of competing pages for each keyword. Click the hyperlinked number if you want to see the search results.

Step 4. Export Results

At the bottom of your list, click 'Export'. Choose the format you'd like and click 'Export' again, then save your results. That's it – click the 'Research' tab to do more keyword research.

Figure 17-4:
Learn how many Web pages compete for those keywords.

To decide how much to spend on each campaign, you need to look at these things:

- Your entire marketing budget
- The minimum cost to do a small campaign in one area
- The number of different types of campaigns you hope to do

  Let's say that you have $1,000, and the minimum banner ad or keyword campaign you hope to run will cost at least $200. Then you know you can do up to five different campaigns.

- The timing of your marketing expense

  Make sure that you have campaigns running when your application is launched into the App Store. Because you'll have to wait for Apple to approve your app, you'll need to check your status often. You should set up your campaigns as much as possible before your expected launch date and be ready to go as soon as you receive word that your app is in the App Store.

For your launch marketing campaigns, make sure that you've done these things:

- ✔ Set up any necessary accounts in advance
- ✔ Defined any keywords or keyword phrases you plan to use
- ✔ Created any graphics necessary for the campaign
- ✔ Completed any payment authorizations or setup necessary
- ✔ Set up all your parameters within the software or Web site

Your goal is to have everything ready so that, when you say "Go", the ad campaign begins. Once your campaigns are running, in some cases, you'll need to monitor results to decide what to focus on in terms of ads. For example, if you're running a keyword ad campaign with Google (see the next section for information on how to set up that campaign), you can actually run multiple ads within one campaign and see results after a day. You can decide to expand the budget for the most successful ads and delete the least successful ads.

If you have extra campaigns to either build up the buzz before your application is launched or announce any new updates or changes once your app is launched, make sure that you've updated all the language everywhere. It's very easy to just repeat something that's already defined, but you may confuse your customers if the message says different things from what you've defined.

Google AdWords

The leader in search engine ads is Google AdWords. You can use this program to create your own ads and bid on keywords that trigger the display of those ads. When a Google user types your keywords in a search, your ad appears on the right side of the results screen in a Sponsored Links box.

Google keeps track of the number of times your ad is clicked, and you pay only for the times your ad is clicked, not the number of times your ad is displayed on the screen. Like other services, AdWords lets you set a budget, so you pay only for the ads you can afford. When your budget is used up, your ad doesn't appear any more. You even specify a daily budget so that your ad campaign budget can't be spent in the first day.

A Google AdWords *campaign* doesn't refer to a politician's run for office; it more commonly means running a specific ad for a given budget. Your ad campaign can consist of one ad running on Google until you spend $100, or a series of ads running for several weeks to promote a new product.

Your customization of the campaign isn't limited to just the keyword. Using Google AdWords, you can pick your target area (a city, territory, or country), and Google targets where the search user is from, whether it's from the search itself, the specific IP address of the computer, or the preferences that the user set up. By using this targeting, you can

- ✔ Show different ads to different territories
- ✔ Offer specific ads and promotions to specific areas
- ✔ Create your own test markets where only a specific group of computer users is presented with a given ad

I discuss Google Ads because it's popular and easy to use. However, all the services work similarly, so just choose the one that works best for you.

If you're interested in setting up your own AdWords campaign, type your keywords and look at the ads that already appear on Google for your targeted subject area. Get an idea of the ads that you're competing against and the words they use to craft their ads. This strategy should give you some ideas for your ad.

Write your ad copy and have two or three people proofread it before building your campaign. Also, take the time to think of the right keywords to use in advance, so you're not guessing when it's time to build the campaign.

When you're ready to build an AdWords campaign, just follow these steps:

1. **Go to `http://adwords.google.com` and click the Click to Begin button.**

2. **Choose between the Starter Edition and the Standard Edition, as shown in Figure 17-5.**

   If you're planning to test the market, pick the Starter Edition. You can then build one text ad and get familiar with the system.

3. **Click Continue.**

   If you picked the Starter Edition, you see a one-page form where you can fill out all the details of your ad. If you picked the Standard Edition, you go to a series of Web pages that focus on one part of the four-part setup process.

4. **Choose the target area of your ad. Click Continue when you're ready.**

   You can pick the country where you want to run the ad, specify a local area, and choose the language to run the ad in.

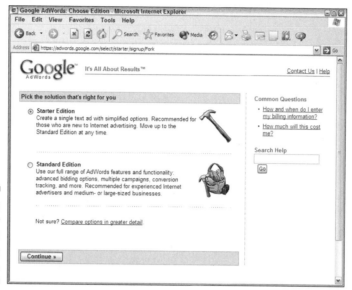

Figure 17-5:
Choose your
level of ad
campaign
on Google.

5. **Specify the Web site address where you want to redirect people who click your ad.**

You don't have to link your ad to your home page. You can specify a special Web page within your Web site so that you can present a special offer to only those people who click your ad. You can easily track the number of people who view that page to see how effective your ad truly is.

6. **Write the ad. Click Continue.**

You can use a total of 95 characters on three lines.

- The headline can contain as many as 25 characters.

- Each of the two lines of text underneath the headline can have as many as 35 characters.

7. **Specify the keywords that will trigger your ad. (See Figure 17-6.)**

You can specify one or more keywords that are related to the product you want to advertise. If you're looking for ideas on what keyword phrases to use, Google displays related keyword phrases based on reading your Web site. You can add those to your campaign.

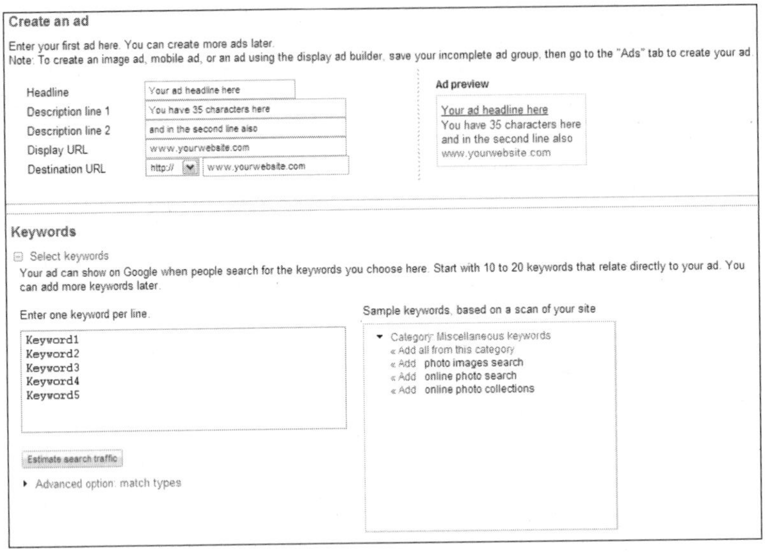

Figure 17-6:
Type the
keywords
that you
want to
associate
with
your ad.

8. **Specify the currency you're using for this ad campaign and then your monthly or daily budget. Click Continue.**

Pick from the options presented, or put your custom ad budget amount in the Budget field provided.

Google prompts you if it thinks that your maximum per-click rate is too low and then suggests a minimum level. If you can't afford a keyword, try to come up with an alternative one.

9. **Choose to receive newsletters, surveys, and other helpful information for future campaigns. Click Continue.**

Leave the box selected if you want to receive this information. If you don't want it, be sure to deselect the box.

10. **Enter an e-mail address and password if you need to create an account with Google.**

Google can tie your campaign to your existing Google account (if you use other Google services, such as Gmail).

11. **Answer the Google security question, and then click Create Account.**

Google sends you an e-mail containing a Web link.

12. **Click the Web link to verify your account and return to Google.**

13. **Log in to your account and provide Google with the billing information for your account.**

Just follow the prompts, or click the My Account tab and look for Billing Preferences. Google asks for your billing country and then your payment information. Read through the Google AdWords program terms and agree to them, too.

After your payment method is entered and approved, your ads begin to appear on Google almost instantly! Go to the main Google page and perform a few searches to see where your ad ends up on the results page.

Banner Ads

Given the colorful nature of iPhone applications and the existing banner ad placement within many iPhone apps already, it makes sense to consider using banner advertisements to help promote your application, on top of other methods like keyword advertising. A banner ad allows you to extend your brand by using the same visual appeal of your app inside the banner graphic, as well as provide animation (in some cases) and a visual cue for how your iPhone application works.

Many Web sites that iPhone owners use still employ banner advertisements. More importantly, the ads that appear inside iPhone applications are banner ads by nature, since the screen is too small to properly display a 25-to-30-word keyword ad along with the app. Therefore, when you create a banner graphic for your iPhone app, you can use it on Web sites, and on iPhone ad networks as well.

Creating your banner ad

When you want to create your banner ad, you have several choices:

- ✔ Design the banner graphic yourself.
- ✔ Hire a (or use an already hired) graphic designer to design it.
- ✔ Pay the banner ad network to design the graphic.

Regardless of who designs your banner ad graphic, use the existing graphics that appear in your application, especially your icon and any other specialty buttons, for example. You want your banner ad to communicate the brand image of your product because you want your potential customers to be able to follow your product from the advertisement to the App Store to installing the app on their iPhones. Using consistent graphics throughout builds familiarity with the app.

You can make your own banner graphic using a program like Banner Maker Pro (see Figure 17-7) or Adobe Photoshop. Your goal is to use as few words as possible and focus on clear, clean graphics because a banner is designed to be viewed quickly, not read like a book.

You may have to scale down your banner for different Web sites' available banner ad sizes. This is especially true if you have to scale down your ad to fit on the iPhone screen in an application.

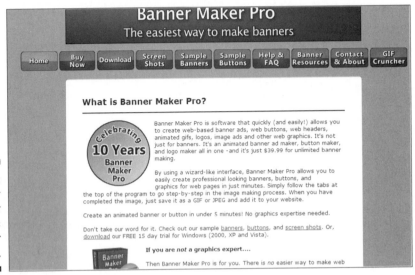

Figure 17-7:
Design your
own banner
ad graphic
with Banner
Maker Pro.

You can also consider making an animated banner ad, which you can think of as multiple image versions that rotate in the same space. (Think of one of those flipbooks, where it looks like something is moving when you flip through the pages very quickly and each image is slightly different.) If you want a quality animated banner ad, I highly recommend consulting a professional graphic designer. (I talk about hiring a graphic designer in Chapter 12.)

When you're making your banner ad, you should keep these design points in mind:

- **Make every word count.** As I said, don't load down a banner ad with lots of words. On the other hand, you can put one to two lines of text in it and still have an attractive and readable banner ad. For banner ads designed to display on the iPhone, one line of text is probably the most you can get away with, and in that case, icons and images are probably your best bet.

- **Leave them wanting more.** Your goal is to get the user to click the ad to find out more (and hopefully, buy your application). Therefore, you've got to entice the user to want to click that ad and read, see, and hear more about what you have to sell.

  If your app has a crucial or breakthrough feature, let your viewers know by hinting at what problems your app can solve, for example. Make the claims that you can back up, and don't be afraid to boast about something that is true and that will get people to notice, like an influential testimonial.

- **Create a call to action.** Sadly, it isn't enough to just get the user excited about your application. You need to present something that actually asks the user to click the banner to do something! In the marketing world, they call this the *call to action*. You're actually calling out for the user to do something besides read the ad.

Maybe your call to action is a mention of how to download a free or Lite application or a free icon or wallpaper. Or it can be the simple "Click here to find out how!" slogan.

Finding the right banner ad network

Even though the iPhone and the App Store are relatively new inventions, there are already lots of options when it comes to finding the right banner ad network to run your ads to reach these iPhone users. One consideration depends on whether you plan to run advertisements inside your iPhone application. If you do run ads within your app, you can consider whether to use the same ad network or platform to run both your general banner advertising and your iPhone in-application advertising.

Here are some ad networks or platforms that can help you coordinate banner advertising within your iPhone application:

- AdMob (www.admob.com)
- Crispin Wireless (www.crispinwireless.com) (see Figure 17-8)
- Medialets (www.medialets.com) (see Figure 17-9)
- Pinch Media (www.pinchmedia.com)
- PurpleTalk (www.purpletalk.com)

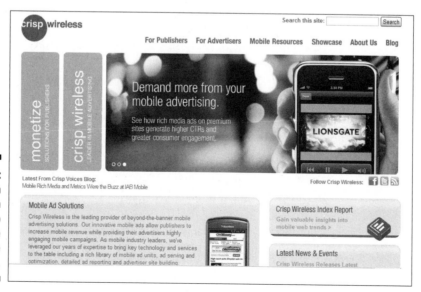

Figure 17-8: You can use Crispin Wireless to coordinate your mobile advertising.

Why pay for ads?

In the early days of the Web, small businesses would set up exchanges, or networks, that would work like this: A business would agree to run a banner ad on its Web site that would show other network members' ads. Every time a user would click the ad from your Web site, for example, you would get a credit and your ad would show up on someone else's Web site (in the network). Every click you helped generate translated into one of your banner ads showing up online. The idea of the exchange now comes to the iPhone, in the form of AdMob's Download Exchange, as shown in this figure.

Download Exchange allows you to show ads inside your iPhone application (ads from other users in the network). As your users click those ads, your banner ads show up in other applications. In fact, you can even control how many of the ads displayed in your application are network ads and how many are paid ads from AdMob's general ad network, which allows you to generate some revenue from advertising instead of just exchanging ad space.

AdMob works with you to get the highest click-through rates possible and gives you the option to filter out any ads you don't want. (For example, you would probably want to filter out any potential competitors because your goal isn't to support their business.) They will also design the ads for you!

You can find out more by going to www.admob.com/exchange.

Test the efficacy of your banner ads. As your ads run on these networks, you should see what your click-through rate is and, in many cases, which of your multiple banner ads are performing the best (and worst). And you can take action on that. You're looking to maximize your click-through rate, and you should look for an ad network that helps you do that, along with providing the tools and interface to monitor your banner ads, rotate out different ads to see which ones are the best, and allow you to test multiple campaigns.

You can take your banner ads to the next level by hiring a firm like VideoEgg (see Figure 17-10) to create rich media ads that include animation, video, and sound. They can create an ad that really pops from the screen and captures a users' attention. You can expect to pay more per ad for a rich experience like this, but hopefully, your response rate (or click-through rate) will greatly improve and therefore make up for the higher cost.

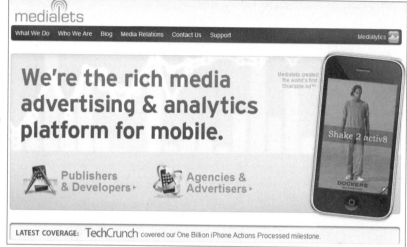

Figure 17-9: Medialets can increase the effectiveness of banners.

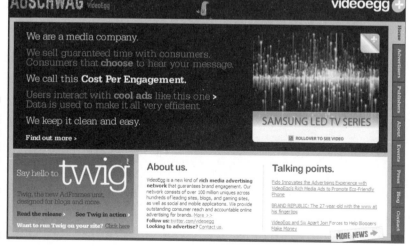

Figure 17-10: Create a powerful video ad with a company like VideoEgg.

Chapter 18

Planning Your Next Project

*W*hen you conceive, develop, post, and market your first application, you definitely gain an appreciation for the entire application development process. After you complete the cycle, the question you may ask yourself is, "What's next?"

If you are like many who have had success in the App Store, your mind has already been contemplating your next effort. At this point, you have the infrastructure in place and you have familiarity with getting an app off the ground. Now your challenge is to learn from past mistakes and make your next offering even better, or translate the momentum of a recent success into a business model. You'll probably do a combination of both. First, you'll need to think in broader terms.

Building Your Brand

Your company's brand identity is the foundation of the story you tell to new investors, partners, the media, and your customers. If you followed our advice in Chapter 5, you've built a brand identity for your company as well as your app. If not, now is the time to start.

If you haven't yet invested in the process of envisioning and developing your company, you can start by identifying the unique attributes of your current app in relation to your overall vision. Think of it as the first piece in a puzzle you are about to put together. What picture is on the puzzle box? In other words, work on creating a vision for your company that includes and goes beyond your first app.

While you develop your brand, consider your core offering to the consumer. Your apps are the products you are giving them, but your *core offering* is often distinct from the mechanics of your apps — that is, the emotion or experience that customers have when interacting with your company and products:

- ✔ Cruise lines offer adventure.

- ✔ Perfume manufacturers offer romance. Specific perfumeries embody their own distinct spin on romance — classiness, sexuality, sophistication, warmth, and so on.

- ✔ OmniGroup, the maker of OmniFocus, offers fun, simple ways to be productive (see Figure 18-1).

- ✔ McDonald's offers fast, reliable "food, folks, and fun."

- ✔ Ferrari offers status, sexiness, power, and speed.

- ✔ Electronic Arts offers top-notch interactive entertainment.

Figure 18-1: OmniGroup has built its brand on a series of simple productivity apps.

Distill what you want your core offering to be. Try to make it something that encompasses the app you released and allows you room to grow while you put out more apps. Make it something that gets you excited and that you would want from a company. When you come up with an offering that you can express in a few words, use that to describe your company in your marketing. You can even use it as a tag line. Remember "GE. We bring good things to life"?

If you haven't had a chance to apply the concepts in Chapter 5, we highly recommend that you go back and do that now; then come back to this chapter.

Keeping an app ideas inventory

When you came up with your first idea, your app concept ideally came from a large pool of ideas that was funneled into the app you finally developed based on a process of elimination. An app ideas inventory allows you the creative freedom to come up with ideas without tossing out a brilliant one, and to be discerning so that you develop only ideas you can see a market for and that align with your core offering.

Perceptive Development accomplishes this by keeping a shared spreadsheet (by using Google Docs) that anyone in the company can add to. (See Figure 18-2.) When ideas come up, any team member can post the idea on the spreadsheet and send an e-mail to the team for discussion. Then, the team can play with and vet the idea based on whether it's been done before, how excited about it they are, how feasible it appears, and what kind of market there might be for it.

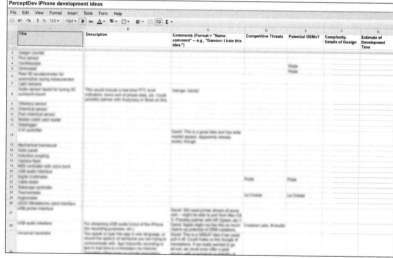

Figure 18-2:
Keep a running inventory on new application ideas.

Picking an app idea that fits your brand

If you went through a brainstorming process like the one we outline in Chapter 4 to come up with your first app, chances are ideas came out of the process that you can pick up and take a second look at. If your original idea came to you in a single flash of inspiration, you may be starting from scratch. On the other hand, you might have an inventory of ideas.

In any case, your next app idea will be strengthened if it connects in some way with the core offering that underpins your first app. This allows you to extend the foundation you started rather than creating islands that you have to bridge together. If you can connect with and extend your core offering with your next app, you'll enjoy these benefits:

✔ A built-in customer base that is already onboard with that core offering

✔ A coherent story that you can write another installment for rather than starting from scratch

✔ An organizational knowledge base about your software content that you can extend rather than reinvent

✔ A platform for cross promoting: "AppX users should try its companion app, AppY!"

✔ A relationship with your product mavens (see Chapter 16) that you can leverage

Everything that you learned and developed for your first app can be used to propel interest in your next app. Going in a completely different direction won't deprive you of *all* that foundational work, but it won't leverage the synergy you can develop between apps that have a common purpose.

After you've built a few apps with a common core offering, branching into new territory can provide a welcome and exciting twist to your corporate narrative, but if you haven't managed to build a corporate narrative yet, you'll risk appearing random — and random is weak.

Consider what kind of attitude you want your company to exude. Here, we don't mean a bad attitude, but rather Oxford's definition: "A settled way of thinking or feeling about someone or something, typically one that is reflected in a person's behavior." Do you want to be the trippy techies who keep doing cool "out-there" things or be the bread-and-butter productivity people? Do you want to be the sports fans who are rockin' their iPhones at the game or be the post-teen gamers who believe in the *Legend of Zelda* more than the legend of Zeus?

Apple's attitude in the consumer-level space is that of the helpful young smart people who probably know more than you do, but are happy to help you be as savvy as they are without making you feel uncomfortable. To pros, Apple's attitude is that of helpful leaders and collaborators working with developers to create the computing future together.

Who you and those you have working with you are can be described as an attitude. Also, what attitude does your existing app(s) exude? Pose these questions to a group of users in the form of a survey. When you're looking at new app ideas, try to find ways to continue that attitude into the next project along with your core offering. This further helps you differentiate yourself in the marketplace.

For example, OmniGroup's attitude is that of light-hearted problem solvers. If you combine its attitude with its core offering, it is "light-hearted problem solvers who offer fun, simple ways to be productive." Looking at its apps at www.omnigroup.com, you can see that each one fits that attitude, and (almost) all of them have the core offering in common. OmniGroup has been developing applications for Mac OS for more than 15 years. It is a leader in third-party Mac software, and its $20 iPhone app OmniFocus is consistently in the top ten in its category. Clearly, choosing to develop apps that contribute to and extend its core offering, and express its attitude has paid off for OmniFocus.

Partnerships and joint ventures

After you launch an app, you might find yourself in the company of developers and owners of businesses similar to yours. Eventually the opportunity may present itself to team with another company, or enter a partnership with another person.

These opportunities can be very exciting and open doors to you that you might not have considered. The opportunity to share the load with another person or company can also come as a relief. Partnering is a terrific way to extend your offerings without having to take on more employees and expenses, or stretch outside your comfort zone.

Many partnerships fail because people go into them thinking, "We'll just do everything together" only to find out down the road that the expectations or desires of one or both partners haven't been fulfilled and are the basis for mistrust and miscommunication. Like ending a romantic relationship, breaking up a business partnership can get ugly fast or torture you slowly.

The remedy for this is to establish very clear roles, responsibilities, and rewards in the beginning so that when the inevitable misunderstandings arise, you have a template to refer to for clearing them up. This also limits assumptions, which are deadly in business. Make everything you are thinking about the partnership explicitly clear on paper so both entities can review and agree to the terms. In the excitement of collaboration, you often feel like the relationship is so good that no one will let the other down and whatever might go wrong is fixable with good will. You also might not want to strain the new friendship with a bunch of legalese and signatures. However, when the shiny newness of the relationship wears off, you'll be working with these people under the pressure of deadlines, difficult software challenges, finances, and risks. Three factors are going to be critical at that time:

- ✔ Genuine generosity and good will toward each other that you express in actions, not just words

- ✔ Explicit agreements that each of you can fulfill to move the project forward

- ✔ An established leader who ultimately sets the direction and tone rather than two "equally important" partners playing clash of the titans

One workable structure is to develop partnerships with other companies in such a way that, on a given project, one company is the lead and the other is essentially the contractor. That way, there is a clear hierarchy of roles and responsibilities. The companies may share some of the risks and rewards as far as profit is concerned, but the contracting company is guaranteed the fee agreed to initially, which should cover its development costs. The roles may vary from job to job, one company playing the lead on one project, and the other company leading on the next; but for any given project, someone being in charge reduces chaos.

The benefits of partnering with other companies can be profound. No company can do everything. Our company, for example, is composed mostly of engineers, not marketers and designers, so we partner with companies that are marketing and design-centric to augment that aspect of our business — from the look of our apps to our branding and Web presence. This allows us to get into the projects that require heavy lifting while still having a professional image and well-designed apps.

Identify your team's core competencies. What areas could you fill through healthy partnerships with other companies or individuals?

If you don't already know companies or people to partner with, make yourself more of a presence at the WWDC and other events. You can meet many people that way.

Using Your First App to Promote Upcoming Applications

Assuming you follow our advice and make your next app continue or augment the core offering of your first app, the promotion for your new app is as simple as letting your customers know it exists and educating them about how it can help them acquire more of your core offering. You have a number of ways to do this:

- ✔ Promoting your new app in the description of your existing app on the App Store

- ✔ Putting banner ads in your existing app for your new one (assuming you have an ad system in your existing app)

- ✔ Promoting your new app with the mailing list that you developed with your existing app (assuming you found a way to gather those e-mail addresses!)

- ✔ Making your new app interoperate with your existing app so that having one is augmented by having the other

Surveying Your Existing Customers

Assuming you built a mailing list with your first app, you now have a powerful market research tool with which to gather inspiration for your next app. However, getting people to take part in surveys can be difficult. Here are some ideas for gaining participation:

✔ **Find a reward you can offer.** If you have digital content for sale, offer them some of it free. Try to offer something that is free or cheap to you, but has value to them. Not everyone will care about your "carrot," but it can boost your response rate.

✔ **Make sure to make it clear that you're gathering ideas for a new product.** People love to contribute to something new, but don't enjoy feeling like marketing guinea pigs. Involve them in the story of your entrepreneurial adventure.

✔ **Keep your survey short and make it known right away.** Almost all companies say their surveys are short, so be specific. For example, "Answer our 5 question survey."

✔ **Ask customers for stories involving your existing app and for features they'd love to see in a new app.** The Obama administration does very well at collecting information about its constituency this way. People feel like they are contributing by telling you about themselves. You can use these stories to glean new insight into how your app is used and see opportunities for new applications.

Generating online surveys has become quite easy. Some of the e-mail marketing systems we outline in Chapter 16 offer surveying, such as SurveyMonkey (see Figure 18-3) or Constant Contact (see Figure 18-4). Here is a short list of some of the solutions available:

✔ SurveyMonkey — www.surveymonkey.com

✔ ZAPSurvey — www.zapsurvey.com

✔ Constant Contact — search.constantcontact.com/survey

✔ Icebrrg — www.icebrrg.com

Some sample questions you can ask:

✔ What feature do you like most about AppX?

✔ If you had a companion app for AppX, what would it do?

✔ What do you wish you could do with AppX, but can't?

✔ If you could create an app for yourself, what would it do?

✔ What's your favorite app after AppX?

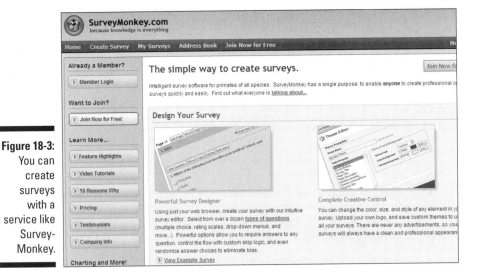

Figure 18-3:
You can create surveys with a service like Survey-Monkey.

Figure 18-4:
Constant Contact can help you survey customers.

Planning Your Future

In this book, we advocate you include your app within the larger context of creating an iPhone app company. This isn't the only way you can go, however. It might fit your vision better to make "one off" apps for specific purposes. If you're an independent developer, you might want to create apps from the context of your personal résumé, rather than for a corporate portfolio. Later, you might consider making a company out of it, or trying to get hired by an existing company.

If you decide to create an iPhone app company, look at the corporate vision you've developed, your core competencies (those things your company is best at doing), and your core offering for opportunities to expand while keeping these elements in focus. Perhaps you can offer hardware that supports the software you develop. Perhaps you can port your software to other platforms. Perhaps you've found a niche, such as the personal planning and organizing company, Franklin Covey, which provides a multitude of products across many media.

When you create a company, you must consider other long-term benefits. A larger company that wants expertise and credibility in your niche might acquire your company. For example, Blackboard focused on providing education technology on a global scale. It decided to create a division called MobilEdu to extend its brand and offerings to the iPhone market (see Figure 18-5). To accomplish this, Blackboard acquired a small iPhone app company, Terribly Clever, in July 2009. (See Figure 18-6.) Terribly Clever built its reputation writing iPhone apps for such universities as Stanford, Duke, Texas A&M, and others. Specifically, the company wrote iPhone applications that were used by the students at these universities to support their academic and campus life activities. This kind of expertise was exactly what Blackboard was looking for, and now Terribly Clever brings its technology to a wider base of institutions.

Consider the iPhone platform as only the base of your enterprise's exploits. When you hit on something special, look around and see how you can expand your market into other areas. If you're successful, you can inform those new customers about your iPhone apps and your app customers about your new venture. The iPhone is a lifestyle product that exists in a product ecosystem. Can you develop a product ecosystem that supports, and benefits from, your iPhone apps?

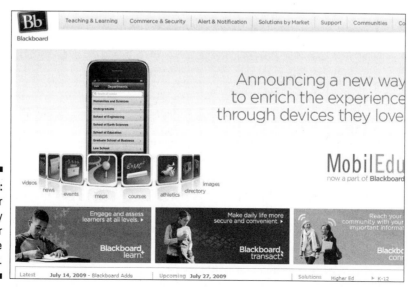

Figure 18-5: A larger company can enter the iPhone app market.

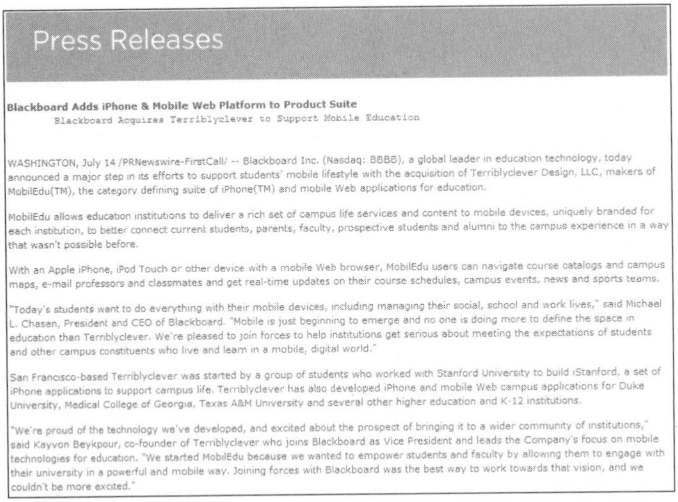

Press Releases

Blackboard Adds iPhone & Mobile Web Platform to Product Suite
Blackboard Acquires Terriblyclever to Support Mobile Education

WASHINGTON, July 14 /PRNewswire-FirstCall/ -- Blackboard Inc. (Nasdaq: BBBB), a global leader in education technology, today announced a major step in its efforts to support students' mobile lifestyle with the acquisition of Terriblyclever Design, LLC, makers of MobilEdu(TM), the category defining suite of iPhone(TM) and mobile Web applications for education.

MobilEdu allows education institutions to deliver a rich set of campus life services and content to mobile devices, uniquely branded for each institution, to better connect current students, parents, faculty, prospective students and alumni to the campus experience in a way that wasn't possible before.

With an Apple iPhone, iPod Touch or other device with a mobile Web browser, MobilEdu users can navigate course catalogs and campus maps, e-mail professors and classmates and get real-time updates on their course schedules, campus events, news and sports teams.

"Today's students want to do everything with their mobile devices, including managing their social, school and work lives," said Michael L. Chasen, President and CEO of Blackboard. "Mobile is just beginning to emerge and no one is doing more to define the space in education than Terriblyclever. We're pleased to join forces to help institutions get serious about meeting the expectations of students and other campus constituents who live and learn in a mobile, digital world."

San Francisco-based Terriblyclever was started by a group of students who worked with Stanford University to build iStanford, a set of iPhone applications to support campus life. Terriblyclever has also developed iPhone and mobile Web campus applications for Duke University, Medical College of Georgia, Texas A&M University and several other higher education and K-12 institutions.

"We're proud of the technology we've developed, and excited about the prospect of bringing it to a wider community of institutions," said Kayvon Beykpour, co-founder of Terriblyclever who joins Blackboard as Vice President and leads the Company's focus on mobile technologies for education. "We started MobilEdu because we wanted to empower students and faculty by allowing them to engage with their university in a powerful and mobile way. Joining forces with Blackboard was the best way to work towards that vision, and we couldn't be more excited."

Figure 18-6:
An existing iPhone app company can be acquired.

Creating Your Own iPhone App Consultancy

You may find that you are so good at, and enjoy, the process of developing apps and/or hardware that you want to offer these services to other individuals and companies in addition to creating your own apps. Creating an iPhone consultancy can be very rewarding:

✔ You have the opportunity to be involved in many diverse projects.

✔ You can hone new skills.

✔ You get to use other people's ideas and resources.

✔ You can collaborate with all kinds of artists, technicians, and business minds.

If you develop a consultancy, you need to constantly develop new relationships and promote your services, similar to what Raven Zachary is doing for his firm. (See Figure 18-7.) Having meetings in which you seek to understand your clients' needs and interests and crafting proposals for them will become part of your routine. The benefits are that you'll be constantly surfing the edge of new technology, constantly keeping yourself in the loop of new trends, and constantly helping to lead the way in the mobile computing revolution!

Figure 18-7:
Promote
your own
iPhone app
consultancy
instead of
a specific
app.

raven.me. iPhone intelligence.

My name is Raven Zachary. I help people create, develop, and launch iPhone products and services. I work with dynamic, creative, market-driven organizations on iPhone strategy and product development.

I believe that the iPhone platform represents a major shift in mobility and provides a compelling opportunity for businesses to deliver products and services, whether native or web-based, in new and exciting ways to a global audience. I have solid experience advising businesses on the iPhone platform.

If you're interested in creating iPhone products and services and are looking for someone to get you up and running quickly and sustainably, I may be the person you are looking for. You can take a look at my iPhone Projects page for a list of the iPhone-related projects I am working on or the iPhone Services page for the type of work I provide to clients.

Blog

13 January 2009
Who says Lite apps don't work?!

12 January 2009
Featured in App Store 2009.01.05

5 January 2009
iPhone Activities @ Macworld

28 December 2008
Segment-Changing Arranged

27 December 2008
Palm's Third Act

>> More Blog Entries

Press

D: All Things Digital. Pre and Web
Longtime Palm Developers Soun

Touch Arcade: From the Expo:
Game-Focused iPhone Intelligen
Party

Ars Technica - Infinite Loop: Apple
allows devs to offer promo copies
iPhone apps

Events

SXSW Interactive, March 13-17, Au

Think Mobile, March 18-19, Austin

Where 2.0, May 19-21, San Jose

Part VI
The Part of Tens

The 5th Wave   By Rich Tennant

In this part . . .

You make lots of lists when you want to create an iPhone application. Sometimes, these lists can seem really long, and other times, maybe not as long. We present you with some lists that can be helpful instead of daunting.

In the final part of *Starting an iPhone Application Business For Dummies,* we leave you with the Part of Tens. In this part, you'll find chapters that list ten helpful items — advice, tips, and references that fit best in a ten-item list format.

Chapter 19

Ten Traits of Highly Successful Applications

• •

As you go through the process of creating, developing, and marketing your iPhone application, keep in mind this list of the ten traits that we have seen in highly successful apps. Not all successful apps have all these traits, but most have a number of them.

Great Design

As we discuss in Chapter 10, the importance of design can't be overstated. The Apple brand is all about form meets function, so the expectations of Apple users are very high as far as aesthetics are concerned. However, design doesn't boil down to just how good an app looks. It also has to do with how the design connects with the subject matter and audience for an app. For example, Dizzy Bee (which we discuss in Chapter 4) has a very child-like design. Comparatively, Whole Foods Recipes has a design that evokes hominess and freshness, which are two strong traits of the Whole Foods brand.

Design also blends ease of use and how fun an app is to use, which we discuss later in this chapter. The following design aspects blend to create the overall design of an app:

- ✔ **Graphic design:** The imagery, colors, fonts, and textures used.
- ✔ **User interface design:** The layout of the functions of the app onscreen, how the functions operate, and how screens transition between each other.
- ✔ **User experience design:** How the app is perceived, learned, and used. In other words, it is that high-level design direction that determines how an app fits into the users' life in context with the rest of their life rather than just what appears onscreen and how it is used.

Most great apps have been created with all these design elements brought to the forefront and explored thoroughly; then executed by inspired design experts. There are certainly apps that fall short in at least one of these aspects of design, but you would be hard-pressed to find one that falls short in all aspects.

Include sound design. For some apps, particularly games, great sound design can take your app to a whole new level. Even the dubious (but popular) iFart app excels in design for those who have fun making farting noises! Annoying sounds, however, can be a turnoff. If you're unsure about reaction to the inclusion (and choice) of sound, survey the sounds in your app with users. Ask users whether they find the sounds annoying.

Many developers don't use sounds because of the potential to annoy. As long as they're not annoying, however, sounds that are well crafted and integrated with the app can enhance "stickiness" and user experience, which we discuss later in this chapter.

Unique Data and/or Functionality

Many great apps capitalize on the fact that they offer something unique, such as data or functionality:

- **Whole Foods Recipes** can leverage its own supply database to offer an app that's perfect for Whole Foods shoppers to put together meals on the fly while shopping at the store.
- **Howcast** streams custom-produced tutorial videos.
- **Ocarina** relies on the unique functionality of playing the iPhone like a wind instrument.

Almost anything you create can be copied by others unless you own a patent or copyright on your material. However, if you get out there in the forefront with your app, you can stay on top by virtue of doing it right first. Just make sure that you do all you can to make your app excellent in other ways as well, though, so that you don't leave the door to competition open on quality. If you can recoup your development costs on your initial rollout, you'll have a better chance to compete with any latecomers on price as well.

Connectivity

The iPhone is a mobile Internet device in its soul. Finding a way to make your app cleverly capitalize on that is often going to increase its usability tremendously because you are using to your advantage the iPhone's identity as a node on a vast mobile network:

- **Use cloud computing** to leverage the computing power of a Web server to perform calculations that would be too strenuous for the iPhone and simply serve the results back to the application over the Internet. This capability allows Google to process your speech into search commands, for example.

- **Crowd-sourcing** uses the Internet to get lots of people to provide various functions, such as providing answers to questions. The app then gives users access to this data all in one place.

- **Connectivity** gives access to databases of information in ways that are fun and easy to use. For example, Gigotron uses an expanding database of live music events to help users to find concerts in their area, buy tickets, and share them with friends. Gigotron also uses connectivity to track users' interests and behavior for targeted advertising.

- **Social networking** is a useful connectivity tool on the iPhone:

    - **Loopt** links a social networking function with geolocation. You can see existing friends on the map and find new ones based on how close they are to you.

    - **GoodFood** is a restaurant location app that leverages users' relationships to allow them to post and share reviews with each other.

Connectivity isn't only linking to the Internet. Since iPhone 3.0, the device has been able to connect over Bluetooth as well. Many games are now multiplayer with people in your immediate vicinity. You can even send real-time audio between phones in your app.

Stickiness

Almost every great app is *sticky:* That is, users keep coming back to use it. A sticky app isn't one of those apps that was downloaded, opened once, and forgotten about. "Stickiness" fuels word of mouth because iPhone users are prone to share their favorite apps with each other. It also garners higher ratings and general awareness of an app.

For productivity or lifestyle-oriented apps, stickiness results from

- Understanding well the wants and needs of your audience

- Finding recurring needs, such as tracking time and getting news

- Filling those needs concisely and completely so that your app becomes the "go-to" tool to accomplish the task at hand

For socially oriented apps (think Facebook and Twitter), stickiness has to do with giving users a way to communicate with each other that is quick, easy to use, and relevant. Rather than guessing what users want and pushing hard to get them to accept it, however, try to identify patterns in social behavior and mimic or enhance them. In other words, when it comes to social applications, developers have had much more success "going with the flow" and finding a way to make naturally profitable the communication methods that users tend to gravitate toward rather than trying to promote their way into acceptance. For more background on this topic, search for *dodgeball versus twitter* in your favorite search engine.

For games, stickiness comes down to a great user experience and a reason to keep playing. If you make a game that's fun to play but doesn't give an interesting goal to work toward or enough variety so that users don't feel like they've seen it all before, you might have some initial success, but the app won't be sticky. A sticky game essentially creates addicts, which is why some games even advertise themselves as addictive. Game addicts can't wait to get back to their favorite game because they feel that they're on a worthy quest that they can't bear to step away from in order to deal with the real world. A game like this inspires them to want to get their friends involved. So if you have a game that allows multiple players, or is massively multiplayer (like *World of Warcraft*), the stickiness of your game can also make it go viral.

You could make a game that has a great plot and plenty of ways for players to expand and invest themselves in game play, but if the experience of playing the game isn't great, it won't become sticky because users won't like it in the first place.

Wings Galaxy: Space Exploration is a great example of a game that has a great user experience and keeps the user wanting to keep playing.

Specific Purpose

iPhone apps are the sushi (or *tapas*, for Spanish cuisine fans) of the application world. Each app is like a small yet complete bite of something. iPhone users' expectations are to have an app for individual things that they do or games they play. Just like cheap, mail-order, multifunction kitchen devices, apps that try to be too many things tend to sink to the bottom of consumers' awareness.

This concept ties in with branding. Consumers want to put an item in a category so that they can relate it with other things in their experience. If you try to defy any category with your app, you defy consumers' ability to understand how your app relates to them. If you have an idea that encompasses many distinct areas, consider splitting your app idea into several sister apps. You then have the opportunity to cross-market them as well, which can give you more marketing opportunities.

Some examples of great apps that stick to their specific purpose are Timewerks (time and billing), Weatherbug (weather updates), and Around Me (location-based services directory).

Ease of Use

Any successful app is easy to use. That doesn't mean it can't have deep and complex functionality. Your designers and developers just have to engage in some inspired interface design if that's the case. Essentially, the iPhone is used on the go, and iPhone users aren't generally interested in reading a user's manual.

If the function of your app takes longer than it should or is counterintuitive, your users will quickly start to skim the App Store for another one to replace it. After all, time and sanity are at a premium when it comes to operating the iPhone. Remember that your users might be pulling up your app for two minutes on a bus ride or even using it while driving. They want to be able to skim through your app for what they want while having a conversation over dinner, so the app had better be easy to use.

Great apps utilize conventional ways of getting things done (navigating a form, for example) to increase familiarity while spicing things up with great graphics or interesting transitions. If you want to include a more unique interface *paradigm* (way of doing things), test it with a number of people who have never seen it before. Is it easy for them to figure out how to do "it" without you telling them anything? Do they need more than one try? How long do they have think about it?

Include directions in your app if necessary, but try to make them appear at the exact interaction step rather than buried in a long document. In other words, if you have to tell the user how to do something, pop a bubble up onscreen that states only how to do that thing right when at certain points in the app. If you have to use more than two short sentences, your directions are too long, and you should rethink that part of the app. Having said that, having to give directions at all is a sign that your user interface design might not be as strong as it should be.

Your app shouldn't require much additional thought for users to operate beyond what it takes for them to decide what they want to do with it. If learning *how* to do it isn't very straightforward, go back to the drawing board.

Correct Pricing

Optimal pricing isn't based on cost of production as much as the perceived value of a product. What a customer thinks your app is worth is far more important than what you think it's worth or what you invested in it.

This can work both ways:

- ✔ You might produce an app that costs you relatively little but is so unique and valuable to users that they are happy to pay you a relatively high price for it.
- ✔ You could invest a lot of time and money into an app only to find that users don't happen to think it is worth much.

In either case, the correct price is one that most users find appropriate for the app. We take a much more sophisticated look at pricing, including methodologies with which to determine your optimal price, in Chapter 3.

Many successful app makers use pricing as a marketing tool. *Wings Galaxy*, for example, features a prominent quote on its App Store page that states: "If you sell this for less than five bucks, this will be the best value on the App Store." They priced the app at $1.99. Reading the quote boosts the perceived value of the app. In that context, the actual price seems like a bargain (which it is).

Pricing your app below perceived value isn't always the best option, however, because the price itself can factor into the perceived value of a product. This is evident on Madison Avenue, where clothing priced hundreds or even thousands above market value is held in high esteem, partly because of its high price. If you have an app that fills a specific niche frequented by power users or aficionados, you can use this to your advantage by appearing to be the best in your category, as indicated from your higher price. You'd better be able to justify it with higher quality or unique features, though! The Twitter client Birdhouse is an example of being successful charging more than the competition. The app actually has fewer features than many free competitors, but offers some unique features for power users that justify the price for them.

Smart Use of iPhone Features

iPhone users love the unique features of the iPhone, such as its accelerometer, GPS, multitouch screen, and ability to connect with hardware devices. Making clever uses of these features can take your app from good to great. If your app relates at all to a user's physical location, be sure to utilize the GPS.

One way to make a game viral is to integrate player's physical position into gameplay, for example. If the user could interact with your app by rotating or shaking their phone, consider using those capabilities. The extended capabilities of the iPhone all have to do with making the device more tactile or more connected to other devices and information. The more you take advantage of these capabilities, the more "iPhon-y" your app will be, and the better it will fit into the iPhone culture.

Some examples of great uses of the iPhone's features are

- *Touchgrind*, a game that makes innovative use of multitouch
- **iChalky**, which makes clever use of the accelerometer and physics calculations to animate an onscreen stick figure.
- **AP Mobile**, which targets news articles to your geolocation.

Fun to Use

The iPhone is a lifestyle device. Apps that bring a smile to the face become users' favorites because they enhance the period of time the user spends with them. A lot of time and attention is put into computing these days. One of the foundations of the Apple brand is creating user experiences that are enhancing and fun rather than boring and dry. This approach actually enhances the lives of users because they spend so much time with their computers and mobile devices. A fun app is like a fun friend.

Even successful utility apps are fun to use. Take Weightbot, for example. This app simply allows users to input their weight and track it over time. The app is very fun to use, though, because of its highly stylized design. Users feel like they're operating a futuristic robotic device. Transitions are clever, and sound effects are used to enhance the experience. The app makes you wish you could track your weight more than once a day just to play with it.

Likewise, Loopt is fun to use because of its capability to see friends on a map and send and receive updates based on location. Google Earth is fun to use because of its interaction paradigm. Scrolling and zooming around Earth on your iPhone is an incredible experience.

What makes an app fun to use is a combination of the other factors we describe through this chapter. Inspired design, the right fit for the audience, ease of use, clever use of iPhone features, and stickiness all contribute to the fun of an app. Some of these qualities simply make an app worth using and others push it over into the fun category. In the case of Weightbot, user interface, graphic design, and sound design make an otherwise standard app unique.

Special Sauce

Every successful app these days needs a little "special sauce": that little extra something that no one else thought of that makes the app fit its niche better, be more fun to use, be more interesting to look at, and so on. What makes your sauce special is going to have to be up to you because it should be unique.

Some apps that exhibit special sauce are

- **TweetDeck:** This very clever interface helps you keep a multitude of Twitter-related activities organized, usable, quick, and fun.

- **Overnight:** Yummy design puts this useful shipping tracking device over the top.

- **FourTrack:** Four-track recording on the iPhone looks and feels like you're using a real musical hardware device.

- **Topple:** A simple but clever premise combined with great design and cute characters give this game uniqueness and flair.

Extra credit: Great marketing

It's not enough anymore to make a great app: You need to get noticed. Because of the volume of apps being produced, waiting for Apple to feature you is not a sound marketing strategy. But marketing doesn't have to mean a huge ad buy, either. Ben Satterfield, creator of Gigotron, remarks that every marketing effort he made has resulted in an increase in his sales, no matter how small. Getting friends to mention you in blogs, submitting your app for reviews, and cross-marketing with other apps all can give you the bump you need to get your sales up.

If you want to advertise, go after those demographics that are very relevant to your app. Do short runs first and test the results; then do bigger buys in publications that gave you results.

Whatever you do, don't put all that blood, sweat, and tears into building an amazing app and then get shy when it comes time to release it. Read the chapters in Part IV about marketing, do further research, and get out there and trumpet your release to the world!

Chapter 20

Ten Influential Review Sites

*G*etting your iPhone application reviewed on the major Web sites that review apps is an important way to stand out over the tens of thousands of iPhone applications so that prospective customers notice you and, you hope, buy or download your app. (We mention this topic in the Marketing section of this book.) Therefore, this chapter points out ten of the biggest or more prominent iPhone app review sites to aim for in your marketing efforts. We list them in alphabetical order so that we don't imply a favorite. Use one or use them all, but get out there and see what people are saying about iPhone applications..

148Apps

www.148apps.com

When Apple launched its App Store, site founder Jeff Scott decided to launch a Web site focused on reviewing iPhone applications and providing news and information about their availability. The name of his site, 148Apps, comes from the maximum number of applications that can be installed on an iPhone. Each of the 9 storage pages can hold 16 apps (9 x 16 = 144) plus the 4 you can store on the static bar at the bottom, for a total of 148 (144 + 4 = 148). That's almost 50 percent more than you see on the standard Top 100 lists. Jeff's site not only reviews iPhone apps (with a separate section dedicated to games) and reports news, but also maintains lists of the most popular-selling apps, the newest apps to hit the App Store, and price changes.

The reviewer's e-mail address is review.monkey@148apps.com.

AppCraver

www.appcraver.com

On the topic of following the "iPhone app economy," AppCraver calls itself "obsessively dedicated" to iPhone applications. Founded by Fred Krueger and Clark Landry, the site does more than provide reviews of iPhone apps. It features the usual editor's picks and reviews both free and paid apps, but its Worthwhile Apps section also tries to recommend apps that cost $2 or less. The site features extensive interviews with iPhone app developers and people involved with the iPhone, reviews of iPhone accessories, and forums in which site visitors can discuss anything in the iPhone world.

To submit your application for review, send it to `www.appcraver.com/contact`.

Apptism

`www.apptism.com`

Although some sites focus only on iPhone reviews, Apptism compiles all sorts of information about every application it tracks, becoming, in effect, an "iPhone app activity aggregator." From launch dates to iTunes Store rankings to notes about related upgrades or articles, everything is tied together with the application description and review on Apptism. Visitors can find out all about iPhone apps they want to download, by sorting or filtering searches on a number of criteria, and even see previews of upcoming applications. To submit your application, visit `www.apptism.com/previews/new`.

AppVee

`www.appvee.com/reviews.php`

AppVee focuses on telling application shoppers what they want to know: whether an app is worth downloading or buying. The site distinguishes itself by providing numerous video reviews on top of written reviews. (In January 2009, AppVee had already served up a million views on its own YouTube channel.) Though AppVee is adding a division to review Google Android apps, its main focus continues to be iPhone application reviews. The site is supported by an active blog and user forums. To submit your app, visit `www.appvee.com/dev_contact.php`.

Gizmodo iPhone App Directory

`http://gizmodo.com/tag/iphone-apps-directory`

Gizmodo started as, and remains, a blog about gadgets and technology. Since 2002, it has become one of the largest blogs about this topic, registering 100 million page views per month, according to the site. It has an extensive iPhone application directory and offers reviews of those apps in addition to descriptions from developer and a comments section for user ratings. The site's simple, clean interface and continual posts ensure that a healthy audience will see your app if Gizmodo reviews your application.

To submit your app, send a tip to: `tips@gizmodo.com`.

Macworld

`www.macworld.com/appguide/index.html`

Nobody has covered the world of Apple longer than *Macworld* — the magazine (founded in 1984) has talked about everything from the Apple IIc to the latest iPhone, iMac, and iPod models. The site's iPhone Central covers all sorts of news about the iPhone and iPhone apps, and it even recommends selected apps over the preinstalled Apple programs. Sample review categories are How I Spent My Summer Vacation and Endless Summer Reading. If you're looking for an authoritative site for news and reviews about the iPhone, *Macworld* is the place to go. Scroll down the page at `www.mac world.com/contact.html` to submit your app.

Major Newspapers

Today's big newspapers are content haven for information and news. Thanks to the advent of technology, newspapers no longer review only the newest books or Broadway plays and instead review technology devices and the software that runs them — such as the iPhone and its applications. Though the size of the audience your app is exposed to is greater than at the most targeted micro-niche sites, the downside to fame and exposure is that reporters cannot possibly review every suggested application. Check each site's contact page to find out how to submit your app.

- *New York Times* Tech section: `www.nytimes.com/pages/technology/index.html`
- *USA Today* Tech section: `www.usatoday.com/tech/default.htm`
- *Wall Street Journal:* `http://online.wsj.com/public/page/personal-technology.html`

The Apple Web Site

www.apple.com/iPhone

What discussion of iPhone Web sites would be complete without Apple.com? The iPhone maker maintains on its Web site an extensive iPhone section that not only displays lists of the top 100 paid and free apps but also posts its own review categories, such as Apps for Traveling or Apps for Going Out. Read about the weekly featured iPhone app, and check out the Top Tips and Tricks section. To have your app featured at this site, simply submit your app and follow our advice to gain Apple's attention.

The Unofficial Apple Weblog (TUAW)

www.tuaw.com

The official iPhone site is Apple.com, but it also has an unofficial site: The Unofficial Apple Weblog, or TUAW, started in 2004 and now part of the AOL Tech Network. With an army of bloggers and an editorial team behind it, TUAW not only reviews iPhone apps but also provides iPhone news, tips, analysis, and opinions about anything related to Apple. Every post allows for vibrant comments from its community of readers. Based on the level of traffic and the number of postings and reviews, the site, though unofficial, is definitely authoritative. To request a review of your application, visit www.tuaw.com/apprequests.

Wired Gadget Lab

www.wired.com/gadgetlab

This popular online blog reviews all sorts of technological goodness, and the iPhone hasn't escaped its attention. The site regularly reviews new apps and iPhone models and accessories, and its monthly traffic numbers suggest that someone is paying attention. Remember that one extra kudo from getting a positive review on the Gadget Lab blog is a possible, very possible, mention in their glossy print magazine. You get no guarantees, but you can certainly have at it. To request a review, send a letter to the associate reviews editor, as mentioned on the home page:

www.wired.com/services/feedback/letterstowriter

App Store Submission Checklist

The following checklist is a carefully compiled list of things to do and to avoid in the process of submitting your app.

The beginning of each section contains a brief description of what to look out for.

Application

Your application needs to be a polished gem. It should have clean, consistent graphics and no rough edges. It should be as snappy as possible, work as intended on all the devices for which it is being shipped, and have all routine bugs eliminated.

- ✔ No broken links in application, internal or external.
- ✔ The word *beta* is not used anywhere, no matter what it refers to.
- ✔ Any accessories to be used with the application are authorized by Apple.
- ✔ Application interface is intuitive and smooth (follows Apple Human Interface Guidelines).
- ✔ No long load times.
- ✔ Resource utilization is well within bounds and does not make the platform laggy.
- ✔ Application is sufficiently different from preexisting applications.
- ✔ Application does not simply duplicate functionality of Apple applications.
- ✔ Application does not use trademarks of other companies (or similar names).
- ✔ Application does not interfere with iPhone functionality (such as draining battery life).
- ✔ Application has a complete and functioning feature set (is a demo or full app, not a beta).

Application Metadata and Application Web Site

The *metadata* (data about data, such as product names, company names, descriptions, and the like) are a key part of marketing the application.

- ✔ Primary language chosen.

- ✔ Company name specified.

- ✔ Encryption: U.S. Department of Commerce approval obtained if encryption is used for anything other than authentication.

- ✔ Application name set.

- ✔ Application description set.

- ✔ Application description contains just enough copy for a concise but full description and easy viewing on the iPhone/iPod itself (one to five paragraphs).

- ✔ Application categories and subcategories chosen.

- ✔ Copyright string defined.

- ✔ Version string defined.

- ✔ Version number is less than 1.0.

- ✔ Application/company landing page URL defined.

- ✔ Application/company landing page URL works and is stable.

- ✔ Support URL defined.

- ✔ Support URL works and is stable.

- ✔ Support e-mail defined.

- ✔ Support e-mail works and is ready to respond to requests.

- ✔ EULA written and defined (if needed).

- ✔ EULA (if defined) is consistent with iTunes minimum terms and conditions.

- ✔ If user must accept EULA, app is set up so user does so within app itself.

- ✔ SKU/UPC code (if defined) specified.

- ✔ Supported devices selected.

- ✔ Game and Content Rating advisories defined.

- ✔ Distribution regions chosen.

- ✔ Payment information defined on iTunes Connect.

✔ Price tier chosen.

✔ Marketing collateral is not misleading in any way.

Application Name

Anyone with experience in marketing knows the power of a brand. Attention to detail in naming, describing, and differentiating your application is an important ingredient of success.

✔ App name can be found easily with appropriate search terms.

✔ App name doesn't exceed character and space limits.

✔ No version number in app name.

✔ No other brands or trademarks (for example, iPhone) in app name.

✔ App name is simple, concise, and relevant.

✔ App name is not too similar to the name of another product.

Application Icon

Part of the reason applications sell well is because of their beautiful icons. iTunes customers are used to album art as a visual reward for their intangible digital asset purchase. Steve Jobs once spoke of OS X having an interface so beautiful that someone wanted to lick it. The iPhone carries on that lickable tradition, and using gorgeous, compelling artwork for your icon is a key part of delivering that experience.

✔ App icon is gorgeous.

✔ Icon conforms to Apple Human Interface Guidelines.

✔ Icon is not scaled up from a smaller icon.

✔ Icon text (if any) is easily legible.

✔ Icon is universal (is understandable worldwide).

✔ Icon is appropriate (no violence or nudity).

✔ Icon is clean, and no effects applied (no rounded edges, no shine, no drop shadows, and so on).

✔ A 57 x 57 application icon created.

✔ A 512 x 512 version of app icon created from same art (JPEG or TIFF format).

Screen Shots

Along with the icon, you need to show your application in action. The app store provides a digital display case for you to vend your wares, and it's up to you to create the application screenshots that will put your best features forward and sell the app.

- Primary screen shot created.
- Primary screen shot shows what app is and does.
- Primary screen shot is best available shot.
- Up to four additional screen shots created.
- Additional screen shots support primary screen shot.
- All screen shots are high quality.
- All screen shots are easily legible.
- All screen shots are appropriate, both culturally and in terms of maturity.
- Status bar removed from all screen shots (if present).
- Screenshots are TIFF or JPG (not PNG).
- Each screen shot has correct size:
    - Portrait, status bar removed: 320 x 460
    - Portrait, full screen: 320 x 480
    - Landscape, status bar removed: 480 x 300
    - Landscape, full screen: 480 x 320
- Localization Application URL localized for all languages.
- Languages chosen for localization.
- Application name localized in all languages.
- Application description localized in all languages.
- Application URL localized for all languages.
- Support URL localized for all languages.
- Support e-mail localized for all languages.
- Screen shot(s) localized for all languages.
- App binary localized to support all languages.

✔ All elements in a given language are appropriate to all cultures that use that language (Spanish for Mexico, Spain, and so on).

✔ All localized elements are also tailored to target culture.

✔ Background for fully designed product page is in 900 x 530 layered PSD format.

Build

Building and uploading your application are the final steps of your application launch sequence. Make sure you've double-checked all the settings before you announce "All systems go!"

✔ App ID defined in iPhone Developer Program Portal.

✔ App-specific Distribution Provisioning Profile created in iPhone Developer Program Portal.

✔ App ID applied to app in Xcode.

✔ Xcode: Active SDK = Device.

✔ Xcode: Active Configuration = Release.

✔ Xcode: Code Signing Identity = Distribution Identity (not Development Identity).

✔ Xcode: Code Signing Provision Profile = Distribution Provisioning Profile.

✔ App built for release.

✔ The .app file compressed as .zip.

✔ Binary size is minimized.

✔ App binary is no larger than 2GB.

✔ For apps targeted for download via cell networks, binary is no larger than 10MB.

✔ Compressed app binary uploaded.

Index

• B •

Business/Accounting & Bookkeeping

Bookkeeping For Dummies
978-0-7645-9848-7

eBay Business
All-in-One For Dummies,
2nd Edition
978-0-470-38536-4

Job Interviews
For Dummies,
3rd Edition
978-0-470-17748-8

Resumes For Dummies,
5th Edition
978-0-470-08037-5

Stock Investing
For Dummies,
3rd Edition
978-0-470-40114-9

Successful Time
Management
For Dummies
978-0-470-29034-7

Computer Hardware

BlackBerry For Dummies,
3rd Edition
978-0-470-45762-7

Computers For Seniors
For Dummies
978-0-470-24055-7

iPhone For Dummies,
2nd Edition
978-0-470-42342-4

Laptops For Dummies,
3rd Edition
978-0-470-27759-1

Macs For Dummies,
10th Edition
978-0-470-27817-8

Cooking & Entertaining

Cooking Basics
For Dummies,
3rd Edition
978-0-7645-7206-7

Wine For Dummies,
4th Edition
978-0-470-04579-4

Diet & Nutrition

Dieting For Dummies,
2nd Edition
978-0-7645-4149-0

Nutrition For Dummies,
4th Edition
978-0-471-79868-2

Weight Training
For Dummies,
3rd Edition
978-0-471-76845-6

Digital Photography

Digital Photography
For Dummies,
6th Edition
978-0-470-25074-7

Photoshop Elements 7
For Dummies
978-0-470-39700-8

Gardening

Gardening Basics
For Dummies
978-0-470-03749-2

Organic Gardening
For Dummies,
2nd Edition
978-0-470-43067-5

Green/Sustainable

Green Building
& Remodeling
For Dummies
978-0-4710-17559-0

Green Cleaning
For Dummies
978-0-470-39106-8

Green IT For Dummies
978-0-470-38688-0

Health

Diabetes For Dummies,
3rd Edition
978-0-470-27086-8

Food Allergies
For Dummies
978-0-470-09584-3

Living Gluten-Free
For Dummies
978-0-471-77383-2

Hobbies/General

Chess For Dummies,
2nd Edition
978-0-7645-8404-6

Drawing For Dummies
978-0-7645-5476-6

Knitting For Dummies,
2nd Edition
978-0-470-28747-7

Organizing For Dummies
978-0-7645-5300-4

SuDoku For Dummies
978-0-470-01892-7

Home Improvement

Energy Efficient Homes
For Dummies
978-0-470-37602-7

Home Theater
For Dummies,
3rd Edition
978-0-470-41189-6

Living the Country Lifestyle
All-in-One For Dummies
978-0-470-43061-3

Solar Power Your Home
For Dummies
978-0-470-17569-9

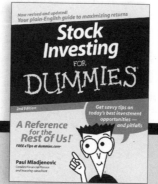

Internet

Blogging For Dummies,
2nd Edition
978-0-470-23017-6

eBay For Dummies,
6th Edition
978-0-470-49741-8

Facebook For Dummies
978-0-470-26273-3

Google Blogger
For Dummies
978-0-470-40742-4

Web Marketing
For Dummies,
2nd Edition
978-0-470-37181-7

WordPress For Dummies,
2nd Edition
978-0-470-40296-2

Language & Foreign Language

French For Dummies
978-0-7645-5193-2

Italian Phrases
For Dummies
978-0-7645-7203-6

Spanish For Dummies
978-0-7645-5194-9

Spanish For Dummies,
Audio Set
978-0-470-09585-0

Macintosh

Mac OS X Snow Leopard
For Dummies
978-0-470-43543-4

Math & Science

Algebra I For Dummies
978-0-7645-5325-7

Biology For Dummies
978-0-7645-5326-4

Calculus For Dummies
978-0-7645-2498-1

Chemistry For Dummies
978-0-7645-5430-8

Microsoft Office

Excel 2007 For Dummies
978-0-470-03737-9

Office 2007 All-in-One
Desk Reference
For Dummies
978-0-471-78279-7

Music

Guitar For Dummies,
2nd Edition
978-0-7645-9904-0

iPod & iTunes
For Dummies,
6th Edition
978-0-470-39062-7

Piano Exercises
For Dummies
978-0-470-38765-8

Parenting & Education

Parenting For Dummies,
2nd Edition
978-0-7645-5418-6

Type 1 Diabetes
For Dummies
978-0-470-17811-9

Pets

Cats For Dummies,
2nd Edition
978-0-7645-5275-5

Dog Training For Dummies,
2nd Edition
978-0-7645-8418-3

Puppies For Dummies,
2nd Edition
978-0-470-03717-1

Religion & Inspiration

The Bible For Dummies
978-0-7645-5296-0

Catholicism For Dummies
978-0-7645-5391-2

Women in the Bible
For Dummies
978-0-7645-8475-6

Self-Help & Relationship

Anger Management
For Dummies
978-0-470-03715-7

Overcoming Anxiety
For Dummies
978-0-7645-5447-6

Sports

Baseball For Dummies,
3rd Edition
978-0-7645-7537-2

Basketball For Dummies,
2nd Edition
978-0-7645-5248-9

Golf For Dummies,
3rd Edition
978-0-471-76871-5

Web Development

Web Design All-in-One
For Dummies
978-0-470-41796-6

Windows Vista

Windows Vista
For Dummies
978-0-471-75421-3

How-to?
How Easy.

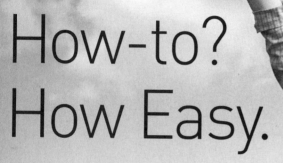

From hooking up a modem to cooking up a casserole, knitting a scarf to navigating an iPod, you can trust Dummies.com to show you how to get things done the easy way.

Visit us at Dummies.com

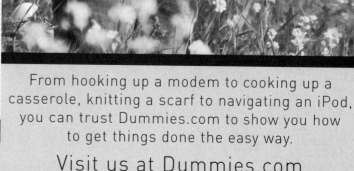

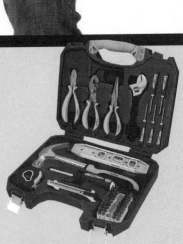